KU-354-546

Victorian Vogue

· · · ·

British Novels on Screen

Dianne F. Sadoff

University of Minnesota Press
Minneapolis
London

The University of Minnesota Press gratefully acknowledges the financial support of the School of Arts and Sciences and the University Research Council of Rutgers, The State University of New Jersey, in the publication of this book.

Portions of chapter 2 were published as "Looking at Tess: The Female Figure in Two Narrative Media," in *The Sense of Sex: Feminist Perspectives on Thomas Hardy,* ed. Margaret Higgonet (Urbana: University of Illinois Press, 1993); copyright 1993 by the Board of Trustees of the University of Illinois; reprinted with permission of the University of Illinois Press. Portions of chapter 4 were published as "'Hallucinations of Intimacy': The Henry James Movies," in *Henry James at the Movies,* ed. Susan M. Griffin (Lexington: University Press of Kentucky, 2002), 254–78; as "'Appeals to Incalculability': Sex, Costume Drama, and *The Golden Bowl,*" *Henry James Review* 23 (2002): 38–52; and as "'Intimate Disarray': The Henry James Movies," *Henry James Review* 19, no. 3 (Fall 1998): 286–95. Portions of the Epilogue were published as "Becoming Jane Austen at the Megaplex," *Novel: A Forum on Fiction* 42, nos. 2/3 (2009).

Copyright 2010 by the Regents of the University of Minnesota

All rights reserved. No part of this publication may be reproduced, stored in a retrieval system, or transmitted, in any form or by any means, electronic, mechanical, photocopying, recording, or otherwise, without the prior written permission of the publisher.

Published by the University of Minnesota Press
111 Third Avenue South, Suite 290
Minneapolis, MN 55401-2520
http://www.upress.umn.edu

Library of Congress Cataloging-in-Publication Data

Sadoff, Dianne F.
Victorian vogue : British novels on screen / Dianne F. Sadoff.
p. cm.
Includes bibliographical references and index.
ISBN 978-0-8166-6091-9 (hc : alk. paper) —
ISBN 978-0-8166-6092-6 (pbk. : alk. paper)
1. English fiction—19th century—Film and video adaptations. 2. Motion pictures and literature. 3. Film adaptations—History and criticism. I. Title.
PR878.M73S33 2009
791.43´6—dc22
2009030042

Printed in the United States of America on acid-free paper

The University of Minnesota is an equal-opportunity educator and employer.

16 15 14 13 12 11 10   10 9 8 7 6 5 4 3 2 1

6140078747

79١
·436
/Sad

VICTORIAN VOGUE

LEARNING AND INFORMATION
SERVICES
HAROLD BRIDGES LIBRARY
LANCASTER

Contents

Acknowledgments

I BEGAN THIS BOOK, IN EARNEST, while on leave of absence from Miami University, Ohio, and I am grateful to many people for providing me the time and funding that made this work possible. First and foremost, I thank then dean of the College of Arts and Science, John Skillings, who generously offered support during the years I served as chair of the Department of English at Miami and afterward. The interim dean of the college, Steve DeLue, and chair of the Department of English, Keith Tuma, later assisted as I finalized the manuscript. I am grateful, in particular, to Skillings and DeLue; it has been the joy of my academic life to work with them as a chair and an associate dean.

Many friends and colleagues supported my work during the writing of this book. I am grateful for help with funding, from Richard E. Miller, chair of the Department of English, and Veneeta Dayal, Dean of Humanities, School of Arts and Sciences, at Rutgers University, New Brunswick. I thank my new colleagues at Rutgers University, New Brunswick, and members of the Rutgers British Studies Project for their feedback, including John Kucich, Seth Koven, Michael McKeon, Carolyn Williams, Henry Turner, Rebecca Walkowitz, Jonah Siegel, David Kurnick, and Stacy Klein; with his usual alacrity and acerbity, William Galperin graciously read and commented on the chapter on Jane Austen. At the Temple University Nineteenth-Century Forum, I benefited from comments by Peter Logan and Kate Thomas. My former Miami colleague Kerry Powell read the chapter on Oscar Wilde and contributed astute commentary. Audiences at the University of Louisville, University of North Carolina–Chapel Hill, Rutgers University, Indiana University–Bloomington and IU–South Bend, University of Michigan, and the University of Toronto asked stimulating questions, often driving me back to my desk with newly clarified thoughts. To the Six Jolly Victorianists at the National Humanities Center (which included Harriet Ritvo, John Kucich, Ginger Frost, and Molly Rothenberg), I am grateful for early feedback. Friends have been there throughout:

Michael Staub and Dagmar Herzog, Emily Bartels, Marty Petrone, Charles Ganelin and Patty Klingenberg, and Sarah Knox.

I received research help from a number of libraries and librarians. William Wortman, humanities librarian at Miami University, gave me extraordinary aid; without his help, this work would have been much more difficult to complete. At Duke University's Lilly Library, Kenneth Wetherington and Kelley Lawton generously allowed me to check out VHS and DVD adaptations. At Rutgers's Alexander Library, Kevin Mulcahey is a worthy successor to Bill Wortman.

This book would not have been possible without the generosity of mentors and coworkers. I thank J. Hillis Miller, whose National Endowment for the Humanities Summer Seminar at Yale University in 1977 changed the course of my professional life; I cannot imagine a more generous, thoughtful, caring mentor than he. To Paul Hammond, director of Digital Initiatives at Rutgers English and the Plangere Writing Center, I am grateful for creation of the book's digital stills. To Jay Clayton and an anonymous reader for the University of Minnesota Press, I offer thanks for help with reframing the book. At the Press, Douglas Armato provided caring editorial guidance. Nancy Sauro, Susan Doerr, and Lynn Walterick smoothed my way during final editing. Kristin Petersen Gagliardi, at Miami, tirelessly checked my quotations and notes. Finally, I am fortunate to have as my husband and sometimes cowriter John Kucich, who read every word, reread many more, and, as always, helped me structure the argument, foreground the important ideas, and make my prose readable. He makes work, life, and love joyful.

Cultural Work at the Millennium

The historical novel—and its related emanations, such as the costume film—has fallen into disrepute and infrequence, not merely because, in the postmodern age, we no longer tell ourselves our history in that fashion, but also because we no longer experience it that way, and, indeed, perhaps no longer experience it at all.

—Fredric Jameson, *Postmodernism*

Against sentimental and intellectualised accounts of an unlocalised "Old England," we need, evidently, the sharpest scepticism. . . . What we have to inquire into is not . . . historical error, but historical perspective.

—Raymond Williams, *The Country and the City*

KEN RUSSELL CONCLUDES HIS CHEEKY FILM about the Byron circle's Villa Diodati ghost-story contest with a twist. In *Gothic*'s (1986) penultimate sequence, Byron (Gabriel Byrne) assures Mary Godwin (Natasha Richardson) that the night's revels bear no relation to the morning's calm. As Byron and Polidori (Timothy Spall) sprawl on pillows in the foreground, the mansion solidly anchors the background. Voice-over: "Three years after that fateful night, Mary Shelley's son, William, was dead." The nineteenth-century figures dissolve out, twentieth-century figures dissolve in; the stately mansion remains exactly as it was: in a long low-angle shot, women and men, adult and adolescent, parade across the screen, foreground and background, in a queue that ends at the mansion's entrance. Cut to tourist boat, with voice-over: "That same year, Allegra, Claire Claremont's daughter by Byron, died. . . . Byron survived her by two years. . . . Eight years after that night at Villa Diodati, only Claire and Mary remained alive." The camera zooms across the water to a close-up of the corpse of a drowned baby boy: "But something created that night 170 years ago, lives on, still haunting us to this day: Mary Shelley's Frankenstein."

This faux British heritage film about the English cultural tradition's immortality, produced by Americans and starring British actors with bona fide heritage-film star images, packages Englishness for middle-class consumers in search of a high-cultural sexual thrill and for Americans anxious to locate in nineteenth-century English literature a heritage of their own. Yet it does so self-consciously, even parodically, for Russell's Diodati tourist-visitor stands in for his film's spectator, who metaphorically visits a heritage site that reinscribes Britain's national heritage, gains visual access to privately owned cultural treasures, and acquires the capability to practice aesthetic tastefulness. This heritage tourist/spectator may later purchase tie-in souvenirs or cultural products associated with the ghosts of Byron at the museum shop, box office, or video store, for the cultural marketplace now serves these multiple touristic niches. Indeed, Russell's film suggests that middle-class tourists, literary readers, and independent-cinema fans—whether up- or down-market—may, by viewing, acquire and enhance their store of cultural and symbolic capital. Despite their torn blue jeans and unfashionable shoes and handbags, his film's pictured heritage fans suggest Russell's spectators' desire to see the stars of past historical moments, acquire knock-offs of cultural icons, and display their take-home heritage kitsch.

Yet heritage culture, both satiric and nonsatiric, also aims to educate the citizens of a no-longer-new nation in their now residual old-country culture, whether print, architectural, landscape, or celluloid, even as it hopes to provide period pleasures, contemporary cultural insight, and historical analysis of the national past. Fredric Jameson's diagnosis of postmodernism as a period of waning or blocked historicity, as my first epigraph demonstrates, bemoans the loss of history as an imagined plenitude and the historical imagination as a situated awareness of genealogical linkage and geopolitical organicism. Yet this apocalyptic sense of history's late-century enfeeblement, of historicity's failure for postmodern subjectivity, announces the present as itself historical, as Jameson elsewhere notes; the awareness of the present as participating in a historical trajectory or genealogy burdens its subject with anxiety about belatedness even as it is constituted by living memory. Raymond Williams suggests, in my second epigraph, that the fear and certainty that a once-communal past is, in fact, lost necessitates scrutiny, for historical perspective situates this loss as signifying a slippage, an always moving, moveable, and retrospective reconstruction that Williams calls the "nostalgic escalator." Williams traces the historical shift from "reflection to retrospect," spawned by and based in the "ideology of improvement" that gradually constituted, during the late eighteenth and early nineteenth centuries, "a conventional structure of retrospect" (*Country* 74, 61). In the late twentieth century, heritage film depicts this historical perspective, sometimes romanticizing the backward glance even as it submits it to skeptical analysis. Presenting history as a situated retrospection in tension with the needs of the present, heritage film may productively address, on screen, the disjunction between past and present that nineteenth-century narratorial consciousness once recounted.

I open this book with Ken Russell's parody of literary production (and, implicitly, filmic adaptation) because Russell, often reviled by reviewers as a producer of kitsch, is smarter about history and literary periodization than his detractors admit. Likewise, heritage film is both smarter about and more embedded in history than its critics have alleged. Thus Jameson's 1990s notion that historicity was waning or in crisis seems, in retrospect, paradoxically appropriate for and anachronistic to a decade in which heritage film posited history as central to culture, both visual and literary. The 1980s detractors of heritage film, such as Andrew Higson, who viewed it as commodifying a simplistic version of history, or Cairns Craig, as packaging a nostalgic desire for earlier days of aristocratic ease and imperial largesse, likewise failed to understand its historical embeddedness and, at the same time, its often skeptical take on such historical fixing or location. Indeed, the salient ideological forces that constitute heritage film's textual field sustain multiple processes of meaning production. The historical imagination, moreover, has changed during the twentieth century; I situate heritage films within a particular yet polyvalent history of historical consciousness, in different decades of heritage cultural production. In turn, these shifts in historical consciousness produce differing versions of the literary classics that lend their stories to the screen. Playing off the 1930s and 1940s against the 1980s and 1990s, I restore the historical situation of heritage film—and the dialogue these films undertake with the decades during which their source narratives were created. This interdisciplinary perspective, which calls on literary, historicist, and cinematic discourses central to the study of heritage film, can produce historically nuanced readings of the cultural forces operative during a source novel's writing and a film's remediation, as well as its commentary on its cinematic precursors: interdisciplinary discourse restores to heritage film its own multiple heritages.

Several principles ground this work:

The cinematic is always already literary. Film adaptations of classic literary texts cannot be interpreted apart from their source narratives. Although this seems axiomatic, indeed banal, two camps have contested the issues that intersect in the matrix of historical, cultural, and industrial forces that constitute the field. Literary critics may sniff haughtily at the popular, middlebrow versions of their canonized favorites. Garrett Stewart, for example, accuses Ken Russell of turning D. H. Lawrence's *The Rainbow*, a "mysteriously effective novel," into "motel-room pay-per-view soft-core." This terse evaluation situates Lawrence's novel as high culture and Russell's film as "pure cinematic kitsch" (172). Film critics, by contrast, often elide or suppress the classic literary texts from which these films are dramatized, adapted, or remediated. Julianne Pidduck productively maps the gender, sexuality, and cultural concerns of 1980s and 1990s costume film, a picturing—and sometimes radical reading—of spaces and places that confine, constrain, and repress female desires, yet her sketchy rendering of these films' literary sources and their historical situations robs her readings of full analytical power. John Hill also elides heritage films' literary originals by focusing on the ways they reside within "specific socio-historical contexts" and are situated within "specific circumstances" of production and circulation (*1980s* xi). This industrial and reception context is crucial to the study of heritage film's reemergence in the 1980s, under the regime of Margaret Thatcher, and to its renaissance in the 1990s, and Hill's sociohistorical thinking inspires my work throughout. Yet this framework for analysis removes from consideration the historical, industrial, and cultural moment during which the adaptation's source text was produced and circulated, and that historical situation must likewise inform our understanding of literary film adaptations.

"Always historicize!" Although I do not adopt Jameson's Marxist-historical dialectic as theoretical paradigm, his well-known slogan shapes my thinking (*Political* 9). Yet the recent critical focus on user pleasure and intertextuality in adaptation studies often reduces history, deconstructively, to little more than another text. For Julie Sanders, adaptations do not undo history but question its stability, making history into textuality and story; although tales are told by "particular tellers" from and in

"particular ideologies and contexts," Sanders's take on adaptation recalls theories of postmodern simulacra, removed from history and an incommensurable "reality" (143, 146). In Linda Hutcheon's model of cultural transmission, historical change becomes, by analogy, a Darwinian survival of the fittest; in this "process of mutation," adapted stories demonstrate "longevity," "fecundity," and—here, Hutcheon smuggles back into her model what she claims to have discounted—"copying-fidelity" (31–32, 167). Adaptation thus removes narrative from history, as storytelling mutates into "some kind of human universal" (175). Robert Stam views literary film as framed by "large-scale historical events," especially global colonialism (16), yet his multicultural dialogue between literature and film focuses more forcefully on narratological and generic categories than on historical thinking. Vincent Leitch's notion of the paradoxical impossibility and necessity of rewriting texts erases historical change, turning a deconstructive aporia—reading not what an adaptation "faithfully reproduces" but what it "leaves out"—into the motive force behind historically distinct acts of adaptation (*Adaptation* 18). Reminding us that formalism and aestheticism were both "historically situated ideologies," James Naremore, on the contrary, calls for a theory that studies "recycling, remaking," and "retelling" in the "age of mechanical reproduction and electronic communication" (15).

The resurgence of nineteenth-century novels as sources for late twentieth-century film, however, must be viewed historically. For these narratives sought, during the moment of their production and circulation, to posit an "imaginary resolution of a real contradiction," as Jameson notes; thus a text's "symbolic efficacity" for any cultural group in a specific historical moment must be grasped through formal reconstruction, "as a determinate structure of still properly formal *contradictions*" (*Political* 77). Literature thus constitutes a "symbolic act, whereby real social contradictions, insurmountable in their own terms, find a purely formal resolution in the aesthetic realm"; the aesthetic act is itself ideological, and the "production of aesthetic or narrative form" constitutes "an ideological act" whose function is to invent "imaginary or formal 'solutions' to unresolvable social contradictions" (79). Several chapters of this book reconstruct the symbolic aesthetic and ideological acts that specific nineteenth-century novels perform, yet heritage film and its literary source novels not only— and not necessarily—resolve seemingly irresolvable social contradictions but, in addition, propose opposing modes for such resolution, or repeat such problematics for a new historical moment. Thus, the production, distribution, and exhibition situations of films that adapt classic novels constitute a homonymic symbolic act or field, both aesthetic and ideological, which may seek or fail to resolve structurally similar yet historically very different social contradictions. Seeming equally intractable to late twentieth-century cinemagoers as did their earlier positing to their nineteenth-century book-buying or book-borrowing predecessors, these contradictions create the conditions in which cultural texts may work on, complicate, or repeat them.

Heritage film (and heritage culture as well, although this larger material-cultural formation is outside the parameters of this book) becomes a dominant cultural form during modern and postmodern ages of anxiety. Although W. H. Auden coined the phrase "the age of anxiety" in the 1930s, Marshall McLuhan locates its emergence as coincident with the telegram's first transmission (1844), as modern communication technology was born. In McLuhan's mid-twentieth-century melancholic meditation on media, technological subjects respond to stress in their environments by drawing their subjectivity inward (and, by implication, constituting the nineteenth-century interiority we associate with the scene of reading and the consumption of literature) and then projecting amplifications of an organ, sense, or bodily function back into the world; in an age of anxiety, this "autoamputation" produces apathy and drives the unconscious (172, 47). Technologically produced anxiety in all its forms constitutes what N. Katherine Hayles calls "cyborg subjectivity," Scott Bukatman, "terminal identity," or Sherry Turkle, "MUD life." In heritage film, a "morph aesthetic" seeks to work on this version of late-century anxiety, especially in heritage horror. Interestingly enough, several modern ages of anxiety—the 1930s, the 1980s, the 1990s—are the historical moments, broadly interpreted, in which film most often dramatized, adapted, remediated, and remade classic nineteenth-century literary texts and their earlier versions.

Recall the cultural precursors. Much work on heritage film concentrates on the 1980s and 1990s, yet the post-Victorian obsession with nineteenth-century literary culture and the concomitant explosion of film adaptations cannot be understood without retrospective reference to their predecessors. Critics of heritage film must ask why late-century filmmakers remade Depression-era genre pix on a grand scale. If filmmaking represents an aesthetic and ideological symbolic act that seeks to resolve seemingly intractable social contradictions, these decades' economic, political, and postimperial uncertainties demanded cultural remediation, both literary and cinematic, that addressed the anxieties experienced by North American and British subjects during these historical moments. Each of my five chapters differently addresses its precursors, sometimes shuttling between the 1930s and 1990s; sometimes proceeding by metaleptic temporality, as the films of the 1990s open a chapter and the 1930s appear in flashback; sometimes they recount straightforward chronological genealogies, occasionally eliding the 1930s in favor of the 1950s or the 1970s. Like the 1930s "vogue of the Victorian age" that F. R. Leavis reviled, in *Scrutiny*'s pages and later in *The Great Tradition* (1948), as linked to the minor novel and to popular fiction, the 1990s fashionability of the Victorian is historically overdetermined and shaped by its industrial and material modes of production, its cultural forms of distribution, circulation, and exhibition (1).

Find the niches. Although Higson thought, in the 1980s, that heritage film solicited a primarily British domestic audience, we now know, on the contrary, that heritage film "travels." Soliciting an international or transnational niche market, heritage film knowingly constitutes itself apart from the saturation-booking one-weekend, repeat-viewing youth-cult blockbuster or the "rootless global 'event' movie" set in a cinematic world with "no distinct sense of place" (Hirschberg 91). As Pidduck correctly notes, contemporary costume films travel because they "deploy, rework and sometimes subvert foundational English cultural references and discourses"; culled from the English novel's "canonical traditions" or theater's bardic texts (the Shakespeare films likewise exploded on the cultural scene in the 1980s and 1990s), these references form a "common postcolonial cultural legacy for English-speaking audiences" (12). Although Tom O'Regan writes not about heritage but about national cinema, his notions apply equally well to heritage, for O'Regan reminds us that national cinema—a formation that includes film texts, industries, and their cultural contexts—always exists "in conversation with" Hollywood and is a "manifestation" of cinema's internationalization, its globalized marketplace at the millennium (115, 97). Often coproduced, occasionally across national boundaries, heritage is an especially ancillary-resistant mode of independent filmmaking infrequently available at video rental chains, advertised on television, or sold in large syndication packages. According to the producer James Schamus, independents must therefore presell rights, self-license, compete at international festivals, and negotiate favorable profit splits in order to earn the box-office receipts necessary to repay investors (95–96). In a move to appropriate public-domain intellectual properties with already secure audiences—such as the Austen novels, the Janeites—the independents also seek the popular, prestigious, and quality stories already available to the English and North American cultural imaginary: novels by Austen, Henry James, E. M. Forster, and Mary Shelley, among others.

Merchant Ivory, perhaps the champion of this cinematic sector, has produced and filmed in New York, London, Paris, and India and debuted in domestic, export, and cosmopolitan markets around the globe. Using Ismail Merchant's talents at rounding up the investors, Ruth Prawer Jhabvala's at screenwriting, and James Ivory's at directing, this cosmopolitan, transnational, migratory company has scripted, shot, and distributed some of the most critically acclaimed box-office hits in the independent cinema sector and heritage mode. Yet Merchant's untimely death signaled the end of an era—or coincided with the emergence of a new cultural and industrial heritage mode. Whereas the 1980s small independents have mostly gone out of business, the biggest independents were bought by the majors and are again being shut down or sold. In 1993, Disney acquired Miramax and Turner Broadcasting Corporation bought New Line Cinema (Wyatt 76; Schatz, "New Hollywood" 34). Although Disney had partnered with Merchant Ivory in 1992, Miramax continued to dominate the prestige and high-culture end of the market even as it added genre films to its product lines (Balio, "Trends" 166). As the mid-sized specialty-division picture has increasingly saturated the independent cinema sector, the production, distribution, and exhibition networks for independents have shrunk or atrophied even as a glut of product has damaged profits. With the advent of IMAX and the rapid growth, since the 1980s, of the shopping-mall multiplex and freestanding megaplex—originally built to serve the multiple markets for adult and family cinema—independent film seems confined to a slowly eroding marketplace.

Critical attention to independent, national, and heritage cinemas must thus address the problem of cultural work at the millennium. Rather than constitute disciplinary combatants, literary, cultural, and film critics must now collaborate on cultural projects. We must ask: What constitutes cultural work at the millennium? How best may critics address heritage's contradictory ideological projects? How best to disseminate high-cultural products to larger audiences while preserving and circulating them via school and other institutions? How best to finance culture of all kinds, via national government funding, corporate underwriting, television sponsorship, philanthropic endowment, box-office purchase, or a mix of these? Although I seek to ask these large cultural questions, even if sometimes implicitly, I also understand the dangers attendant on this kind of interdisciplinary, indeed, cross-disciplinary, work: the methodological complexities of doing historically and culturally comparative work, given one's disciplinary training; the extraordinary difficulties of researching "real" audiences and consumers, whether Victorian or contemporary; the almost involuntary urge, by literary critics, to value print over visual- and popular-cultural texts; the impulse to generalize about nonprint media from too few examples. I seek to avoid these pitfalls by triangulating in each chapter literary texts, a problem in film studies, and a set of historically located discourses to quiz and complicate our notions of heritage and fidelity aesthetics, technologies of the body and look, practices of marketing sex, and the queering of heritage. Film adaptation is a culturally inflected process in an industry that creates the heterosexual romantic couple, that pictures cultural anxieties regarding the body-technology matrix, that practices self-censorship yet spawns pornography, and that suppresses yet markets emergent queer cultures. These historically, discursively, and aesthetically linked perspectives collide in a matrix of cultural forces that shape the ways we imagine and film our world.

Two chapters that address central problems in the study of literary film adaptation open this book. Chapter 1 assesses and moves beyond the heritage debate, in which 1980s television and film critics denounced heritage visual culture for its neoconservatism, its apparent complicity with Thatcher's heritage acts and enterprise economics. Based on anti-Thatcherite polemics by Robert Hewison and Patrick Wright, this critique originated with writers such as Higson, Craig, and, on the televisual side, Monica Lauritzen. During this historical moment, heritage culture and film and British national cinema were excoriated for picturing for a middle-brow audience the privileged lives of the English upper classes; for endorsing country ideology—the belief in the correctness and viability of social rank—in its various retrospective and nostalgic twentieth-century guises; for applauding private ownership of stately mansions as "a question of national prestige" (Hill, *1980s* 77–78). Yet the professional-managerial middle class, this culture's primary users, consumes heritage film because its members' fears about their shaky class position makes heritage film's

occluded but omnipresent status anxiety seem fascinating yet worrisome, especially its representation of the upper class and its social codes
of paternal benevolence, deference due to rank, and social restraint. The
Austen novels also barely occlude an omnipresent status anxiety invoked
by the historical shifts taking place during the Regency, a worry linked to
both rank mobility and marriage. The films of Jane Austen's novels, appearing between 1993 and 2005, remediate their source texts for a middle-
class audience fearful of geopolitical and national instability, anxious
about corporate downsizing and possible downward class mobility, and
later, about fiscal constraints during the worst financial crisis since the
Great Depression. In the 1980s and 1990s, the country-house film became
so popular precisely because it expressed late-century angst about the
nation's preeminence, about economic globalization, and about the future
of high culture.

In chapter 2, I argue that fidelity aesthetics must itself be historically
situated. Recent scholars seek to overturn the notion of fidelity aesthetics
that until recently governed the conversation about adaptation. Thomas
Leitch and Imelda Whelehan, for example, argue respectively that literacy
studies and cultural studies more appropriately represent the literature/
media exchange; other scholars, however, move beyond this impasse.[1] For
Sanders, "infidelity" to the original produces the "most creative acts of
adaptation and appropriation," and the cultural consumer's pleasure—
the "sense of play" between texts, the "interplay of expectation and surprise"—governs his or her experience (20, 25). Hutcheon, too, focuses on
modes of audience engagement, defining adaptation as "repetition with
modification" or "without replication"; adaptation's "knowing" consumer
experiences pleasure in the oscillation between recalled source and newly
experienced text, as "comfort of ritual and recognition" joins "the delight
of surprise and novelty" (167, 149, 120, 173). John Glavin argues, against
fidelity, that film (here, of novels by Charles Dickens) as a now-dominant
fictional mode shapes the ways late twentieth-century spectators read
nineteenth-century fiction (3, 5–6).

Other critics of fidelity aesthetics subvert fidelity by foregrounding
theory rather than comparative study. Stam wonders whether "strict fidelity is even *possible*," substituting "intertextual dialogism" for "the aporias
of 'fidelity'" (3–5). Leitch denounces "adaptation study under the sign of
literature," with its "fetishization" of fidelity, which enforces passive reading; like Sanders, Leitch calls for a "'pro-creational adaptation'" that freely

invokes and enacts the necessity of "rewriting" (*Adaptation* 16, 19). Yet Leitch seeks to "construct a systematic grammar" of modes of "intertextual reference," repeating earlier critics' now tired efforts to list the multiple strategies screenwriters and filmmakers deploy to adapt literature (*Adaptation* 20). Stam, on the contrary, uses film to map the multicultural history of the novel, whether realistic or magical or reflexive. Together, these critics privilege form to create an archive of adaptational modes. Nevertheless, nineteenth-century and early twentieth-century novels are apt for film adaptation precisely because, given their ambivalent commitment to narratological realism and experimentation, they suggest the impossibility of faithful remediation, of re-creation or re-production in a new medium. Fidelity aesthetics is always a shifting and malleable notion: as cultural values and sexual mores change from one historical moment, political situation, or national setting to another, the concept of fidelity shifts as well.

In chapter 3, I suggest that the 1990s remediations and remakes of gothic horror tales and flicks display and displace the human-machine matrix to address anxieties about the morphed, prosthetic, or ectogenous body. Renewed interest in all modes of cinematic horror during the decade served to arouse and alleviate the public's worry about new reproductive technologies (NRTs), genetic engineering, cyborgs, and cloning. Indeed, the cinematic apparatus and film's visual- and special-effects technologies serve as other machines that reproduce even as they threaten the body's integrity. Monsters and vampires fascinated nineteenth-century readers because they helped resolve problems associated with distributed maternity and paternity, historically specific ways of doing kinship, and the possibility of scientific body engineering and artificial procreation. These anomalous figures were deployed to imagine solutions to the problems of body replication, technological emergence and reproduction, and transnational flows of bodies, blood, illness, and mortality. In appropriating Victorian canonical fiction for the post-Victorian moment, the 1990s heritage gothic-horror film focused late twentieth-century fears about the status of the physiological body, mediated ways to do kinship, and the misuses of sexual—or technologically assisted—reproduction; horror addressed anxieties about the ways information, communication, and visual-cultural technologies extended or usurped the body's sense organs even as they glamorized these effects. These late-century gothic-horror films also managed the anxieties they stimulated, for as a genre, horror reconfirms heteronormative, often conservative, political values and gen-erates apathy, complacency, and self-protective numbness during decades of social and cultural dislocation.

Heritage film, I argue in chapter 4, shapes and serves niche tastes even as it deploys a crossover aesthetic to enlarge its market share. The Henry James films' uneasy position in the new Hollywood accounts for their problematic reception, for the James filmgoers, like the readers of the novels themselves, have never constituted a mass audience. Indeed, James's ambivalence about his lack of cultural popularity is a critical com-monplace. Independent producers and directors understand, as did he, the demand for cultural, here box-office, success, for it enables them to choose projects, acquire funding, find distributors, and secure the market-ing and publicity necessary to get exhibited on the art-house or indepen-dent cinema circuit. Because mass popularity often eludes heritage film, the James adaptors knowingly chose to shoot the sex scenes at which James only hinted—or at most represented through veils of narratorial consciousness—to create audience buzz. Although James's high-cultural novels hardly seem apt for remediation, on film they define the 1990s middlebrow, a cinematic aesthetic and market niche central to indepen-dent film's efforts to cross over to mainstream success without the advan-tages of saturation booking, television advertising, and easy access to ancillary markets, while competing with other cultural products in a seg-mented, highly diversified, yet market-saturated and conglomerated new Hollywood industry. The Henry James movies' failure was thus overdeter-mined, as independent heritage film sought to go mass market by shoot-ing and selling sex.

In chapter 5, the country house becomes queer-heritage icon. Late-century heritage film remediated late nineteenth- and early twentieth-century novels and plays to picture a sentimental sisterhood and male homosociality, to perform and undermine marginalization, oppression, and the demand for gay self-censorship. Distinct styles of homosexual effeminacy and connoisseurship as well as aesthetic responses to the exigencies of gay life, these cultural projects mix modes, fashion malle-able icons, and open a space for middlebrow, avant-garde, and biopic experimentation. Sentimental queer heritage film also interrogates the values associated with heritage: social restraint, deference due to rank, and paternal benevolence. Even as social restraint morphs and becomes "unspeakability," however, these films solicit a homospectatorial look as they display the eroticized male body. The paradoxical model and mediator in the genealogy of such gay male projects is, of course, Oscar Wilde; as figure, Wilde structures my account of queer-heritage remediations, in which a cross-historical cultural cluster or assemblage of texts appropriates Wilde to sentimentalize life in the country house.

In the millennium, the globalization and mass marketing of heritage film signals a cultural, historical, and aesthetic shift. Heritage film has gone Bollywood, as world English has disseminated classic British narratives to audiences in, say, South Asia, via colonial university curricula as well as alternative sites of consumption. Heritage and Bollywood films share a dedication to hybrid aesthetics, and both modes manage audience affects by mixing genres, marketing star images, and spectacularizing mise-en-scènes. Despite heterogeneous production practices, Bollywood, like Hollywood, creates the heterosexual couple, here, in a *masala* genre mix of sentiment, melodrama, and romance. No longer solely national, Bollywood's millennial audience is diasporic, for the postcolonial Indian "nation" is among the most complex and heterogeneous of communities. In addition, a new round of adaptations has begun appearing at the megaplex and on the small screen. Even as the BBC and WGBH's *Masterpiece Theatre* treat middle-aged professional-managerial fans to new versions of Austen, Forster, Dickens, Emily Brontë, and Elizabeth Gaskell, they solicit a younger audience for heritage film with an updated, more quickly paced story: dramatizers familiar to heritage devotees and upstart millennial-generation British filmmakers now adapt classic fiction for the graying domestic audience and the global teenaged set. As Elinor and Marianne go Bollywood, as Lizzie gets hitched to a hunky American hotel magnate or brooding, upper-class Brit, the Jane Austen movie enters a new historical moment.

As millennial culture goes high-tech, digital, Web-based, and virtual-reality, film will continue to remediate a now-residual print culture for a North Atlantic community hooked on quality, middlebrow, and high-camp pleasures. Heritage culture, in general, and heritage film, in particular, are complex formations whose texts are embedded in and are about our own embeddedness in history. As such, this cultural mode is not symptomatic of postmodern temporal dissociation but is a cultural indicator of how post-Victorian culture operates on and through history to address its most pressing crises. Neither monolithic nor politically conservative, heritage film presents us with the reason to keep studying it: not because it adapts or remediates Jane Austen, not because it franchises gothic horror, not because it challenges heteronormativity, but because it reminds us of our own historical situatedness. The cultural work of the literature/film intertext, then, is to invoke the history of historical consciousness, to picture the historical imagination at work on social contradictions. Heritage film morphs, travels, and productively forces us to imagine ourselves in different but not unrelated historical dilemmas and difficulties as we seek to live within and survive our own millennial age of anxiety.

CHAPTER 1

Heritage Film, Classic Serial, and England's Jane

The national heritage of this country is remarkably broad and rich.... Its potential for enjoyment must be maintained, its educational value for succeeding generations must be enriched and its economic value in attracting tourists to this country must be appreciated and developed. But this national heritage is constantly under threat.

—First Annual Report, National Heritage Memorial Fund, 1980–81, *Britain's Heritage*

When we say "Jane Austen" everyone knows what we're talking about. Austen means class, literature, virginity, and family viewing.... "We love Jane Austen because she's Heritage."

—Fay Weldon, "Jane to Rescue"

THE NATIONAL HERITAGE MEMORIAL FUND'S First Annual Report identifies the conservative uses for contemporary culture of imagining the past, the ways audience enjoyment may be mobilized to consolidate national cultural hegemony, and the ways anxiety about perceived threats to national heritage may be aroused. Seeking to stimulate tourist traffic at Britain's museums, historical attractions, country houses, and on preservation lands, adherents of heritage culture generally take retrogressive positions in the ongoing debates about public access to and private ownership of estates, gardens, and cultural treasures, disputes that, in the eighteenth and nineteenth centuries, took place in print and through political speechifying. As John Hill notes, heritage culture is widely thought to feature the "privileged lifestyles of the English upper classes, elite institutions[,] ... the country (and country house), the Home Counties, and ex-colonies" to applaud private ownership as "a question of national prestige" (*1980s* 77–78) and, as Andrew Higson argues, to present as national the heritage of a fractional upper class ("Re-Presenting" 114). The professional-managerial middle class, this culture's primary users since the 1970s, consumes these texts, artifacts, and experiences because its members, unsure about their class position's stability, find heritage culture's occluded but omnipresent status anxiety attractive yet worrisome, especially its representation of rank and elite social codes, of the nation and its geopolitical power. The 1980s and 1990s country-house films became so popular precisely because, like the Heritage Memorial Fund's Report, they expressed late-century fears about the future of high culture, the nation-state's continuing preeminence, and economic globalization's threat to personal and national financial stability.

Although filmmakers may use heritage culture's codes and conventions to endorse conservative values, they may also critique, reassess, rehistoricize, or lampoon notions of the nation, tradition, and rank. Dynamic rather than monolithic, heritage culture enables consumers to interpret its discourse from multiple perspectives: to celebrate or question its representations of paternal benevolence, deference due to rank, and social restraint; to glorify or interrogate the value of upper-class ownership of cultural treasures; to document the labor histories of the middle and working classes for its late twentieth-century professional-class consumers. Heritage film's prestige, moreover, serves to differentiate its texts from Hollywood's products—the global blockbuster, the special effects testosterone flick—in an international multimedia marketplace that must increasingly meet niche demands. Late twentieth-century heritage films instruct their spectators in the many ideological uses of heritage culture: consume this film as icon in an endangered cultural tradition; use it as a form of tourism or class snobbery; make it camp and give it edge. Neither inherently nor essentially conservative, the heritage film, and the country house as its icon, may contest what Dror Wahrman calls "country ideology" for the contemporary moment, may even herald or record the "collapse of deference" (22; Cannadine, *Class* 164). Politically complex and multivalent, heritage film may promulgate liberal or conservative political messages in a highly segmented cultural marketplace, may display the value of its literary source to document its prestige, or may expose the impasse at which neoliberalism's mid-to-late-century ideological projects arrived.

The debates about high-cultural ownership and public access to those treasures, about deference due to aristocratic rank and the value of social restraint, about social class as an indicator of taste, and about cultural consumption in the service of social distinction express the worries of their historical moments and global locations. In each, the figure of Jane Austen signals apprehension about cultural value and possession. Austen's stories enable middle-class readers or spectators to cope with economic difficulty or to celebrate moments of conspicuous yet tenuous financial success, invariably limned with shadowy fears of failure. In the first section of this chapter, I argue that the 1990s films and classic serials of Jane Austen's novels critique the conservative version of Austen to expose heritage film's present uses of the political and historical past. In the second section, I consider Austen's country-house novels, which inscribe for late twentieth-century readers what Lawrence and Jeanne Stone define as an occluded but omnipresent status anxiety (*Élite* 423–24). Indeed, the heritage audience's position in a professional-managerial middle class structurally resembles Austen's own as member of a well-educated, professional middle class invested in the culture of patrimony, a fragile class position that overdetermined Austen's socially insecure fiction. In the third section, I look back to the decades of prestige pictures and of the BBC classic serial to argue that Austen's stories were used to arouse and allay interwar fears about post-Depression penury and worries about a newly declared war in Europe, or, at late century, to provide an acute analysis of neoliberalism's ideological impasse. At chapter's end, I show that, no less than the members of the National Trust, twentieth-century guardians of the literary canon view classic culture as under threat and in danger of being eclipsed. Heritage-culture fans and protectors of the canon worry equally about the public's ignorance of literary, artistic, or architectural culture and, paradoxically, its commodification and defacement by overly easy access.

This tension between the demand for cultural preservation and the fear of degraded popularity through public access drives the contradictions that shape heritage culture's apparently contradictory ideological projects. The Jane Austen films, as a group, likewise display this tension: they secure spectators access to heritage-culture sites and classic literary stories to enhance social and cultural capital; they incorporate and seek to surpass, pay respect to, and spoof the famous spinster writer. Although it began in the 1930s, the critical fear of mass culture's attack on Englishness reappeared in the 1980s as neoconservative antagonism about cultural illiteracy and canonical ignorance. In the ebullient 1990s, the Jane

Austen boom signaled a similar yet displaced worry about the continuing viability of print culture, the widening appeal of visual and technological culture, and the seemingly forbidding future for cultural workers, teachers, and specialists alike.

The Jane Austen Decade

According to research on the professional-managerial class's nonwork pastimes, heritage culture's middle-class users value the knowledge that provides them cultural capital; indeed, this sector of the tourism and leisure industry continues to expand. As Pierre Bourdieu claims, these cultural workers' occupations in the presentational and representational fields of media, teaching, advertising, and design means they create, disseminate, and market symbolic goods. In their lifelong labor of cultural acquisition and self-improvement, they accumulate, so as to transmit and convert, social capital; serving as cultural intermediaries and gatekeepers for aspiring others, they consume, produce, and specify new knowledges. The disposition to collect and the cultivation to discriminate among cultural goods, although marked by its early familial conditions of acquisition, thus requires the expenditure of time, energy, labor, and already accumulated cultural capital, and this consumption necessitates a class position consistent with patterns of high-quality spending.[1] Like Bourdieu, John Urry links British cultural-consumption patterns to taste and class hierarchies and identifies those who work in "'education, health, and welfare' public services" as consumers not of "middlebrow" but of high art.[2] As Richard Prentice's sociological research on tourism also indicates, British and American members of the professional, nonmanufacturing class consume heritage culture, usually while on holiday, to "produce beneficial feelings" of, say, inspiration and relaxation (225–30).

These critics assume, as does Bourdieu, that a "socially recognized hierarchy of the arts" corresponds to a "social hierarchy of [its] consumers": that taste functions as a marker of class (*Distinction* 1–2). As Sharon Zukin notes, however, Bourdieu's "snapshot" of midcentury social life "presents a rather quaint image of *la France éternelle* familiar from school French texts" (38). Indeed, Bourdieu often fails to indicate the historical moment in which his familial, class, and institutional analyses are located.[3] His disdain of the late-century shift from domestic and familial cultivation to educational acquisition of competency skews his 1960s research on social

distinction, which demands updating for a millennial moment characterized by rising educational achievement, the emergence of technological
and digital hardware, and a continually evolving new media culture. Even
in a 1980s study of Scottish women readers Bridget Fowler found that
although Bourdieu was correct that the "market for culture is deeply segmented" and that inherited economic capital or family class standing
"provides the 'habitus', or situation plus dispositions" to acquire "legitimate taste," increased access to educational resources had created a "new
stratum" populated by service-class public-sector administrators and pro-
fessionals that consumed culture and had acquired "legitimate taste,"
broadly defined (170). According to Michael Kammen, after midcentury
in the United States, "direct correlations between social class and lifestyle
became progressively more elusive" (243). At century's end in Britain,
taste hierarchies no longer "exactly correspond[ed] to social distinctions"
among the classes but were linked instead, as Sue Harper suggests, with
a sense of "status, intellectual pretensions, and definitions of culture"
(56). Not only family of origin and early schooling, Bourdieu's primary
determinants of social distinction, but also gender, race, age, marital status, geographical location, postsecondary educational opportunity, and
attitudes toward financial risk affected cultural attainment and shaped
taste (Harper 136–53).

Thus the late-century professional-managerial middle class, with which
I am concerned in this chapter, may cross taste cultures as it consumes
products within a highly differentiated and commercialized global marketplace. Yet that middle class was itself segmented and diversified at century's
end. In Britain, Higson reports, professional educators as a middle-class
fraction prefer art-house films, whereas corporate managers choose mainstream entertainment; moreover, since the 1980s, a "slight upmarket trend"
has produced an "increasing embourgeoisement" of the UK cinema audience (Heritage 102–3). According to David Cannadine, "the overwhelming majority" of U.S. citizens now "regard themselves as middle class," and
the century-long expansion of the middle class (and creation of its frac-
tions) means that, although cultural stratification and differing taste levels
exist in the United States, their ranks are increasingly "permeable" (Class
190; Kammen 73). American baby boomers "prefer a more diversified
cultural menu than their parents did," and their "bicultural" purchase of
cultural products makes their straddling class boundaries likely (Kammen
254, 244).

Zukin argues, moreover, that late twentieth-century cultural purchase and use is "consumption-biased rather than demand-led" (39). Not conditioned by the urge solely to acquire and possess beautiful objects or to engage in heritage tourism, cultural consumption in the service of social distinction is now shaped by the industry's marketing strategies, and culturally dominant narrative-genre products, such as film, currently serve to advertise other products and so become themselves consumption-biased sites. Period films do so less often than those set in contemporary time; whereas network television now incorporates advertising into the show, the period film sells a less identifiable product, the disposition to acquire legitimate taste, to appreciate and take pleasure in canonical literary texts adapted for the screen. Zukin also emphasizes that the culture industries produce "*real* cultural capital." Bourdieu's term "cultural capital," she insists, must be expanded to refer not only to knowledge, possession, and mastery of cultural goods but also to the "capital invested in culture industries, from film to food, magazines, architecture, and decor." "'Symbolic consumption practices'" thus "provide a 'real' base" for "capital accumulation" (38).[4] Although Zukin neglects to ask who benefits from such accumulation, the fact of this capital investment—for the film industry, funding for technological innovation, expansion of exhibition outlets, and massive advertising in print and other media—demands that we now understand cultural texts as "software" in a global-technological marketplace. Bourdieu himself recently admitted that "social capital" is never "completely independent" of economic capital ("Forms" 51).

The 1990s heritage films and serials of Jane Austen's novels display and thematize cultural consumption: the disposition to practice the habits of good taste, the real value of acculturation as an investment that could produce economic returns; the formation and enhancement of social capital—the unceasing effort of sociability and the continuous exchanges that, deploying specific competencies, promote the creation of (in Austen's novels, familial and class-based) aggregates. The spectator who purchased a ticket to an Austen film, tuned in to a serial, or bought or rented a DVD thus practiced cultural acquisition and identified with pictured sociability, herself participating in cultural-capital accumulation. If she had read Jane Austen's novel, her cultural capital compounded; if not, she earned it through having purchased a twentieth-century remediation.[5] Nonetheless, this 1990s spectator watched films about the acquisition and ownership of cultural treasures, the tutelary imperative that the female introject a man's tenets of taste so as to prove herself worthy of a well-born husband of rank by reproducing his taste aesthetic through her education.

The Jane Austen decade opened and closed with two ideologically contradictory adaptations of *Pride and Prejudice,* one critiquing, the other eroticizing the values of cultural acquisition and accumulation among the upper gentry. Andrew Davies' classic-serial dramatization (1995), for example, displays the patriarchal estate as a repository of cultural treasures and its master as a model of paternal benevolence and social restraint. Yet this Darcy awaits Elizabeth Bennet's miraculous, transformative power, although she will bring to the upper gentry Austen's omnipresent status anxiety. On a tour of Derbyshire, Lizzie and her aunt and uncle Gardiner visit Pemberley and so introduce to the estate Lizzie's soothing yet agitating presence. As Darcy (Colin Firth) rides a white horse across his land and toward his country house, Davies crosscuts to Elizabeth (Jennifer Ehle) walking the picture gallery, a parade space that demonstrates Darcy's ancestors' dedication to cultural acquisition; cut to the estate shot from Darcy's (and the spectator's) perspective. Cut to the master's portrait in the gallery; to Darcy, disrobing; to Elizabeth, looking bemusedly at the portrait; to Darcy in shirttails and breeches as he dives into a pond and then swims, shot underwater, toward the camera; to Elizabeth, admiring the park's gardens; to Darcy, now walking, with shirt out, muscular body visible through his clinging wet shirt—as he meets Elizabeth, with surprise.[6] "I can't imagine what has effected this transformation," Elizabeth exclaims, as Darcy—once dressed—invites her to meet his sister, Mr. Gardiner (Tim Wylton) to fish on his lands, and all to have supper at Pemberley. Immersed in Pemberley's ponds and entranced by Elizabeth, Darcy emerges altered, the sequence suggests, playing on a tension between self-possession or authenticity and public presentation. Indeed, the scene asks, how may the filmmaker accurately map cultural representations onto real—or pictured—bodies? The partially dressed figure the spectator looks at necessarily represents, as do his estate and cultural acquisitions, the Darcy persona's properties—and property.

Director Simon Langton pictures the historical links among cultural capital accumulation, the country house or estate, the privileges of rank, and the virtues of upper-gentry paternalism. As the sequence suggests, the cultural apparatus of the Regency ruling class—the capability to collect and display art collections for selected visitors at stately homes—demanded leisure, a fashionable aesthetic education, and nearly boundless funds.[7]

During the late eighteenth and early nineteenth centuries, Linda Colley claims, members of the landed establishment, arguing that patrician art collections served a "public benefit" and were "an asset to the nation," began to open their country-house art collections to "acceptable members of the public" (175). By the 1770s, what Adrian Tinniswood calls the "polite tourist"—no longer a connoisseur or antiquarian—sought to develop, by visiting houses and gardens, his or her taste and to refine his or her sensibilities.[8] Eighteenth-century domestic tourism mobilized the lesser gentry into the English countryside's privately owned spaces, provided access to the estates and homes of the wealthy, and "seduc[ed] them into an identification with the tastes and interests of the landed rich," creating a fantasy of ownership and possession, of "shared participation" in an aesthetic space that glorified and idealized the region and, later, the nation (Fabricant 257). By the nineteenth century, the country house had become a repository for works of art and their collections, a matter of "public benefit" and an "asset to the nation"; the new private galleries, moreover, enabled the gentry to view art without questioning cultural private ownership as an economic principle that governed the

A wet-shirted Darcy strides across fields and by ponds to Pemberley—and Elizabeth. (Pride and Prejudice, *1995*)

emergent European art market (Colley 175–76). In the nineteenth century, financially strapped Italian princes and continental royalists and aristocrats sold their riches abroad, as Europe's art treasures began their slow migration west. In the twentieth century, they would move west once again, to U.S. museums and private collections (Cannadine, *Aspects* 27), and, in the twenty-first century, begin to be repatriated eastward, to Italy, Greece, and Austria.

Even as it displayed and constituted social distinction during Jane Austen's time, domestic tourism served to sustain appropriate relations among members of the fractional gentry class. At least in part to create a socially stabilizing consensus between the gentry and the emerging middle class and to maintain their own privilege, the landed elite participated in constituting country ideology, which depicted eighteenth-century social structures as rightfully hierarchical. Yet the wars with revolutionary America and France, the demands of a massive new empire, the pace of "administrative and industrial" life at home, all proved a "corrosive challenge to patrician confidence and authority" as the century ended (Colley 152). During the 1780s, denunciation of the landed elite entered the political mainstream, as even conservative middle-class commentators railed against patrician degeneracy (Colley 154). By the 1790s, the attribution of middle-class virtues had become a rhetorical strategy appropriable by "competing political camps," although this rhetoric was neither unified nor coherent (Wahrman 179, 36–55; see Spring). Nevertheless, new forms of civil society, Miriam Hansen argues, based on an "autonomy grounded in the private realm" and constituted via "the intimate sphere of the nuclear family" also created new norms of social interaction, which included "equality, mutual respect, general accessibility, and potential openness" among family members and affiliates (8). Aristocratic social relations—paternal benevolence, deference accorded to rank, and social restraint—thus began to decline, as values that governed the public sphere entered the private domain, and new protobourgeois social relations—the increasing power of daughters to choose marital partners, for example—emerged in turn. Thus, Elizabeth Bennet and her aunt and uncle Gardiner might visit Pemberley to view its pleasant grounds, well-proportioned rooms, and elegant but not bedizened furnishings.

In the sequence in which the tourist Lizzie and the disheveled Darcy meet, Langton updates Austen for the millennial moment, displacing concerns about private ownership of and public access to cultural treasures onto the late twentieth-century fascination with sexuality and gender relations. Written and shot as "serious adult drama," Sue Birtwistle, producer of *Pride and Prejudice* and *Emma*, declares, the late-century classic serial focused on sex and money, the postmodern equivalents of rank aspiration and landed-estate ownership (Giddings and Selby 118, 104). The cuts between Darcy's portrait and his gradually exposed body; between Elizabeth, looking, and Darcy, soliciting the look; between house, with picture gallery, and landscape, with park, gardens, and pond, all suggest the fertile, "natural" penetration of estate by polite tourist, upper by lesser gentry—and, paradoxically or psychically, male by female, who surprises Darcy, disrobed. Davies maps the male body onto landscape, estate, and nation as Darcy's torso displays an "erotics of nationalism" that exposes and interrogates the class and social boundaries his rank seeks to command (Hayward 97). Welcoming tradesmen to his estate, endorsing the housekeeper's tours for bourgeois interlopers, and so facilitating a historically emergent tourism of his country house and its gardens and galleries, Darcy is recruited out of his prideful social restraint and into a gentrified generosity, out of public assertion of patrician essence, cultural and estate ownership, and into private (here, possibly sexual) intimacies. Only when this transformation has occurred may an aspiring lesser-gentry daughter without brothers enter the country house, meet the family, and fantasize her figure into its spaces and among its figures. Langton's wildly popular upmarket serial solicited spectatorial delight in the social distinction Lizzie would acquire by aligning herself with that hunky, upscale, and eroticized male body.[9]

Roger Michell's theatrically released teleplay, *Persuasion* (1995), rehistoricizes a period Jane Austen to display her nostalgic yet uneasy take on the decline of a land-based social hierarchy, the fragility of cultural capital, and the disappearance of rural England for cultural consumers themselves worried about fiscal constraints and class status. When Sir Walter (Corin Redgrave) leaves Kellynch Hall, he exudes patrician essence, failing to see the people who work the land as other than submissive caricatures; these servants and peasants, shot in close-up from his perspective via glance/object cuts, wear appropriately impassive facial expressions (for deference was, by 1817, already on the wane, even in the country, and merit was emerging). When Anne (Amanda Root) leaves Kellynch, by contrast, a hand-held camera shoots the carriage and its cargo of caged pigs and ducks; cut to Anne's sad face, then to shots of the countryside from her point of view, the camera mimicking her bumpy ride, her jumpy sight of fields, sheep, horses, and trees; a backward, retrospective look at Kellynch; and—after a long pan—another field of grazing sheep. As the carriage enters Uppercross, Laycock Village—the film's location setting—resembles a relic of English country life, complete with sheep in the rutted dirt road. Yet Michell's rural panorama self-reflexively depicts mid-twentieth-century nostalgia for a coherent national past even as it exposes that nostalgia as located in a particular retrospective glance and historical vantage point. Anne possesses the film's historical awareness, which is represented by the long point-of-view shot that identifies her look as structuring this sequence and, in particular, by her backward glance. Historically in crisis, patrician arrogance will fail to deny the gentry daughter's emergent, postaristocratic, and protobourgeois perspective. Here, Austen depicts the moment in which country ideology becomes residual and a middle-class future is fashioned out of the multiple structural relation of present distress, past unattainability, and bourgeois future making. Remediating country ideology via point-of-view shots, Michell alerts the spectator that she, too, participates in ideology through the mediating structures of his historically analytical film.[10] For the late twentieth-century spectator, a coherent rural England is still disappearing.

Michell also repoliticizes Austen for a 1990s audience anxious about the relevance of an apparently out-of-date nationalism in a period of strategic warfare, excess expenditure, and relative economic decline. The brilliant credit sequence sets a bifurcated world of men at sea against that of women and dandies at home: a crane shot of sailors rowing; a shot of elegantly dressed people exiting from (and later entering into) estate doorways that echo the screen's (constraining) frame; a low-angle shot of a sailor climbing the ship's ropes; hand-held shots of the Elliots jumping into their carriage to escape dunning creditors; tracking shots of Admiral Croft surveying the troops and of men at sea toasting their fortunes below deck: "Gentlemen, the war is over." In shots of Anne Elliot's family at Bath, Michell critiques a dandified Regency notion of status and distinction, presenting as residual an insistence on deference and submission, rank hierarchy, and paternal benevolence. His camera tracks around the cold, elegantly furnished rooms, the clothing-sheathed people positioned singly on upscale Regency chaises; circling behind them, the camera pictures their isolation within a regime of patrician essence exposed as anxious rank maintenance: will they be snubbed by genteel relations?

Later, the Bath family genuflects and grovels to these estranged aristocratic cousins as Michell's mise-en-scène parodies their acts—framed by hung "curtain"—as performances. The film thus rewrites the novel's historical concerns by imagining patrician snobbery (and anxiety) from the present's skeptical perspective. It juxtaposes the dominance of the British Navy with supercession of the gentry estate and affirms the rise of the middle-class professional while ironizing the aspiring midcentury bourgeois man who has gained entrée to the military officer corps. Michell interprets Austen's novel as weighing the world of debt-ridden and entailed estates, inauthoritative fathers and dysfunctional families, fashionable women and shopping daughters against that of professional men at sea, traveling the world, making their fortunes, and bringing their wives with them aboard ship.[11]

The figure of the gentry daughter is the fulcrum on which this critical and historical lever works.[12] The traveling daughter and the moving wife depict an emergent form of bourgeois womanhood. When Louisa Musgrove (Emma Roberts) jumps from the Cobb at Lyme Regis, a remarkable low-angle, slow-motion shot of her body falling, the camera seeming to tilt up her dress as she falls—first feet, then petticoat ruffle, then skirt, bodice, and finally face—illustrates the dangers of female travel to a then medicinal but soon-to-be pleasure-seeking setting where men and sea meet ladies and land. Literally "throwing herself" at Frederick Wentworth (Ciaran Hinds), Louisa displays the historical emergence and the danger of such seaside notions of flirtation (see Urry, Gaze 16–39). Point-of-view and slow-motion shots accentuate, by contrast, Anne Elliot's function to locate perspective, constitute critique, and imagine a dynamic future. After her narcissistic father and sister "retrench" to Bath, Anne closes up Kellynch Hall before the estate's new tenants arrive: Admiral and Mrs. Croft (John Woodvine, Fiona Shaw), a Navy man and his globe-trotting wife. As a servant throws sheets over the furniture, a remarkable shot from a chair's point of view pictures Kellynch's sad state before the sheet closes over it, whitening the frame.[13] In a filmic reversal that ironically attributes to the country house the subjective qualities of vision, the estate's objects see Anne's loneliness, whereas her rank-bound father sees a flaw in her complexion. The transformation of country house to rental property, the displacement of the gentry family to lodgings (even if only to recuperate their finances), and the daughter's apprehensively having to support, even cause that move, both portray Austen's view of the historical estate's endangerment as anxious—despite its attraction to daughters who desire to have and inhabit one.

Michell's movie, then, sets the country estate, created through condensation as the seat of patrician essence, against the fortunes of the professional man and bourgeois daughter. The film associates occupational enterprise with manhood, publicity, and landlessness even as it displays a historical shift away from patrician essence, deference hierarchies, and paternal benevolence. Having once broken her engagement to Wentworth because, as Lady Russell counseled, he had "nothing but himself to recommend him," Anne Elliot eagerly accepts this professional man when, after accumulating the spoils of war in the Caribbean theater, he is "no longer nobody" (*Persuasion* 19, 165).[14] Indeed, he has been promoted due to his merit in a system opposed to one of heredity, which Anne's ineffectual father represents (McMaster 121). As Michell's *Persuasion* ends, the public staging of private intimacy successfully challenges residual forms of civil interaction and social restraint: Frederick and Anne kiss on the Bath Circus, as a historically accurate yet literarily anachronistic circus parade—of freaks, jugglers, and clowns—passes the kissing couple.

Lady Russell consoles Anne Elliot as Kellynch Hall is let to Admiral and Mrs. Croft. (Persuasion, *1995*)

Choosing to leave her (endangered) country estate, choosing to marry down in rank, Austen's Anne Elliot is situated during the historically salubrious emergence of professionalism and conjugality alongside the questioning of deference hierarchies and country ideology. In a later moment of post-welfare-state economic distress in the United Kingdom, of dot-com boom and bust in the United States, Michell's Anne justifies the rise of the twentieth-century middle class and hails its status-anxious members to the box office.

In the millennial *Pride and Prejudice* (2005), Joe Wright displays country dinginess and maternal monetary worry during a decade of North Atlantic fiscal anxiety and fear of downward mobility. Amid Longbourne's domestic clutter, its untended grounds and workers' cottages, Wright pictures the Bennet girls as desperate for rescue from estate-entailed impoverishment. Charlotte (Claudie Blakley) tells Lizzie (Keira Knightley) that she's twenty-seven, a burden to her parents, and likely to be as happy with Collins as any other: "Don't you dare judge me," she commands; cut to Lizzie's visit and, as she and Charlotte settle in the drawing room exclusively for her use, Charlotte sighs, "Oh, Lizzie, how I love managing my own home." Wright's more-than-slightly hysterical Mrs. Bennet (Brenda Blethyn) reproves a critical Lizzie: "When you have five daughters, you'll think of nothing but marriage," she yells up the stairs, shot from the landing above her and through banisters, signs of her fiscal fear and constraint. Recuperating Austen's quietly practical—certainly not embittered—analysis of an unmarried, lesser-gentry female future, Deborah Moggach's screenplay rewrites Lizzie's story of upward mobility as a tale of overt status anxiety and envy of rank and wealth.

Wright's adaptation foregrounds class antagonism. Caroline Bingley's (Kelly Reilly) intervention in her clownish brother's tepid flirtation with shy and sweet Jane (Rosamund Pike) has never been cattier, colder, more cutting; Mr. Collins's (Tom Hollander) assessment of Longbourne's worth and sizing up of Bennet girls as possible wives—whispered to Mrs. Bennet as rack focus and glamour lighting sharply etch Lizzie's profile—never crasser. When Elizabeth visits her sick sister at Netherfield, hair streaming and hem muddied, she enters a drawing room markedly different from Longbourne's. Wright's mise-en-scène, like Michell's Bath scenario, features a sparely furnished, upscale room, with exquisitely tailored furnishings much marveled at as "expensive" by Mrs. Bennet and her girls; liveried servants—gentler than the aged, tattered, and rude variety at

Longbourne—introduce "Mrs. Bennet, Miss Bennet, Miss Bennet, . . . and Miss Bennet"; cut to Mrs. and Misses, plopping on settee. "I'm just admiring the general splendor," Lizzie gawks. The visit to Pemberley increases Lizzie's admiration. As she and her aunt and uncle Gardiner enter the stately mansion, Lizzie's look structures the sequence.[15] Here, the tourists look not at portraits but sculpture, as Lizzie eyes reclining chivalric male, supine pulchritudinous female: embodied cultural capital. With Lizzie (in foreground), the Gardiners, and Mrs. Reynolds (in background), she looks wistfully at Darcy's bust. Hardly a polite tourist, Lizzie wanders alone through the house, gazing admiringly at ceiling murals, elegant furnishings, and flowers and fingering desk, vases, and bust: the aesthetic goods that index Darcy's status, taste, and rank (here significantly higher than in Austen's novel) are evidence of the estate's monumentality, its extravagant cultural and real capital accumulation. Lizzie wanders to a window, out onto a balcony, to a balustrade; glance/object cut to the patterned garden, with fountain, as rack focus brings it into clear view. Harpsichord music wafts onto sound track, as Lizzie turns, reenters the mansion, examines more cultural goods (as do we), moves to an open door and listens; cut to a girl, playing, shot from the back and reflected in a mirror; to Lizzie, looking into the room, door ajar; to back of a masculine figure, entering frame left; to Lizzie, in close-up, watching; to girl, leaping up, and man desperately hugging; the two turn and see Lizzie, looking; cut to extreme close-up of Lizzie's eyes; to Lizzie, running, to terrace, only to be followed by Darcy (Matthew Macfadyen). Here, Elizabeth's voyeuristic, envious, implicitly self-aggrandizing looks exhibit her identification with rank and connoisseurship, her estate envy, the almost crass materialism of a soon-to-be impoverished girl—unless she marries up.

And marry she does. Moggach's ending, without precedent in the novel, supplies a "post-coital clinch" that serves the teenaged imaginary and the American market alike (Stanley, "Yes"). Kneeling on a balcony that overlooks the park's lake, lit by torches, Darcy asks Lizzie what he shall call her; when he's "incandescently happy," she says, "Mrs. Darcy"; as the camera tracks in to close-up, he alternately kisses and proclaims her marital state. Borrowing strategies from the romance genre, Moggach truncates Austen's plot to feature the heterosexual couple's inevitable coupling: trimming details of Jane's visit to London, Lydia's to Brighton, and Lizzie's flirtation with Wickham; telescoping into montage Mary's embarrassingly bad pianoforte playing, Collins's courtship of Lizzie, the Bennet family's response to Collins's proposal to Charlotte, and Lydia's and Kitty's flirtations with officers. Deploying follow focus at the crowded Netherfield ball, cinematographer Roman Osin tracks figural interaction (father silently soothing a distraught Mary, Collins plucking petals from a daisy, Kitty and Lydia whispering) that suggests subplots yet does not distract from Lizzie and Darcy's centrality. Cast for elegant neck, collarbone, and pout, Knightley postures and preens, always aware of her beauty, courting Darcy's look, arousing the female spectator's envy and anticipation of the male viewer's look. More Brontë than Austen hero, Darcy proposes to Elizabeth in a Palladian folly, in a rain-drenched park, lake in the background; screaming her rage at his arrogance, Elizabeth leans against a column, spent, as he stalks off in the storm. Wright's romance exploits the status anxiety everywhere apparent in Moggach's lucid analysis of female endangerment under primogeniture, reworks it from a perspective on class antagonism rather than a postfeminist focus on gender.

These heritage films and serials of Jane Austen's novels, then, need not be viewed as necessarily nostalgic or politically conservative. In the

Newlyweds Darcy and Lizzie kiss at the climax of Joe Wright's Pride *and* Prejudice *(2005).*

1980s, Higson claimed that heritage film commodified the British past so as to articulate a "nostalgic and conservative celebration of the values and lifestyles of the privileged classes" (*Heritage* 12).

Higson invoked Cairns Craig, who likewise viewed heritage film's pictured "country houses," "panelled interiors," and period costumes as fashioning a "perfection of style" that denied the "difference of culture" during the "last great age of the English *haute bourgeoisie*" (10–11). Martin Hipsky dismissed heritage film as "upmarket escapism" that produced a "sanitized, guilt-free nostalgia" (103–6). Yet Raphael Samuel argues that heritage is a "nomadic term" that "register[s] changes in public taste" (205, 211); Peter Mandler, that nineteenth-century "popular and national history" shaped heritage (*Fall* 4). For Claire Monk, the 1980s heritage-film debate is itself a "historically specific discourse, rooted in and responsive to [the] particular cultural conditions and events" of Thatcherite conservatism, the passing of the National Heritage Acts of 1980 and 1983, and 1980s British media politics ("Debate" 177–78). As Hill demonstrates, the 1980s British educational and arts communities opposed Thatcherism for its "apparent philistinism" and "hostility to public provision for the arts," showing an intellectual disdain for the "divisive consequences of Thatcherite economic policies" (*1980s* 30). For Alison Light, "the return to Edwardian England in the '80s [was] as much a rejection of Thatcherism and its ethics as a crude reflection of it" (63). Failing to historicize their own ideologically inflected discursive position, the 1980s heritage critics sometimes misread the analysis of status anxiety as complicity with Thatcher's political program.

Spectators in the 1990s, like post-Depression moviegoers and 1970s and 1980s television viewers, avidly consumed adaptations of Austen's novels to indulge and alleviate status anxiety, a powerful boom-and-bust fear in a financially extravagant yet downsizing decade. These films and classic serials address and seek to resolve some of the same, or cognate, structural problems of class and social privilege for their historical moments that Austen's novels did for the Regency. Because heritage culture focuses on issues of class and rank, of cultural ownership and acculturation, heritage film, its visual mode, appropriates or remediates Austen's novels, retrospectively reinterpreting her tales in light of present needs. The films' semiotic productivity and multiple ideological uses make them meaningful for the late twentieth-century cultural consumer, as the novels did for their readers.

Novels, Nobles, and Mobility

The Austen films and serials appropriate, rewrite, and visualize novels that worried about the Regency's politics of hierarchical rank, benevolent paternalism, and landed-establishment cultural ownership. As Lizzie notices when touring the Pemberley estate of which she might have been mistress, this English country house is located on "rising ground," surrounded by "a beautiful wood, stretching over a wide extent"; with a very large park, a "great variety of ground," and handsome prospects; and among streams with tasteful, rather than ragged, banks and bridges. The travelers enter the park at "one of its lowest points," a vantage guaranteed to produce picturesque delight and so to aestheticize the landscape, without its seeming "artificial," "formal," or "falsely adorned" (*Pride and Prejudice* 219). Elizabeth had "never seen a place for which nature had done more, or where natural beauty had been so little counteracted by an awkward taste" (219). Although Austen remains silent about visitors' having paid fees or left tips for the privilege of viewing house and gardens, when these polite tourists apply for entry, Mrs. Reynolds shows the house's public spaces, those "open to general inspection" (225). Elizabeth and the Gardiners admire inside and out, respecting the country house's spatial boundaries, practicing decorous restraint, and admiring the material, social-positional goods—including art, furniture, and decor—that index status (see Fabricant 254–56). Elizabeth views the "lofty and handsome" rooms, their "furniture suitable to the fortune of their proprietor," their views with beautiful prospects, from which the window-framed landscape seems, however shifting, "a beautiful object." Admiring Darcy's taste—"neither gaudy nor uselessly fine"—Lizzie takes "delight," sees and perceives "real elegance" at Pemberley, and so distinguishes herself as likewise capable of taste (220). Mrs. Reynolds praises her master's paternal benevolence, and her commendation—which alerts Lizzie that she has misread Darcy's character—glorifies his beneficence and civility as brother, landlord, and master, his "guardianship" of the poor, his tenants, and his sister (224). As Elizabeth looks at Darcy's picture in the portrait gallery, she "fixe[s] his eyes upon herself" and imagines his "regard" (both look and respect) with a deep "sentiment of gratitude" (224). In this scene, the narrator seems to endorse and Lizzie to appreciate the deference hierarchies, condensed paternal essence, and social civility of the landed gentry, for she shares Darcy's cultural taste and refinement—and identifies with it, too.[16] Yet she also reverses the look, commanding the portrait to look at her, as she looks at it, and so acquires a kind of female cultural stature, albeit a passive, even compliant one.[17]

In this "most famous of country-house visits," as Tinniswood calls the Pemberley tour, Austen suggests the estate's elegant commerciality, the social and class relations appropriate to its monumentality, and the extent of its cultural and real capital accumulation (102). Indeed, the gentry daughter's function to extend "respectable alliances" becomes a figure for *embourgoisement,* the penetration of lesser gentry daughters into the country house through the acquisition of legitimate taste. The tutelary picturesque also prepares the Austen heroine indirectly for marriage, for by introjecting upper-gentry tenets of taste, she proves herself worthy of a well-born husband of rank by "acquir[ing] certain elements of his education" or "learn[ing] to reproduce his taste" (Armstrong, *Age* 54). As Vivien Jones reminds us, eighteenth-century novels helped effect an "alliance between old property and new money" that depended upon and was consolidated by the learned skills of women like Fanny Price, Elinor Dashwood, or Elizabeth Bennet (130). Clara Tuite identifies Austen as member of a hybrid "'middle-class aristocracy'"; invested in the "mystique of patrimony," Austen's middle-class fraction reformed and renovated paternal culture through upward mobility of the educated, taste-capable lesser-gentry female (*Romantic* 143). This doubly invested position produced a "socially insecure fiction," for Lizzie's, Fanny's, or Elinor's marital mobility everywhere evoked for the rank-anxious reader the ever-present possibility of fall, failure, and middling vulgarity (6).

Tourism and the acculturation it stimulated enhanced the rank-anxious gentry appreciator's taste. The picturesque aesthetic in turn spurred the domestic tourism industry, for William Gilpin and Uvedale Price wrote guidebooks for travelers such as Elizabeth Bennet and her aunt and uncle Gardiner who, on their Northern tour, viewed landscapes, gardens, and country houses in "pursuit of novelty and amusement" (*Pride and Prejudice* 216). Whereas Marianne, Elinor, and Edward Ferrars debated the picturesque's cultural status in *Sense and Sensibility* ("I know nothing of the picturesque," Edward demurs, preferring a landscape of "beauty with utility" to one with "rocks and promontories"), in *Northanger Abbey,* Henry Tilney instructs Catherine Morland in history and picturesque aesthetics ("fore-grounds, distances, and second distances—side-screens and perspectives—lights and shades") with the "eagerness of real taste" (*Sense and*

Sensibility 97; *Northanger Abbey* 76). Yet most domestic-tourist destina-
tions—the Lake District (which Lizzie and the Gardiners had been
"obliged to give up" for a "more contracted tour"), North Wales, and
the Scottish Highlands—enabled not only views of picturesque British
landscape but tours of country houses (*Pride and Prejudice* 215).[18] This
cultured, professional gentry class thus enjoyed a new geopolitical mobility; its capability to share aesthetic pleasure with the ranks just above
or adjacent to its own enabled the tradesman's *and* lesser gentry's identification with an aristocratic class, despite their lack of arts, estate, or land
ownership.

By the long eighteenth century's end, rank's privileges and powers
were being debated in Parliament, in the public sphere's emerging cultural
spaces, and in the rural lanes. Challenges to patrician aesthetic dominance
likewise marked the period. During the 1790s and first decade of the
1800s, Raymond Williams argues, a conceptual shift altered the meanings
of "taste," "artistic," and "aesthetic" away from general human skills usually associated with rank and toward specialized textual repositories or
categories of appreciation. Whereas "taste" and "sensibility" had begun
as "categories of a social condition," they became individual and discrimi-
native; they named selective skills possessed by especially sensitive persons with civilized sensibility who could thus consume aesthetic objects,
improve estates, and admire beautiful gardens or sublime landscapes.[19]
Whereas legitimate taste had once been the "'perquisite of the gentleman,'"
education enabled middling and lower-gentry sons and daughters likewise to acquire it: it had become a "bourgeois categor[y]."[20] The aesthetic
shift to which Williams refers was contemporary with the late eighteenth-
and early nineteenth-century fascination with picturesque aesthetics,
which, Peter Mandler notes, renewed an interest in English art (*Stately*
13), and which, Nancy Armstrong argues, reshaped the look, representation, and consumption of nature. As the cultural geography of England
began to shift toward the commercial centers, such a sociospatial change
"required a standard of taste capable of refiguring the English countryside
as a space at once therapeutic and aesthetic." England ultimately consolidated taste "in a traditional land-owning class, albeit one whose boundaries were made permeable to some degree by education, on the one
hand, and by capital, on the other"; as this shift occurred, the look of landscape changed, becoming itself an item of cultural even as of real capital,
as the gentry traveler viewed and sketched it, spending money freely along

the way (*Age* 57, 54). The picturesque aestheticizing of nature as a "frameable possession" enabled members of the middling sort to realize, Ann Bermingham believes, that "aesthetic judgement was not the gift of a privileged few but could be learned by anyone and applied to just about anything."[21]

Nevertheless, the wars with Canada, the United States, and France first threatened and later refurbished the landed establishment's sense of cultural and political power. Supported and sustained by "peerage mania," peripheral and professional intermarriage (especially with the Irish and Scots, and daughters with the gentry's younger sons), the capitalizing of agriculture, an upsurge in country house building and renovation, enhanced dominance in Parliament and an enlarged state bureaucracy, and increasingly conspicuous consumption of the arts, the British landed class "renewed, extended and recreated" itself as a supranational elite of wealth and power, enjoying a historical and cultural renaissance that enabled its continued dominance until around 1880.[22] Yet the late nineteenth-century collapse of agricultural prices and the resulting depression—which drove rents and land values down and expenses up—and the late nineteenth and early twentieth-century imposition of death duties, the Great War's astronomical elite mortality rate, and the disappearance of the servant class saddled England with, as Lawrence and Jeanne Stone say, "far more great mansions than it knew what to do with" (*Élite* 424–25; see Cannadine, *Decline* 25–28; Mandler, *Stately* 254–63). Only massive land sales and teardowns and creation of the postwar stately home business helped resolve the modern economic and social problem of the country house— and served, as well, to fashion it as an icon in an emergent heritage culture. That the country house as social and economic institution survived the early century demographic crisis (in which "declining nuptiality, rising mortality, and declining marital fertility" endangered direct inheritance from father to son), 125 years of war with France, and the early nineteenth-century industrial and commercial revolutions attests to it owners' strategic creativity as well as to their power and authority to govern in county, region, and nation (Stone and Stone, *Élite* 100).

Despite the country seat's splendor in *Pride and Prejudice,* in *Mansfield Park* Austen depicts the landed establishment's vulnerability to political agitation, scion corruptibility, and gossip or publicity. Although the Park's "grandeur" terrifies poor relation Fanny Price, she soon grows accustomed to her unheated garret room, Aunt Norris's affected condescension, and

Sir Thomas Bertram's arrogance. Fanny, he affirms, is "not a Miss Bertram," for his daughters' "rank, fortune, rights, and expectations . . . will always be different" from hers (14, 10–11). After Maria Bertram agrees to marry Mr. Rushworth for a "larger income than her father's" and a "house in town," the young people play tourist, and Mrs. Rushworth displays Sotherton Court, the family's "capital freehold mansion" (38, 82). Unlike Pemberley's or Mansfield's, Sotherton's furnishings are out of date, its art pedestrian, and its chapel decommissioned. Sotherton's grounds likewise fail to please, its situation and views tedious or nonexistent, for the terrace, the bowling green, and the railing-lined walk contradict Regency aesthetics, as does the less displeasing planted wood, with its small trees and excessive regularity (90). Having been neglected by a now-late patriarch and once modernized by a wastrel younger son, the Rushworth estate is an "ancient manorial residence" no more (82). "Every generation," the charming bounder Mary Crawford sneers of the chapel's uselessness, "has its improvements" (86). In this scene of prenuptial tourism, the narrator implicitly exposes girls with rank but no "disposition" for the "acquirements of self-knowledge," fiancés with money but no taste, and social climbers eager to seduce eldest sons (19). Silent while other girls banter, flirt, and argue, the meritorious Fanny unaccountably possesses the real "delicacy of taste, of mind, of feeling" that her cousins and companions lack (81).

In this late novel, Austen represents the English country house in decline as a comedic icon and status anxiety as rampant. Maria Bertram Rushworth's elopement with the impetuous Henry Crawford and Julia's with Tom Yates, moreover, fashion Fanny the daughter that Sir Bertram always wanted. Although Fanny does not marry the heir to Mansfield Park—she is, after all, too good but too middling for the recuperated Tom—she weds his younger brother and so, assimilated back into Mansfield Park, acquires an adequate rural home (472). When, after Dr. Grant's unfortunate demise, Sir Bertram gifts the living to Edmund, the parsonage "soon grew as dear to [Fanny's] heart, and as thoroughly perfect in her eyes, as every thing else, within the view and patronage of Mansfield Park, had long been." Her sister, Susan, becomes the Park's "stationary niece" in her stead, for Susan will not enjoy her sister's upwardly mobile assimilation, the reader is led to believe, even as her position as Fanny's double cements the new wife's conjugal and figuratively consanguineous place (463, 472–73). Although Fanny marries a younger son, she nevertheless facilitates many readers' fantasies that she has inherited or may one day inherit the Park after all; Edward Said calls her its "spiritual mistress."[23] This novel's portrait of the estate as inscribed in Britain's imperial history also foresees the impending peril to the landed establishment's economic and cultural capital, for two rounds of war with France plus depression at home and in the British West Indies endangered landholder prosperity even as it stimulated renovations of glory and power. Said hyperbolically claims that the English novel "opens up a broad expanse of domestic imperialist culture without which Britain's subsequent acquisition of territory would not have been possible" (95). Postcolonial criticism's focus on slavery, colonialism, and race in the New World has since occluded the landed establishment's historical fate, an essential aspect of British imperialism's rise and fall.[24]

In *Persuasion*, the country house gives way to British seaside resort, as gentry geographical mobility goes middlebrow. Although the Holiday Act of 1838, which made rail travel less expensive, would remake the seaside resort a pleasure-space accessible to the urban laboring classes, Lyme Regis in Austen's time provided gentry and gentlemen alike the medicinal benefits of sea bathing. Looking with a "stranger's eye," Anne Elliot plays gentry tourist, noticing the "sweet retired bay," the "beautiful line of cliffs" stretching behind, its picturesque "green chasms between romantic rocks" and "extensive sweeps of country" (64). Gentry girls and navy captains visit during the off-season, when assembly rooms are shut up, lodgers and bathing machines gone. The "unaffected, warm, and obliging" Harvilles live in "rooms so small," moreover, that Anne imagines they must "invite from the heart"; despite their meanness, Captain Harville's lodgings nevertheless represent "the picture of repose and domestic happiness" (65, 66). Unlike Lizzie's and the Gardiners' rural visit to Pemberley and the Bertrams' and Crawfords' to Sotherton, this middlebrow tourism endorses neither symbolic capital nor real expense, neither deference hierarchies nor gentlemanly rank, neither art collecting nor patrician benevolence. Instead, on this visit, the captains and girls go slumming. Anne Elliot's fantasy, "these would have been all my friends," endorses not a lesser-gentry girl's fantasy of maritally possessing landed estate but her willing fall, for love, out of the upper gentry and into the professional set that values heartfelt homeliness. Although Wentworth has earned £25,000 through manly "merit and activity," and Anne will inherit £10,000, should her father not squander it, Austen's heroine desires "no landed estate, no headship of a family" and no baronet for husband, much to sister Mary's dismay (165, 166). Although Austen presciently depicts the country house's sad abandonment, her narrator values Anne's escape from the stifling, solipsistic regime of lodgings, from the affected condescension of patrician relatives in Bath, into a possible and more modest haute-bourgeois future.[25]

Jane Austen's novels thus chart the decline of the country house at the century's turn, and the estate's later disposition confirms her anxious suspicion about its future. Despite the post-1880 decline of aristocratic rank, privilege, and governing power, despite twentieth-century country-house teardowns and massive land and estate sales, the matrix of forces I have been examining reappeared, albeit reconfigured, in the mid-twentieth century. Peter Mandler's account of the legal, cultural, and political skirmishes that shaped the country house's emergence as heritage icon concludes with the 1980s, a decade that capped the century-long, unevenly developing emergence of interest in historic preservation, alongside the decline of antiaristocratic agitation. During the decade that swept the stately home into megapopularity in tourism and on film, the country house was transformed, as past economic became (real) cultural capital (*Stately* 329–53). Austen's novels about undoweried daughters, class aspiration or descent, and cultural capital accumulation became stylish, as the British public turned against modern architecture, worried about the environmental future, and listened to the country-house lobby (Mandler, "Nationalising" 113).

The Austen novels' semiotic productivity enabled dramatists and adaptors to position twentieth-century spectators in the space the Pemberley-touring Lizzie occupies, soliciting 1990s hybrid-class professional identification with wealth, or, during periods of financial stress and market downturn, arousing and allaying apprehensions of its loss. In the 1930s, for example, when a global Depression created anxiety about class status, economic and cultural capital, and geopolitical mobility, and again in the 1980s, when Margaret Thatcher's political agenda sought to redress Britain's perceived economic decline and the nation's deteriorating imperial projects around the world through privatization, heritage enterprise, and restoration of Victorian values, heritage film and classic serial once again appealed to spectators eager to enjoy a romance with rank yet needing to alleviate their own bouts of status anxiety.

Precursors: Jane Austen in Hollywood and on the Beeb

Robert Z. Leonard's post-Depression spoof of wealth in *Pride and Prejudice* (1940) lampoons Lizzie's fantasized identification with the privileges of rank and wealth. Jane Murfin and Aldous Huxley's screenplay, adapted from Helen Jerome's dramatization, sets Austen against the backdrop of economic depression at home and the blitz in England, the very England the opening film credits refer to, ironically, as "Old" and so implicitly "Merry" (Belton 177). Shaped by the economic and social upheavals of the 1930s, Huxley and Murfin's screenplay rewrites Austen's novel as a Depression-era story about "women, money, and marriage" (Brosh 19). The film criticizes female cultural consumption and taste acquisition as vulgar consumerism even as it seems wholeheartedly to endorse both, for rather than debate the virtues of Scott and Byron, these Bennet girls go shopping.[26] After the credits, the camera tracks across the quaint village set onto the back of straw-bonneted Mrs. Bennet (Mary Boland), who, turning, brags that Meryton's visitor, Darcy, is richer than Netherfield's new tenant. Cut to Lizzie (Greer Garson), first in close-up, then through the shop window, framed as the desirable, even glamorous daughter; to Mrs. Bennet and Jane (Maureen O'Sullivan), examining expensive fabrics guaranteed to attract rich husbands of rank. Thoroughly out of place among her shopping sisters, Mary (Marsha Hunt) buys "Burke's essay on the sublime and beautiful." Gathering her gaggle of undoweried girls, Mrs. Bennet bundles her daughters into a barouche; cut to slapstick carriage chase with rival Lucases: the goal, marriageable men. At home, a phalanx of girls marches into the foyer; "Look at them!" Mrs. Bennet commands her husband (and us), as the full-frame double parlor doors open onto a tableau of well-groomed girls already aging into "penniless old maids."

Using mise-en-scène to endorse capital acquisition, with a wink, Huxley and Murfin also satirize American values. Set not in the Regency but the 1830s, Leonard's film creates a historically inappropriate "hybrid style" that enables the U.S. spectator imaginatively to escape the post-Depression 1930s and the British spectator, the impending war, by "viewing an earlier, more romantic period" located without political and historical specificity (Balio, *Grand Design* 92–94; Maeder 12–13; see Laver 155–68). Wardrobe stylists clothed the Bennet sisters in "formula makeup and wigs" that suited the studio's modern lighting technologies and faster film stock yet alluded to the "romantic" fashions of an earlier century (Annas

74). Adrian, MGM's costume wizard and media star, re-created the studio's glossy style through lavish display, eschewing Regency single-feathered headdresses and slim Empire-waisted gowns for "excessive and decorative" 1830s costumes that featured wide-brimmed and feathered straw hats, abundant leg-of-mutton sleeves, and ruffled, crinoline-held skirts (Maeder 13). Hairstyles and makeup preserved Garson's newly minted celebrity image, for once created by a studio's dentists, cosmetic surgeons, and cosmetologists, a star's look could not be "sacrificed to history" (Annas 58).[27] Shot in MGM's "opulent and sophisticated" house style, with brilliant high-key lighting and Academy Award–winning art direction by Cedric Gibbons, this film made wealth glitteringly attractive and, at the same time, laughable (Balio, *Grand Design* 96, 87–88). Like other late-1930s class-conscious quality comedies, Leonard's film indulged dreams of wealth and upward mobility, delivered pleasures of diversion and escape, even as it mercilessly exposed the smug, often ignorant, affectations of the rich and well-born (Pells 281–83).

Murfin and Huxley's representation of rank depicts social distinction as snobbery, as it seeks to transform British aristocratic values into something

Unmarried daughters look shocked as Mrs. Bennet presents to Mr. Bennet their futures as penniless spinsters. (Pride and Prejudice, *1940*)

like American egalitarianism (Belton 183). Lizzie overhears Darcy and Bingley at a ball: "What arrogance! what snobbery! London fashions we do not admire," she exclaims; "every Hottentot may dance," Darcy sneers, likening the provincial to the racialized primitive. In Huxley and Murfin's screenplay, the tour of Pemberley becomes a garden party. While other girls mince and scrape, Lizzie battles Darcy at archery, scoring three bull's eyes. Here, the writers rewrite Lizzie as the uppity broad of 1930s screwball comedy, whose snappish responses to gentlemanly pride, whose skill and drive, gain her power and admiration, even from the upper-class doyenne as future mother-in-law. "She's right for you, Darcy," Lady Catherine announces of the girl who hates her taste in architectural arches; "you need a woman who will stand up to you. You've found her." Read as post-Depression-era escapism, this Hollywood version of *Pride and Prejudice* stimulates a fantasied identification with upper-class cultural acquisition and accumulation; read as cultural critique, it satirizes the same as vulgar expenditure, consumerism, and gold digging.[28]

Huxley and Murfin thus updated Austen for an audience still fearful about the bottom line and unemployment yet worried about a new war in Europe. Filmed during Hitler's march through Belgium and the Netherlands and opening at the height of the Battle of Britain, the film idealized the British rural and middle classes to argue for "Anglo-American solidarity in times of crisis" (Belton 186). British actors and writers working in Hollywood, including Laurence Olivier and Greer Garson, sought to encourage America's support of its ally, already at war while the United States remained neutral (Brosh 22). Moreover, Hollywood had not yet recovered from the Depression's economic ravages. Hays Office censorship, the bureaucratization of studio management, and threats of court action against the studio's practices of full-line forcing, block booking, clearance and zoning, and admission-price discrimination made Hollywood's financial state in 1940 "shaky at best" (Balio, *Grand Design* 13–26; Schatz, *Boom* 11). The Depression had halved national income between 1929 and 1932, and the average theatergoer responded by cutting entertainment expenditures; after bankruptcies and receiverships, the big eight studios needed desperately to produce higher profits and so overproduced a "glut of 'quality' pictures" (Schatz, *Boom* 12). *Pride and Prejudice* did good business at the box office despite Hollywood's woes and in the face of a strong British industry stimulated by the necessity to shoot quota quickies.[29] The screenplay's double motive to please and criticize nevertheless drenched the dramatization with status anxiety, even as it sought to allay economic and class apprehension.

The BBC classic serial likewise evoked and soothed status anxiety, for it rose to popularity as the modern professional-managerial class claimed social power during post–World War II prosperity. In the 1940s and 1950s U.S. mass-production technologies made television possible, postwar prosperity made TV ownership imaginable, and the promise of mass viewership made television attractive to cultural producers accustomed to recycling literary products for different media and audiences. Worried about social mobility, professional overcommitment, corporate routine, and lack of leisure, the conforming American man in the gray flannel suit and his equally anxious suburban wife, as well as the British postwar worker and his wife, displaced and made poorer by the war's ravages, turned to 1950s television for education, information, and entertainment. Since midcentury, moreover, film and television synergies have shaped the heritage-cultural marketplace. After the 1948 Paramount decision, which dismantled the studios' vertical integration, television emerged first as a competitor, then as a new mode of and market for film exhibition; by the 1960s, the film and television industries began consolidating, as hardware and software convergence (among film, televisual series, and, later, computer and video games) exploited the new multimedia exhibition outlets, and the Hollywood majors claimed television as a lucrative ancillary market for film (Maltby, "Post-Classical" 29–31). In the 1980s, technological and market synergy made UK film dependent on TV; government funding, the "modern successor" to "private patrons of the past," Hill notes, helped ensure that, as Mike Leigh claimed of Britain in the 1980s, "'all serious filmmaking was done for television.'"[30]After the TV series and miniseries had earned major market shares in the 1980s, the classic serial (on film rather than video) returned to prominence in the 1990s under auspicious market conditions.

Classic serial's emergence in the early twentieth century, its cultural dominance at midcentury, and its renaissance in the 1990s identifies it as a remarkably flexible genre for reaching a culturally literate and socially aspiring small-screen audience. As cultural product, classic serial fulfilled the BBC's ongoing public-service mission to disseminate and provide knowledge of national culture and its traditions.[31] In the United States in the 1970s, WGBH's *Masterpiece Theatre* offered the BBC a "'wedge into the American TV market,'" entertaining viewers worried about the unwinnable colonial war in Vietnam, about the oil embargo, the Iran hostage crisis, severe recession, and double-digit inflation (Jarvik 31, 33–44). Anxiety about oil, in particular, facilitated the emergence of corporate underwriting on public television; fearing stricter governmental controls, Mobil Oil sponsored *Masterpiece Theatre* at least in part to present itself as a responsible company interested in natural resource preservation by analogy to classic culture. In Britain, Shell Oil undertook a similar campaign.[32] In doing so, these multinational corporations sought to add "cultural prestige" to their corporate brand, to reach through public-service television a "prized target demographic," the status-anxious, often highly educated professional disposed to enhance his or her cultural capital and to enjoy period pleasures.[33] By the mid-twentieth century, control, accumulation, and sponsorship of North Atlantic community culture had shifted from upper-class Britons, with art collections and country-house galleries, to the transatlantic boardrooms of multinational corporations. In both countries, the *Masterpiece Theatre* amalgamation of British and American "national myths," Timothy Brennan argues, sought to "strengthen imperial attitudes in an era of European and North American decline" (374). This was especially the case for Britain. Although during her regime Margaret Thatcher attacked British television's long public-service tradition by submitting it to threats of censorship, to government bullying, and to competition in the marketplace, Channel 4, which debuted in 1982 as a period of "wide-ranging . . . unease in liberal circles" began, nevertheless supported and sustained British cinema's 1980s renaissance by financing independent product providers.[34]

Although televisual heritage culture thus served the interests of government or corporate projects in advertising, culture, and ideology, its dramatizers and directors produced serials that might be read by its professional middle-class audience as criticism of those very conservative values. In his massive study of nineteenth-century autodidact print culture, Jonathan Rose discovers that when scores of working-class readers encountered writers such as Sir Walter Scott, Thomas Carlyle, and Jane Austen, reading facilitated their "indispensable skill" of "straddl[ing] the working and ruling classes" (50). In the United States, a heterogeneous group of mid-twentieth-century consumers likewise used popular culture in ways different from those their creators had intended. John Fiske argues that female viewers of the *New Newlywed Game* appropriated wife-participants' exposure of their husbands' sexual, household, and cultural weaknesses to create for themselves a sense of empowerment. Noting that popular is not mass culture—which he calls commercialized and com-modified—Fiske identifies the popular text as a cultural resource to be "plundered" or "poached" from, to provide viewers everyday kinds of uses and pleasures (331–32). Despite his often idealized perspective on "the people," Fiske indicates the ways televisual cultural texts—like Rose's nineteenth-century print texts—may, because they are internally contra-dictory, be read oppositionally. Like the midcentury game show, the clas-sic serial made possible a "struggle for meanings" (332).

Fay Weldon's faithful dramatization of *Pride and Prejudice* (1979) dis-plays this struggle for meanings, this dynamic interaction between oppo-sitional and ideologically normative stagings of classic culture. Director Cyril Coke pictures, for example, the constraints, two-dimensionality, and depthlessness of paternal essence as well as the daughter's efforts to escape the father's drawing room—only to find another version of father and imprisonment. Although filmed shots of country house and estate serve as establishing shots or sequence-framing devices, the videotaped and sound-staged parlor is this serial's primary setting. The small-screen's relatively open frame enables entrances into and exits from the parlor where daughters read or sew, but its depiction of gentrified social restraint produces for the spectator a suffocating affect. As in popular 1950s melo-drama, the "frame of respectability" carefully delineates and limits the "range of 'strong' actions." Thus the telling "social gaffe"—Darcy's refusal to dance with Lizzie—or the not quite "hysterical outburst"—Lizzie's re-buff of Darcy—often expresses a female's efforts to escape from a stifling everyday scene, a "'closed' world" or "genteel prison" (Elsaesser, "Tales" 56, 61; Sales 25). The settings, moreover, expose these characters' social fixations and emotional fixity: the serial's low budget gives it an aura of shabby hauteur rather than aristocratic gloss; although the sets, props, and costumes have a genuine period look, the Chippendale furniture, recycled from set to set, appears used rather than elegant; the costumes, likewise reused, seem threadbare, as does the serial's family and marital ideology, which, in Austen's time, was already being challenged from within, as was the middle-class Eisenhower-era family. As Simon Langton, director of the 1995 *Pride and Prejudice,* said on re-viewing Coke's adaptation, its unidirectional lighting, set fragility and instability, fixed camera, and clash of video (in parlors) with film (in establishing shots) make Coke's *Pride and Prejudice* look "'artificial'" to the contemporary viewer who had grown accustomed to high production values, even on the small screen (Giddings and Selby 105). Sarah Cardwell notes that limitations of early television technologies—the "relatively still camera, infrequent changes of *mise-en-scène* and lack of post-production editing"—produced the classic-serial aesthetic and its dedication to fidelity, which now looks "staid and rigid" ("Small Screen" 185).

Deploying Austen's semiotic productivity, Weldon's dramatization and Coke's direction suggest liberalism's social and political impasse as a new, conservative decade began.[35] Claiming that she "lift[ed]" *Pride and Prejudice* from the page, "adding and subtracting scarcely a word," Weldon insists on her devotion to fidelity, an aesthetic that enables serial to be "classic" even as it provides viewers the tools for oppositional reading ("Jane" 2–3). Indeed, classic serial's capacious length, languorous pacing, and serial sequencing and repeatability facilitates its fidelity to literary sources. Eschewing scene dissection via shot/reverse shot and shooting primarily in medium waist-up and two shot, Coke interrupts spectator identification and keeps the viewer at a distance from the characters; a relatively immobile camera shoots the stationary and frontal performances characteristic of "live" early TV serials (Giles 80). David Rintoul's acting style sustains the serial's suffocating sense of a closed world. With his highly gestural movements and clipped elocution, Rintoul's Darcy recalls a talking marionette: turning on his heel, he stands poker-straight, chin first, speaking at rather than to Lizzie (Elizabeth Garvie). Ever the perfect representative of upper-class social restraint, Darcy hardly seems attractive—never mind glamorous, as would Colin Firth in Davies' later dramatization. Indeed, he looks the prideful prig for which non-Janeite viewers might mistake him. The horrified TV viewer watches the parlor bind Lizzie, from the comfort of, and in a space analogous to, her own midcentury living room.

Yet in this *Pride and Prejudice,* as in Austen's novel, Elizabeth exemplifies a new, hybrid class style. Negotiating "between aristocratic refinement" and her family's "middle-class coarseness," Lizzie maneuvers herself out of the lesser-gentry parlor and into the country house (Litvak 15–16). Identifying with Lizzie, the liveliest of characters, the viewer may well believe in her uniqueness, rightful penetration of the upper class, and apt appropriation of its style and taste. As women entered the workplace in record numbers during the 1970s, they found a heroine of their own in TV's Lizzie, who moves up in rank through marriage without threatening—because becoming educated into and never violently rebelling against—status and taste hierarchies. Indeed, Lizzie's hybrid identity as the serial ends positions her, like her viewer and like Austen herself, as member of a cultured, professional middle class. Like Austen's narrative, the classic serial reproduces so as to reform and renovate paternal culture through the educated, taste-capable, lesser-gentry female's marital mobility; it likewise evoked for the status-anxious late 1970s viewer the fear of entrapment by middle-class tastelessness. For its professional North Atlantic community audience, Weldon's *Pride and Prejudice* portrayed class status and social restraint as both desirable and deadly.

Unlike Coke's *Pride and Prejudice*, David Giles's *Mansfield Park* (BBC, 1986) shoots the upper gentry enjoying the naturalized pleasures of country sociability. Unlike Weldon's, Ken Taylor's dialogue is neither self-consciously elocutionary nor modernized, as is Emma Thompson's in *Sense and Sensibility*, but is conversational, albeit formal. Production technologies changed dramatically during the early 1980s, and Giles's serial looks and sounds like film rather than video. Shot in the sound-staged drawing room, billiards room, patriarchal closet, library, schoolroom, and on the central stairway, the many luxurious sets and glamorous Regency costumes look authentic and upscale. Location shots picture the upper class at play outdoors as well as in the drawing room. When Mary Crawford (Jackie Smith-Wood) quizzes Edmund (Nicholas Farrell) and Tom Bertram (Christopher Villiers) about whether Fanny (Sylvestra Le Touzel) is "out," they stroll a rural lane; when Edmund consults Fanny about Mary's character and decorum, the cousins walk in the park's wood, through the shrubbery, and into a sundial-bearing clearing; the young people ride to Sotherton in Henry Crawford's (Robert Burbage) barouche and, viewing the house and park, take a pedestrian tour through wood and climb over a gate while Fanny rests on a country bench. For Fanny's coming-out ball, Giles cranes over a large cast of extras, elegantly costumed (note women's fans and men's gloves), as they pass into the ballroom, circling through a great hall across a circularly patterned marble floor, under an exquisite chandelier.

This regal classic serial may be read as endorsing the values of paternal benevolence and country ideology or as deploying glossy style to display patrician superficiality. Either way, this is a kinder, gentler Jane Austen, one appropriate for the Reagan-Bush era of corporatization and merger mania, the Thatcher era of privatization and wealth generation. Rather than coercive autocrat (as Harold Pinter would later play him), Sir Thomas is a well-meaning and freely spending patriarch: he surely ordered a fire to warm Fanny's garret chamber; his demand that she accept Crawford's marriage proposal displays paternal solicitude for a poor relation (despite his crass reminder that Fanny may ever remain single); although Aunt Norris blames Fanny's refusal for having caused Maria's (Samantha Bond) seduction, Sir Thomas blames only himself. His fond good-nights after Fanny's coming-out ball; his insistence, despite Aunt Norris's parsimony, that *his* niece shall not walk to a dinner engagement; his admiration of Fanny when he returns from Antigua, all indicate his generosity. Taylor's dramatization and Giles's direction likewise stylize Austen's narrator's acerbic take on Mary's crass attitude toward matrimony. Everyone should marry "as soon as they can do it to advantage," the practical Mary notes; she scolds Fanny—but lovingly, as a future sister—for having declined Henry's proposal; she soothes the poor cousin who refuses to act in *Lover's Vows*. "Yes, she was very kind," Fanny confesses under pressure from Edmund. Moreover, Mary's strategy for protecting Maria after her elopement with Henry seems less vulgar than it does in Austen's novel: that Sir Thomas shall be silent, the divorced Maria and Henry forced to marry, that their good dinners and large parties shall restore their social acceptability seems almost caring, although coy. The non-Janeite viewer feels surprised that Edmund criticizes and rejects this attractive and energetic Mary.

Unlike Patricia Rozema's pert, shrewd, and rebellious Fanny, to whom I will return in chapter 2, Taylor's heroine is the demure, modest, and often silent poor relation, thankful for avuncular benevolence. Whereas the novel's free indirect discourse betrays Fanny's early and growing love for Edmund, her judgments of her theatricalizing cousins, and her jealousy of and rage against Mary Crawford, Taylor's screenplay refuses to voice Fanny's thoughts, unconscious desires, and moral hesitations. As a result, the non-Janeite may not know that Fanny rejects Crawford because she loves Edmund. In two parallel scenes, Fanny's silence enhances her gratitude and her surrogate family's kindness. One: Edmund follows Fanny up the grand staircase and, at the top, the two discuss Edmund's quandary about whether he—a younger son bound for the clergy Mary despises—will be accepted by her. Shot not quite beside one another, each in profile as he or she looks decidedly not at the other, the cousins talk: "Don't tell me anything" you might later regret, Fanny says; Edmund,

"You are the only person I would have talked to"; Fanny, "You can tell me anything." Here, a conversation each cousin identifies as intimate appears decorous and formal, as well as contradictory. Two: Fanny shot in profile, looking out the drawing room window; Edmund enters, and the two talk about his decision not to wed Mary. "I will tell you everything," he avers, he and Fanny in profile before the glowing window; "You were not deceived. What should I do if you should ever go away?"; "I shall never." Cut to two hands, as his hand moves ever so slightly to cover hers. Dissolve to the cousins' previously unspoken-of wedding.

Behind the elegant, sophisticated mise-en-scène, this graceful Mansfield Park nevertheless houses a compromised patriarch, spendthrift eldest son, shrewish widowed aunt, and disreputable daughters, all of whom demand reform. Yet the teleplay's silenced heroine and the glossy visual style cover over criticism of this degraded and historically endangered upper gentry. As Susan (Eryl Maynard), Edmund, and Fanny ride Sir Thomas's elegant coach down the avenue, a glance/object cut displays the country house in all its glory. "Oh, Fanny," Susan sighs, "it is beautiful; I never thought it would be so grand." Although the Park's grandeur ironically indexes its moral inauthenticity and Sotherton Court's dilapidation, its decay, Giles shoots the Mansfield dinner table overloaded with luxury plates, elegant food, and silver candelabrum; Aunt Norris urges Rushworth to employ Humphry Repton to improve Sotherton, as Mary agrees and the moralizing Edmund expostulates. Austen's mood of omnipresent status anxiety is likewise soothed, for cross-class marital relations at the parsonage, adjacent to and within the estate of Mansfield, appear morally less compromised than does life at the country seat. "Ah, the sweets of housekeeping in a country village," Mary sighs skeptically; at serial's end, Fanny says in voice-over: "Happy . . . we remain together within the view and patronage of Mansfield Park." Retaining the privileges provided by patrician benevolence and power, however chastened, Fanny and Edmund begin their moderate, modest housewifely and clerical lives. Shot for a 1980s North Atlantic audience accustomed to the ideological denial of crass class strife even as those at the top got rewarded, this Mansfield Park consolidates and makes pleasant patrician essence.

In 1996, two Emmas proposed diametrically opposed readings of Austen's novel. Diarmuid Lawrence's televisual Emma glorifies patrician essence and Englishness for a North Atlantic audience; by contrast, Douglas McGrath's upscale feature-film Emma, which I discuss in chapter 2, endorses the taste-capable daughter's saucy renovation of paternal culture. Lawrence shoots girls in period costume taking country walks through golden corn, hilltop vistas of a palatial Donwell Abbey, and landed-gentry rural parties, depicting country ideology as a unified and naturalized cultural formation. In this neoconservative serial, social relations of inequality are made to appear legitimate, for Lawrence's *Emma* insists that a historically out-of-date patrician marriage constitutes around itself an organic and natural society of ranks based on trust and obligation. Judging the novel's ending uncinematic, Andrew Davies (now a BBC and big-screen cultural icon) wrote a new conclusion, without precedent in the novel, for his screenplay; the film thus ends with an orgy of premarital bliss, as Knightley (Mark Strong) throws a harvest supper, attended by peasants, workers, newly engaged daughters of nobody, and gentry alike (see Birtwistle and Conklin 57). By candlelight, Knightley asks his tenants to "drink the health of the lady who has made me the happiest man on Earth." He guarantees, "There will be stability. There will be continuation—though my life is to change" (Birtwistle and Conklin 151). Led by the three happy couples from three different classes, the concluding ball, like the marriages it anticipates, serves to consolidate social relations and heal class divisions under the sign of paternal benevolence.

Here, Davies invents a regional society imagined as a condensed and displaced picture of the nation. England endured no revolution, Davies has said, because the British landed establishment was not composed of decadent, nonresident landlords but effective estate managers: "'It's like old-fashioned conservatism really,'" he says of his screenplay's conclusion (Birtwistle and Conklin 58; see Spring 64–66). Alun Howkins views the rural ideal, which animates Davies' dramatization, as enabling the transformation of eighteenth-century patrician essence into nineteenth-century ideologies of traditional continuity and harmonious community, images of which Davies' adaptation provide an excess. Embedded in Lawrence's romanticized pasts of candlelit evening gatherings and suppings, of rural English landscape and village, is a retrospective fantasy that imagines country ideology as enhancing an "organic and natural society of ranks" that, despite its portrait of social and economic inequality, is believed by all strata and status groups to be based on "trust, obligation and even love." Forging an image of national unity out of multiple figural identities, Davies seeks to resolve the class differences his source novel has identified by subsuming them within a rural version of Englishness characterized by "a special kind of classlessness."[36] Lawrence's portrait of gentry paternalism reminds us that 1990s middle-class television viewers may have taken a pleasure different from the bumptious jolliness that satisfied 1940s Hollywood audiences or the glossy style preferred by culturally aspiring 1980s television viewers. Identifying with patrician figures, these spectators enjoyed a retrogressive bond with rank and its notions of honor, respect, and gentility. Even in this idyllic view of England, however, Davies frames the teleplay with chicken thieves, suggesting that the harmony Knightley voices may well be purely ideological (Cardwell, Davies 123).

Misunderstanding Austen's appropriateness for multiple ideological projects and different audiences, liberal 1980s cultural critics impugned all classic serial as pandering to middle-class tastes. Accusing the mode of standardization, historical nostalgia, a monolithic and uniform conception of periodicity, and exaggerated faithfulness to its novelistic source, Paul Kerr denigrated classic serials by invoking the horror of popularity, the lowbrow generic conventions of melodrama, the audience of weeping women that consumed the pop-cultural product, and the naiveté of the scripts' adherence to fidelity aesthetics: their "homogenisation" and aesthetic "flattening."[37] Monica Lauritzen deplored classic serial's generic look and unsophisticated historical periodicity: "'Sometimes you feel as if the same serial has been going on for five years,'" she quotes the film critic Ruth Halldén as saying; "'Some time ago it was called *Portrait of a Lady*, then *Pride and Prejudice*'"; still later "'they called it *Middlemarch*'" (30).

Yet, as I have suggested, classic serial provided multiple quality pleasures and created different ideological readings to serve different audiences. These critics' clear disdain for classic serial as product and for its consumers nevertheless sought to index their own good taste and skills of discrimination even as it betrayed their anxiety about the Reagan-Bush and Thatcher era's uses of the past, the widening appeal of visual culture, and the decline of canonized classic culture. Writing from within the 1980s debate about a privatized infrastructure, public access to cultural goods, and heritage culture's enterprise economics, liberal commentators such as Kerr and Lauritzen expressed ideologically driven anger at what they perceived to be widespread indulgence of benighted middle-class tastes. Writing after the millennium, however, Cardwell revalues the "classic-novel adaptation" by noting its exploitation of televisuality, its emphasis on performance and intertextuality, and its self-referential postmodernity:

"there is no monolithic ideological bias" inherent in classic serial, she emphasizes.[38] Despite liberal writers' criticism, Thatcher challenged the 1980s welfare state's hegemony by instituting conservative market-oriented policies. After postwar relative economic decline, Britain had fallen behind its European neighbors in manufacturing, productivity, and exportation; even as Britain's economy failed to grow as fast as, say, France's and Germany's, colonial territories challenged the British empire, as new independent states and markets emerged (Gamble 2–10; M. Williams 107–17). The 1970s global oil crisis, the 1980s miners' "insurrection," and expanding unemployment, health, and housing costs opened a space for Thatcher's monetarism and macroeconomic management, her tactics of privatization, welfare rollback, and triumph over the trades unions (Cannadine, *Class* 182). The government also sought to strengthen state power in the interests, Hill maintains, of "national regeneration, social order, and discipline" (*1980s* 8). Thatcher's political, economic, and ideological agenda nevertheless produced mixed results. Despite family-values rhetoric, the divorce rate rose; despite a rise in worker productivity, increased unemployment costs undercut the effort to reduce public expenditure; despite enhanced oversight of public media institutions, the BBC muddled through (Hill, *1980s* 11, 6, 30). As nationalized industry was sold (in part to augment state coffers, in part to sell stock shares to the stakeholding public), political rhetors speechified and cultural consumers worried about the nation's future. For Stuart Hall, the late-century debate about economic decline could not be separated from "the question of an embattled national identity," although this "worr[y]" often went unspoken (109). Still, Thatcher's notions of "national sovereignty and identity" were at odds with the "globalizing economic and cultural forces" that the emergent European Union represented, and they were eventually her undoing (Hill, *1980s* 15).

It's not surprising, then, that Thatcher presided over passage of the National Heritage Acts of 1980 and 1983, which sought to preserve the nation's traditions in the face of globalization. Because Victorian social and environmental critics founded and early supported the preservation cause, moreover, Thatcher presented the Acts as a crowning achievement that, like her other policies, reinvigorated "Victorian values."[39] Nevertheless, Cannadine notes, Thatcher's dedication to British middle-class values of "thrift, hard work, self-reliance, independence and responsibility" did not recall Victorian ethics but enshrined an idealized childhood memory of "Grantham shopocracy" (*Class* 178). Yet heritage's historical origins are indeed Victorian. Established in 1895 during a period of economic downturn, the National Trust bought and held land, buildings, and rural open space inalienably and privately—and continues to do so in the twenty-first century—in "the national and public interest." The Trust's rhetoric, which articulates the public's right to visit privately owned landscapes and estates, thus negotiated the conflict between private property and public access, but it did so "at a displaced level."[40] After the 1980 and 1983 Acts, Thatcher's government encouraged heritage enterprise; tourism, in particular, flourished.[41] In the media sector, the BBC, which once enjoyed a monopoly on program production and distribution, experienced ratings competition, and, with its licensure status threatened, classic serial became, as it had been decades earlier, a staple BBC product (Giddings and Selby 124). During the 1980s "culture wars," Thatcher sought to ensure that culture, although it belonged to the nation, was paid for through individual, perhaps corporate, enterprise but not by the government.

Anti-Thatcher cultural critics not only attacked the Heritage Acts and classic serial but raged against "the heritage industry" as promoting the display, exploitation, and commodification of the UK's national past and traditions. According to Robert Hewison, heritage culture staged authenticity, created standardized objects and homogenized period concepts to exhibit and sell the past (137); to Patrick Wright, it promulgated a "golden age" or "rural idyll" and made visible images of plenitude without picturing past conflict or "colliding self-interests" at the public, national level (20). Marxist critics excoriated heritage culture's display of residual "patrician essence" in a mythological "arcadian English" that occluded class and regional divisions (Nairn 36–37, 46–47, 43). Yet Peter Mandler notes that nineteenth-century heritage consciousness, in opposition to elite fashions, enfranchised popular culture as part of the nation and righted the class-based "social imbalance[s]" of the eighteenth century (*Stately* 21). John Urry rejects Hewison's and Wright's view of the Heritage Acts as massive public relief programs for aristocrats who could no longer afford to maintain their estates; defining tourism broadly, he argues that, in the 1980s, leisure activities other than country-house visiting—such as ecotourism and "pedestrian touring," modern forms of nineteenth-century rural rambling—emerged or flourished as tourism studies began to consider questions of sustainability, carrying capacity, and the suburbanization of rural spaces (*Consuming* 197, 202, 206). The heritage-industry critique thus ignored new and expanding patterns of popular consumption, aesthetic pleasure, and user interpretive capability, as well as the heritage industry's environmental goals. "There is no singular discourse of National Heritage," say Bommes and Wright.[42] Anxious about consumers' lack of or promiscuous cultural taste, apprehensive about the nation-state's future, and worried about the link between cultural consumption and social distinction, twentieth-century literary critics played their own part in the debates about cultural acquisition and dissemination. Although I will not discuss the 1980s skirmishes among Allan Bloom, Dinesh d'Souza, and others, since they are well known, the century's culture wars, from a millennial perspective, betrayed critical anxiety about what class rightfully possessed, financed, and should preserve literary high culture and whether the hoi polloi should have access to it.

Scenes of Reading: The Critics at Work

Literary reading in Jane Austen's novels invariably educates the capability skillfully to interpret and judge, to define morality, sensibility, or ethics, and thus determines romantic fate or class position. That Sir Walter Elliot reads only the Baronetage or that Darcy takes pride in and expands Pemberley's library demonstrates one's neglect of his estate, the other's improvement of its cultural holdings. That Willoughby joins in Marianne Dashwood's love of Cowper and Scott identifies him as a potential—but perhaps overly sensitive—lover; that Captain Benwick, a "young man of considerable taste in reading, though principally in poetry," enjoys Scott and Byron reveals a refined sensibility in need of educating; that Edmund Bertram and Fanny Price, discussing improvement, quote Cowper underscores their suitability as marital partners (*Sense and Sensibility* 47; *Persuasion* 67; *Mansfield Park* 56). Because they are readers with the disposition to practice social distinction, Anne Elliot and Benwick—who compare and rank "the first-rate poets"—display and exercise taste appropriate to their social ranks, consuming texts already privileged in the English imaginary, taking pleasure in aesthetic experience, enabling the reproduction of status, and sustaining the newly emergent technologies of social classification (*Persuasion* 67). Because her characters themselves practice literary criticism, Austen seems the perfect figure to stand as placeholder for

nineteenth- and twentieth-century anxieties about the disposition necessary to acquire cultural distinction, the rightful collection and possession
of cultural treasures (both real and symbolic), and the urge to canonize
and preserve literary culture.

When critics compare and rank writers, judge texts, and create a canon,
Austen often stands in as a figure for anxiety about the tradition's history.
Depending upon the critic's own historical position, Austen appears at
the origin, climax, or center of the novel's trajectory as it becomes a dominant literary form. After Richard Bentley's 1833 *Standard Novels* marked
Austen's "formal inclusion in the canon," William Galperin notes, her
writing has often been "deemed a culmination" in the "rise of the novel"
(*Historical* 75, 120–21). F. R. Leavis's 1930s "great tradition" took shape
around Austen's fiction, as her novels retrospectively "created" the genealogy that "lead[s] ... down" to her and so established a historical continuity:
"as we look back beyond her," Leavis says, acknowledging his retrospective reinterpretation, we see "significances" that only she makes possible (5). At midcentury, Ian Watt positioned Austen at the "climax" of
the eighteenth-century novel; Austen anticipated, enabled, and signified
"English pre-eminence in the genre" (296–99). As an overdetermined figure of authorial eminence, Austen demonstrates, by analogy, the critic's
educated discrimination, elegant taste, and cultural power, for "[s]tandards
are formed in comparison," Leavis announced, among "the pre-eminent
few" (3; see Mulhern 256–63). Austen likewise represents the critical
effort to protect high culture from popular-cultural encroachment. Anxious about the inroads against the classics made by popular and mass culture, Q. D. Leavis feared that the "standardising forces" of "cinema, radio,
large-circulation newspapers," and the lowbrow bestseller have "destroyed
traditional culture" (193). These literary intellectuals thus sought to set
the cultural agenda, inculcate critical taste, and display the capacity appropriately to evaluate and consume cultural objects.[43] Austen's hypercanon-
ization sustained this cultural work.

In the 1980s culture wars, liberals and conservatives alike expressed
anxieties about the public's access to cultural knowledge. Unlike Leavis and
Watt, John Guillory views the canon as "itself a historical event" (244).
Guillory exposes the classificatory scaffolding that girds the structures
of canonization. Stressing that the canon has been selected, transmitted,
and consolidated through the cultural practices of literacy, the schools as
institutions, and the curriculum and syllabus as their instrument, Guillory

argues that the school "reproduces the stratified structure of the social order," as the English curriculum measures individual "educational acquisition" (243, 242). Acknowledging that the "novels of Jane Austen" entered the canon as women began to be taught to read and write, Guillory represents their author as figure not of origination, climax, or continuity but of worry about cultural and linguistic literacy; the classics, he notes, originally entered university curricula to teach proper language, and so class and gender, skills. E. D. Hirsch, by contrast, blames a national decline in U.S. cultural literacy on a late-century refusal to teach the canon and to value good taste. Contemporary Americans should know Jane Austen, he avers, but because citizens may learn about the classics from conversation, cinema, or television, they may know only "Jane Austen," the name of an author who wrote about romance in nineteenth-century England, as they know Sherlock Holmes via Basil Rathbone's acting (156, 147). Indeed, literate persons who know anything about the contents of Austen's work represent for Hirsch "specialists" of a sort; the TV- and film-educated folks who know only the quotable and recycled "Jane Austen," nonspecialists (31–32). In Hirsch's hands, the canon is not a historical event but a list of "guideposts" identified by titles and terms. For Guillory, the canon is an ideological construct that protects the elite against encroachment by the nonliterate into their culture; for Hirsch, the canon must be defended to preserve past cultural goods, enhance linguistic norms, and maintain national cultural hegemony.

The cultural battle between neoconservatives and liberals was anxiously waged throughout the twentieth century. The 1930s and 1980s literary-critical skirmishes betray the same tension that subtends the heritage-culture and heritage-film debates: the worry that lack of access to classic literature or lack of capability to read it endangers the cultural tradition, set against the fear that mass availability will cause degraded popularity. Yet in these two historical moments, literary critics themselves deployed culture to acquire social distinction and achieve class mobility. In the 1930s professionalization of literary studies, Claudia L. Johnson argues, a "middle-class professoriate wrested Austen from upper-class Janeites" ("Divine" 27). Indeed, the Leavises lived through the transition from an "old, imperial literary culture" of patrician intellectualism to a petty bourgeois, grammar school– and university-educated professionalism that brought class upstarts (like themselves) into what had been a national literary aristocracy (Mulhern 262; Appleyard 309). As a cultural professional,

E. D. Hirsch enjoyed the genteel, black-tie culture of Albemarle County; Guillory, the class ascendancy of Yale. The literary gentleman (for he was a man—or a distinguished man's wife—in the 1930s and 1940s) modeled professional powers of discrimination for the modern, canon-making moment, when distinctions between high and low culture, civilized sensibility and popular pleasure, and elite and mass forms of consumption mattered and were being constituted and worried about in Charlottesville, New Haven, Cambridge, and beyond.[44]

Literary-critical adoption of Austen as figure for anxiety about the canon and about culture's uses results in part from her narratives' semiotic productivity. Austen's texts enable critics both neoconservative and liberal to "project contemporary anxieties and controversies" onto her novels, John Wiltshire argues (*Recreating* 134). Whereas subversive readers view Austen's heteronormative endings with dismay, Johnson notes, and find in the novels evidence of protolesbian, postimperialist, and anticonformist leanings, conservative readers celebrate Austen's novels as exemplary documents of Englishness, mannerliness (that is, social restraint), and rural pleasure (or country ideology). Subversive readings recuperate Austen's divine ideological promiscuity, her capability to be "popular and canonical, accessible and complexly inaccessible" yet also "amenable to shifts of sensibility and cultural assumptions" (*Austen* v). Postmillennial critics have historicized Austen's novels' ideological malleability. Deidre Lynch describes Austen's interwar mobilization as an English "national asset" as serving to articulate the "shifting boundaries between elite and mass culture"; Galperin notes the "constitutive *instability*" of the midcentury professional middle class that "adopted Austen as its own," transforming her into a "fundamentally conservative novelist" rather than an anxious "historian of her milieu" (Lynch, "At Home" 162–63; Galperin, "Readers" 90, *Historical* 217). This historical instability makes Austen available for "modern projections," Johnson claimed in the 1980s, due to our own "decidedly modern nostalgia for an unalienated relationship to a calmer, more manageable world" (*Austen* xix).

Modern anxieties about the cultural function of classic literature resonate with worries about the nation's economic future. The Leavisite project to "restore integrity and order" to the British literary tradition and to guarantee the "notion of an abiding, self-evident Englishness," Francis Mulhern maintains, depended upon an appeal to "England's 'national greatness,'" for Leavis celebrated "English" as "exclusive, socially and morally," and as the "instance of a 'human norm'" that demanded "rigorous discriminations" and hard intellectual work (259–62). Indeed, the early twentieth-century literary-critical taste aristocracy personified by Leavis and "nourished by the international eminence of the British state" gave way as British imperialism crumbled and a "new, American hegemony" emerged (261–62). Hirsch's very American late-century apprehension that visual culture, gossip, and the tabloid press would eclipse the Western cultural tradition, moreover, not only repeated and updated Q. D. Leavis's 1930s anxiety but silently invoked the terrible fate of a dumbed-down nation. Print culture's demise, Hirsch feared, would undermine the stable elements of a national vocabulary, which he viewed as the core value of cultural literacy; produce a decline in cultural memory, as a skills- rather than a content-based curriculum sidelined the literary tradition; and create and sustain a growing corporate need for "cultural non-specialists" (29, 113, 31). From this anxious millennial perspective, literary culture might well not survive the next half century (McLemee A1, A16; Zill and Winglee).

Anxiety about national preeminence also informs the heritage-film debate. Calls for a revitalized national cinema contend with hoots that heritage cinema is class-bound, aesthetically inferior, and produced for middlebrow, generally female, spectators. Heritage is often misread by cinemagoers as coterminous with British national cinema, Hill maintains, because British films have circulated "quite limiting and restricted versions of 'Britishness'" ("National" 17, quoting Elsaesser). Yet Hill argues persuasively for a new national cinema that provides the moviegoing public with "diverse and challenging representations adequate to the complexities of contemporary Britain," a "nationally specific" cinema that is neither "nationalist" nor "attached to homogenizing myths of national identity" ("National" 16). Like Higson and Craig, Hill here conflates aesthetics with ideology, suggesting, as well, that the heritage icon—the country house—is transcendent, essentialized, and ahistorical, notions that betray inattention to historical patterns of class formation and decline, to the legal specificities of land and property ownership. National identity, moreover, is no more natural, no more a timeless essence than is the landed estate; instead, it is a fluid historical product, constituted anew during moments of political and ideological contestation. As Susan Hayward notes, the imaginary nation may be used to "revalue the concept of national cinema," to problematize the nation as a geographically continuous territory, a singular linguistic, religious, or ethnic community (93, 101). Despite our current and fashionable intellectual skepticism about the nation, nationalism, and national identity; our endorsements of hybridity, boundary crossing, and imagined community, national cinemas—and British heritage film—nevertheless contend in a global cultural war with Hollywood's dominance of the world's markets. As Tom O'Regan says, national cinema—a formation that includes national film texts, industries, and their cultural contexts—always exists in "conversation with" Hollywood (115). British heritage and national cinema thus provide diversity of global media product, stimulate middle-class professional cultural consumption, and encourage intellectual debate about the value of high culture in a globalizing, technologizing, late-capitalist North Atlantic community.

North Atlantic economies, moreover, slumped and then boomed during the 1990s, paradoxically stimulating cultural consumption throughout the decade. As 1980s free-market enterprise in Thatcher's Britain and corporate-merger mania in Ronald Reagan's and George H. W. Bush's United States gave way to a downsizing economy in the early 1990s, heritage film's project to reinvent a national culture seemed less ideologically complicit with New Right policies than it had a decade earlier. The elections of Bill Clinton in the United States (1992) and Tony Blair in Britain (1997) shifted the terms of 1980s political rhetoric, even if, as leaders, they were seen as compromising with Republican and New Right politicians. Later in the decade, as the stock market expansion produced financial speculation by pension managers and individual day-traders, excess expenditure by corporations and conspicuous consumption by individuals, the fin de siècle glow of financial well-being made heritage film and classic serial hip. I do not mean to glorify the 1990s "wealth effect"—now seen from a vantage point of the worst financial crisis since the Great Depression to be the outcome of corporate fiscal impropriety and accounting misconduct (see Galbraith 168–70; Baker 98–104). Nor do I mean to idealize consumer "choice," the policies that enable it, or its political and economic consequences. Choice is never exercised outside the operations of historical constraint, and, as a concept, it may be deployed by conservatives and reformists alike to serve their political and ideological interests. Yet the 1990s made highbrow and heritage culture popular beyond Jane Austen's wildest dreams, as profit making and profit taking fueled and sustained a romance with rank and its aesthetics, a euphoria appropriate for a gilded-age culture of taste acquisition, social distinction, and geopolitical mobility.

The advent of world markets nevertheless nurtures global industrial fears of U.S. cultural imperialism in the millennium. In the 1990s, Hollywood's long-term strategy to "build on a strong base of operations at home while achieving a 'major presence in all of the world's markets'" forced independent production companies and filmmakers in Britain, the United States, and other nations to enhance opportunities to coproduce, exploit niche markets, and advertise in multiple exhibition windows; to develop new economic and industrial-production strategies such as transnational coproduction, global theatrical release and exhibition, and the preselling of distribution rights.[45] Still, film culture has changed since 1970s art-house cinema and, paradoxically, soft-core pornography helped to create an intellectual film audience of cinephiles, located primarily in large- and mid-sized cities and university towns. At the millennium, cultural liberals worry about the loss of locally produced and regionally oriented product, as the global blockbuster erases geopolitical visual or rhetorical signs from film and the mid-sized specialty-division Hollywood flick saturates the independent cinema sector. As the independent production, distribution, and exhibition sector shrinks and the major studios spawn their own indie look-alike divisions, the millennial heritage-oriented moviegoer must seek out cultural product by a new generation of filmmakers. He or she must also continue to participate in the public debate about the value of culture and its popular visual mode, heritage film. To do so is crucial to the future of culture and cultural workers in the North Atlantic world.

CHAPTER 2

Being True to
Nineteenth-Century Narrative

*In the ... 1990s, Hollywood produced numerous filmed versions
of classic novels, [with] a particular vogue for the novels of Jane
Austen. . . . Some of the adaptations are quite free, but (except for
the odd* Clueless*) the Austen films, whose popularity swept the
others aside, are historically accurate in costume and setting and
very faithful to the original novels.*

—J. David Bolter and Richard Grusin, *Remediation*

*There is no period look. The period look was invented by
Hollywood.*

—Jane Campion, *Interviews*

ABOUT HER DRAMATIZATION OF *Pride and Prejudice* (1980), Fay
Weldon claims, "Not a word was said—well, only about 20—that
wasn't in the book, nor a scene either—well, only one or two" (quoted
in Ozick). Jane Campion maintains that she and her screenwriter were
"broadly faithful" to Henry James's *Portrait of a Lady*—a "damn extraordinary book" and her favorite novel (*Interviews* 196, 177–78). Lindsay
Doran and Emma Thompson hoped that people who "love Jane Austen"
would find their film of *Sense and Sensibility* faithful to the novel's "humour
and wisdom" (*Screenplay* 16). Yet the avant-garde filmmaker Sally Potter
hates "slavish" adaptations; seeking to find a "live, cinematic form," she
"ruthless[ly]" altered *Orlando* (MacDonald 212; Potter, "Immortal" 58).
Dramatization, adaptation, transformation: despite their differing, often
ambiguous or unreflective commitments to fidelity aesthetics, most filmmakers seek to respect a classic narrative even as they re-create it in a new
medium. This group implicitly addresses the question central to film adaptation of literary classics: how to shoot on film the no-longer contemporary stories so dear to readers yet so foreign to nonreaders.

Brian McFarlane distinguishes between the ways film "transfers" some elements from fiction and "adapts" others. Deploying the theories of Roland Barthes and Seymour Chatman, McFarlane differentiates "cardinal functions" or narrative "kernels" (story events that produce "cruxes" and serve as "hinges in the narrative") from "catalysers" or "satellites" (which elaborate, and deletion of which would not disturb the "narrative logic" [Chatman 53–54]). For McFarlane, the "hinge-points" of narrative, which introduce into stories moments of "risk" and provide "'chronological functionality,'" may be transferred from one medium to another; the satellites, which "root cardinal functions in a particular kind of reality" and introduce "'areas of safety, rests, luxuries,'" must be adapted. The filmmaker who shoots a faithful adaptation must, McFarlane maintains, "seek to preserve the major cardinal functions" of his or her source novel (13, 14). As McFarlane states, however, fidelity is only one way—and "rarely the most exciting" or useful way—to theorize the intertextual relations between source-text and film adaptation, dramatization, transformation, or remediation (11).

During the 1990s Victorian vogue, feminocentric plots of courtship, marriage, seduction, abandonment, and betrayal attracted filmmakers because they thematized the problem of fidelity and infidelity with which filmmakers struggled. Indeed, Virginia Wright Wexman notes that Hollywood movies must, for market purposes, create the romantic, heterosexual couple. Yet classic Hollywood and new Hollywood films narrate the couple very differently (Bolter and Grusin 34). In their landmark look at classical Hollywood cinema, David Bordwell, Janet Staiger, and Kristin Thompson argue that classical form depends upon story causality and character motivation; plot and story comprehensibility (flashbacks, durational strategies, and crosscuts); spatial organization (framing, frontality, roundness, and continuity editing); shot establishment and scene building, development, and sequencing; and a range of nondisruptive differentiations (film noir's challenges to style, story, and heterosexual romance, for example) (12–95). Classical Hollywood stories thus relate consequential events that are dependent upon causal logic, on characters' alteration by the acts they undertake, even as those events react, in turn, upon them. Most studio-era genres (except perhaps the gangster movie or western) involve a romantic plot or subplot, often to entice female spectators to the theater; fulfilled or thwarted by narrative teleology, the classic Hollywood couple thus mates and weds or self-destructs at story's end, via song-and-dance seduction, in nightmare noirish vituperation, or after screwball-comedy sparring and sparking.

New Hollywood movies easily absorb studio style even as they innovate stylistically, whereas hypermediated films disrupt these features of classical Hollywood storytelling, calling attention to their own remediation. As Geoff King suggests, new Hollywood cinema combines narrative with the pleasures of action or motion, star performance, spectacular vista, and emotional intensity yet offers the spectator a "'different economy of pleasure'" via a nonlinear plot often punctuated, fragmented, or sensationalized by spectacle (185). New Hollywood, like classical Hollywood cinema, nevertheless serves up narrative enigmas and questions, story hooks, partial answers and delays, additional enigmas, and redundancies to build suspense and "ensure maximum comprehensibility," for despite the pressures of corporate financing, merchandizing, and product placement, narrative fails to dwindle under the regime of spectacle (181, 185–87, 200–204). King takes as his example the masculinist, action-packed, late twentieth-century blockbuster; this exemplary new Hollywood product clearly subordinates the female in any coupling plot trajectory, making special effects rather than romance narratively productive. Hypermediated product, on the contrary, combines the logic of immediacy, or immersion, with the logic of hypermediacy, in which multiplied signs of mediation (appropriated bits of text, graphics, split screen, voice-over of source narrative, and so forth) "rupture" an illusion of immediacy, acknowledging and making visible multiple acts of representation. This self-conscious text "undercut[s] the desire for immediacy," indulging in the spectator an attitude of play or subversion as he "acknowledge[s] the medium as medium" and takes "delight in that acknowledgment" (Bolter and Grusin 33–34, 41–42). Thus, the visible disarticulation of figures or bits of text from their original context facilitates irony, parody, pastiche; plot teleology may deploy narrative enigmas, questions, decoys and delays, and redundancies, but it also eschews maximum comprehensibility. This filmic mode, often practiced in independent cinema, with its "canny cross-generational appeal," perfectly captures the niche market between the "global mass audience" and avant-garde film's "coterie of cinephiles" (Scott). Although boy may get girl at the story's end, certain knowing female winks, direct addresses to the spectator, or historical self-situatings may supervene, undercutting the spectacular masculinity of new Hollywood romance.

The filmmakers I examine in this chapter adapt nineteenth-century fiction to thematize the late-century problem and aesthetic of fidelity as they create—or fail to create—the romantic, heterosexual couple. They shoot feminocentric stories about early-century women in love who are faithful beyond their—and our—wildest expectations; about women who mistake their own perceptions, interpretations, and representations of love and so must be educated into being faithful; about midcentury women unhappy with or enraged by demands for fidelity; about late-century women who struggle against or question the concept of fidelity altogether. These nineteenth-century narratives depend upon, respectively, the causal logics of courtship, marriage, and occasionally, childbirth, and of romance or seduction; they propose enigmas about which sexual actions or events occur first, which second, and so forth. Filmmakers deploy the romance genre, moreover, to showcase their fidelity to source novels—or to flaunt their own faithlessness. The filmmaker who, like Campion, reverences her nineteenth-century source is invariably drawn to novels *about* fidelity—or about the thrills, risks, and dangers of infidelity. The story about faithful women and seducing or bigamous men enables the filmmaker to represent to interviewers, reviewers, other cultural gatekeepers, and audiences alike his or her allegiance to the author and adherence to the story's teleology and thematics. Stories about infidelity, by contrast, may suppress the film's relation to its source novel so as to showcase auteurism and vaunt individual talent.

In this chapter, I argue that the uses of Jane Austen's, the Brontës', Charles Dickens's, and Thomas Hardy's novels for prestige visual culture is precisely to raise the question of whether film can be faithful to an original novelistic conception of, say, identity, passion, or destiny, in a narrative trajectory that seeks to create the normative heterosexual couple.[1] In this chapter's first section, I suggest that Jane Austen's courtship plots offer the filmmaker who shoots a film faithful to his or her source many cardinal functions that readily transfer to film. These same plots, however, also provide the opportunity for adaptation, for updating the courtship plot as late-century gender interrogation or sex game. In the second section, I argue that the 1940s Brontë films trim events in their source novels' plots through narrative transfer of strictly selected cardinal functions to feature the romantic couple; claiming fidelity to the romance plot even as they prune its seeming illogic, these films indulge spectatorial fantasy yet inoculate against its dangerous passion. Nevertheless, 1990s filmmakers restore events once edited from the Brontë tales but paradoxically suppress romance fantasy. In the third section, I sketch the late-century shift from passion plot to anxious tale of sexual encounter or hookup, both of which vex fidelity aesthetics and narrative conclusion, as the figure of promiscuous girl allegorizes the auteur's infidelity, originality, and celebrity. In conclusion, I examine self-conscious hypermediations of Jane Austen's novels that declare the romantic couple outmoded and identify source novels as sites for plunder.

Fidelity aesthetics, then, is a more problematic and capacious concept than it has been thought, for adaptations may never be wholly faithful or unfaithful to their originals. Moreover, fidelity aesthetics can never be theorized apart from cultural and historical situations, production and distribution regimes, and the careers of dramatizers, directors, and screenwriters. The 1990s repurposings (that is, rewritings for a different market) of heterosexual romance serve spectators in an age of conspicuous consumption and excess expenditure; their 1940s precursors were made in an age of post-Depression and interwar gender and financial anxiety. Fay Weldon's notions, however equivocal, that a film could achieve period authenticity or capture the source novel's spirit, misrepresent the matrix of forces that intersect to produce a film's fidelity—whatever that is—to a literary classic.

"True Readings": Fidelity and Adaptation

To what, McFarlane asks, should a filmmaker be faithful in adapting a novel? As Campion notes, "the period look" retrospectively reinvents the details of historical setting (170). "Exhaustive attempts" to "create an impression of fidelity to, say Dickens's London or to Jane Austen's village life," McFarlane adds, may "produce a distracting quaintness," for the classic novel can never appear to the contemporary filmmaker, cultural gatekeeper, or spectator as it did to the author, critic, or reader of its own time (9). Peter Bogdanovich's *Daisy Miller* (1974), McFarlane argues, demonstrates the difference between fidelity to narrative and "the period look"; although Bogdanovich claimed that his mixed bathing scene was "authentically of the period," this invention—an "irrelevant fidelity"—misrepresented James's fictional settings (9). The "time lag" between a novel's publication and its adaptation's (or remake's) release, in addition, affects the re-creative process and the film's style. Thus "conditions within the [film] industry" and the "prevailing cultural and social climate at the time of [a] film's making" shape and determine the kind of adaptation a filmmaker shoots. Among the former, McFarlane lists items such as a studio's dominance or house style, a director's commitment to genre conventions, and the effects of certain stars' images; among the latter, the economic and propaganda exigencies of wartime or changing sexual mores from decade to decade (21–22). Thus the cultural and historical situation in which remediation occurs shapes the filmmaker's reworking of narrative in a new medium.

The *"kind* of adaptation the film aims to be," MacFarlane notes, determines how faithfully it "reworks the original" (22, 202; emphasis in original). Because fidelity aesthetics relies on an impressionistic sense of novel and film, critical appraisal may mistake subjective responses for directorial intentions; viewer pleasure in having read the novel, moreover, may produce wildly variable responses to the movie. McFarlane resolves this problem by sorting the aspects of fiction that can be *"transferred* [to film] and those which require *adaptation proper"*; the former concern *"narrative,* which functions irrespective of medium" and the latter, *"enunciation,"* elements of which achieve "different means of signification and reception" and evoke, in a faithful adaptation, affective responses similar to those in the viewer's memory of the "original text" (195, 21; emphasis in original). Narrative, then, or what happened in a fictional text, can function independently regardless of medium; the screenwriter may extract cardinal functions or narrative kernels so as systematically to transfer hinge-points—those events that necessarily alter the outcome of the story—from verbal to visual medium. Yet "character, atmosphere, tone, [and] point of view" are "intransigently tied to the medium [that] displays them" (196). These functions require adaptation, and it is here that the filmmaker invests a story with his or her style and intention and "reproduce[s] certain thematic and affective elements of the novel" in a different medium (197).

Nineteenth-century narratives thus enable filmmakers to problematize the intersection of narration and enunciation. For Barthes, a narrative's cardinal functions and hinge-points necessarily create sequences of other events and actions, the entailment of which creates the reader's questions about possible outcomes or consequences. Literary (and film) texts thus propose enigmas; the reader's (or spectator's) response—his or her questions about and answers to enigmas—constitutes the narrative contract, the desire to continue reading (or watching). The narrative ends that confirm the value of beginnings and middles may look structurally homologous in book and film, but visual style may contradict—ironize, subvert, or question—the efficacy of narrative disclosures (75, 84). In Austen's courtship plots, cardinal functions produce multiple enigmas about wooing, about whether narrative ends will produce weddings. Cardinal functions, which are transferred from novel to film, structure enigmas about courtship and affective constancy; visual style, which is adapted, seeks symbolically to resolve questions about sexual and gender relations for late twentieth-century audiences, for a historical and cultural moment when the meaning and significance of marriage has radically changed.

Because her stories' enigmas inevitably produce the happy heterosexual pair, Austen's novels are especially suited for faithful adaptation. Anne Elliot's, Elizabeth Bennet's, and Fanny Price's stories, for example, evaluate the quality and nature of female fidelity narratively necessary to produce appropriate marital choice. Each novel plots tales about the misjudging woman, the excessively sensible girl, the rational Jane Austen stand-in, the (surrogate) father and mother, the jilting girl, the seductive Regency cad, the babbling woman, and the man who seeks family reconciliation. Some of these figures, especially the villains, facilitate even as they delay the plot, decoy the heroine and the reader/spectator, and foreground the near misses of the courtship plot. If misjudging or misreading, these women are educated so as to earn their happy endings; if seductive or jilting, they get their comeuppance in broken engagements and near brushes with spinsterhood; if constant and rational, they are rewarded with betrothal and the certainty of weddings. Indeed, as Martin Amis says, only a little reductively, "all Jane Austen's comedies are structurally the *same* comedy" (32).

Despite narrative delays and blockages, Austen's plots deliver on female fidelity. *Sense and Sensibility,* for example, diachronically juxtaposes two plots, each of which involves a secret about who is engaged to marry one of our heroines. In the first, the narrative enigma is "are Marianne and Willoughby engaged?" Marianne keeps the fact secret, even from Elinor and her mother. In the second, the enigma is "shall Lucy Steele, who is secretly engaged to Edward Ferrars, marry him?" Having vowed to Lucy her faith, Elinor keeps the secret engagement mum, despite the humiliations and false friendship Lucy visits upon her. Marianne's story reveals that Elinor's suspicions of Willoughby's "inconstancy" are unfounded;

Marianne confesses that he never "'professedly declared'" love, despite his having acted the part of admirer (*Sense and Sensibility* 186). Elinor's story exposes Lucy, moreover, as that inconstant creature, the jilting girl. When Mrs. Ferrars disinherits Edward because he is engaged to this woman of inferior family and position, Lucy quickly marries his brother, Robert: when Edward tells her this news, Elinor runs from the drawing room in tears of joy that he is still unmarried (357–60). Moreover, Elinor learns that after Willoughby marries, he feels remorse at having injured Marianne. His heart, he claims, "'was never inconstant to her'"; her own constancy and "'faith in [his] constancy'" grieves him, he says, even now. Although he has since married, she is "'dearer to [him] than ever'" (330, 326, 330). Perhaps, Austen wittily suggests, constancy can be taken too far.

Sense and Sensibility thus endorses fidelity even as it questions its reliability and its capability to generate story outcome. Elinor has been luckily mistaken in her wise pragmatism about attachments, marriage, and connection: "'After all that is bewitching in the idea of a single and constant attachment, and all that can be said of one's happiness depending entirely on any particular person,'" she tells Marianne reasonably, "'it is not meant—it is not fit—it is not possible that it should be so.—Edward will marry Lucy; . . . and time and habit will teach him to forget that he ever thought another superior to *her*'" (263). Despite Elinor's scolding— that, visiting at Norland, he "'must have felt his own inconstancy'"— Edward will marry Elinor, his "second choice," and will criticize his first engagement as the result of early and inconstant attachment. Marianne, who romantically refuses to "'approve of second attachments'"—despite her father's having taken two wives, the narrator wryly observes—suffers "an extraordinary fate": at the advanced age of nineteen, she must submit to "new attachments" and "give her hand" to Colonel Brandon, who has "suffered no less than herself under the event of a former attachment" (368, 55–56, 378). As Ruth Perry notes, Austen thus participates in the moral debate about the "inalienability of women's love"—and mocks it (*Novel* 251).

Despite their near misfires, Austen's courtship plots create the normative heterosexual couple. Through plot satellites, each narrative deploys a different form of decoy, delay, or blockage; each narrative, too, uses satellites to portray the cultural politics of matrimony, the novels' wished-for conclusions. *Pride and Prejudice*, for example, functions on the decoy of entailment, for the unctuous Mr. Collins may, Mr. Bennet laughs, "'turn you all out of this house as soon as he pleases'"; but Charlotte (not Lizzie) accepts Mr. Collins, and Mrs. Bennet imagines the betrothed curate viewing Longbourne's furnishings "'as his own future property'" (*Pride and Prejudice* 54, 58).[2] Lady Catherine de Bourgh may put her property in trust for her daughter, Mr. Darcy's apparent future bride, which later will affect not the rank but the wealth and social position of our heroine. *Sense and Sensibility* opens with the feared usurpation: because Mr. Henry Dashwood's old uncle entailed his estate to his son by his first marriage rather than leaving it in trust to his otherwise impoverished three daughters by a second marriage, his grandson, John Dashwood, complicitous with his wife's greed, denies these half sisters annuity or allowance. The story spins out the consequences of this disfranchisement, and its plot hinges on one heroine's possible misalliance and the other's likely spinsterhood. In *Persuasion,* Lady Russell's accusation that Frederick Wentworth has "no connexions" and no income but from an "uncertain profession" produces the novel's plot through narrative delay; only eight years and many marital enigmas later (will he marry Louisa or Henrietta?) may Frederick meet Anne again and confess that "he had been constant, unconsciously, nay unintentionally" to her all those years, despite his intent to forget her (19, 161). In a public proposal and spectacular betrothal, heterosexual coupling finally wins out over narrative delay and detour.

The Regency cad also facilitates narrative delays and blockages, for the fates of Bennet, Dashwood, and the Bertram girls hang on whether they fall victim to their passions for the Wickhams, William Elliots, and Henry Crawfords of their circles. *Pride and Prejudice:* Mr. Darcy's sister, Georgiana, nearly elopes with Wickham, who later seduces—and, due to Darcy's "in *loco fraternis*" generosity, eventually marries—Lydia, Lizzie's sister (Perry, *Novel* 153). *Sense and Sensibility:* Colonel Brandon's first love Eliza, who was married against her will to Brandon's abusive brother, "fall[s]," sinks into a "life of sin," and ends up "confined for debt"; Brandon cares for her daughter, offspring of Willoughby, Eliza's first seducer (205–11). *Persuasion:* Mrs. Smith's ruined widowhood, caused by William Elliot's urging of Mr. Smith to overexpenditure and so penury and death, and Elliot's continuing disposition to "every gratification of pleasure and vanity" makes him woo Anne, hoping to marry for money (139–40). Although these embedded seduction stories are recounted by figural first-person narrators, all but Lydia's seduction remain restricted from the narrative economy of entailed actions; as catalyzers or satellites, they cooperate with plot kernels so as to end blockages and delays. To marry the hero, Austen's heroine must possess the ability to read Regency men as appropriate or mistaken marital partner, even if she must become narratee in a storytelling situation that self-referentially stands in for the narrative's methods and cultural uses.

Case Study: The Plots of Sense and Sensibility and Emma

Jane Austen's plots' major cardinal functions are few and their settings restricted. Nevertheless, *Sense and Sensibility*'s opening is rich in narrative kernels, in story events that change the direction of characters' lives: Henry Dashwood dies (but offstage); the entailment enables John and Fanny Dashwood to move into Norland; Fanny persuades John not to provide his "mother" and half sisters with annuities; Elinor, meanwhile, becomes attached to Fanny's brother, Edward Ferrars; Fanny suggests to Mrs. Dashwood that Edward's expectations preclude his marrying a penniless girl; when Sir John Middleton offers to let Barton Cottage, Mrs. Dashwood accepts; by the next chapter, the female family has relocated. After this opening sequence, however, most narrative actions serve as satellites that root the action in the social and cultural life of the times (invitations to visit; paying calls, meeting cousins, attending balls and parties, and walking or riding to and from these events). These satellites, moreover, often begin with unmotivated actions: Sir John calls—yet again—to invite Elinor and Marianne to Barton Park; Willoughby hangs around the cottage—still—as he calls on Marianne; Marianne or Elinor takes her—daily—walk in town or neighborhood or garden. Here are the novel's central cardinal functions:

1. The family relocates to Barton Cottage (the sequence includes the functions listed above).
2. On her morning walk, Marianne falls, and Willoughby, passing by, rescues her and carries her home.
3. The group plans a party to Whitwell; while at breakfast prior to departure, Colonel Brandon receives a letter, leaves the room, then announces his departure for town.
4. Mrs. Dashwood visits Lady Middleton; Willoughby calls while she is out, and, as mother and eldest daughter return home, Marianne bursts from the parlor, crying.

5. Lucy admits to Elinor that she has been engaged to Edward for four years; Lucy asks Elinor to request that John Dashwood give Edward the Norland living when he becomes a clergyman.

6. Marianne and Elinor spot Willoughby at a ball; Willoughby snubs Marianne; Willoughby sends a letter confessing that he is engaged to another woman.

7. Colonel Brandon tells Elinor that Edward may have the Delaford living, but she must offer it to him.

8. Fanny discovers that Lucy and Edward are engaged; Mrs. Ferrars disinherits Edward.

9. Marianne catches a cold; Colonel Brandon fetches Mrs. Dashwood.

10. During her convalescence, Marianne transfers her affection to Colonel Brandon.

11. The family learns that Lucy has married Mr. Ferrars; Edward calls, and tells them Lucy married *Robert* Ferrars; Edward and Elinor marry; Mrs. Ferrars forgives them.

12. Marianne and Colonel Brandon marry.

These actions provide a skeleton of the novel's events. Although in her screenplay Emma Thompson eliminates the latter parts of 11, she transfers the other cardinal functions directly to the screen. The settings remain the same: one drawing, ball, or breakfast room after another; one assembly hall, and so forth.

Thompson does not simply dramatize *Sense and Sensibility* as did Fay Weldon *Pride and Prejudice*. She rearranges several cardinal functions and shuffles virtually all satellites, so as to tighten the narrative's causal logic, render the action more comedic, and enhance figural emotion and spectatorial affect. She places function 7 after 8 rather than before, to prepare for Elinor and Marianne's exchange; their filmed fight about Elinor's hard-heartedness in tolerating Lucy's engagement to Edward—a sotto voce exchange in the novel—depends upon Elinor's knowledge of the secret betrothal. Thompson also alters the narrative shape of satellite functions:

- adds events at beginning of narrative to characterize Edward Ferrars;

- introduces Lucy and Robert Ferrars earlier in the story, so they may dance together at a ball and tumble out of the Dashwoods' townhouse, when Fanny throws Lucy out;
- alters Fanny's persuasion of John Dashwood, who invites Lucy rather than the Miss Dashwoods to town prior to their ball, so Lucy will be available for comic tumble;
- telescopes narrative events, as Mrs. Ferrars breaks in on Lucy, Edward, and Elinor to inform them of Willoughby's impending wedding to Miss Grey, rather than days later;
- dramatizes rather than recounts, as Lucy whispers her secret to Fanny, who screams, "Viper in my bosom!" before she throws Lucy out;
- cuts Willoughby's self-justificatory visit to Cleveland;
- intensifies figural affects of envy, rivalry, and jealousy, as Elinor, Lucy, and Edward or Colonel Brandon, Willoughby, and Marianne talk as threesomes;
- adds and crosscuts to enhance dramatic and comic tone: Marianne walks into rainstorm, Elinor tolerates screaming Palmer baby;
- adds scenes, as Colonel Brandon picks Marianne up and carries her home, exactly where she met Willoughby and as he had done; the stage directions reinforce this added and plot-shaping repetition: "It is like seeing Willoughby's ghost" (Thompson 179);
- pictures Marianne's and Colonel Brandon's wedding as conclusion.

Because Austen's novel lacks sufficiently motivated action, causal logic, and pictorial drama, Thompson speeds the narrative pace by combining, trimming, and tightening the actions within scenes; she joins, in addition, groups of scenes into one dramatic scene, deepening the intensity of characters' qualities—Marianne is *really* overly expressive, for example—and intensifying figural affects. The dialogue, although trimmed, tightened, and modernized, sounds faithful to Jane Austen, without seeming to have been lifted from the novel.

Thompson's screenplay nevertheless radically alters Austen's atmosphere, tone, and perspective. The novel's tone is rancorous, as the narrator rages at female shallowness and the constraints of social routine. By the time Elinor and Marianne meet the Miss Steeles, the novel's reader is bored to death with visitors, balls, and calling, with female sentimentality, babbling, and vapidity. "This specimen of the Miss Steeles was enough," Elinor says after one visit, as Austen consigns the reader to more narrative encounters; the reader, too, is sick of innuendos, manipulations, and deceit and joins with Elinor, who could not observe Mrs. Ferrars's "studied attentions" to the Miss Steeles "without thoroughly despising them all four" (Thompson 94, 175). To alter this catty aspect of the novel—unsavory to a largely female contemporary audience—Thompson rewrites Elinor as a shrewd observer of the sexual scene. Thus, the Regency rake who comes calling in barouches, gifts wild posies, and whirls a girl around while adoring her humble cottage is a bad bet for a walk down the aisle. The sly and satirical Elinor asks, "Is he human?" when the glorious Willoughby brings a dripping, crippled Marianne home after having rescued her from a fall. "Good work, Marianne," she wryly comments, after the sensitive seducer reads her Shakespeare's love sonnets (a felicitous switch from the now-unread Cowper and Scott); "another meeting will ascertain his views on nature and romantic attachments and then you will have nothing left to talk about and the acquaintanceship will be over" (Thompson 89, 101). Using the tools of adaptation proper, Thompson updates Regency romance for the 1990s.

Thompson's screenplay, moreover, cannily adapts the passive male characters to alter the novel's perspective on sexual relations and gender arrangements. The film's sexy men seem—like 1990s guys—commitment phobic. The only marriageable heartthrob empathizes with women and likes little girls. As Thompson invents and elaborates the opening sequences, Edward Ferrars quietly refuses to displace the youngest daughter from her room with a view; sympathizes with the girls who have "just lost their father" and instructs *his* sister that "their lives will never be the same again"; protects the traumatized Margaret—a character Thompson enhances—by creating a playful geographical game with Elinor that draws her little sister from under the library table; and hands the weeping Elinor, who listens as Marianne plays the pianoforte, his handkerchief—it was "father's favourite," she blubbers. Suggesting some gender-bending games of S&M and B&D, Ferrars "fences" with Margaret in the garden under Elinor's gaze, gets "run through" by the girl while waving at the looking woman, and tells Elinor that he will accompany Margaret on "an expedition to China" as a "very badly treated" servant whose duties will be "sword-fighting, administering rum and swabbing" (Thompson 41, 45, 48).[3] Played by the mugging "matinee idol" Hugh Grant, Edward Ferrars is a successful single gent only because he's feminized (Thompson 219). "Why did we cast him?" Thompson wonders when he arrives on the set; "he's much prettier than I am" (Thompson 212).

In adapting the novel's perspective on sexual relations, Thompson sensibly replaces most marriageable men with sisters, for a sister is much more dependable than a bachelor.[4] The film reserves terms of endearment such as "dearest" and "my darling" for sisters, and Marianne and Elinor share the most intimate of conversations and scenes. Framed in two shots, Thompson and Kate Winslet lie seductively on the luscious bedcovers of four-posters, costumed in nightclothes, with the scenes lit by candles and the dialogue whispered. "Is love a fancy, or a feeling?" Marianne reads to Elinor before jumping into bed with her; at Barton Cottage, they undress, keep their underclothing on, and play footsie under the covers (Thompson 53). Yet when a man comes between these sisters, they do battle. Marianne refuses to tell Elinor whether she is engaged; bound by her vow to Lucy, Elinor does likewise. "We have neither of us anything to tell," Marianne states icily; when Marianne demands of Elinor, "Where is your heart?" Elinor rages, as Marianne weeps, but the sequence ends with the sisters' embrace (Thompson 146, 167). Framed by two sequences shot in bed, the sisters' intimacy, withdrawal, and return to intimacy climaxes with Marianne's fever. Shot from overhead, Marianne lies unconscious in bed, Elinor in frame right; Elinor walks slowly to the bed, crying, "Marianne, please try—I cannot—I cannot do without you"; "please, dearest, beloved Marianne, do not leave me alone" (Thompson 54, 184). These sequences suggest a sororal homosociality that might be read as erotic (girls are safer sexual partners than men), or as preliminary to marital choice (girlish hugs prepare for later heterosexual intercourse), or as postfeminist polemic (girls are better partners than men).

Thompson adapts the atmosphere and perspective of Austen's novel to depict a deep cultural anxiety about the difficulty of 1990s sexual arrangements. The film transfers to the screen the novel's narrative delays, caused by passive males' inability to declare love or confess sexual infidelities, by women's refusal to kiss and tell or not kiss and not tell. But the film's enunciation foregrounds anxiety about the making and keeping of vows. As Edward and Elinor stroll in the gardens, the watching Fanny Dashwood assures Mrs. Dashwood that the compassionate Edward "would never go back on his word"; when Lucy insists to Elinor that Edward is capable of "making a woman sincerely attached to him" (of which, as the spectator knows, Elinor is fully aware), she gives Lucy her "word" not to tell a soul. Although Willoughby has "broken no vow," the sensitive Edward turns out to be a hero because he refuses to break his promise to Lucy, has "stood by her" and so been "cut off without a penny" (Thompson 57, 126–27, 148, 165). In a climactic, long two shot, strikingly sans the slow track-in that indexes intimacy, Elinor tells Edward he's been given a curacy; "you honour your promises," she says and wishes him and Lucy joy (Thompson 172). Mainstream Hollywood cinema hands the heroine to the hesitant but sensitive lover precisely and paradoxically because he won't break it off with a bimbo. The film celebrates this stubborn, nearly pathological insistence on keeping one's promises even as it exhibits fidelity's fragility. The C-word has become a social problem, and Thompson's adaptation depicts 1990s heterosexual worry about vows as performative speech.

Like *Sense and Sensibility*, *Emma* produces the proper heterosexual couples but is about matchmaking and so self-consciously reflects on the

Elinor, Marianne, and Mrs. Dashwood dream as they watch Willoughby leave Barton Cottage after his first call on Marianne. (Sense and Sensibility, 1995)

procedures that create the couple. As such, it serves as a perfect allegory for Hollywood's dominant ideological uses of wedding as narrative closure. In each volume of *Emma*, an enigma structures the story's events, as narrative blockages, decoys, and misfires nearly prevent the wished-for conclusion: the vow. Volume 1: Emma instructs Harriet to read riddles rightly (not "trident," "mermaid," or "shark" but "courtship" is the answer), yet she herself misunderstands the meaning and significance of romance clues and representations (69). When she paints Harriet's portrait, Emma imagines Elton's admiration expresses his love for the sitter; when he journeys to London to purchase a frame, Emma attributes Elton's frivolity to his love for her newly found friend; when during the coach ride to the Coles' party Elton grabs, gleefully, the woman whom he believes has encouraged him, Emma is aghast. Volume 2: During a game of anagrams, Emma misreads "blunder" and "Dixon" as signifying a rival's illicit love for surrogate father rather than as alibi for a secret engagement (321–22); she misapprehends a love token, the piano, purchased during Frank Churchill's trip to London, that operates the same decoy; she willfully misunderstands Frank's visit to Jane Fairfax, when Frank examines Jane's eyeglasses before an awakened babbling aunt and newly arrived Emma. Volume 3: Emma misinterprets Harriet's story about her rescue from a gypsy attack as signifying her love for Frank rather than Mr. Knightley; she serves at Box Hill as butt of a party conundrum: "what two letters of the alphabet . . . express perfection?" Mr. Weston asks (answer: "M" and "A" [343]); yet when Emma attacks the penniless spinster, Miss Bates, "it was badly done, indeed!" Knightley reproves (347). Despite Harriet's figural function to question the viability of romantic choice across boundaries of birth, rank, and wealth, Austen's novel maintains that such boundaries must not be abrogated.

Emma's plot functions because free indirect discourse shapes the narrative's enigmas, decoys, and alibis. By positioning the misjudging woman as the story's focalizer rather than as sister, surrogate mother, or friend in omniscient narration, the novel seduces heroine and reader alike, for Austen's use of narratorial restricted consciousness and free indirect discourse forces the reader to know no more about the characters' romantic entanglements than does Emma. Identifying with Emma, seduced or led astray by the novel's riddles, ruses, and enigmas, missing the clues hidden in plain sight, the reader misinterprets *Emma*'s courtships and is educated in romance as is the heroine. Despite her narcissism and misjudgment, the plot develops Emma's character so as to educate her for the creation of the heterosexual couple: the socially correct husband and wife of the upper gentry.

Because film cannot *transfer* narratorial irony, free indirect discourse, narrative focalization, and verbal double signification to film, McGrath uses disjunctive edits to adapt Austen's verbal as visual wit. He sutures together, for example, Emma's (Gwyneth Paltrow) disdain for the Coles' party with her demand that she be invited, using the sound bridge to ironize Emma's self-importance. "As friends of the Westons," she tells her father over chess in front of the candlelit hearth, "they should have the courtesy to extend an invitation—unless they don't want me, but I—." Cut to Emma's greeting at Mrs. Cole's door, "—but I cannot tell you how delighted I am to be invited." At tea, the new and clearly vulgar Mrs. Elton (Juliet Stevenson) tells Emma how pleased she is to have made the Westons' acquaintance; moreover, "Knightley" arrived while she was visiting, she whines, "quite the gentleman." Cut to Emma, head turned, sipping tea, in voice-over: "Knightley? Never—." Cut to Emma riding in her barouche, with Harriet (Toni Collette): "—Never seen him before, and she called him Knightley!" In one long sequence, McGrath introduces Jane Fairfax (Polly Walker) via complex cuts and sound bridges. Miss Bates (Sophie Thompson) tells Emma, "You must sit right where you are, and you must say . . ." Cut to Emma, in the same dress, saying (to Jane Fairfax, although the spectator does not yet know it): "We are so glad to have you with us. How were you able to get away?" As Jane responds, Emma's voice-over replaces Austen's indirect discourse: "Hmm, she is more giving than I expected. I take it back, she is—." Cut from Miss Bates's drawing room to Hartfield's conservatory, as Emma tells Knightley (Jeremy Northam), "—absolutely impossible. She wouldn't tell me anything about Frank Churchill." Here, McGrath sutures scenes with sound bridges to picture Emma's misjudgment, narcissism, and social pretensions.

The disjunctive edit serves McGrath's use of adaptation proper to expose marrying up in rank as Emma's displaced desire, projected onto other, less privileged women, as he creates the multiply layered, ambiguously located, and ironically inscribed effect of free indirect discourse through edits, sound bridges, and voice-over effects. Moreover, the disjunctive edit joins sequences that represent different settings (often involving members of differing ranks) yet signal the likelihood of misreading.

McGrath concludes Harriet's (recounted) attack by gypsies: her helplessness accentuated by the film's only point-of-view shot (hers), a glance/object cut pictures her rescuer, Frank Churchill (Ewan McGregor), in low-angle shot, as he extends to Harriet his gloved palm; cut to the two hands clasping in extreme close-up. Cut to the same still-clasped hands, now ungloved; the camera tracks out, and Harriet sits, rescued, on Emma's Regency chaise, firelight glowing over the warm and cozy red damask interior. McGrath here depicts the full force of Austen's verbal wit: the watching Emma thinks Harriet ready to fall for the cad, Frank Churchill, whom she has decided in her multiply mirrored, diary-writing, voiced-over self-reflection scene that she herself could never love. Later, when Knightley tells her that Mr. Elton (Alan Cumming) has married, Emma cries, "I don't know what to say—"; cut to Harriet, in the rain, dripping wet, as Emma continues (but now about Knightley rather than Elton) "—except I'm in a state of complete shock." Cut to Harriet's recounted meeting with Mr. and Miss Martin at Fords, in which she voices over to Emma the Martins' conversation, which shifts into pictured action and spoken dialogue in a remediated scene. The spectator is educated—as was the Regency reader—to see that farmer Martin (Edward Woodall) is every bit the appropriate partner for the daughter of nobody knows whom, as McGrath ironizes the ideological assumption that partners choose one another freely, without withstanding historical, social, or class constraints.

McGrath knowingly submits the heterosexual couple to a scenario of "old-fashioned emotion and post-modern cool" as he updates coupling for the new Hollywood (Scott). Eschewing period Regency "wet nightgown" dresses, Jenny Beavan and John Bright costume Paltrow in high-waisted dresses and slim, draped skirts, with décolleté plus fichus and shawls (day) or displayed cleavage (evening), and bonnets galore; Jeremy Northam, in English country waistcoats, long-tailed and cutaway coats, walking or riding boots, double button-fronted trouser fly, and countrified top hats (see Laver 152–62). Glamour lighting haloes Paltrow's curled and coifed blonde hair that bares her neck and throat as the Regency gowns bare her chest. To index allure, firelight flickers on profiles of Knightley and Emma, Emma and Mrs. Weston (Greta Scacchi), Emma and Harriet; sunlight glitters off a stream by which Knightley and Emma stroll. This highlighting displays and eroticizes the female figure and helps produce the "happy ending," the traditional Hollywood kiss, a "privileged moment of romantic bonding" in which the heroine surrenders to the "erotic will" of her hero (Wexman 18). Yet McGrath eroticizes Knight-ley's figure as well, for Northam dances sensually, as Paltrow's body moves to the frame's margins; fade to black, a standardized punctuation of clas-sical style little used in late twentieth-century Hollywood. This cinematic style serves McGrath's kind of adaptation, a midsized movie distributed by Miramax—and first of the late-century Austen feature films—that drenches the flirting couple in old-fashioned emotion even as its dis-junctive edits, embedded and remediated scenarios, and glossy lighting and costumes stylize the couple with postmodern cool. Artfully adapt-ing Austen's novel about matchmaking into new Hollywood spectacle with canny cross-generational appeal, McGrath perfectly captures the specialty-division niche market and entices to the theater teenaged girls and Janeites alike.

Together, *Sense and Sensibility* and *Emma* demonstrate the kinds of ways filmmakers may make movies faithful—in its most capacious sense—to their source novels, whose courtship plots, driven by enigma, decoy, and delay, nevertheless produce the perfect heterosexual couple of rank. Yet using the tools of adaptation proper, these filmmakers update Austen's courtship stories for audiences in a decade rife with anxiety about couples and coupling, about dating and "hooking up," about STDs and AIDS. Due to the different historical situations these novels and films address and the different cultural work they undertake, the films of Austen's novels cele-brate saucy female opposition to the conventions of courtship.

Romance: The 1810s and 1990s

In perhaps the most notorious scandal—and the most widespread popu-lar agitation—of Austen's time, the Prince Regent, who had flaunted his marital infidelities and sexual exploits with married actresses and with Maria Fitzherbert, to whom he was secretly married and had set up a shadow court, sought to divorce his wife. Despite her apparent unpopu-larity with the English people, Princess Caroline, estranged from her hus-band, separated from her daughter, and insufficiently financially provided for, aroused widespread public sympathy. "Poor woman," Austen wrote to Martha Lloyd, after having read Caroline's letter to her husband in the February 1813 *Morning Chronicle*, "I shall support her as long as I can, because she *is* a Woman, & because I hate her Husband—but I can hardly forgive her for calling herself 'attached & affectionate' to a Man whom she must detest. . . . I am resolved at least always to think that she would have been respectable, if the Prince had behaved tolerably by her at first."[5] Although Austen died before the regent became king and so prior to the royal divorce case, both in 1820, other literary women followed the "Trial of Queen Caroline" closely. Fanny Burney wrote, "We are all, and of all classes, opinions, all ages, and all parties absolutely *absorbed*" by the royal divorce (quoted in Perkin, *Women* 38). Indeed, the Prince Regent had transgressed the social rules for keeping adultery within the family, which demanded considerable "delicacy and finesse" (Lewis, *Family* 39). As Joan Perkin argues, the case of Queen Caroline served, through the medium of public opinion, to expose social conditions that subverted the romance story's causal logic, for rather than produce happiness, this scandal recounted acts of adultery and ended in marital estrangement. The legal reforms sought soon after the royal divorce depended upon this public debate (40). Yet Austen's jokes about parents' and suitors' fears of scandalous publicity indicates her awareness that sexual scandal was a feature of Regency life.

Austen's novels endorse the new styles of courtship even as their plots often produce traditional courtship outcomes, such as marrying up in rank or into the landed establishment. According to historians of love and marriage, this shift began to take shape during the seventeenth century and, by the beginning of the eighteenth, romantic love seemed a "necessary ingredient" of a "successful marriage" (Perry, *Novel* 204).[6] Whereas Britons and Americans often viewed romance as "childish, uncontrolled, and unreliable" and novel reading as a source of erotic fantasy, by the turn of the nineteenth century, few "questioned that love was required for marriage" and fewer imagined that "marriage might not necessarily follow from love" (Rothman 39–40, 57). As the American practice of "bundling" declined with "the invention of petting," sexual expressiveness was constrained, since intercourse was reserved for married couples, and love emerged as a culturally valued motivation for marrying (Rothman 44–55; Laudermilk and Hamlin 76–79). In England, too, notions of romance shifted between 1760 and 1860. Whereas early in that period, families thought a daughter's "lukewarm respect and regard" for a possible mate and his "attachment" to her satisfactory for marriage, by 1860, a girl might engage in "ardent pursuit of romantic love," a value generally endorsed by her parents. Although expectations and rhetoric may have changed more than experience, the development of national marriage markets in London and

Bath enabled girls seemingly to choose their partners, and parents to "relinquish the appearance of arranging marriages without sacrificing" their control of their daughter's choice (Lewis, *Family* 18–19, 20, 31). As Austen wrote to her niece, Fanny, in 1814, "Anything is to be preferred or endured rather than marrying without Affection" (*Letters* 280). Indeed, Perry notes that marriage for love as the "standard good of fiction" was so pervasive by 1790 that Austen's juvenile parody, *Love and Freindship*, could satirize it (*Novel* 217). Throughout Western Europe, "personal choice of partners had replaced arranged marriage as a social ideal," and "individuals were encouraged to marry for love" (Coontz 145–46). By the late nineteenth century, David R. Shumway notes, the "fight for spousal choice [had] been won" (49).

In Austen's time, however, daughters were the instruments of advance in ambitious families, the figures behind whom resources were mobilized, for marriage was the fulcrum on which social power and economic advancement were leveraged. Mothers and their surrogates—although often pilloried and satirized as matchmakers (witness Mrs. Jennings)—nevertheless dutifully urged introductions, chaperoned calls, and supervised the preparation of balls and card parties—even, against all dictates, unobtrusively slipped out of drawing rooms when declarations seemed imminent. Daughters of aristocratic families with landed wealth often exercised less marital choice than did gentry girls and could find themselves affianced without their consent (Laudermilk and Hamlin 76–79). Once choice had been exercised or match made, nevertheless, marital sexual arrangements in Regency England were flexible and fidelity, permeable—if the proper delicacy and tact were observed. Should marriages prove disappointing, gentry or aristocratic husband and wife could live separately within their domicile and had the prerogative to take lovers, as long as they remained discreet in public (Perkin, *Women* 89–96). Although women who eloped to the Continent, were divorced, or remarried suffered social isolation, men might with impunity develop affective relationships with their mistresses and illegitimate children; both aristocratic mothers and fathers could "pass off" bastards as legitimate offspring, and fathers could settle marriage portions on illegitimate daughters so as to enable their own romantic marital choices (Lewis, *Family* 39–42; Perkin, *Women* 66–67, 6). Although divorce was unavailable for all but the richest Britons—those who could afford the high cost of a private Act of Parliament—informal divorce was widely practiced by the middling and laboring classes, members of which might simply move away from, sell at market, or desert a spouse (Lewis, *Family* 38–39).

In the 1990s, on the contrary, the rules of courtship had never been less clear, and the self-help dating book unscrambled the chaos for a post-feminist age. Dr. Joy Browne's *Dating for Dummies* moans, "There aren't any rules" (1); Dr. Aaron T. Beck whines that men and women dare not break the unspoken marital "rules" they absorb from their parents (53–66). As Shumway argues, the self-help literature's rhetoric ranges from case-historical to instructional, its psychological bent from psychoanalytic to cognitive-behavioral, its intended readership from couples or partners in couples to singles (149). Whereas the case-historical, psychoanalytic mode assumes monogamy, values communication, and proposes "peer relationship" rather than marriage as paradigm, cognitive books assume marital pathology, acknowledge adulterous passion, and demonstrate the incompatibility of marriage and romance (144). "One of the most profit-able product lines in contemporary publishing" as early as the 1920s, mar-ital advice books loaded the shelves of the local chain bookstore, big-box discounter, or public library during the sex-obsessed and sexually anxious 1990s (63). Authored by suburban New York or LA wives, medical pro-fessionals, couples therapists, or call-in radio psychotherapists, cognitive books became the decade's bestsellers. Ellen Fein and Sherrie Schneider nurture dating anxiety (and demand for their book) as they promulgate a postfeminist sexual double standard: Girls never mention "the *M* word," act "wifey," or sleep with a man before the fourth date (nevertheless, "men want as much as they can get on the first date"). But "if you play your cards right," they tell their reader, "you can have sex with him every night for the rest of your life when you're married!" (61, 78, 81). Although the authors confess that their book seems so, "well, '50s," it's really written for 1990s girls who, although they don't want to give up liberation, enjoy sex *and* long to marry the man of their dreams (2). Despite their deeply conserva-tive notions of gender expectations and arrangements, these self-help dat-ing books nevertheless speak to women living in the age of AIDS and HPV, psychotherapy and Prozac, personals ads and date rape, health clubs and hooking up; they imply that sex and intimacy have never been more dangerous.

The self-help literature exploited metaphors of survivalism, the jungle, and gaming during a decade of "unbridled [economic] greed," as men and women competed in the boardroom and in the bedroom (McGee 84–88).

For Browne, animal, childhood and historical pasts determine men's behavior. Her pop-cultural translation of historical data relies on rates of increased life expectancy, nearly universal use of birth control, falling rates of fertility, and female financial independence. Her metaphors—men in packs lock horns, mate, roar, and control the lair—inscribe incommensurability between the sexes even as her book pretends to ameliorate the difficulties such difference entails (*Jungle*). Fein and Schneider agree: "Men love a challenge," they claim; "that's why they play sports, fight wars, and raid corporations" (36). Writing not for women but men, Warren Farrell—once a 1970s pro-feminist and "liberated man"—blames "our evolutionary past" for dysfunctional sexual relations. "*Our genetic heritage,*" he explains, "*made it functional to kill the criticizer before the criticizer killed us*" (41, 23; emphasis in original). Farrell's atavistic maxims blame women without quite naming them and justify men, whom he views as the new victims of discrimination in domestic abuse, no-fault divorce, and contemporary child-custody cases. The consolidation of sexual difference in popular 1990s dating books guarantees that men and women hail from different cultures or species, if not planets; that dating is dangerous and so needs to be ritualized; and that sexual, bodily, and social ritual is both essential and arbitrary.

The history of self-help manuals demonstrates decreased parental and increased peer control over adolescent social codes, physical intimacies, and marital choices. According to Beth L. Bailey, modern sexual experts emerged when the nineteenth-century courtship system of "calling" gave way to the early twentieth-century system of dating. By 1915, the forces of urbanization and industrialization, the democratization of education, and the emergence of a national culture created the circumstances in which rule-bound, domestically located forms of courtship moved out of the parlor and into the public spaces available to a youth-centered culture. Whereas Victorian calling was controlled by women, primarily mothers, modern dating "shifted power from women to men" (20). Girls could no longer ask men to call, and men's expenditure on dates meant that girls owed them sexual favors, yet the double standard meant that girls had to decline men's erotic advances (13–24). Asymmetrical gender roles, John Modell argues, structured the new dating system, yet, even under the double standard, girls gained more from the dating system than did boys because it was "considerably less restrictive" than was calling (102). Between roughly 1920 and 1965, Modell notes, the success of the dating system "placed a downward pressure on the age of marriage"; as material affluence and marital timing brought wedding closer to school-located dating, popularity became "prescriptive for girls," gossip and "cattiness" began to govern female databality, and "rating-and-dating" success precluded for girls ambitions beyond those of their peer group. Popular girls at midcentury married young and had few objectives beyond marriage; their marital choice was "sharply constrained by the asymmetries of contemporaneous marital roles" (124–25).

After the 1960s sexual revolution, however, dating became as old-fashioned as calling had been in the years after 1910. Shumway charts the emergence, during and after that decade, of a new discourse of intimacy, which competed with even as it incorporated the historically earlier discourse of romance. The emergence of "new theories and practices of psychoanalysis" in the 1950s and women's changing roles after second-wave feminism caused this historical shift (133–36, 139). The professional middle class, Shumway argues, was "positioned economically and educationally to develop new [notions] of love and intimacy"; this class's expansion throughout the twentieth century "enabled the discourse of intimacy" to evolve—and after the 1960s it fueled the shift toward explicit (if simulated) sex on screen (7). In Anthony Giddens's idealized version of contemporary "malleable" sexuality, women were the avatars of modernity and feminism the cause of the long twentieth century's transformation of romantic love into intimacy (15, 53–63). The sexual revolutionaries' children—often born later in their parents' lives as women pursued professional options—practiced additional, and different, social and sexual experiments. Millennial undergraduates told Dana Mulhauser, for example, "There is nothing in between . . . random hook ups" and commitment to "ultra-serious relationship[s]" (A52; see also Seaman, chapter 2).

The emergence and development of cultural media helped to consolidate these historical shifts in coupling conventions. The sex experts who emerged in the 1920s as commentators on and arbiters of the dating system published in the new mass-market youth-oriented magazines and, at midcentury, taught and wrote the textbooks for the sex-education courses they innovated at U.S. universities. Early cinema as a technology of leisure provided commercial entertainments for, Hansen suggests, an "ethnically diverse, socially unruly, and sexually mixed audience" (16). The magic lantern, stereopticon, nickelodeon, penny arcade, dime museums, amusement parks, and vaudeville and variety shows offered "short-term and excessive stimulation," and, at the dance hall or cinema, young immigrant Americans practiced what Hansen calls "the styles of a heterosocial modernity" (29–30, 104). Although strict standards excluded women from traditionally male working-class entertainments, the dance hall and cinema attracted young, female first-generation Americans; at the cinema, cheap and safe entertainment unsupervised by parents allowed young people to mix with "friends, acquaintances, and even strangers" (105). By midcentury, the movie date had become the norm, as young people practiced in darkened theaters the new and relatively "safe" styles of sexual relations, French kissing and heavy petting (Rothman 293–94). Despite the constraints imposed by parents—curfews, moral invocations, threats about pregnancy—throngs of American teenagers learned about sex at the movies, as well as about the "delicate standoff between sensual indulgence and constraint" that petting represented (Modell 95).

The 1990s Hollywood films of Jane Austen's novels update matchmaking and courtship for a decade rife with confusion about romance, wedding, and sexual fidelity. Yet these films glorify class-appropriate courtship and marital choice even as they celebrate female resistance to such arrangements, enabling safe examination of gender and sexual relations. Although Ang Lee *(Sense and Sensibility)* and McGrath *(Emma)* shot different kinds of adaptations, their films cautioned that courtship needs rules. Whether in the 1810s or the 1990s, the narrative's cardinal functions maintain, women must not pursue men or misrule will follow. In *Sense and Sensibility,* Marianne fails to secure Willoughby because, believing that "to love is to burn," she takes romantic sensibility seriously and forgets that good girls don't chase guys. Whether rushing across a crowded dance floor to meet her man, allowing him prematurely to cut a lock of her hair (a tongue-in-cheek reference to 1990s "date" rape), riding too fast in his barouche, and visiting too precipitously the estate he will inherit, Marianne expresses her feelings and so gets dumped. Yet Emma Woodhouse rightly repudiates Elton as beneath her social rank, does not abandon the power and position of mistress at Hartfield, despite her marriage to Knightley and the consolidation of their estates. Although their plots conclude with the end of courtship misrule, each of these films of Austen's novels depicts courtship for a late twentieth-century social climate in which vexed sexual relations demand adaptation proper. Despite the plots' seeming conservatism, cultural and social uncertainty about sex at the time of the films' making shaped the kinds of adaptations Lee and McGrath shot.

Creating the Couple: The Problem of Narrative Transfer

In the 1940s, filmmakers faithful to the Brontës' novels truncated and trimmed their 1840s source stories to feature the romantic couple's "twisted passion" (Berg 320). William Wyler's *Wuthering Heights* (1939) ends, midnovel, with Cathy's death; no second generation assimilates Grange and Heights characteristics to create the tutelary wife and cultivatable rube, to restore to its former but now decidedly leveled glory the ancient paternal name. Ben Hecht and Charles MacArthur's screenplay, Tino Balio says, went "'straight to the heart of the book'" by performing "major . . . surgery on the novel" (*Grand Design* 206). For A. Scott Berg, the screenplay "neatly extracted the heart of the dark romance," "stripping away" extraneous characters and "telescoping the passage of time."[7] John Houseman and Aldous Huxley's screenplay for *Jane Eyre* (1944) likewise trims Charlotte Brontë's narrative to feature the romantic couple. Gone are the subplots of Jane's uncle Eyre in Madeira, her unconscious delay of her marriage, and the inheritance that makes her an independent woman; gone, St. John, Diana, and Mary Rivers, the three cousins with whom Jane shares her new wealth and the family she belatedly acquires; gone, the courtship elaborations of charades and gypsy impersonation; gone, the madwoman's mirrored pantomimic shredding of Jane's wedding veil; gone, the scenes of red-room torture, Jane's eerie sketches, Bessie's visit to Lowood and her mention of Jane's kin, the coachman's tale of Thornfield's burning, the struggles between and near betrothal of Jane and St. John Rivers. These films rewrite as paeans to the heterosexual couple Emily Brontë's refashioning of regional identity through domestic regeneration, Charlotte's chastisement of the female heart through sadomasochistic struggle. Yet Wyler's vain heroine and Huxley's domineering hero delay and nearly subvert the wished-for narrative conclusion, monogamous heterosexual coupling, indulging even as their larger plots disavow perverse pleasures antithetical to wedded bliss.

These films exploit fantasies of masculine dominance and female submission to lure women to the theater and secure spectatorial identification. As U.S. women entered the Depression-era and wartime workforce, their low-paying jobs more stable than those of professional-managerial male workers, hostility to women wage-earners coincided with anxiety about married women at work; as men lost corporate jobs and militarism increasingly came to define masculinity, fears about male competency to support women and families created a crisis of masculinity (Brosh 27–29). By the end of the decade, Britain was at war and enduring compulsory blackouts, food rationing, and transportation restrictions. Moviegoing exploded, as competing middle-class entertainments were curtailed by nighttime darkness and rationing (Lant 19–29). The hard-working female spectator demanded pleasure, escape, and sexual fantasy from her cultural expenditure; the immigrant or wounded veteran male spectator demanded manly dominance, which rationalized male control of women and work. Although it supports and sustains creation of the heterosexual couple, 1940s heritage romance seeks to address and resolve these gender difficulties, reversing "instances of male brutality" into expressions of "overwhelming desire and love" (Modleski, *Old Wives* 49).

Hecht and MacArthur's, Houseman and Huxley's screenplays participate in this ruse by elaborating or inventing scenes that heighten the hero's power and the heroine's submission. "'Who knows, but your father was Emperor of China, and your mother an Indian queen,'" Nelly conjectures of Heathcliff's origins in the novel (*Wuthering Heights* 67); "You're a Prince in disguise," Cathy (Merle Oberon) adds in the film; she, his "Princess of Yorkshire" and "Queen," yet "still [his] slave." In *Jane Eyre,* a fallen horseman commands Jane to hand him his whip and get out of his way; snaps his fingers, requesting that Jane "amuse" him; pleads, "Do you find me handsome?" and "Is my life worth saving?" Joan Fontaine's Jane sits silent, bows her head, says "yes, sir" and "no, sir." She watches as a costumed bride charades wedding; looks out windows as carriages arrive for a ball to which she's not invited, out at Rochester's horse galloping away over the snow, out at the battlements, as Bernard Herrmann's ominous music threatens. Jane's periodic voice-over—which speaks the highlighted pages of a spurious *Jane Eyre*—psychologizes and moralizes Rochester's class and gender perversity: although he appeared "proud, sardonic, and harsh," behind the "harsh mask he assumed lay a tortured soul, fine, gentle, and kindly."

These fantasies express female complicity with even as they rage against male brutality, a hostility that threatens to disrupt the plot's promise of faithful coupling. The romance spectator is thus "inoculate[d]" against male power even as she indulges an "infantile" "revenge fantasy" against it (Modleski, *Loving* 43, 45). Returning to the Heights from her "new life at the Grange," Cathy initiates the violence between herself and Heathcliff (Laurence Olivier), ordering him to wash because she is "ashamed" of him, once beggared, before Edgar.[8] "That's all I've become to you, a pair of dirty hands," he yells, slapping her face and running to the stables, where he breaks the window and, looking/reaching out, bloodies his hands. Cut to pier-glass scene, as Cathy looks at her gentrified reflection in the full-length mirror, metaphor for her effort to wrest dominance from the men around her; weeping, she tears off hat, dress, and crinoline; cut to peasant-garbed girl, running to Pennistow Crag. In a later scene, Cathy rages at Isabella (Geraldine Fitzgerald); "He's been using you to see me," she screams, as Isabella smiles at her own vanity-mirrored reflection; then the two cats fight, slapping one another and rolling on the floor. Later, Isabella plots with Hindley to kill her new husband (but claims she has not); "My dear wife, your loyalty is touching," Heathcliff sneers. Female anger shames the once dominant male, gets displaced onto another woman or otherwise disavowed by the plot; later, a male restored to power punishes the woman for her passion and power grabbing. Even so, Cathy remains the romance heroine, an ambiguous figure of complicity and rage that invites female spectatorial identification.

Jane Eyre likewise enacts such fantasies of inoculation and reversal in the service of romance coupling. At Thornfield, Rochester (Orson Welles) challenges Jane's training in female morality. "I like to serve you, sir, in everything that's *right*," the compliant Jane tells Rochester. When her master asks Jane to forgive, love, and stay with him at Thornfield despite his mad wife's presence in the attic, Jane rejects his claim that they would hurt no one. In the novel, Jane struggles, as her "conscience, turned tyrant, held passion by the throat": "'you shall, yourself, pluck out your right eye,'" conscience demands; "'yourself cut off your right hand: your heart shall be the victim; and you, the priest, to transfix it'" (254). This metaphor for the chastisements meted out to masturbating boys—and girls—means Jane may marry her master only when the madwoman in the attic, Jane's alter ego, assumes to herself the heroine's fantasied self-mutilation. As Carla Kaplan notes, romance at once arouses the desire for and allays female anxiety about male dominance and adoration. Even as it normalizes and affirms heterosexual coupling, the Brontë romance thus compensates for lack of female marital satisfaction by criticizing heterosexual gender norms (73).

Although gothic-romance filmmakers, like novelists, must unite the heterosexual couple, *Wuthering Heights,* like other 1940s romances, "equate[s] satisfactory closure" with the death of the "excessively desiring woman" even as it glorifies a perverse version of fidelity (Doane 118). "I've no more business marrying Linton than being in heaven," Cathy tells the listening Nelly after she accepts Edgar's proposal, an event that traditionally signals narrative conclusion but here hints at death. Track in on Cathy at window: "He's more myself than I am"; "I am Heathcliff!" Shots of lightning flash outside the windows, thunder peals on sound track. No wonder, then, that at film's end, this rude couple plights their troth, as they had when children. "I'll never leave you again," Heathcliff whispers, bent over his beloved's dying figure and acknowledging his departure as narrative delay. "I'm yours, Heathcliff," Cathy moans, as he carries her to another set of windows, intercutting the looking couple with scenes of Pennistow Crag. "See our castle?" Cathy asks; "I'll wait for you." As Mary Ann Doane suggests of other 1940s gothic-noir love stories, this romance ending fails to conclude and, indeed, activates an apparatus of "waiting, near misses, [and] separations," all in an attempt to derail even as it fulfills the classic Hollywood story of the captivated desiring female (112). Here, the thematic of waiting resists "any notion of progression" in plotting; whereas waiting cannot be an appropriate subject for narrative, Doane argues, it can be "productive *of* narrative" (109, emphasis in original). In death, Cathy will be captured and Heathcliff will wait, a feminine state displaced from the heroine onto the hero.

Paradoxically, however, Cathy's promise to wait confirms the coupling conclusion and so transforms the unhappy into a happy ending. "She's mine now," Heathcliff snarls to the returning, submissive husband. As Edgar kneels to pray, Heathcliff utters Brontë's famous last words: "Catherine Earnshaw, may you not rest so long as I live on. I killed you, haunt me then. . . . Take any form, only do not leave me in the dark alone so I cannot find you. I cannot live without my life. I cannot die without my soul." Cut to the Heights' hearth, to the pictured storytelling situation, in which Nelly (Flora Robson) recounts this tale to the wandering stranger and narratee, Lockwood (Miles Mander). "Cathy's love was stronger than life itself," Nelly intones. Dissolve to the ghosts of Heathcliff and Cathy. Nelly's voice-over: "Good-bye, Heathcliff, good-bye my wild, sweet Cathy." When sneak-preview audiences panned the film as difficult to follow and overly gloomy, Samuel Goldwyn ordered William Wyler to reshoot a happy ending; when Wyler refused, Gregg Toland superimposed Olivier's and Merle Oberon's ghostly doubles onto the set for Pennistow Crag, curiously endorsing the perverse romance fantasy (Berg 328;

Freedland 159). "He's not alone, he's with her," Nelly claims; "They've only just begun to love."

To support and sustain these fantasies, the 1940s Brontë romances cast as their romantic leads actors characterized by "exemplary" and "spectacular masculinity" (Radway, *Romance* 128). In a complex set of negotiations with David Selznick, Orson Welles demanded credit as star, coproducer, cowriter, and codirector; he then dominated the film's production. Lighting Welles with selective eye highlights, cinematographer George Barnes heightens his power; shooting the short actor towering over diminutive, submissive, and passive Joan Fontaine, he eclipses Brontë's demure governess.[9] René Hubert costumes Welles in slimming and glamorous coattails and heightening heels, in monarchical dressing gowns and cloaks decorated with dazzling gold chains. Shot either in extreme close-up, from low camera angle, or in darkened gothic interiors—complete with wooden beams, winding staircases, ominous battlements and towers, and noirish shadows—the film's focus on "gaslight" gothic-romance conventions problematizes the story's ending: will the charismatic male love or kill his bride? In *Wuthering Heights,* Laurence Olivier, already known for his Old Vic Shakespeare and brooding good looks, misbehaved on the set, angered by Wyler's insistence on multiple retakes, fighting with Oberon, and longing for his absent mistress, Vivien Leigh. With the release of *Wuthering Heights,* Olivier found himself a "dashing, sought-after young sex symbol," besieged by fans outside the New York stage door where he was playing. Boorish, sour, and angered by his "mass popularity," Olivier had nonetheless become an icon of spectacular masculinity, a role he would again immediately assume in *Rebecca* (1940)—on the set of which he tormented the still-inexperienced Fontaine—and *Pride and Prejudice* (1940), in which he brought brooding male sensuality to the role of Darcy (Holden, *Olivier* 136–40, 153; Spoto 130–32, 139).

The Brontë novels proved to be privileged heritage icons for the 1940s, for the films indulged female attraction to, anxiety about, and rage against spectacular masculinity even as they reaffirmed sexual fidelity for a post-Depression and an interwar era anxious about fiscal constraint and indebtedness, worried about women at work, and fearful of increasing strife in Europe. The 1840s novels portray the humbling of male passion through the retrospectively reimagined clash of cultures and the consolidation of rural classes following the American and French revolutions and the wars with France. The 1940s films rewrite these cultural and historical narratives to expose and ameliorate anxieties about social upheaval after the Depression and as the Second World War took shape. In the United States, money was still scarce, women still worked, and men, lately come home from war, would soon be dispatched to another; in Britain, the Depression was less severe but its burdens distributed over the country unevenly, with the south and west enjoying prosperity, the north enduring hunger marches and severe unemployment (Brosh 65–67). Picturing the pleasures of middle-class domesticity (doing needlepoint, playing the piano, sitting in the drawing room) and female anger about such constraint, the films catered to the female spectator's desire—*she* was unable to enjoy such pastimes—yet instructed her to be satisfied with marital fidelity. For Janice Radway's Smithton readers, romance indulged sexual fantasy, yet it also "legitimate[d]" the heroine's heterosexuality, "underscore[d] and shore[d] up the very psychological structure that guarantee[d] … women's continuing commitment to marriage and motherhood," and this fantasy likewise sustained the 1940s Brontë spectator (*Romance* 149). The eventual coupling of hero (who, beneath his reserved and cruel

Selective lighting and actor placement enhance Orson Welles's power as he proposes to Joan Fontaine's Jane Eyre. (Jane Eyre, 1944)

exterior might be or become, as another figure, "compassionate and kind") and heroine (who, despite her refusal to be silenced by male autocracy, eventually espouses the domestic role, however ambiguously) reassures the spectator that sexual fidelity is essential to "true love," that masculine promiscuity does not threaten marriage, that female infidelity is lethal. The romance imperative, shaped by the tensions of the post-Depression historical moment, thus fascinated the female spectator and encouraged her identification with the ambiguous heroine (Doane 122).

The romance came of age as changes in the publishing industry and as Depression-era bookselling strategies shaped the buying of books and so readership. These changes began in the 1840s, with Charles Dickens's early-career spin on the sporting news, and continued as a gradual process, as technological invention and shifts in industrial production enabled the emergence of serial publication, the triple decker, household reading, the lending library, and the mass-readership periodical. During the 1840s, as Radway demonstrates, books were believed to be written by "learned gentlemen of independent means"; a century later, the book had become a "saleable commodity"; early technological advances in publishing—the invention of rotary presses, synthetic glue, and perfect binding—spawned a sudden surge in innovation, enabling large print runs. The necessity to avoid overproduction created "category literature," a form whose (here, female) audience could be calculated and specified (*Romance* 20–22). The new book series enabled successful and continuous sales to a "huge, heterogeneous, preconstituted public," and, in 1939, the debut of Pocket Books heralded "successful paperbacking" in the United States (Radway, *Romance* 28–29; Simonds 98–99). As women entered the public sphere during the 1930s and 1940s yet continued to be responsible for domestic labor, the gathering of a potential gothic-romance audience in drugstores and supermarkets provided publishers easy access to consumers and consumers easy access to inexpensive books. Commodity packaging achieved "mass sales," and a "non-advertising mode of reaching women readers" enabled producers easily to attract "more than half of the book-reading public" (Radway, *Romance* 42–44). Romance fiction's rise to preeminence in mass-market category publishing depended on technological, marketing and readership-predictive activities made possible by advances in book making, distribution, and, later, in the 1980s, computerized data gathering.

The gothic romance's popularity on film likewise depended upon producers' capability to market, distribute, and exhibit prestige pictures within the regime of studio production. While the studios amassed fortunes in the 1930s, Hollywood's independent producers struggled against the vertically integrated industry that prevented easy access to theatrical booking and control of distribution networks (Schatz, *System* 10–11). Selznick and Goldwyn, who developed *Jane Eyre* and *Wuthering Heights* respectively, did battle with the studio behemoths.[10] Selznick's *Gone with the Wind* (1939) and *Rebecca* (1940) "redefin[ed] the limits of prestige and profitability in Hollywood filmmaking"; after 1939 and 1940, production values and marketing would never be the same (Schatz, *System* 292–93). Although Goldwyn outdid the major studios in prestige authenticity, he could never better Selznick's marketing genius, which enabled Selznick to reach the wide audience that would guarantee box-office success, critical acclaim, and industry awards.[11] Despite Frank Nugent's *New York Times* review, which named *Wuthering Heights* "one of the most distinguished pictures of the year," Goldwyn lost the 1939 Academy Award to Selznick, whose *Gone with the Wind* earned eight Oscars, including Best Picture, and who would go on to earn Best Picture again in 1940, for *Rebecca* (Berg 332; Freedland 160). In the wake of *Rebecca* and *Suspicion,* moreover, *Jane Eyre* was marketed as a noirish female gothic and, although it did "solid business," barely broke even; *Wuthering Heights,* attractive to "class" but "too heavy" for "general" audiences, grossed $1.2 million in the United States but still did not make money.[12] Despite its acclaim and success at the box office, 1940s heritage romance failed to gain a wider audience paradoxically because it was marketed as gothic romance.

Half a century after the first wave of prestige adaptations, the romance continued to attract both "class" and general female spectators and readers. Yet as sexual relations and marriage changed, so did the romance genre. In the 1980s, Carol Thurston argues, romance novels depicted as "the norm" a "balanced power alignment" between men and women (8). Working women readers bought books about independent women who, like themselves, had highly skilled professional jobs, earned good incomes, and had sex with whomever they chose. Reading romances for "entertainment, relaxation, fantasy, and escape," these readers, like 1940s romance spectators, had entered the labor market, this time as career women whose income was essential to maintaining their families' middle-class consumerist lifestyles (86–88, 115–35). The late-century romance, moreover, crossed taste cultures, portraying, for example, "single parenthood" for "niche markets," multiethnic stories for African American, Latino, or religious readers. Commercial publishers cultivated crossover writers, who could quickly sell their books to Hollywood (Rosen 37–38). Creating an "extensive web of psycho-media" in magazines, advice-giving audio- and videotapes, soap operas, and self-help books, the updated romance thus penetrated film, television, and video markets, appearing in multiple windows across cultural boundaries (Simonds 132, 218). The postmodern romance genre thus complicated ideologies of male dominance and female submission, producing newly fashioned fantasies for working women and entertainments appropriate for multiple niche markets.

To feed this burgeoning market for a revised romance, late-century filmmakers remade the 1940s Brontë films. Rather than reproduce female complicity and rage, or domineering, spectacular, and anxious masculinity, the 1980s and 1990s films repurposed the Brontës for a new Hollywood and millennial audience. These remakes seek to "get [the novels] right," as do all remakes, by shooting an "authentic" Brontë (Braudy, "Afterword"). Restoring narrative events truncated in 1940s gothic romance— restoring second generations or discovered cousins that classic cinema once disavowed—1990s directors flaunted their fidelity to Charlotte and Emily during the heyday of heritage even as they adapted character, atmosphere, tone, and perspective to create an updated period look. Remaking spectacular masculinity and feminine complicity as period fantasy, the 1990s films of the Brontë novels reshaped spectatorial desire and identification for a postfeminist, antiromantic age.

Julian Amyes's *Jane Eyre* (1983) seeks to get Brontë right as only classic serial can. Alexander Baron's dramatization restores scenes and sequences that Huxley and Houseman expunged in 1944: Jane's fantasy that her uncle, as ghost, will rescue her from the red room; conversations with Miss Temple; Jane's sketches; Rochester's references to himself as sufficiently old to be Jane's father, and to young Jane as kin to him; the courtship games of charades and gypsy impersonation; Bertha's shredding of Jane's wedding veil; Jane's letter to Uncle Eyre, which makes Mason appear, as an impediment to Jane's marriage; the inheritance subplot; and, although this sequence is trimmed, Jane's discovery of cousins at Moor House and near marriage to St. John. In Brontë's novel, the figurative heart structures Jane's and Rochester's courtship; rewriting a faithful dramatization of Brontë's narrative, Baron thematizes fidelity as central to his project, exploiting romance's central metaphors. When Jane (Zelah Clarke) refuses to marry Rochester because his "wife is living,"

Rochester (Timothy Dalton) acknowledges that he "should have appealed to [her] heart": "I should have asked you to accept my pledge of fidelity, and to give me yours: Jane—give it now"; when Jane calls her master "a married man—or as good as a married man," claims that she has "as much soul" as he and "full as much heart," he offers his hand, his heart, and a share of all his possessions. After she returns to her master, Baron's Jane, like Brontë's, declares herself an "independent" yet faithful woman; Rochester accepts her proffered "heart," and her "I do" invokes the wedding ceremony, as she becomes "bone of bone" and "flesh of flesh" of her beloved master. In this scene of reunion, Baron displays his fidelity to his source novel and implicitly condemns his predecessors' disloyalty to the original.

Loudly proclaiming their fidelity to the Brontës' novels, Franco Zeffirelli and Peter Kosminsky fail to make romance credible for a postromantic age. Zeffirelli boasts that his "abiding love of British culture" and passionate immersion in "the period [and] the place," guarantee his films' "essential 'rightness'" and "fidelity" (19, 85–86, 93). Zeffirelli's credits, like Amyes's, offer "special thanks" to the Brontë Society and the Brontë Parsonage Museum, Haworth, as the author's house, writer's relics, and society's archive warrant his film's authenticity. Peter Kosminsky's title, *Emily Brontë's Wuthering Heights* (1992), brands his film as genuine, as credits roll over shots of a hooded female figure, "Emily Brontë" (Sinead O'Connor), as she walks the moors, explores a ruined castle, and wonders who lived there.[13] Her authorial voice-over repeatedly summarizes character motivations and explains cardinal functions; her presence implicitly claims the film is faithful to the writer's original novel. Casting British heritage stars Joan Plowright, Fiona Shaw, and Amanda Root in minor parts, Zeffirelli imagines Mrs. Fairfax as jolly, even cuddly, in frock and mobcap, Mrs. Reed as unredeemably wicked, Miss Temple as thoroughly innocent and caring. Casting Ralph Fiennes as Heathcliff (shot in profile, blue eyes blazing), French crossover art-flick beauty Juliet Binoche, as Cathy (who, in addition to her atrocious English accent, laughs inanely through much of the film), and heritage hunk Jeremy Northam as a vaguely revolutionary Hindley, Kosminsky updates heritage with a self-conscious period look. Yet Zeffirelli's and Kosminsky's gestures toward credibility in period costume, stately house settings, and heritage casting scream frock drama. Despite the urge to authenticate and update by returning to the novels, the new Hollywood Brontë looks decidedly unsexy.

Suppressing the sexual fantasies that drive the romance genre, Zeffirelli and Kosminsky seek to make romance palatable to postfeminist female spectators. Yet Zeffirelli merely modernizes female submission; Kosminsky reinscribes male domination. Charlotte Gainsbourg plays Jane Eyre as independent woman: the gray governess has ready energy and wit; William Hurt plays Rochester as tender and sensitive. The cleft-chinned, intellectual heartthrob mumbles, "I feel like I have a string tied from under my left rib where my heart is, tightly knotted to you." Rewriting Rochester as a "thoroughly modern neurotic" rather than as a charismatic, domineering brute disables romance's disavowal of male brutality, even rape, as an expression of overwhelming desire and devotion, disables female complicity with and rage at male power. The great romance between master and governess becomes a sappy story of "embittered angst" (Holden, "Jane"). Kosminsky's film, by contrast, displaces romance's rage from women to men, as Fiennes and Northam battle for ascendancy. Remasculinizing Brontë, Kosminsky tells as a tale of surly male greed Brontë's story of regional English family life interrupted and destroyed by a waif from the colonial periphery. Although Kosminsky flaunts his fidelity to Brontë, *Emily Brontë's Wuthering Heights* ironically recalls Luis Buñuel's *Abismos de Pasión* (1954), a European art film (but made in Mexico) that adapts Brontë's novel's violence for a Roman Catholic, masculinist culture.[14]

The 1990s Brontë romances seemed immediately outdated because they failed to repurpose the sexual fantasies their prewar predecessors so successfully exploited. The few and generally tepid reviews earned by these films highlight their aesthetic failures. Roger Ebert called Zeffirelli's remake "recycled Gothic Lite"; Stephen Holden longed for the "dear old golden-rule days of feminine propriety" after viewing it.[15] Unlike the 1990s Austen films' saucy, savvy heroine who gets her man despite narrative decoys and near courtship misfires, these heroines' passivity failed to ignite spectatorial desire and identification; unlike the dominant and nasty, yet loving, heroes of the 1940s Brontë films, these pallid, dour, growling, and snarling heroes also disappointed. I am not endorsing the sexual fantasies these films inscribe, or fail to inscribe, nor do I celebrate or judge their unconscious content. Nevertheless, the 1940s perverse sexual scenarios indulged female fantasy even as they enhanced masculine power. This mix served wounded, impoverished, and worried midcentury males and fearful and overburdened females. During a consumerist and spendthrift decade

of post–Gulf War self-satisfaction, however, it failed to arouse female desire or to attract postfeminist men.

Fidelity and Culture at the Millennium

In the twentieth century's last decades, the sex scene replaced the Hollywood kiss as signifier of devotion, and the romance genre shifted as the
seduction plot became more popular than ever. As the heritage heroine's
body becomes the erotic look's overt object, the narrative spins alternative enigmas: May a sexually experienced heroine marry? Will the victimized girl give birth or be spared that consequence? If not, will the narrative
scapegoat her figure? Will her sacrifice purify the cultural imaginary?
Thomas Hardy's enigmas presage death, for their cardinal functions
feature mishap, delay, and detour that cannot be undone by wedding;
Charles Dickens's deeply troubled couplings contaminate the joy associated with happy endings. In order to adapt these mid- to late nineteenth-
century novels, screenwriters again trimmed and telescoped narrative to
focus on the heterosexual couple. Asking whether fidelity suits a modern
or postmodern world, these adaptations link star images and specialty-
division style to imagine romance not as courtship or perverse passion but
as lethal, often fatal. Shot in an increasingly eroticized cultural climate,
they picture heterosexual coupling for a nonmarital age by again invoking
the "twisted passion" of forties romance.

Plot and discourse bedevil the director who adapts Hardy's novels.
Plot: how to transfer to film the narrative's cardinal functions, when
Hardy's lovers' sexual and affective fidelities, however spiritually desired,
fall victim to intellectual crosscurrents in modernity, social and religious
traditions or superstitions, and their own vacillations? Discourse: how to
adapt the narrator's distant observational stance yet intimate focus on his
characters' mishaps? In *Tess* (1979), Roman Polanski shoots mishap and
enigma as period romance that displays one but barely occludes another
perverse fatality; in *Jude* (1996) and *The Claim* (2000), Michael Winterbottom prefers rural period realism as the canvas for characters over-
whelmed by the forces of modernity. Changed sexual mores, moreover,
enable Winterbottom to shoot as explicit scenes Hardy's circumspect
sense of sex; Polanski prettifies atmosphere, as sexual encounter becomes
enigmatic and seduction perverse. Hardy's stories, nevertheless, disable
creation of the Hollywood heterosexual couple, as women are sacrificed

by choice or circumstance and men bring adversity upon themselves as conclusion. How faithfully to turn Hardy's melancholy, even perverse, tales into conventional Hollywood romance torments these filmmakers, as they shoot films for a decade in which sex cannot guarantee wedding as ending.

Hardy's *Tess* produces the heroine's image through what J. Hillis Miller calls "the optical detachment of [a] spectator narrator" (50). Superimposing perspectives of sweeping landscape and small rural moment, Hardy's narrator's "double perspective" requires the narratee to look closely and from a distance, portraying him as a sympathetic yet "alien observer" (52). Viewed from the "summits of the hills that surround it," the "ungirdled and secluded" vale of Blakemore remains untrodden by London "tourist or landscape-painter"; the coastal traveler, neither despoiling by looking too closely nor appropriating by looking too distantly, may behold below him the "delicate," virginal Vale (*Tess* 22–23). The reader as rambler, moreover, first sees Tess being looked at by others. Tess "exhibit[s]" herself at the May Day dance for a series of "on-lookers" at the "spectacle of a bevy of girls dancing without male partners"; Angel Clare "glance[s] over" the women, fails to choose Tess, exchanges a look with her as he departs (hers reproachful, his sorrowful), and, looking back, sees Tess's white shape standing apart from the dancing figures that seem already to have forgotten him (24, 26–29). Understanding Hardy's doubled perspective and the desiring intimate backward look (a look that likewise seals the fates of Jude Fawley and Sue Bridehead), Polanski shoots this reciprocal look as central to the narrative's structures of desire, with Hardy's Wessex as backdrop.

Michael Winterbottom's *Jude* and *The Claim* also capture on film the double perspective of Hardy's observing narrator. The camera shoots widescreen landscape and then obsessively focuses, via close-up, on melancholy late-century men and women who escape, approach, or follow one another across the countryside. In both Hardy films, modernity remaps the rural landscape and structures the story, as the railroad speeds across country space or, in scenes of laboring, is built across continent. Winterbottom shoots Jude (Christopher Eccleston) looking out train windows, the landscape whizzing by, from his point of view (POV). When he learns that Fawleys are not "meant for marrying," Jude screams, in close-up, then runs howling through woods; cut to railroad tracks, to a close-up of Jude, framed in a train window, to his POV of countryside.

In *The Claim*, a town's fate hangs on the railroad's arrival: in long shot, men sledgehammer in snow and lay track, as the train snakes around mountain, across river, and, from Dalglish's (Wes Bentley) POV, past Half Dome; yet the Central Pacific Railroad bypasses the mountain town and locates in the valley.[16] Kingdom Come, moreover, is a town of laboring men and the prostitutes who serve them, as Winterbottom shoots a form of heterosocial modernity appropriate to *The Mayor of Casterbridge* as North American revivalist western. Ironizing the wife-and-child-selling male hero as "defender" of "community and family," Winterbottom adapts Hardy's tone, atmosphere, characters, and perspective, recasting the novel's national setting and reconstituting its historical moment (Neale, "Westerns" 30). Winterbottom's visual mapping of rural England or crossing of American continent pictures a soon-to-be—or already—gone landscape punctuated by the close-ups and howls of modern lovers frustrated by the failures and impossibilities of modern sexual intimacy.

Polanski alternates landscape long shots and figural close-ups of his beautiful heroine for a seductive scenario. "Hardy was clearly in love with Tess," Donald Hall writes of *Tess of the D'Urbervilles*, "and he leaves his male readers in the same condition" (424). In correspondence with Sir George Douglas, Hardy wrote, "I am so truly glad that Tess the Woman has won your affections. I, too, lost my heart to her as I went on with her history" (I: 249). Roman Polanski, who reread *Tess* until he "knew it almost by heart," likewise adored Tess. "I've loved her since I first read [the novel]," he told Mitchell Glazer—who would later pen Cuarón's screenplay for *Great Expectations* (Glazer 41). Framed by shots of early roses, the scene in which Alec (Leigh Lawson) feeds Tess (Nastassja Kinski) strawberries depicts her, in shot/reverse shot, from Alec's perspective. As the camera tracks Alec's hand picking and then offering the red fruit to Tess, in close-up, she looks down, looks up at Alec from under her country hat, attempts to dissuade him from feeding her, then accepts the strawberry into her pouting, red mouth. This close-up serves as index to the woman's penetrability. Whereas Alec's violation of the sleeping Tess occurs in Hardy's narrative gap, in Polanski's scenario, rape becomes romance. "You're bleeding," she whispers as they embrace tenderly; soft focus visualizes moonlit, misty aura; dissolve to Tess's accepting Alec's gift—given in exchange, the spectator presumes, for her maidenhead. Montage condenses their encounter, again, into romance: Alec rows Tess on a pond as light reflects off the water; swans surround the skiff as the music swells; Tess looks down under her parasol, an index, once more, of her hesitance and her permeability.[17] Later, confined in Alec's house, dressed by the finery his ersatz wealth has purchased, Tess finally becomes a kept woman. Hating his heroine's victimage and sacrifice but himself identifying with the seducer, Polanski turns Hardy's tale into a "'beautiful, tragic love story'" in a "'romantic, even sentimental'" mode (Glazer 41).

Hardy's story submits Tess to the seduction plot's tropes of *bildung* as fatality (N. Miller). Although he tastefully shoots the one night of idyllic married bliss when Angel (Peter Firth) and Tess flee from the law, Polanski, like Hardy, disallows marriage as narrative closure, as unable to fix the social order and undo the D'Urberville repetitions Tess has unwittingly put in play. Liza Lu, virtually effaced from Polanski's film, cannot redeem Tess's "fall" or sublate her sacrifice. Polanski's romance, moreover, allegorizes not only a cultural shift from romance to seduction but the Manson family's attack at Cielo Drive, and so his personal myth of adoration as modern victimage. Bearing the dedication "To Sharon," *Tess* represents as period romance the violence done the woman who loved both Polanski and Hardy's novel and who would have played the part of Tess; the dairy maids, the Manson family women, dominated by and obsessed with the filmically flaccid hero; Angel as villain, Manson; Alec, Polanski himself, seducer of the actress who did finally play Tess after his wife's murder (Polanski 382; see Glazer 42–44). Nevertheless, in *Tess*, constables hunt down not the man who has "unlawful sexual intercourse" with an "innocent" girl but the girl herself, who, having killed the man who had violated her, then pays for her spoliation and her murder with her life. Polanski called *Tess* the "story of innocence betrayed in a world where human behavior is governed by class barriers and social prejudice" (Polanski 405). Rooted in the late-century seduction plot, Polanski's film eschews Hardy's consolatory suggestion that Alec and Liza Lu couple at the story's conclusion and heralds the death of the heterosexual marital couple.

With his adaptation of *Tess*, Polanski seeks at midcareer to out-Hollywood Hollywood. Despite its having been shot in France, despite Polanski's having been on the lam from criminal prosecution in the United States, the director hoped, with *Tess*, to recapture the recognition he had achieved with *Rosemary's Baby* (1968) and *Chinatown* (1974), the latter a signal movie in the new Hollywood renaissance. Seeking to attract the audience that had made his earlier films box-office hits, Polanski's award-winning *Tess* eschewed grit or shock and anticipated the 1980s

European heritage explosion. Released five years after *Jaws* and three years after *Star Wars*, *Tess* entered the U.S. cinema marketplace when film producers had begun to bankroll, and distributors and theater owners to exhibit, blockbuster fantasy, disaster, and exploitation pictures. Knowing his film a commodity, as were those genre pix, and aware of his laboring position as alienated because of his status in Hollywood as foreigner, cosmopolite, and pervert, Polanski needed his film's spectator to desire its heroine's star image and so be widely consumed (Polanski 311, 352–57, 377–83). "Dedicated to the consumption of female flesh," Polanski's romantic, even sentimental film also allegorizes the ideological work of film adaptation in late-century commodity culture (Polanski 182). The seduction plot on screen, as adapted from an 1890s narrative about female penetrability, thematizes, pictures, and mimics the seduction necessary to secure a theatergoing audience. This film, like Winterbottom's, pictures solicitation as an allegory of Hollywood culture, itself dedicated to advertising, marketing, and selling female flesh on screen.

Unlike Polanski's tasteful montages, Winterbottom's sex scenes make explicit Hardy's modern anxiety about bodily intimacy. Hossein Amini's screenplay telescopes Hardy's narrative events, as Jude takes a Sunday walk with Arabella and seduces her in the barn the same night. Janty Yates costumes Rachel Griffiths in country décolletage to show off her cleavage; Arabella, the modern tramp, removes from and returns to her breasts the egg she's hatching: "It's natural for a woman to want to bring live things into the world." When Arabella later returns to England from—significantly—Australia and seduces Jude, Winterbottom shoots him fumbling and humping, on top and then next to her, sleeping, his head on her chest, her large left breast and nipple drawing the spectator's anxious look. When the "delicate" Sue finally has sex with Jude, Winterbottom shoots a long take of Kate Winslet's full body, naked, as Jude enters frame left, also naked, and crawls on top of her; cut to his kissing Sue's mouth, then nipple, then torso.[18] Cut: Sue cooks breakfast, in a scene without precedent in the novel; fast track to Jude behind her, kissing her; "You're looking pleased with yourself," she smiles. Yet Amini denies Jude either Arabella or Sue as loving wife. As the film ends, Jude walks Christminster's streets and byways, finally approaching a black-garbed Sue, who kneels by their children's snowy graves; they kiss. Sue walks away, shot from behind, snow rising in clouds around her feet and hem; cut to high-angle shot of a powerless, pitiful Jude, screaming after her, "We are man and wife if any

two people are on this earth," as the camera tracks out, leaving Jude solitary, stark, and small against a field of snow. Ending in a palette of blacks
and whites (much as it began, filmed on grainy black-and-white film stock),
Jude declares the death not of the hero himself, as in Hardy's novel, but of
the once-conventional heterosexual couple in heritage film.

In *The Claim*, sex is sadistic, fetishized, and commodified, as extreme
close-ups replace full body shots. A woman's back, camera in tight, a
match lit; track up to her image shot in a mirror, Dillon (Peter Mullan)
behind; cut to close-up of his unlacing her corset; the woman's reflection,
as she turns, looking at him and the camera. In tight close-up, he un-
laces her boots, kisses; intercuts between figures struggling on the bed in
medium long shot and extreme close-ups of faces, a kiss; "you like to hurt
me," Lucia (Milla Jovovich) whispers; "no," Dillon responds. Later, the
half-dressed Dillon enters Lucia's bedroom, gives her the deed to the house
as a "settlement"; "I'm not a whore," she screams, as he exits to begin his
second courtship of Elena (ironically, Nastassja Kinski once again). Later
still, mother-daughter embrace replaces heterosexual sex scene. Close-
up of Elena's face at foot of bed; the camera tracks up the bed and down
her body; Hope (Sarah Polley) crawls onto the bed, as the camera tracks
to an extreme close-up of the dying mother cuddled by her daughter, shot
upside down, faces together. Dillon keeps watch, but hardly as voyeur.
Here, Winterbottom adapts Hardy's wife-sale as frontier divorce, settlement, and claim-payment. Sex is always implicated in these commodifying circuits.

Like Frank Cottrell Boyce's for *The Claim* and Amini's for *Jude,* Mitchell
Glazer's screenplay for Alfonso Cuarón's *Great Expectations* (1998) trims
its source novel's narrative, telescoping some events and eliminating others, to foreground romance. But the heterosexual couple has changed
since Dickens's day and David Lean's. Although his screenplay transfers
Dickens's novel's primary cardinal functions from verbal to visual medium,
Glazer rewrites the dialogue, changes the setting, and locates the action
in the 1980s, the decade of "Reaganite entertainment," of corporate mergers and takeover bids in the culture industries, as in others (quoted in
Keathley 305). Self-consciously historically locating itself, it specifies its
aesthetic as *not* period costume drama: "It *is* the '80s," Estella (Gwyneth
Paltrow) sneers when Miss Dinsmore (Anne Bancroft) asks about her
evening's escort. Adapting character, atmosphere, tone, and perspective,
Cuarón updates romance for a late-century commodity culture.

The sex scenes celebrate, even as voice-over criticizes, the romance as hookup. Foregrounding Gwyneth Paltrow's reedy body and fetishizing body parts (eyes, mouths, throats, collarbones) in extreme close-up, Cuarón pictures the look the star body/image solicits, for here the hero is a New York artist.[19] The American queen of 1990s heritage romance, Paltrow disrobes, her body tastefully morselized by extreme close-up not of breast or pubis but eyes, mouth. Cuarón intercuts sexual moves with shots of Finn's (Ethan Hawke) look: she, robed in strapless, ruffled organza dress, aggressively moves her knee into Finn's hands; his palm, moving up her thigh, touching panties, produces a series of extreme close-ups of Paltrow's face, head back, eyes closed, mouth open, in the soft-core look of female arousal; dissolve to kiss; in close-up, her hair brushes his hand. Abruptly, Paltrow stands, turns, and walks away. A later sequence in which Finn sketches Estella begins with Finn's sleep-drenched POV of Paltrow's legs striding horizontally across the screen. "Don't you want to paint me?" she asks. Close-up of hands unbuttoning shirt, tilt down; framed in a medium-long shot by huge rounded window, she drops her shirt; she turns, in a black bra and tube skirt, which she pulls off; later, a close-up of her shoe, dropping from her foot; bra off, medium shot from back; panties drop as the camera tilts down her legs. Alternating shots of the naked Paltrow posing—cross-legged on bed, smoking, as traditional yet novel odalisque—Finn, looking; of his hand drawing—first nipple, then pubic hair. Suddenly, Estella rises and, having dressed, departs; her reflection flashes on the glass door as she exits. When the two later make love, Estella moans like a liberated nineties girl, "I want you inside me"; cut to kiss, dissolve to white.

This Reaganite love story updates romance's primary metaphor, the heart, for a materialist age. When Finn first meets Nora Dinsmoor, the boozy, frowzy, singing-and-dancing version of Miss Havisham puts the boy's hand on her breast. "What is this?" she asks; the boy responds, "your boob"; "my heart," she corrects, and "it's been broken." As he later bids her goodbye, Finn puts her hand on his chest; "you know what this is," he says; "it's my heart, and it's broken." "Estella will make men weep," Dinsmoor later warns Finn; "she'll break your heart." Indeed, Estella's abrupt exits signify her heartlessness, her role as hurt little girl become affectless, wounding woman. Although the screenplay slashes subplots (a Hispanic bride without narrative function replaces Biddy; Arthur Lustig is not Estella's father; Miss Dinsmoor's relationship to Estella goes unstated;

gallery director, hangers-on, and the social elite in New York replace the Pockets), Glazer captures Dickens's second ending's ambivalence, as Finn goes home, visits Paradiso Perduto, follows a hallucinated Estella around the decayed mansion, and meets the real girl onshore, with her own daughter. "Can you ever forgive me?" Estella asks, as Finn's voice-over concludes, "I always had. It was as if it had never been; it was just my memory of it." Shot from behind, the two take hands as music swells and the credits roll.

Jill Greenberg's casting celebrates celebrity as sexy. Paltrow is pure star image in *Great Expectations;* the spectator never forgets that he or she looks at a heritage star who can cross over into multiplex romance, who was born and bred in Hollywood, who can sell a flick whether she strips or speaks the King's English. Although an Academy Award for *Shakespeare in Love* validated Paltrow's acting in 1998, her career trajectory has alternated between midcult heritage films and romantic comedies. Robert de Niro as the Magwitch figure remains one of Hollywood's consummate tough guys, for his face recalls streetwise kid, savvy boxer, hoodlum, Vietnam vet, rapist, and, later, heritage monster.[20] This male type—of "violence, aggressivity, callousness and brutality," especially against women— is nevertheless champ, hero, buddy, and common man, an image that amalgamates American masculinity's contradictions when in cultural crisis, as in the 1990s and the Great Depression (Dyer, *Stars* 55–56). Dinsmoor, the harridan boozer, is 1960s superstar, Mrs. Robinson, and Helen Keller's teacher.[21] Grotesquely made up with wrinkled, rubber face mask and white pancake foundation, wicked-stepmother eyeliner, and outmoded bouffant wigs, Bancroft is shot, in one scene, applying makeup, fantastically misshapen close-ups of eye, cheek, mouth, and beauty mark flashing into and out of the magnifying mirror; "I've gone red," she cackles at Finn, flashing her face and flaming hair at the camera. Earlier, she dances, drunk, flabby body poured into a green, sequined gown. These high-profile, genre-pic, star images—the hag star past her prime, the heritage queen gone cock tease, and the woman-hating tough guy with a heart of gold— alert the spectator that Cuarón means to criticize Hollywood's notion of glamour celebrity even as he glorifies it. Adapting character, atmosphere, tone, and perspective, Cuarón shoots Finn's expectations in glitzy, big-studio style, as romance feeds female rapacity and masculine delusion.

The Hollywood heterosexual couple, as these films suggest, is no longer romantic, nor does the story necessarily end happily ever after. To earn top box-office dollar, millennial romance mixes the love story with other genres; the publishing industry does likewise. As readers get older and young consumers plug in rather than read novels, romance becomes hotter or sweeter, more inspirational or paranormal, to target new demographics. As Harlequin Books' CEO Donna Hayes says of the company's new marketing schemes, "Our intention is to . . . serve all readers across [the] whole spectrum," for romance consumers—highly educated, motivated readers and loyal customers—need to feed their "fantastic addiction." Hayes justifies the marketplace, claiming that "romance readers, generally speaking, have much better sex lives than people who don't read romance" ("Harlequin" 1–5). Whether a version of Austen, Dickens, or Hardy; whether hot or chaste, this contemporary romance knows itself a commodity and so solicits consumption. Yet however it is distributed, marketed, and sold, the romance's declining market share of the cultural consumer's dollar, like that of literary texts, according to the National Endowment for the Arts, coincides with electronic media's emergence and rise to dominance (Romano).

Hypermediated Romance

Remediation, Bolter and Grusin claim, "is a defining characteristic of the new digital media" (45). Although film is not a digital medium, its recent appropriation of video technology heralds the end of celluloid. Because they remediate literary texts, however, adaptations necessarily represent one medium in another and may also acknowledge and make visible multiple acts of representation (33–34). Whereas televisual film reviews, movie trailers, interactive film posters, or Web sites hypermediate text or film by exhibiting clips, print, graphics, and photos in multiple windows, film remediates literature by embedding metaphors for or pictures of the book, often the source novel (as in the 1940s Brontë films) or in voice-over of its often ersatz original. Because historically older media, such as film, must prove their continuing cultural and aesthetic relevance within digital culture, new Hollywood independent cinema often deploys the "double logic of remediation"; gratifying the spectator's longing to multiply its access to media, such films exploit, at the same time, the desire to "erase" the media the spectator enjoys consuming (5). Watching heritage film, like reading books, may operate the logic of immediacy by making viewers experience "immersion," feel as if they are "'really' there"—in

Bath, for example, with Anne Elliot—even as they consume a cultural product; yet playing off spectatorial desire for "transparent presentation of the real" against pleasure in a medium's "opacity," heritage film may also satisfy an audience's desire as well for dislocation and pastiche (5, 21). The spectatorial oscillation between the logics of immediacy and hypermediation, Bolter and Grusin maintain, is "key to understanding how a medium refashions its predecessors and other contemporary media" (19).

Although in my epigraph to this chapter, Bolter and Grusin call the Austen films "historically accurate in costume and setting and very faithful to the original novels" (44), they bracket the "odd" one, Clueless, that flaunts its infidelity to Jane Austen. Patricia Rozema's Mansfield Park acknowledges its borrowings not only from Austen's novel but also from letters, nonfiction, and early journals, whereas Amy Heckerling's Clueless erases all traces of Emma from its mise-en-scène, repurposing Austen for a popular-cultural audience of teenaged girls. Heckerling's tongue-in-cheek film captures the "real" world of Los Angeles rich kids, invoking (for valley-girl viewers) the logic of immediacy; Rozema's film upscales the Regency romance for media-savvy millennial spectators. In Mansfield Park, the heroine's self-reflexive address to the camera disrupts narrative continuity, destroying the seamless viewing experience that simulates the engaged, fantasy-driven reading of romance novels. Writing letters, telling stories, Rozema's Fanny fashions herself a modern, female author. In a postmodern pastiche that literalizes repurposing, Heckerling's Cher refashions her girlfriend, Tai, from hopeless hick to spandex-clad, buns-of-steel babe, as Clueless rewrites Austen's matchmaking mishap as a makeover gone awry.

These odd film adaptations deploy the logic of hypermediacy by multiplying media in their mise-en-scènes (Bolter and Grusin 45). Mansfield Park opens with long, languorous shots of something approximating bodies: shapes move and flow; textures, rivulets, and dark markings emerge, as do almost inaudible murmurings. The spectator gradually identifies handwritten, graphic shapes or "letters," hears the whispers of girls reading aloud personal letters. Acknowledging its incorporation of earlier media, Rozema's titles insist upon this medium's materiality: paper's heft and texture against the hand, cursive script as translated by eye and brain; the female voice, invoking presence, intimacy, and immediacy. Freely refashioned from the novel and Austen's childhood stories and juvenilia, the sound track's "letters to Susie" disrupt the spectator's expectation for realistic representation. Instead, satiric snippets of Austen's "History of England" recount stories of women degraded by men, as Fanny alters historiography to suit a sisterly audience; parodic children's stories reshape the destinies of women—one, seduced and abandoned, is later eaten by her sons (an allegory of the link between classic and popular culture via the metaphor "gobbled"). Rozema's film repurposes the narrative technologies that produce cultural discourse; the storytelling situations repackage the social networks in which it is constituted and consumed. At film's end, Fanny's doting husband finds a publisher for her collected stories: Our storytelling heroine's emergence as author—if only in a limited printrun with a vanity press and little chance of profit—figures her filmmaker's cultural function as refashioner of classic novels into hypermediated visualcultural products.

Rozema's film submits desire to the double logic of hypermediacy. Mary Crawford (Embeth Davidtz) asks Fanny to rehearse August Kotzebue's eighteenth-century drama *Lover's Vows* in her garret, imploring Edmund (Jonny Lee Miller) to watch: "We all need an audience." Mary touches, seduces, and embraces Fanny (Frances O'Connor), who reads Mary's "male" lover's lines. Track out to include Edmund, watching. Later, the players prepare to perform: they make up, practice dialogue, and grope one another; pan to Rushworth (Hugh Bonneville) reflected in pier glass, narcissistically trying on a very large codpiece; cut to Lady Bertram (Lindsay Duncan), engaging in sex play with her lapdog. Watching these filmed rehearsals and backstage behaviors, the spectator oscillates between love of theatrical immediacy and delight in the logic of hypermediacy, for we know this embedded amateur theatrical figures and makes fun of the period look. Whereas Austen repurposes in narrative an earlier print medium, drama, Rozema refashions staged theater on celluloid. Immersing the spectator in the pictured "real," cinema's darkened auditorium dissolves spectatorial awareness of the moviegoing situation; dramatic performance, on the contrary, breeds mindfulness of other spectators, the curtain's rising and falling, the costumes' rustling, the actors' bodies spitting, sweating, and heaving. Rozema's film makes visible the spectator's oscillation between this desire for immediacy and a fascination with media.

Like *Mansfield Park*, *Clueless* opens with a montage that allegorizes media's fascination for the spectator. After the credits, Heckerling craneshoots kids in a Jeep convertible. Cut to Cher (Alicia Silverstone) dangling shopping bags; cut to a slow-motion montage of Cher and Dionne (Stacey Dash), walking; cuts and pans to kids laughing, splashing, and playing at a pool party. Guy "falls" from rocks, over artificial waterfall; Amber (Elisa Donovan) paints her nails, left, opposite a poolside classical bust with straw hat, frame right. Cut to Cher, licking ice cream off her finger; pan to girls atop waterfalls; tilt down bared legs in close-up, up other legs to girls donning suntan lotion while balancing cell phones. Cut to ice cream social: multiracial girl threesome; cut to montage of thighs bared below miniskirts, in close-up; to girl feeding whipped-creamed cherry to soda jerk. Cut to pool: more legs in close-up, more cell phones. Close: the gang sings, "We're the kids of America." Voice-over, by Cher: "OK, so you're going, is this, like, a Noxema commercial or what?" Heckerling spoofs Hollywood's use of the female body as spectacle: these "girlie shots" bare, fragment, objectify, and make consumable the teenaged female body, as though it were ice cream and tasty; displaying the camera's shots and cuts, the edit's suture, they make visible the viewer's look. Yet Heckerling also indulges her spectator, who, male or female, enjoys watching these morselized body parts and pix. Heckerling's montage thus

Fanny Price plays the male lover to Mary Crawford's beloved when the two girls rehearse Lover's Vows, as Edmund Bertram watches. (Mansfield Park, 1999)

displays its visibility, inciting visual curiosity and providing pleasure both visual and sexual.

Heckerling's film paradoxically appropriates the technologies of a historically later medium, television. In this opening montage, Heckerling deploys the techniques, practices, and spectatorial relations of MTV's "excessive, highly self-conscious video style" (Bolter and Grusin 53). This historically asynchronous remediation of TV by film appeals to a target audience of teenaged girls by making them comfortable with a visual style to which they are accustomed, one that displays its borrowing of televisual aesthetics. Unlike the cinematic look, MTV's "aesthetic of the glance" directs the spectator's attention "here and there in brief moments," oscillating between immediate engagement with the glanced-at leg and delight in fast pans, quick cuts, and the capacity for intercut (Bolter and Grusin 53–54). The glance feeds the millennial spectator's hunger for attraction—a popular form of immediacy, Heckerling suggests—and for visual sexual arousal—a perverse practice of MTV viewers and romance consumers. The target spectator's familiarity with MTV style normalizes practices of lateral marketing (product placement in films, and tie-ins), strategies everywhere apparent in this teenaged-market niche movie. Heckerling's film, for example, wittily pictures couch potatoes, as Josh and Cher catch some TV, eating snacks and watching ads; Tai sings along with Mentos gum ads. In the opening montage, the camera zooms in on a product name, "Jeep," after the crane shot. However odd an adaptation Heckerling's *Clueless* might be, it takes to the limit a media-saturated culture's gleeful repurposing of classic culture as content/software for advertising.

Clueless and *Mansfield Park* allegorize their own repurposing procedures. Heckerling transfers from *Emma* each narrative kernel, every cardinal function, even as she freely adapts character, atmosphere, tone, and viewpoint on girls' culture. The narrative kernels, transferred: Emma's portrait of Harriet becomes Cher's photo of a made-over, rose-sniffing Tai (Brittany Murphy); Knightley's dancing with the rejected Harriet, Josh's (Paul Rudd) good-deed dance with Tai; Harriet's ambush by gypsies, an attack on Tai by male mall rats. Regency rake becomes "cakeboy," "Oscar-Wilde reading," "friend of Dorothy"; Emma's insult to Miss Bates becomes Cher's thoughtless assumption that her Hispanic housekeeper speaks "Mexican"; Frank Churchill's and Jane Fairfax's secret engagement—the crux of Austen's narrative—Christian's (Justin Walker) openly secret homosexuality. These kernels mobilize the plot: the portrait of

Harriet, the ambush by gypsies, the secret engagement, all produce as consequence Cher's misinterpretation of her or Tai's objects of desire. Tai's photo, the slackers' mall ambush, and Christian's homosexuality create Cher's confusion about whether she will find the right boyfriend—itself a refashioning of the print-cultural romance's courtship plot. Refashioning Austen for a teenaged target audience, Heckerling foregrounds her own style and intention, her power to shape character, atmosphere, tone, and viewpoint for a millennial audience weaned on consumerism, multicultural politics, and media saturation. Thus, Heckerling winks at her baby-boomer Janeite spectator, narrative transfer may be faithful even as adaptation evacuates narrative content, changes historical and geographical location, and alters perspective on the narrative's material. Playing with the double logic of remediation, Heckerling satirizes fidelity aesthetics.

When romance matchmaking becomes teenaged "makeover," the look that structures female popularity becomes visible and rivalrous. When Tai appears at Bronson Alcott High, the camera tilts up her blue-jean clad body, as Cher and Dionne assess her looks. Suggesting the rituals of adolescent popularity, this tilt stages the figural, and allegorizes the spectatorial, look. Coloring hair, redoing makeup, redressing the body, Cher and Dionne make Tai over in montage; the spectator watches the remakers, reflected in a full-length mirror, as they watch the reflected or assess the bodily Tai: "I'm going to be a supermodel" plays on the sound track; "everyone will want to look just like me." Taking pleasure in this rivalrous structure of looking, the spectator participates, by implication, in Hollywood's cosmetic, surgical, and stylistic production of star images and bodies. The body-morphing practices of workouts, plastic surgery, dieting, and adolescent bulimia likewise remake these female bodies: feeling like a "heifer" after having eaten five M&Ms, wanting to blow "chunks" or "rolf," Cher controls her body and its image, upon which her popularity rests. The film's best joke: after rhinoplasty, Amber tells the butch tennis teacher, "My plastic surgeon doesn't want me doing any activity where balls fly at my nose"; Dionne responds, "There goes your social life." Heckerling displays Hollywood's primary spectatorial technology even as she spoofs classic Hollywood cinema's courtship plotting, its studio-era insistence on normative heterosexual coupling, its production of star images, and its tendency to repurpose earlier media technologies to perform new cultural work.

Rozema sends up the romance conclusion as Hollywood's late-capitalist commodification of the heterosexual couple. In *Mansfield Park*'s brilliant final sequence, as Fanny watches a flock of birds fly past the Park's second-story window, the camera seems, too, to take flight, speeding across streams and meadows, up to a stone house and into its window; Aunt Norris has gone to her niece, Fanny's voice-over knowingly tells us; we watch a still of aunt and niece beside table, stiffly looking away from each other; "It could have turned out differently"—Fanny hesitates—"but it didn't." The camera speeds out the window, across hedges and fields, into a garden party: a still of Henry and wife, Mary and husband, spaced around a table, a flirtatious look passing between nonmarried spouses; sister and brother have "found partners who shared their more"—Fanny falters—"*modern* sensibilities"; "It could have turned out differently, but it didn't." Rozema's birdlike camera, speeding across English landscape and penetrating into rural gardens and houses, satirizes the estrangement of loving couples, the loneliness of family life, and the consequential logic of the courtship plot. Only Edmund and Fanny, mirrored by Mansfield Park's reflecting pool, plight their troth—and as her beloved kisses her in

Cher Horowitz and Tai Frazier consult the mirror as Dionne assesses the makeover's success. (Clueless, 1995)

shot/reverse shot, Fanny looks over his shoulder at us, smiling knowingly. As the crass but entertaining Mary Crawford says in her "proposal" for rehabilitating Maria after she has abandoned her husband and eloped with Henry Crawford, "This is 1806, for heaven's sake; it's not the first time this has happened in the world, nor the last." Situating herself as modern, Mary winks at the audience, for seduction has a history as well as a future—in Hollywood.

For Heckerling, Austen anticipates the postmodern commodification of romance. Creating the 1990s couple at Bronson Alcott High means shooting couples that boff without consequences, go steady without intimacy, and make sure a pass doesn't stain a designer dress. "Nice stems," Christian says, after the camera has tracked—along with his look—up Cher's bare legs; Cher sends herself candy and flowers, to assure Christian she is sexy; in a skin-tight red dress, she welcomes him for a date, as cookies burn in the oven. At the mall, their "sanctuary," Cher, Dionne, and Tai ogle a cute waiter; "I hate it when their thing is crooked," Tai says, holding up half a large, salted pretzel; Cher is "hymenally challenged" and "saving herself for Luke Perry"; Dionne is "technically a virgin," but her "man has no complaints." "You can see how picky I am about my shoes," Cher proclaims, "and they only go on my feet." Later, as she realizes she loves Josh, fireworks go off, fountains spray in spot-lit colors, in imitation of earlier Hollywood-film romantic realizations. Yet here, sexual intimacy is advanced petting or noncoital orgasmic relations, and love is technologically mediated—by the cell phone, computer, TV, or by Hollywood romance predecessors.

These films' riffs on fidelity aesthetics, then, demonstrate that a film may never be fully faithful to its source narrative. A more capacious term than it is normally assumed, fidelity aesthetics as concept covers a range of remediational motives and strategies. In addition, conditions within the film industry, national economic exigencies, changing sexual mores, or a director's commitment to genre conventions and cinematic styles may affect his or her dedication to fidelity aesthetics. Three key social and sexual changes have transformed the romance of the heterosexual couple in mid- to late twentieth-century film: the postwar and postfeminist entries of women into the workplace, the advent of late-century feminism, and the emergence of the anxious man sensitive to female needs and desires.[22] In the late 1930s and early 1940s, economic constraint and fears of war pressured the conditions and experience of sexual relations; in the 1980s and 1990s, feminism and rising standards of living again returned women to work, making them less economically dependent upon heterosexual and marital relations; and, at century's end, a decade of masculine anxiety problematized male domination of women in the marketplace, workforce, and at home. Concomitantly, on screen, the courtship plot became out-moded unless repurposed as savvy and saucy, and later, the seduction plot rewrote romance as crass, edgy, and even fatal. With the decline in impor-tance of studios and producers, the consolidation of classic Hollywood narrative, the emergence of an independent, and, most recently, specialty-division new Hollywood style, shifting industry economics and techno-logical possibilities also pressured sex on screen. Filmic representation of the heterosexual couple, of marital or sexual fidelity, alters not only due to social and cultural changes but also to Hollywood and heritage film-makers' malleable notion of fidelity aesthetics.

CHAPTER 3

Reproducing Monsters, Vampires, and Cyborgs

A FRIENDLY WARNING: If you have a weak heart and cannot stand intense excitement or even shock, we advise you NOT to see this production. If, on the contrary, you like an unusual thrill, you will find it in "FRANKENSTEIN."

—Ad for James Whale's *Frankenstein* (1931)

Whatever else it is, the cyborg point of view is always about communication, infection, gender, genre, species, intercourse, information, and semiology.

—Donna J. Haraway, "Cyborg Manifesto"

Sexual reproduction is a bizarre and even perverse way to replicate.

—Ian Wilmut, Keith Campbell, and Colin Tudge, *Second Creation*

DURING THE 1990S AND BEYOND, numerous stories about harvested organs, frozen embryos, cyborg babies, and human and animal clones hit the major newspapers. In 2000, a British widow discovered that her husband's brain had been removed at death and given to Manchester University medical researchers; in 2004, UCLA officials disclosed that the Willed Body Program's director had been selling body parts on a "nationwide black market" (Lyall; Broder; Madigan). In 2003, two British women lost court battles to save frozen embryos because their former partners had withdrawn consent for embryonic implantation ("British Women"); a thirty-year-old cancer patient became, in 2004, the first woman to produce a healthy fetus from her own "frozen and thawed" ovarian tissue (Grady), and in 2009, a transgender man, Thomas Beatie, gave birth to his second child; Nadya Suleman gave birth to octuplets (Tedmanson; Saul).

Louise Brown, the "first test-tube baby," celebrated her twenty-fifth birth-day along with some of the 1,000 other IVF children conceived at Bourn Hall, Cambridge, including her sister Natalie, the world's fortieth IVF baby (Moreton). Two kittens cloned by Genetic Savings and Clone appeared at the 2004 Madison Square Garden cat show, and Dolly the sheep, the "first higher vertebrate cloned from an adult cell" in 1996, was euthanized, after having developed an incurable, precancerous lung infection.[1] On 9 August 2001, President George W. Bush announced that only existing stem-cell lines could be used in government-financed research, and, on 9 March 2009, President Barack Obama reversed Bush's action (Stolberg). In 2005, South Korean scientists claimed they had cloned human embryos and extracted embryonic stem cells, and a different South Korean reproductive-technology researcher left his post after admitting that he had paid female staff members for eggs (Brooke). In short, coverage of these stories or breakthroughs or frauds will continue, as experimenters challenge, rework, or ethically investigate science's limits.

The scientific issues that surround these events have created a media spectacle. Before announcement of Dolly's birth in *Nature,* the Scottish scientist Ian Wilmut recalls, a reporter leaked the story to the press; thousands of phone calls reached Roslin Institute, where Wilmut and Keith Campbell worked; headlines such as "Clone on the Range" and "Will There Ever Be Another Ewe?" hit the front pages. Yet most accounts "skipped past Dolly" to focus "on the prospects of human cloning," against which most, but not all, commentators were "dead set" (Wilmut, Campbell, and Tudge 116, 219–24). Named for Dolly Parton because she was cloned from a mammary gland ("There's no such thing as baa-aa-aad publicity," the singer said), Dolly had become by her death a "diva and a star" and, even after death, the "world's most exalted sheep" that will enjoy "continuing stardom" as a taxidermized museum display (Gillis). In addition, Dolly served "humanity's efforts to master—and manipulate—the molecular details of life"; "engineered" by artificial reproductive technologies, she has stimulated "commercial" cloning (Gillis). Issues of science and celebrity, experimental mastery, body engineering, intellectual property, and corporate profit emerge repeatedly in these stories of body invasion and body-part piracy, transplantation, assisted reproduction, or bodily replication. These early twenty-first-century news items, moreover, emerged after a century-long scientific and public debate about biotechnological intervention in "natural" reproductive and end-of-life events. In the 1990s, this debate took center stage in the popular press and other mass-market cultural media, as print and visual cultures appropriated, supplemented, deployed, and circulated scientific claims to the medical public.

The nineteenth century's most popular gothic horror tales address and seek to resolve historically earlier—and cognate—questions about the human-machine matrix, about sexual reproduction, and about economic worries; these anxieties tapped fears about downward class mobility, corporate profit taking, and migration's effect on financial stability. Mary Shelley's *Frankenstein* fascinated its early nineteenth-century readers because it addressed questions of role-distributed maternity and paternity, historically specific ways of "doing kinship" through marital arrangements, and the possibility of scientific body engineering and laboratory experimentation. By the mid-nineteenth century, print culture addressed new economic problems, as did Charles Dickens's novels about the evils of industrial and professional greed. Britain's "new urban gentry" feared violence by and disease of the "casual residuum": the status of health in London's slums, the growth of mass democracy, and geopolitical class separation; infection by the poor and by immigrants who, with the 1880s suburban explosion, increasingly lived among the middle class.[2] By century's end, Bram Stoker's *Dracula* sought to resolve fears about body replication, technological intervention, and population invasion, about transnational flows of bodies, blood, disease, and death (Valente 1–13).

The late twentieth-century horror movie seeks to resolve dread about cognate bodily, technological, and economic woes. In this chapter, I trace the shifts within and among the historically situated cultural periods of horror's popularity, from the genre's post-Depression exploitation of despair and panic, to the 1970s elaboration of the 1930s hints at sexual arousal, to the 1990s indulgence of excessive sensation and consumption. Whereas Shelley's early nineteenth-century novel alludes to Regency laborer rage at technology and gentry fear of insurrection, James Whale's film allegorizes the 1930s U.S. worry about and obsession with work, (in)solvency, and upper-class regulation (O'Flinn 196). Cinematic horror, like its print cousin, Robert Sklar argues, enjoys its "highest popularity" during "moments of extreme social and cultural dislocation": world wars and their ravages, economic depressions and related diaspora, political upheaval and popular din. For David J. Skal, the monster has always been a "lightning rod for prevailing social anxieties"; for Martin Tropp, James Whale's *Frankenstein* "plays upon" fears about work, gender, and violence that "haunted the Thirties" (*Gothic* 142; Tropp 39, 33). But what of the 1990s, a decade of unprecedented prosperity, even given the 1950s economic boom? As economic exigencies and sexual mores shifted, the vampire became an alluring aristocrat who stimulated female spectatorial swoon; by late century, he seemed a sexy beast, a biotechnological cultural celebrity, a pleasure machine. The 1990s new Hollywood gothic horror exploited spectatorial fears that fiscal affluence, caused by the dot-com boom with its concomitant wealth effect, might produce a period of decadence, on the one hand, or a late-nineties round of economic recession, corporate downsizing, merger mania, and real estate speculation, on the other (Galbraith 113–32).

Yet horror as genre manages even as it arouses anxiety. The horror genre in general, Carol J. Clover argues, inverts gender roles and so indulges spectatorial vacillation between pleasure and pain, multiplying sexual identifications and spectatorial pleasures (*Chain Saws*). These films also situate themselves in a genealogy of genre pix that assures spectator knowingness, as generic conventions make terror into a "quasi-affect" through narrative inoculation against its physiological and psychic sensations (Russell 233). Gothic horror's "morph aesthetic" likewise stimulates fascinated dread and instills even as it undoes physiological and psychic numbness to provoke pleasure, excitement, astonishment, and laughter— for soothing narrative conclusions undermine surprise and suspense. As it satisfies spectatorial greed for sensation, moreover, late-century horror appropriates other genres. Long a "standard Hollywood practice," genre mixing is now "virtually obligatory," Rick Altman claims, to guarantee audiences that cross taste cultures (129–32, 141–42). Consuming across categories, spectators as "active agents" make "productive" meanings, taking "divergent pleasures" from the films they view (Tudor, "Why" 53, 49). As such, genre films exist in a "field of contested . . . images," and neither producers nor consumers can control fully their overdetermined meanings (Braudy, "Nature" 281). Gothic horror films thus "mutate as an entertainment type defined by shock and novelty" even as they—vampirishly— produce active spectators, multiple pleasures, and new markets.[3]

By century's end, a mass audience for spectacular entertainment products had emerged, ready to consume sequels, prequels, action pix, and special-effects blockbusters. The 1990s literary gothic horror film sought to benefit from the 1980s heritage boom by targeting a niche audience of worried independent cinema fans eager to enjoy quality period vampires, yet it also hoped to enter the mass market and cross over to big box-office profits; it did so by spectacularizing the nineteenth-century monster and vampire. Appropriating Victorian canonical fiction for the post-Victorian moment, Kenneth Branagh's film adaptation of *Frankenstein* glamorized star images and special effects to both arouse and soothe late twentieth-century fears about prosthetic or ectogenous bodies, artificial ways to do kinship, and the misuses of assisted reproduction; Coppola's, of *Dracula,* celebrated the ways communication, information, and computer technologies extend or usurp the body's sense organs through fantastic visual effects. Thus heritage and new Hollywood cultures alike morphed and updated Dracula's and Frankenstein's terrors for cultural consumers in a technologically acute, scientifically anxious, and fiscally greedy age.

Science in/as Popular Culture

Mary Shelley's and Bram Stoker's fascination with science is a critical commonplace. Whereas *Dracula* recounts the modern emergence of information and communication technology, as the vampire springs from texts and machines, *Frankenstein* adumbrates the coming of biotechnology, as the monster is born from laboratory instrumentation's reanimation of morselized corpses. Despite their historical location nearly a century apart, these novels' special brand of terror resides in their portraits of beings who represent scientific creativity gone awry, misprized evolution let loose on earth, perhaps to reproduce or replicate a race to threaten the world's peoples. Both texts, moreover, present disenchanted readings of their scientific-technological imaginings. Marshall McLuhan suggests that humans respond to anxiety about their physical and social environment by withdrawing subjectivity inward and projecting amplifications of an organ, sense, or bodily function back into the world as, say, artificial limb, thus numbing their fear through "autoamputation" and projecting technological extensions of the fragmented body outside the self (172). Even clothing, from this perspective, becomes prosthetic skin; such prostheses may protect or aid the endangered body or may extend the fragile body's power over a terrifying world around it. This cyborg body—part flesh, part artifice—alters physiological sense ratios, activates apathy, and stimulates dread in "the age of anxiety and of electric media" (47).

Shelley's and Stoker's novels about science anticipate McLuhan's age of anxiety and of electric media. Saturated by Mary Shelley's fascination with the new electric, galvanic, and chemical technologies, for example, *Frankenstein* extends outside the body and locates in the laboratory the nervous system's flow and charge, the power to animate. Shelley's bio-technological anomaly increases the power and expands the range and speed of physiological action; the monster's apparent ubiquity—leaping the Alps, bending over Frankenstein's marriage bed, swimming near Walton's ship, weeping at Frankenstein's deathbed—uncannily facilitates the monster's bridal murder as well as his later grief. In *Dracula*, the telegraph extends the body's mouth and, placing it outside the organism, speeds up the transmission of messages, extending the voice's range and scope; the phonograph stores speech, waiting to be received by the ear (later, the telephone) and translated into print, via the typewriter, which turns the hand's writing into machine-text (Kittler, *Gramophone* 28). Transfusions place blood outside the tapped body, circulating it through machines and among persons. From these early- and late-century texts about the body's electrical- or communication-technological extensions, twentieth-century film borrows and amplifies the jolt to life of electrified monster, specimen of ectogenous life; the morph of atavistic vampire into degenerate, cyborg, or posthuman organism.

Percy Bysshe Shelley's 1818 "Preface" to *Frankenstein* claims scientific precedent for the "event" on which Mary's novel "is founded," noting, in particular, the work of Erasmus Darwin and German "physiological writers" (5). Anne Mellor adds to those celebrated scientists several that Mary maligned—Humphry Davy, Luigi Galvani, and Adam Walker—for seeking to control or change nature; Marilyn Butler adds William Lawrence, the Shelleys' physician and London neighbor, whose materialist science contested John Abernathy's "spiritualised vitalism."[4] Although critics differ about which scientists Shelley counted as "good" or "bad," "moral" or "immoral," I am interested, instead, in the media presentation of these scientific struggles. Indeed, Shelley's ghost story took shape during and immediately after a series of scientific debates and demonstrations: Galvani's galvanic experiments, which electrically energized dead frogs' legs in the laboratory, published in 1791; Giovanni Aldini's theatrical demonstrations of voltaic efficacy, in which dead ox's heads shook, hanged murderers' corpses quivered, arms lifted, and fists clenched in an "appearance of re-animation," which "made the British headlines" after an extravagant London performance (1802–3); Davy's spectacular public demonstrations of the voltaic pile's power to produce "shocks, sparks, ... loud noises," and gunpowder explosions, which sought to best rivals in the scientific and popular press (1807–11); and, perhaps most important, the "vitalist debate," publicly staged by Lawrence and Abernathy at London's Royal College of Surgeons (1814–19) and later published as lectures, which Percy Shelley purchased.[5] These very public performances, debates, and contestations were disseminated to the British public by "lectures, newspapers, a few accessible books," and "the serious Reviews" (Butler 302).

Shelley's scientific contemporaries, Davy, Lawrence, Galvani, and Aldini, practiced a popular science that helped found the disciplines and constitute the practices of electrolysis, bioelectrogenesis, and electrotechnology. Davy's "public experimental display," for example, demonstrated the "powers of nature" to a wide audience whose role as "witness" could be mobilized to "consolidate and extend" his scientific achievements (Golinski 188–89). Amateur scientists, like Frankenstein's fictional father, replicated these popularized experimental phenomena by reproducing them in makeshift laboratories, and enthusiasts across England— including the Shelleys, while visiting Villa Diodati—likewise practiced galvanic techniques. Indeed, the experimental sciences were being constituted as disciplines throughout the nineteenth century by such display and debate, as science became a knowledge-producing system based on laboratory observations collected over sufficiently repeated trials and tested by comparison of cases, inductive reasoning, and formulation of hypotheses to produce logical, generalized, and generalizable statements about the body's organs, nerves, and internal secretions. Only through this widely disseminated staging could scientific disciplines emerge, for their "boundaries were neither fixed nor impermeable" but were constructed by the rhetoric of scientific conversations, lectures, research publications, and popular periodical essays and cartoons (Golinski 6–7, 204).

Science's social networks and professional rivalries thus constituted in a variety of media the emerging disciplines' tools for experimental observation. Claiming to reproduce natural events in the laboratory, Bruno Latour maintains in his postmodern ethnography of science, the experimental scientist, in fact, fabricated the very laws of nature he presumed to discover. From Latour's late twentieth-century perspective, laboratory observation thus constituted and organized the binarism of natural/social, making it an unstable but structurally consistent mode of scientific representation. Undertaking the "work of purification," which constructed nature and the social as distinct from one another, the laboratory covered over even as it abetted the "work of mediation," the production by scientific practices of the hybrid research subject—part natural, part social. The "work of translation," which guaranteed the transmission of knowledge along professional networks, institutionalized scientific claims, created credibility for findings and constituted hierarchies of merit and distinction. As Latour insists, "No science can exit from the network of its practice. . . . Everything happens by way of mediation, translation, and networks."[6] As N. Katherine Hayles argues, "Culture circulates through science no less than science circulates through culture"; literary texts "actively shape" what technologies mean and the ways "scientific theories signify in cultural contexts" (*Posthuman* 21). Mary Shelley's "hideous progeny" circulated scientific research concepts into literary and popular culture and, participating in the vitalism debates, shaped science's signifying practices through the work of translation and (re)mediation.

Shelley's scientist is, like his creature, a composite of the scientists his creator knew from various media representations. From Davy, whose *Elements of Chemical Philosophy* she read as she completed her manuscript in 1816, Shelley may have learned that scientists such as Waldman became interested in "phaenomena of electricity," including "lightnings . . . taken from the clouds," and galvanism, "which has enabled men to produce from combinations of dead matter effects which were formerly occasioned only by animal organs" (O'Flinn 197; quoted in Golinski 210). From Galvani, that "'animal electricity'" activated nerves and muscles; from Abernathy, that electricity, or "something analogous"—a "spark of life"—could explain vitality; from Lawrence, the ridicule of electricity as mere metaphor for the soul (Butler 306–7; Mellor 303). Frankenstein's education and early career, moreover, mimic Davy's: left to himself as a child and forced into "no particular plan of study," Davy claimed, "What I am I made myself" (Golinski 208). In Shelley's 1818 version of *Frankenstein,* lightning ignites Victor's scientific ardor. "I beheld a stream of fire," he tells Walton, and, as "soon as the dazzling light vanished, the oak had disappeared, and nothing remained but a blasted stump" (23). Victor's father explains, too, the destruction by dazzling light of an oak tree: "'Electricity,'" he declares. He constructs a "small electrical machine" and so "exhibited a few experiments"; made a kite, with wire and string, that "drew down that fluid from the clouds" (23). Later, as a university student, Victor sees a sudden, dizzying "light so brilliant and wondrous" that he knows he will discover the "capacity to bestow animation" on inanimate matter

(30–31). Yet, as Butler notes, Shelley's protagonist "seems to know too little science rather than too much" (307).

Mary Shelley's monster anticipates Latour's postmodern, hybrid research subject, a quasi-object (part natural, part social) fabricated through laboratory mediation and masquerading as natural, as "born." The "component parts of a creature might be manufactured, brought together, and endued with vital warmth," Mary had learned from Byron's and Shelley's late-night conversations about galvanism (172). She thus imagined that, when science manufactured beings from raw bodily materials, laboratory mediation created a "monster": a hybrid quasi-object. She had learned, too, that science had publicly to stage experimental events that had been produced in the laboratory, to solicit an assembled public as potential interest group, as possible adherents outside the laboratory, and as agitators for the research's mission. Her scientist, guilty of the work of mediation, nevertheless rejects the scientific work of translation along scientific networks. Victor shuns his monster, seeking to separate it from the social and consign it to the natural, nonhuman world far from European communities. Shelley, too, expunges this work of translation from the 1831 edition of her hideous progeny, as she demonizes science in the wake of heated public debate.[7]

The electrical wizardry of cinema animates the celluloid *Frankenstein,* linking scientific with cinematic (re)mediation. Although James Whale does not shoot his hero's youthful researches, his adult Frankenstein (Colin Clive) calls experts and amateurs to "witness" his electrochemical experiments. After Victor (named Henry in the novel and played in the film by John Boles), Elizabeth (Mae Clarke), and Dr. Waldman (Edward Van Sloan) journey to the windmill-laboratory, they enter a chiaroscuro, canted-frame world of flying sparks, whirring wheels, and smoking beakers. "I've discovered the great ultraviolet ray that first brought life into the world," Frankenstein tells them; the fabricated body in the lab "has never lived. I created it. I made it with my own hands from bodies I took from graves, from gallows." The spectacular creation scene, whose "picturesque electrical gadgetry" cost a then-whopping $10,000, intercuts among Henry and Fritz, the watching spectators, and the electrical machinery as it snaps, sizzles, and sends bolts of light leaping across the frame. The laboratory table moves up, up, up through the ceiling into the storm, its lightning the natural energy harnessed and reproduced by experimental machinery; it moves down, back into the laboratory; cut to close-up of the monster's hand, moving: "It's alive!" Henry screams. The spectators watch in astonishment.

Whale's *Bride of Frankenstein* (1935) reprises its original's creation scene. Whale's camera, more mobile than in the original, tilts, dollies, and pans around the laboratory that is stuffed, like its precursor, with electrical gadgetry; high- and low-angle shots alternate as the table rises, and canted frames of equipment, scientists, kites, and lightning, edited at staccato pace, picture activity in the lab.[8] Only Fritz, Frankenstein, and Dr. Pretorius witness this work of mediation, yet their collaboration recalls Victor's horrified audience in *Frankenstein,* one member of which—Dr. Waldman, like the spoof Dr. Pretorius—might be mobilized to publicize Henry's scientific achievements. Whale's two birthing scenes, moreover, remind us that we, like Henry's witnesses, watch a brilliantly constructed scenario; that film, like the monstrous body, is sutured and pieced, that, like all media, it demands spectators. As Diana Fuss says, linking the work of mediation to remediation, "Film has always been a technology of dismemberment and fragmentation" ("Monsters" 189). Henry's figural spectators thus stand in for the film's spectators; Whale shoots, he said, Frankenstein's "feverish excitement[,] calculated to carry both the spectators in the windmill and the spectators in the theater with him. . . . The lightning flashes. The monster begins to move. Frankenstein merely has to believe what he sees, which is all we ask the audience to do" (quoted in Curtis 141).

The 1990s celluloid Frankensteins restore to their scenarios Victor's youthful fascination with electricity and, appropriating Whale, repurpose the birthing scenes for heritage horror spectacle or sci-fi extravaganza. In Branagh's *Mary Shelley's Frankenstein* (1994), Victor (Kenneth Branagh), Elizabeth (Helena Bonham Carter), Justine (Trevyn McDowell), and William (Ryan Smith) frolic in the Alps (as though they had waltzed in from *The Sound of Music*), flying kites and inviting lightning to strike. A storm hits; Victor grabs machinery from the picnic basket; in quick shot/reverse shot, he and Elizabeth wire a lightning rod. In overhead shot, the four lie face down in a circle, fingers touching, heads together. Lightning strikes: sparks jump between palms, leap from fingertips. "How do you feel?" Victor asks Elizabeth; "Alive!" she shouts, foreshadowing Victor's later shriek and invoking Whale's invention. Close-up of index fingers touching, as spark of life leaps from Victor to Elizabeth, remediating Michelangelo's *The Creation.* Roger Corman's *Frankenstein Unbound*

(1990) pictures the laser scientist's power to call down lightning. As a storm rages, a gigantic thundercloud breaks, lightning blasts; a barbaric horse and rider descend from the sky, striking John Buchanan, the scientist (John Hurt). Although this figure for electricity's primitive power recedes into the clouds, Buchanan has been hit and so, in a weird plot twist, time-travels to Geneva, 1817, where he meets "Mary Shelley" (Bridget Fonda), "Byron" (Jason Patric), and Shelley's monstrous characters. "I've read your novel," he confesses after seducing the as-yet unpublished author. Later, twenty-first-century laser technology blows the Swiss city to smithereens, as Buchanan departs into a futuristic landscape. Whereas Branagh's heritage period drama pictures electric jolt as mimicking Renaissance models of creativity—a motif to which Branagh will return in his creation scene—Corman's sci-fi laser scenes use computer-animated special and visual effects to portend and spoof global disaster, induce future shock, and prophesy posthuman identity.

Stoker's *Dracula* modernizes electrical science, addressing late-century social anxieties about information-age technologies, about the related discourses of degeneration, criminality, madness, and monstrous reproduction. "'Let me tell you, my friend,'" Van Helsing claims, "'there are things done today in electrical science which would have been deemed unholy by the very men who discovered electricity—who would themselves not so long before have been burned as wizards'" (171). Van Helsing cites Jean-Martin Charcot, the Salpètrière Hospital's galvanic experimenter and magnetic investigator of female hysteria, to justify his desire to hypnotize Mina when the band of men tracks Dracula to Transylvania: hypnotism "'follow[s] the mind of the great Charcot … into the very soul of the patient he influence[s]'" (171). Invoking Charcot's scientific revival of hypnotism as hysteria's therapeutic technology, galvanic probing of symptomatic organs as experimental technique, and magnetic transfer of symptoms from one mapped body location to another as scientific proof, Van Helsing instructs Seward in popular science's genealogy of fabricators, all in danger of retrospective reinvention as magical thinkers, wonderworkers, or madmen. Although by 1897 Charcot's theories had been contested and largely debunked, the charismatic experimental scientist had entered the cultural lexicon and performed well the work of translation; his students and protégés included the scientific inventors of psychology (Pierre Janet), psychometrics (Alfred Binet), and psychoanalysis (Sigmund Freud). Here, Charcot's figure invokes modern electrical science as a knowledge-producing discourse that constituted, through the work of mediation, experimental quasi-objects (his hospitalized hysterics), that contested experimental findings at other sites such as Nancy, that translated laboratory data from the Salpêtrière to other research centers, and that staged performing hysterics for the medical public.[9]

Mina—the agent through whom all knowledge passes and who constructs the novel's narrative from recorded speech, news stories, and graphic texts—also invokes criminal anthropology and degeneration theory to denounce the vampire as an object demanding scientific research, classification, and specification. "'Nordau and Lombroso,'" she notes knowingly, would classify "'the Count [as] a criminal and of criminal type'" (296). Mina cites Cesare Lombroso's photographic archive, in which the criminal, a product of degenerate heredity and pathological milieus, displayed deviant physical, mental, and nervous characteristics. Although Mina does not say so, Lombroso adopted Charcot's (and Binet's) laboratory research procedures: he tested physiological functions, measuring reflex action, visual and tactile acuity, muscular strength, and sensitivity to faradic current; he tabulated the sensory capability of his prostitute research subjects, locating, he said, the female offenders' greatest sensory dullness in their clitorises and least in the palms of their hands (296). Mina also cites Max Nordau's notorious aesthetic theory, which declared Émile Zola and Oscar Wilde "degenerates." Citing Lombroso's and Nordau's popular-scientific mid- and late-century theories, Mina identifies the criminal, the prostitute, the degenerate, and the artist as hybrid figures of primitivity, atavism, and bestiality. These "types" express their cultures' worries about body invasions and panics: the 1890s syphilis epidemic, the public health crisis in London's slums and elsewhere, geopolitical class aggregation or segregation through suburbanization. Degeneracy theory is a "'semiotic' science" (Stepan 113).

Mina's "'lightning flash'" about Dracula resembles Lombroso's own. In 1870, the skull of a "famous brigand" caused the scientist "a flash of insight" about "an atavistic being who reproduces in his person the ferocious instincts of primitive humanity"—"criminals, savages and apes"—and expresses the desire to "extinguish life in the victim, ... to mutilate the corpse, tear its flesh and drink its blood" (quoted in Pick 122). Lombroso's insight outlines the principle of incorporation—the drive orally to ingest, the habitual repetition of past bodily motion—that will define the vampire's bestiality. Mina's notion that Dracula resembles this historically atavistic figure identifies him as a throwback, a common figure in the overdetermined and unevenly developing nineteenth-century "medico-psychiatric and natural-scientific language of degeneration."[10] Yet Mina confounds concepts of biological and cultural heredity. At the end of the nineteenth century, George W. Stocking Jr. notes, habits were thought to become "organized as instincts through the inheritance of acquired characteristics"; through this Lamarckian transmission, "characteristic qualities of civilizations were carried from one generation to another both *in* and *with* the blood of their citizens" ("Concept" 10, 6). As would Lamarckians, Mina imagines Dracula's vampirism as racial, as historically transmitted in and with the blood of his atavistic ancestors to the emergent world of modernity: "'Who was it but one of my own race who as Voivode crossed the Danube and beat the Turk on his own ground?'" Dracula boasts, likewise believing it (34–35). Although outmoded, Mina's theory nonetheless mimics scientific observation and uncannily captures the essence of vampire replication without sexual reproduction: her story makes science look remarkably like vampirism.

Linking degeneracy with electric, mechanical, and information technologies, Stoker's novel also maps the turn-of-the-century break between the industrial age and the emergence of the "graphic age of electronic man" (McLuhan 190). *Dracula* gleefully invokes communication, travel, and medical technologies: typewriter, phonograph, telegraph, shorthand, manifold copies; the underground, the railroad, the Kodak camera; blood transfusion. As electricity and chemistry may animate a morselized corpse in *Frankenstein,* in *Dracula,* electric waves, tool strokes, light exposures, and railroad cars may cross geopolitical boundaries and facilitate transnational flows. Via communication technologies, messages circulate: "I bear messages which will make both your ears tingle," Arthur telegraphs Quincey (62). After listening to Seward's phonographic diary, Mina says, "'I have been more touched than I can say by your grief. That is a wonderful machine.... It told me, in its very tones, the anguish of your heart.... I have copied out the words on my typewriter, and none other need now hear your heart beat, as I did'" (197). Harker's shorthand—"'nineteenth century up-to-date with a vengeance,'" he boasts—supersedes handwriting (40). Thus soon-to-be-residual printed and written communications circulate among soon-to-be-dominant electronically produced messages: Mina Harker's written and Jonathan Harker's shorthand diaries, Dr. Seward's recorded phonograph diary, telegrams delivered late or in timely fashion, memoranda left for one character or another, legal letters delivered or undelivered, clippings from the *Westminster Gazette* and other periodicals, Mina's Traveller's-typewriter-inscribed diary, tellingly gifted by the American, Quincey Morris.[11]

Stoker's paean to modern technology also inscribes anxiety about the power of such machinery, a dread the movies marshal. Jennifer Wicke confirms the resemblance of vampire and the new technologies of mass culture, mass transport, and tourism in Stoker's novel: the vampire is "crucial to the dynamics of modernity," she writes, for "vampirism springs up, or takes command, at the behest of shorthand" (469, 471). Yet vampirism also springs up at the behest of electronic technologies and early psychologies. Whereas vampirism emerged in print to address 1890s fears about disease transmission, growing mass poverty, urban degeneration, and technology run amuck, it was remediated at the movies to salve 1930s worries about economic distress, rural depopulation, and political instability. At century's end, vampirism 1990s-style excites and soothes fears about communication-technological explosion, sexually transmitted disease pandemics, and a sensed impending global and national financial panic. Yet late twentieth-century vampirism also converts worry into an aesthetic of pleasurable fear. Borrowing the codes and conventions of romance, gothic horror stimulates the affects not only of terror but also of sexual arousal and period pleasure. Exploiting the ambivalent fear and joy associated with anxiety about the body/machine interface, gothic-horror-romance makes terror sexy. As such, the genre manages worry by requiring spectators to deploy generic conventions, producing pleasure in knowingness, as sensation pulses and throbs.

Genre Bending: Horror and Romance

In her "Introduction" to the 1831 edition of *Frankenstein,* Mary Shelley anticipates the ways generic codes and conventions arouse and deploy spectatorial affects on and in the body. Retiring to rest at Diodati after the well-known ghost story competition, Mary neither slept nor thought but imagined, in reverie, her scientist and his "hideous phantasm": having mocked his own Maker, the scientist would flee the laboratory, feel fright and terror, but, later, as he awakens, he "behold[s] the horrid thing," which "stands at his bedside, opening his curtains." Like her fantasized scientist, Mary reports having opened her eyes "in terror" on awakening; a "thrill of fear ran through me," she writes; "O! if I could only contrive [a story] which would frighten my reader as I myself had been frightened that night!" (172). Shelley's preface wishfully identifies character, author, and reader, as though all were viewers located in the same position, awakening from dream or reverie, seeing, via the relay of looks, the same scene, the eyes of a terrifying monster, standing beside the bed and peering through the gap in the drapes. Seeking to produce the same affect—fright and terror—in the reader that she experienced when dreaming of her scientist, Mary Shelley deploys the look to link author's and viewer's bodies in an early nineteenth-century aesthetic of pleasurable fear: a "thrill of fear ran through me." Here, Shelley's "drape" anticipates the movie screen, on whose surface the celluloid monster's face will appear, making flesh creep, a physiological and emotional affect appropriate to horror as genre.

As genre, horror functions to arouse terror, manage anxiety, and produce pleasure. For Altman, a genre includes a corpus of texts, is a framework with stable boundaries and identity, and exists across historical and geopolitical boundaries. A genre's individual examples are singular and unique but share "family resemblances" or are akin to one another (98). Genres negotiate the reconciliation of thematic oppositions, Geoff King maintains, and so perform social or cultural work. Horror thus seeks to resolve a binary opposition between "irrationality and the world of the rational"; science fiction, an opposition between "humanity and the products of science or technology" (125). Yet, Hamid Naficy cautions, "genres are not immutable *systems*" but *"processes"* of "structuration" and "variation" that function to produce not novelty or sameness but "regularized variety." Readerly or spectatorial pleasure is produced from the "play, or the slippage" between fulfilled and violated generic expectations, Naficy notes, from the "familiarity and comfort of repetition" experienced when conventions are recognized and "deviations" understood (206). As King argues, a "genre label is an implicit promise"; particular genres, whether literary or filmic, offer "specific pleasures": the pleasure of "being scared, uplifted, thrilled, brought to tears" (120). The generic contract, then, binds authors or filmmakers, texts (whether printed or visual), individual cultural consumers and interpretive communities, and an industry (whether publishing or movie) and its practices (Naficy 206).

The monster's or vampire's appeal, however, depends upon his function as transgressor of binaries and his capability to arouse disjunct emotions. That the monster signals a "category crisis" has become a commonplace in horror criticism. For Berenstein, the monster signifies "a challenge to easy notions of binarity"; it relishes "boundary crossings" and willingly violates limits, questioning the "validity of boundaries themselves" (38–39). For Noël Carroll, the monster is "interstitial, categorically contradictory, incomplete, or formless": a "category mistake" (31–32). The monstrous being "violates, defies, or problematizes standing cultural classifications," transgresses the "deep categories of a culture's conceptual scheme" (Tudor, *Monsters* 53; Carroll 32). For Mark Seltzer, the creature conflates man and machine (12–15); for Rhona Berenstein, male and female, progressive and conservative (4, 10, 23); for Harry M. Benshoff, heterosexual and homosexual (11). Yet Stephen King claims that horror—"as Republican as a banker in a three-piece suit"—reconfirms values and generates "our good feelings about ourselves" (quoted in Carroll 199). The horror flick appeals to us as spectators, then, not only by hammering our "shock reflex" but by reassuring us that we feel only "quasi-fear," a combination of physiological states (increased adrenaline emission) and psychological ones (the sensation of rush) that we nevertheless know will be soothed by the story's end (Carroll 36, 71). Horror offers a "temporary release from everyday identities" even as it consolidates and reproduces normal—King would say, Republican—selves through its narrative contract and generic conventions (Berenstein 38). As genre, cinematic gothic horror arouses pleasurable as well as fearful physiologically based affects.

To entice women to the theater, horror has historically served up romance as part of the gothic-horror mix. The female spectator's investment in the figures of vampire and masterful hero—Dracula, Heathcliff, and Rochester—are not terribly different when horror meets romance, for the female viewer who identifies with the gothic-horror girl takes pleasure when "fiends ... sweep heroines off their feet" (Berenstein 66). Consulting early twentieth-century audience research, Melvyn Stokes concludes that, however limited geographically and by education, age, and sex, 1920s and 1930s spectators were "predominantly female," and, because Hollywood believed women its "primary market," "melodramas and romances" dominated the marketplace (43–44, 47). Although he notes that pre-Code audience composition can only roughly be approximated, Thomas Doherty agrees that, by "common consent," women composed the Depression-era moviegoing majority, and Hollywood "catered to" their interest in melodrama, romance, and sex pictures (*Pre-Code* 126). Much 1930s movie publicity, moreover, targeted prospective female spectators. Marketing wraparounds, such as in-theater stunts and dual-advertising campaigns, gendered the audience and suggested the censorable material only hinted at on screen. Explicitly romantic marketing for Tod Browning's *Dracula* called it "The Story of the Strangest Passion Ever Known," "The Strangest Love Story of All" (Berenstein 13, 66).[12] Opening in New York City not on Friday the 13th as originally planned, but on Valentine's Day—as had the play four years earlier and as would *Silence of the Lambs* in 1991—this love story asked female spectators to experience a "strange" attraction to its vampiric star on a day devoted to love and romance (Skal, *Gothic* 194; Brunas, Brunas, and Weaver 18).

Bela Lugosi—who never escaped his star image as Tod Browning's Dracula—used the romance genre's conventions to glamorize his own celebrity and enhance his horror films' profit. Carroll Borland, would-be actress and Lugosi groupie, called him "the most magnetic man I have ever known. We would just sit in a room and all the women would go . . . whoom" (Skal, *Gothic* 176). Borland's ambiguous term clearly signified a sexual thrill, and Lugosi clearly relished his role as lady-killer. In a 1931 trade magazine, he claimed that "*women* . . . love horror. Gloat over it. Feed on it. Are nourished by it. Shudder and cling and cry out—*and come back for more*" (quoted in Berenstein 88; emphasis in original). Although Lugosi may have projected his own narcissistic self-regard onto his audience, his metaphor imagines gothic horror consumption as vampiristic, with the female spectator both willing victim and vamped fellow practitioner. Lugosi's fantasy scenario solicited repeated viewing, just as the vamped victim, turning vampire, demanded more blood and made more vampires. "Men did not come [to the theater] of their own volition," Lugosi said; "*Women did*. Came—and knew an ecstasy dragged from the depths of unspeakable things. Came—*and then came back again. And again*" (quoted in Berenstein 89; emphasis in original). In this scenario of spectacular projections, the spectator is repeatedly drenched with the orgasmic thrill of the kill. Yet like horror's quasi-fear, gothic-horror-romance's quasi-arousal, which combines physiological (engorgement of blood) and psychological states (the sensation of "whoom"), reassures its spectator that, by story's end, perverse female attraction to monsters will be banished and heteronormativity restored: heroine killed off or normalized; vampire banished or skewered. At *Frankenstein*'s end, the monster thus pulls the (phallic?) lever, blows up the laboratory, and the married couple clinches; at *Son of Frankenstein*'s conclusion, the family embraces.

Yet at *Mary Shelley's Frankenstein*'s end, Elizabeth, made monster's bride, looks from the monster that knifed her to the scientist who made her, and leaps from country-house mezzanine, partially burning it—like Thornfield—to the ground.

Browning and Lugosi nevertheless hint that the vampire's bite is uncanny sex scene, however muted, to elude the censors. Looking back, Skal calls the flesh-and-blood Lugosi, on Broadway, "sexy, and supremely continental"; with slicked-back patent-leather hair and a "weird green cast to his makeup," Lugosi seemed "a Latin lover from beyond the grave— Valentino gone slightly rancid" (*Gothic* 129). On film, the close-ups, crosscuts, and tracks and dollies of a newly mobile camera cooperate to evoke the aesthetic of pleasurable fear, as Lugosi is shot in low-contrast grays, hair glossy, make-up gleaming, dark mouth leering, and eyes highlighted, rendering them piercing, penetrating, and perverse.[13] Lucy (Frances Dade) falls for the aristocratic heartthrob: "he's fascinating," she tells Mina (Helen Chandler), who, jokingly laughs, "Well, Countess, I'll leave you to the Count and his ruined Abbey." Cut to medium close-up of Lucy in bed, crosscut with shots of her bedroom window, a bat hovering outside; Lucy raises her eyes to the bat; cut to its entry through the window; cut to Lucy, track right to Dracula, hands reaching out; dolly behind him to the bed, his face approaches her neck, fingers puncturing pillow. Mina, too, falls victim to Dracula's charms, as her seduction/romance/rape sequence concludes with the count's face, leering in close-up, his head slowly moving down as he disappears from frame bottom, presumably to indulge in censorable sexual pleasures. No spectator during Joseph I. Breen's reign could have missed the suggestion.

Yet Dracula does not discriminate between male and female victims. Hired by Universal to create a patentable intellectual property by merging Stoker's novel and Hamilton Deane and John L. Balderston's play, Louis Bromfield rewrote Renfield as the dapper English realtor who tours Transylvania to secure a lease and who then, vamped by the count, transmutes into madman. This change sidelined Jonathan (here, John) Harker and expunged heterosexual sex from the action. Reading from a 1980s queer-cultural perspective, Christopher Craft names the novel's "pivotal anxiety" as the male desire for "an overwhelming penetration," despite "aversion to the demonic potency" that gratifies that desire (73). Early in the film, when Renfield (Dwight Frye) pricks his finger, Dracula grins lewdly as the camera tracks to his figure; at scene's end, the camera dollies around a bewildered Renfield, as the count bids him goodnight. Cut to Dracula's three brides, who converge on a drugged and dreaming Renfield; cut to Dracula, entering through terrace doors; track to women, backing away from the count's raised hand and, backs turned, toward the camera; track in on vampire and victim, Dracula's hands holding Renfield down in an S&M pose; he bends to the agent's throat—the screen fades to black. Browning's departure from the script's bridal vamping gives the film a "decidedly homoerotic" tone, Skal notes, for the film's real story is Renfield's "unrequited love" for his master (*Gothic* 198–99). "Dracula should go only for women and not men," Universal's chief, Carl Laemmle, wrote disapprovingly on the screenplay, seeking to censor before Breen could object (Skal and Savada 144).

Shot and released during the four-year interval between adoption of the Production Code and enforcement of its strictures, *Dracula* and *Frankenstein* dodged the censors because sex, expunged from other genres, emerged, with a wink, in monster flicks. Yet Depression-era financial exigencies, religious vociferation, cultural and regional sensitivities, and shifting sexual mores constrained and shaped the ways sex was represented on

Selective eye lighting highlights Bela Lugosi's leering sexuality in Tod Browning's Dracula *(1931).*

screen in all genres. As U.S. movie attendance plummeted beginning in
1930 and the debts incurred by the conversion to sound fell due, moral
reformers took on the financially failing studios.[14] In response, Richard
Maltby suggests, the industry sought to self-regulate, disarm the reformers,
and prevent government antitrust legislation by adopting the Production
Code in 1930. The code would ensure that spectators with metropolitan
sophistication, citizens of rural middle America, and "innocent" children
could all view the same Hollywood product; the Code thus served as a
"mechanism" through which multiple viewing positions were inscribed in
one film ("Production" 40). The 1930s war waged against the industry by
the Catholic Legion of Decency and Protestant religious groups, however,
aimed to determine more than whether nudity, adultery, or prostitution
could be depicted, and obscenity spoken, on screen. As Gregory D. Black
argues, the battle pitted "a vocal, powerful minority" against the producers
and studio heads to demand that Hollywood's films uphold "traditional
moral and political views"; it also represented an interdenominational
squabble, since majority Protestants, unlike Catholics, sought government regulation of film content (56; Lewis, *Hard Core* 101). Despite the
reformers' cries that Americans found the movies obscene and disgusting,
however, Hays Office functionaries, movie reviewers, and other witnesses
continually confessed that audiences loved the bedroom comedies, gangster flicks, and literary adaptations dished up by Paramount, Warner Bros.,
and RKO (Black 84–100).

The battle over how much sexual innuendo could be bantered about
in a pre-Code Mae West teaser, whether gangster movies incited teenaged
males to crime, and if faithful adaptations of modern novels could be
brought to the screen represents an early twentieth-century culture war,
one not reenacted until the 1980s, and then not over sexual but political
values.[15] The debate was ideologically driven. Father Daniel A. Lord, a
leading Catholic figure who helped rewrite the Code in 1929, spouted
vaguely eugenic rhetoric: Hollywood must manufacture entertainment
that "'tends to improve the race,'" to "'re-create and rebuild human beings
exhausted with the realities of life'"; if films consistently represented
moral characters, "'they could become the greatest natural force for the
improvement of mankind'" (quoted in Maltby, "Production" 47). Breen,
head of the Hays Office for more than twenty years, was a "rabid anti-
Semite" who laced his language about Hollywood immorality with racial
slurs; his battles against the producers and studio heads, his negotiations

with the Catholic bishops who led the Legion of Decency, were grounded in this belief that Hollywood Jews corrupted American values (Black 170–72; Lewis, *Hard Core*). Although Republican members of Congress were not involved in this early-century culture war as they were in the later, conservative religious, social, and club leaders had the clout to obstruct box-office revenues—and the censorship struggle always involved the bottom line. The 1934 Legion crisis, which forced creation of the Production Code Administration (PCA) and so tightened control over script development and production, gave Breen virtually sole control over the awarding of PCA seals of purity even as it confirmed the continuation of industry self-regulation, a form of mediation and compromise pioneered by Hays in 1927 (Krzywinska 89). Paradoxically, the boycotts, which continued after the crisis, stimulated box office receipts in all but a few overwhelmingly Catholic U.S. cities.

Since the Code did not mention vampires or monsters, the horror genre enjoyed a certain freedom from censorship in the years before the Code's enforcement. This crucial partial restriction pushed the genre toward romance, for explicit sexual material was, by 1934, prohibited from the so-called sex pictures and, although it produced new modes, such as the screwball comedy, it worked in general to shape classic Hollywood narration and to create the heterosexual couple.[16] Universal, which cooperated with the Studio Relations Committee (SRC), regulated monstrous and vampiric sex even as it winked at the censors (Maltby, "Production" 49–50). The horror films of 1931–33, cashing in on Depression-era cultural worry, economic distress, need for escape, and erotic fascination, enabled Universal's Depression-era survival, earning solid profits and "setting the parameters for the studio's signature genre" (Joslin 25; Schatz, *System* 228). *Frankenstein* and *Dracula*, moreover, opened during a time of social turmoil and anxiety about the movies' corrupting influence. Although it was thought to contain "undue gruesomeness" and religious irreverence, *Frankenstein* was nevertheless banned only in Kansas, condemned by the local London County Council, and, after Catholic objections, shown largely intact in Quebec; the famous cutting of the little girl's drowning scene occurred in 1937, at reissue, and the curtain-raiser prologue was added for Canadian distribution (Gardner 67; Krzywinska 86; Skal, *Monster* 137). Although the Motion Picture Producers and Distributors Association (MPPDA) received numerous complaints about *Dracula*, only Massachusetts snipped it (Skal, *Monster* 126). After the successful release of *Bride of Frankenstein*—which broke attendance records and received "among the best [reviews] of Whale's career"—only Ohio demanded "substantial deletions" (Curtis 249–51). Whereas monster and vampire were censored abroad, only one of Hollywood's major European markets suppressed it.[17] Because the Hays Office censored sex, politics, and crime, the horror film had located the Code's "'first loophole'" (quoted in Doherty 297).

In the 1970s, when sexual mores had shifted and censorship had given way to the MPDAA ratings game, gothic-horror audiences demanded sexual scenarios on screen.[18] Remediating not the novel but the Balderston and Deane play, John Badham's *Dracula* (1979) romances the gothic in gothic horror. After dinner at Dr. Seward's (Donald Pleasence) madhouse apartment, the aristocratic count (Frank Langella, star of Broadway's *Dracula: The Vampire Play* [1977] and the embodiment of 1970s sex appeal) ogles the butler as he sucks his cut finger and watches, via glance/object cuts, as Jonathan (Trevor Eve) and Lucy (Kate Nelligan) dance and peck; Mina (Jan Francis), whom he has already vamped, dizzily drops a cup, and Dracula, instructing that she be administered no drugs— "you must not pollute her blood"—hypnotizes her. "Dance with me," Lucy instructs her new neighbor. Cut to close-up of vampire hand on her bared lower back; track to her hand joining his; dolly across the drawing room, past a phallic pillar in the frame plane, as the couple waltzes, then whirls, faster; cut to Jonathan, watching, jealously, then looking away; cut to the count's carriage, careening away into the night. "I'm not good enough for you?" Lucy's lover later whines; why, he asks, is she "hobnobbing with aristocrats?" Cut to Dracula, on upper balcony, watching; to Mina in bed; camera tilts up madhouse as Dracula slithers down the wall. Here, Badham plays the gothic for all it's worth: dark, foggy night; quasi-terror and quasi-desire stimulated by swelling music; exchanged figural glances; close-ups of hands on bodies. This foreplay scene promises to arouse and thrill the female spectator; instead, it may make her laugh—another pleasurable physiological and affective sensation.

Lucy and Dracula's lurid red-and-black bedroom scene turns gothic horror into Harlequin romance. Van Helsing (an older, once sexy Laurence Olivier—and Mina's father in this version) and Dr. Seward (Lucy's father) watch a white horse paw Mina's grave; Lucy sits on her bed, waiting. Cut to Dracula, emerging out of fog and approaching the leaded window, his shirt draped across his bared upper chest; "You will be flesh of my flesh, blood of my blood," he purrs—only Langella's suave star image could carry this off. Cut to Lucy, unbuttoning nightdress; to the count, sweeping off his cape; he lifts Lucy onto the bed; kisses her breasts through diaphanous nightdress; close-up two shot in profile, firelight in background; she gasps as he penetrates her. Cut to black figures against lurid red background; kisses, bats, hands on bodies—triumphant gothic music; cut to Technicolor, as the count slits his chest and bleeds; cut to her face, looking up, drinking from his wound; tilt up to count's face in close-up, his eyelids droop in ecstasy. Together, the lovers slink down the madhouse wall: "You will join me on a higher plane, feeding on them; we will create more of our kind, Lucy." These spectacular scenes of flaming red and deep black mimic a hot romance aesthetic, as the thrill of fear gets R-rated.

In *Bram Stoker's Dracula*, Francis Ford Coppola outdoes Badham by borrowing the trappings of soft-core pornography. Here, Jonathan's vamping is orgiastic. Materializing out of his bed, three bare-breasted brides growl, lick Jonathan's throat, tear his shirt, open his pants, display their fangs, bite his neck: close-up of a bride's face, blood on lips; two brides kiss, in soft-core girl-girl shot, then slide onto Jonathan. Lucy, too, has never been sexier: streaking through darkened garden, in ruched and body-hugging orange dress, she lies on a raised grave, the beast between her legs and her blood on his mouth. Later, Lucy—again in orange nightdress—touches her neck in bed; cut to Dracula, watching, outside the terrace doors; cut to Lucy, camera tracks down as she touches her breast, nipple standing visibly through filmy gauze; crosscut between giant microscopic slide of blood (medicine's and cinema's historically old technologies) and Dracula, looking at Lucy; track of his shadowy hand crossing the wall, flowers wilting (as he becomes erect?). In the transfusion scene that follows, Lucy writhes, bares her breast, profiled beside Dracula's shadow, as her blood drips on the floor. Picturing spoofed arousal on screen, Coppola shoots bodily fluids on the move—which may even provoke spectatorial laughter.

Coppola also mixes vampire tale with beauty and the beast, rewriting Dracula as wronged and haunted prince-lover in this "reincarnation romance."[19] When Dracula (Gary Oldman) finds Mina's photograph among Jonathan's belongings, he recognizes his long-lost Elizabeta and vows to "love again": "The luckiest man on this earth is the man who finds true love," he croons. Yet after stalking Mina (Winona Ryder) to a London street, he nearly rapes her in the cinematograph, the new medium that will once again revive him: "I have crossed oceans of time to find you"; his head turns toward the camera over Mina's body, eyes glow red, teeth grow fangs, and he goes for her neck; but he can't do it, he loves her too much. Later, beauty and the beast swear everlasting love during Dracula's vamping of Mina: he bites, opens a wound in his breast: "Drink and join me in eternal life"; she drinks, she licks, he groans orgasmically. "She is now my bride," he chortles. Here, Coppola rewrites Stoker's heterosexual romance as sappy Hollywood love story. Oldman's star image makes Dracula potential rapist and testosterone freak but also lovelorn solitary, alone and tearful when his beauty betrays him. Genre (like blood) mixing solicits the youth market, where romance-film consumption and quasi-arousal really happen.

As the romance genre shifts with changing social conditions and sexual mores, the on-screen couple also changes: the perversely passionate but chaste duo become partners who have sex, however simulated. Gothic horror likewise morphs, as arousal and soft-core scenario enter 1990s heritage spectacle. Female fans adore it. Brigid Cherry's research on women's consumption of quality, historical, and costume-drama gothic-horror films identified four vampire films as favorites: Neil Jordan's *Interview with the Vampire* (1994) and Coppola's *Bram Stoker's Dracula* (1992) scored numbers 3 and 6, respectively (171). These 1990s fans liked romantic, handsome, exotic, elegant, and sexy vampires, especially aristocratic beaux that expressed erotic feelings for their victims; Milly Williamson's vampire fan-club interviewees in Britain and New Orleans likewise loved the romantic, soulful, sympathetically portrayed vampire (57–66). Gothic horror, Cherry concludes, functions as "a form of erotica for women" (173). Yet these fans also rated *Frankenstein* highly and enjoyed identifying, sympathizing, or empathizing with the marginalized monster in classic horror films. The monster's humanity elicited their own sense of loneliness, social exclusion, "bookish[ness]," and (gendered) "revenge," as they felt a "subversive affinity" with the monster (Stokes and Maltby, 196–99; Cherry 175–76). Although limited by its silence about nonhorror viewers and its focus only on *gothic*-horror consumers, Cherry's ethnographic study—and Williamson's interviews—outline the ways female fans take pleasure in quality period horror-romance, as in rebellious outsider figures.[20] Cherry's research subject refuses to look away (pace Linda Williams), as she seeks the thrill of quasi-fear and quasi-arousal.

Horror mixes with genres other than romance, seeking a mass audience as well as repeated spectatorship. Whereas gothic horror evokes the fearful erotic thrill, science fiction arouses and allays fears about the human-machine interface; the queer spoof elicits laughter; the costume drama provides period pleasures. Operating the permeable, flexible boundaries among horror, sci-fi, romance, parody, and costume extravaganza, the heritage vampire flick deploys a morph aesthetic to undo spectatorial anesthesia; it mobilizes terror at body invaders, pictures splattering blood, and, manipulating POV and rapid cuts, titillates even as it operates the thrill of the kill.

Morph Aesthetics

Francis Ford Coppola's period fantasy *Bram Stoker's Dracula* and E. Elias Merhige's parody of filmmaking as vampirism *Shadow of the Vampire* update Stoker's novel for late twentieth-century spectators worried about the body's integrity and its natural reproducibility. Remediated for film, the post-Stoker vampire and the post-Shelleyan monster stimulate and spoof terror about the contemporary body's instability and permeability, the unclear boundary between life and death, and the possibility of body invaders and panic sex. Late twentieth-century visual culture of all kinds celebrates and glorifies the sensate pleasures that piggyback on these terrors: the thrill of out-of-body and virtual-reality travel, the zing of computer-assisted special effects, the future-shock of terminal identities, the joy-and-pain of sadomasochistic regimes of dominance and submission. At the same time, however, Coppola's and Merhige's films pay homage to their nineteenth-century originals, shrilly singing paeans to fidelity aesthetics, to authentic re-creation of period costumes, sets, and acting styles. Managed by technologically produced authenticity, the 1990s heritage gothic-horror film poses as terrifying, knowingly pictures threats to the body's image, even as its period pleasures alleviate terror, a quasi-affect.

Deploying early cinema techniques, Merhige and Coppola use a period aesthetic to simulate authenticity, even as their films parody the concept of cinematic verisimilitude. Thus Coppola's Dracula, shot with a Pathé camera, walks the streets of London with the "slightly jerky, speeded-up movement of early silents" (Coppola and Hart 76). When Dracula nearly rapes Mina in the cinematograph, the screen flickers with various nudie shorts and with Lumière's *The Arrival of a Train*, exhibited in 1896 at London's Empire Theater. Indeed, Hart's screenplay calls for a projection of Queen Victoria, in carriage, celebrating her diamond jubilee, a festival historically coincident with the invention of cinema, with new camera and film-projecting technology, *and* with the publication of Stoker's novel (Coppola and Hart 83; Thomas 292, 301). Merhige's *Vampire* cheekily depicts the "making" of F. W. Murnau's *Nosferatu* (1922), complete with location scouting, crew shooting, director shouting, and stars kissing, fighting, and biting off screen as well as on. Hoping to re-present the sound and look of Murnau's silent film, Merhige uses "film history as a jumping off point for experimentation." Desiring to "transport" his audience "back to another time," the filmmaker began, NPR reporter Beth Accomondo explains, by "borrowing period wax cylinder recording devices from collectors"; sound designer Nigel Heath then hybridized the mix with digitalizing technologies. The "scratchy sound" would contribute to a sense of "other-worldliness," Merhige said, and provide the spectator the "feeling that [he] listen[ed] to a disembodied voice," a "ghost," or "something from another world" ("Profile" 1–3). That ghost signifies postmodern authenticity, the parodic appropriation of past for present filmmaking. "I scouted locations," Murnau (John Malkovich) says of his search for "Max Schreck" (Willem Dafoe), and "there he was, living in an old monastery": he's "completely authentic." The joke: he is authentic, but members of the crew, not knowing the director has promised the vampire the female star's blood for playing the part of an actor playing the part of a vampire, fall victim, one by one, to his bite.

Merhige allegorizes cinema as vampiristic, then, and those who work on the set as the figuratively undead. *Vampire*'s figural production crew names F. W. Murnau's "real" but now dead (but on film, undead) crew: Murnau, the director; Henrik Galeen, the writer; Fritz Wagner, the photographer; Albin Grau, the art director; "Max Schreck," the actor who plays the vampire. Unknowingly punning on cinema's vampire mechanics, the narcissistic Ellen (Catherine McCormack) whines that the "theater audience gives me life" but film "takes it from me"; she must "sacrifice" for her art, the director insists. In his premiere vampiric act, Merhige's Murnau shoots Count Orlock and his visitor at dinner; the guest cuts, as Murnau talks him through the scene: "Cut a slice of bread, watch your *finger*," he screams, inciting the count to go for Gustav's bloody digit. "Is he even human?" Murnau asks as he starts to shoot this scene, suggesting the vampire star's species violation—and his own knowing transgression of species boundaries to facilitate "life," and death, on the set. During the film, moreover, vampire and director gradually exchange places. The film director is "not so different," "Max Schreck" sneers, from the vampire, who seizes control as he kills off the crew: "This is hardly your picture any longer." As Murnau's filming concludes and Merhige's film ends, moreover, the director mixes genres much as Schreck mixes blood. The vampire pic becomes snuff flick, as Murnau shoots while Nosferatu sucks blood from the drugged star's veins, bodies falling around him on the set, director watching as though he, too, were drinking it in. Merhige's film thus parodies, as Clover says, the "institutionalized sadisms of the movie set" as it portrays the star being vamped and displays the figural director as vampire—himself vamped by his postmodern predator, Merhige (171).

Merhige's film shows, moreover, that cinema creates its cultural authority through citation, an aesthetic form of technological reproduction. Merhige's film remakes F. W. Murnau's vampire, who cannot exist apart from his reproduction not only through blood sucking but also in cultural products. He thus incorporates significant scenes from Murnau's 1922 black-and-white classic, parodically reenacted and sutured into his own Technicolor text: Nina plays with a kitten in her window box (Merhige's modern Murnau voices over "nice pussy," in a double entendre that Murnau's glorified, sacrificial female would never have evoked); Jonathan reads "The Book of Vampires" before the castle's doors open, like a movie curtain or the pages of a book (Thomas 295); Dracula says of Nina's locket portrait, "What a lovely throat" ("Max Schreck" says, "She has a beautiful bosom"); Dracula haunts the *Demeter*'s deck during the night (because "Max Schreck" refuses to sail, the ship sits high on dry land); the vampire dies, back arched, arms raised, and brightly lit, in a frame that replicates F. W. Murnau's but replaces puff of smoke with melting celluloid. This 1990s embedded "remake" openly acknowledges the destabilized position of the "original" that it parodies. Recognizing the complex intertextuality of source novels, first adaptations, and remakes, Merhige's film demonstrates, as David Wills notes, that "there can never be a faithful remake" because there never was "a simple original" (quoted in Braudy, "Afterword" 329). Merhige's film thus acquires authenticity of a postmodern kind by acknowledging that the genuine is a fabrication, a reproduction, rather than a return to or revival of an original.

Whether homage, revival, or rivalrous supplement, the remake situates itself historically, as Leo Braudy says, "in relation to previous films as well as to previous literature" ("Afterword" 328). Some stories do cultural work not only for the historical moment of their production and first consumption but for later, and again later, historical periods and cultural consumers as well. In Merhige's embedded remake of F. W. Murnau's classic, the figural Murnau mumbles, "There is no Max Schreck"; "I found him in a book." Merhige's title, moreover, echoes *Nosferatu*'s final intertitle—"the stifling shadow of the vampire vanished with the morning sun"—and so invokes inscription, with silent film as incorporated source. Indeed, Merhige's parodic remake recalls the studio era, for the primary decades of remakes—the 1930s and 1940s, the 1980s and 1990s—coincide with the dominance of the studio system and the return, via entertainment conglomeration, of studio dominance through creation of specialty divisions, the mini-majors.[21] As a cinematic mode, the remake thus meditates on a narrative's "continuing historical relevance" and takes a stand on, rehearses, or seeks to complete "unfinished cultural business" (Braudy, "Afterword" 331). As Skal notes, although horror's narrative structure and generic conventions change little historically, "our cultural uses" for monsters morph as does Dracula himself (*Monster* 23). Thus the remake functions through appropriation and reappropriation to reproduce, but with new technological and cultural power, the worries of past historical

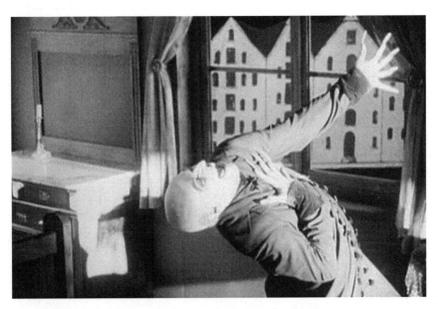

Melting celluloid replaces puff of smoke as Dracula dies in E. Elias Merhige's parodic remake of Nosferatu, Shadow of the Vampire (2000).

moments in light of present needs. Horror's central tropes—"turning back" and "turning away"—combine this retroversive move with the genre's signal spectatorial and aesthetic thrill, shock, to remediate the filmic genealogy that precedes, sustains, and feeds it (Williams, "Looks").

Like Merhige, Coppola plays with the notion of authenticity even as he, too, pays tribute to, yet differentiates his film from, a vampire genealogy of which he is a knowingly belated member. Returning to Bram Stoker's novel rather than Murnau's film, Deane's drama, or Balderson and Deane's American stage play, Coppola claims, "No one had ever done the book." To satisfy Coppola's "ever-present drive to be authentic," according to the film's associate producer, Susie Landau, the staff built barouches to simulate "period movement," trained some actors in Victorian "etiquette," and coached other players in Romanian (Coppola and Hart 3, 78). Researching 1890s aesthetics, they compiled documentary scrapbooks; borrowed from Symbolist paintings by, for example, Gustav Klimt; and produced period artifacts, props, and sets, using nineteenth-century materials where possible (Coppola and Hart 70). "We have tried for a unique, striking visual style that immediately says you are in the realm of magic," Coppola has said; "I want people to understand the historical and literary traditions behind the story." As Landau explains, the crew "wanted to make [spectators] feel that [they were] experiencing the history as it's happening," in an instant in which "past, present, and future meet all at once" (Coppola and Hart 5, 78). This dynamic notion of the present as always already historical disjoins the spectatorial body from its temporal, mappable location, situates it in an ever-morphing moment and space of period magic, cinematic suspense, and future shock.[22]

Coppola's costume horror film puns on and alludes to its source novel even as it everywhere displays its departure from it. Eiko Ishioka's Oscar-winning costumes, violating even as they invoke authenticity, mélange period designs, mingling East and West, male and female, Transylvania and Victorian England. Each figure bears a signature color, as the costumes invent a "symbolic language" of character, period, and "exotic, erotic" style (Coppola and Hart 126–27). Mina wears cool green and blue dresses that signify her schoolmistress status and unspoiled innocence. In Hillingham's conservatory—a fairy land of orientalism where the girlfriends view sexual prints from Sir Richard Burton's popular midcentury *Arabian Nights* and Lucy prattles of what, between a woman's legs, pleases a man—the primly typing and sexually horrified Mina wears a virginal blue, high-necked, narrow-sleeved, leaf-embroidered day dress; Lucy (Sadie Frost) wears a white lace décolleté, off-the-shoulder, *en coeur* costume with leg-of-mutton sleeves. Being fitted for her wedding (and death) dress, Lucy greets Jack Seward in a white lace extravaganza with lengthy train and Elizabethan ruff. Nevertheless, Lucy's signature color is orange, for Ishioka dresses her to express, as Coppola says, her "vixen, leering, slut[ish]" character: the body-hugging, tucked, orange night dress, for example, in which she couples with the vampire on a gravestone (Coppola and Hart 119–20). Dracula's palate: red and gold; his Transylvanian cloak bears an "enormous train" that "undulate[s]" "like a sea of blood"; his crest of intertwined dragons, wolves, snakes, birds, and fire signifies his warrior status, his ancient royalty. For Ishioka, "reference is only reference": her designs invoke authenticity yet fabricate the period look, knowingly invoking faux fidelity (Coppola and Hart 38, 37, 127).

Coppola produces his period look through visual effects.[23] For budgetary reasons, he says, he eschewed the "slick high-tech methods of computer animation [and] 'morphing,'" choosing instead to use "naive," "within-the-camera" early-cinema morph effects. The visual effects designer, Roman Coppola, browsed shops for "old FX paraphernalia"; used multiple exposure, trick shots, and reverse-film and faux frame-of-gravity effects. Yet Michael Ballhaus, director of photography, used more recent postproduction, laboratory-based special effects—front projection, model shots, and matte and mirror effects—to mimic an old-fashioned, mythical atmosphere; Ballhaus's opticals deployed the full range of early-cinema punctuators, including fades to black, wipes, dissolves, irises, freezes, and masks, also now accomplished in the lab, usually by computer (Coppola and Hart 52). Despite Coppola's disingenuous disclaimer, the film's extravagant visual and special effects identify morph aesthetics, so named in the early 1990s, as central to picturing the vampire's power.[24] When Jonathan Harker sups at Castle Dracula and the count recognizes his fiancée, Mina, as his long-lost love, Elizabeta, the vampire's shadow, pictured over a front-projected map of London, reaches for Harker after the count's body withdraws, violating the logic of body and shadow to create an uncanny effect of unconscious vampiristic lust for blood (Prince 50–51). The vampire-as-mist creeps under the window, across the floor, and up Mina's writhing body; here, dry-ice smoke, lit green and superimposed through mirrored front projection and optical FX, shows the vampire's power to morph (Coppola and Hart 133).

Violating the logic of body and shadow, Dracula's shadow attacks Jonathan Harker. (Bram Stoker's Dracula, *1992*)

Coppola's early-cinema morph aesthetic, knowingly invoking the turn-of-the-century spectator's curiosity about the power of an apparatus that could picture movement, superimposition, and special effects, also submits the spectator to the shock of postmodernity. When Van Helsing (Anthony Hopkins) calls Mina the "devil's concubine," the scene cuts to rapid montage:

A hand opens a gun case / a flower blooms through time-lapse photography / maggots crawl on a corpse / Arthur guards Lucy's bedside, with gun, nodding off / a body decays through fast-motion photography / headlong rush through Hillingham's garden: Quincey patrols, cocks his gun / in close-up, Lucy's eyes snap open; she grows teeth, writhes in bed, dressed in red / Dracula attacks Lucy / the vampire throws Arthur backwards across the room through reverse-action / intercut: beams of light break through a chapel window; on sound track, nuns chant; a priest carries a cross, as Mina and Jonathan declare their vows, shot from back / Dracula rushes up steps to window / intercut: Mina and Jonathan stand before the altar, priest blesses / Dracula declares Lucy condemned to death / intercut: Mina and Jonathan drink from chalice / vampire-wolf bursts through window glass

and attacks Lucy / intercut: Jonathan and Mina kiss / in close-up,
Lucy writhes/ Dracula's POV: blood splatters her bed / intercut:
Jonathan and Mina kiss.[25]

This montage leaves the spectator breathless, as parts of it whiz past his
or her eyes in fast motion, yet its over-the-top visual and special effects
may provoke a laugh, as well. It captures vampirism's threat to penetrate
female body, permeate epithelial boundary, free leaky substance of blood,
and tries but fails to allay that threat: Arthur guards and Quincey patrols,
yet one sleeps and so gets knocked unconscious, the other charged by
morphed-to-wolf vampire. This montage also pictures the power and paradox of vampire culture: the imbrication of natural growth with degeneration and corruption (flower blooms, maggots crawl); the articulation of
wedding and predatory sexual degradation (the parallel editing of bridal
sip from a chalice with wolfish blood sucking). Using pixilation in the
vampire POV shots, the camera "click[s] off frames erratically—single
frames and then a burst of several per second," which produces the terror effect of "animal-like sensory perception, something primordial." The
"predator's POV should always be scary," Roman Coppola says, to produce the rush of adrenaline, the fear of being engulfed by morphing bodies, the thrill of crossing boundaries and violating biological classifications,
the dread of undead penetrations (Coppola and Hart 89). The filmmaker's
capability to move viewers through delirious kinetic experiences of motion,
headlong rush, and rapid transformation creates—and spoofs—spectatorial affects of dizziness, shock, and amazement.

Morph aesthetics also mobilize the "astonishment" that Tom Gunning
has argued is basic to early cinema aesthetics. Spectators of Lumière's *The
Arrival of a Train* may well have experienced a "pleasurable vacillation
between belief and doubt" in the onrushing image's reality ("Astonishment" 117); its pleasure depended upon the spectator's belief in its illusion,
whereas its danger depended upon the shock of movement, of visual transformation. Maxim Gorky said of Lumière's train, "It speeds right at you—
watch out! It seems as though it will plunge into the darkness in which you
sit, turning you into a ripped sack full of lacerated flesh and splintered
bones"—yet this was a "train of shadows" (quoted in Gunning 118).
Only the *moving* picture could affect this sensed imbrication of body and
picture through the illusion of motion across space, and Coppola's *Dracula* arouses the spectator's pleasure in this marvelous and terrifying film

magic. As his vampire morphs into wolf and springs through Lucy's bedroom window, as though out of the screen at the spectator, eyes gleaming and tongue dripping, the picture proposes that the spectator's body may be penetrated, like Lucy's neck, to the bloodied holes in which the sequence cuts. Merhige's vampiric filmmaker likewise knows the power of cinema so to excite *and* to cite. In a parodic allusion to Lumière's *Train*, his figural Murnau, on the rails to a location shoot, calls the director a "scientist engaged in the creation of memory"; as Murnau's face dissolves in and dissolves out, his voice-over details the spectatorial affects aroused by the panoramas Merhige shoots: the play of light on faces registers laughter and agony, that, like the vampire, "will neither blur nor fade." Thus the modern aesthetics of astonishment morphs through horror, fashioning a special-effects "aesthetic [of] pleasurable fear" (Sedgwick, *Gothic* 10).

This morph aesthetic of pleasurable fear remediates the vampire, making the spectator aware of the play of media. In Stoker's *Dracula*, media, or technological prostheses, consume essences (the Kodak), mediate exchanges (Mina's photograph, blood transfusions), facilitate global flows (telegrams, phonographs), or themselves replicate (the manifold copies). Although Stoker does not include film among his media, the cinema as technological invention and Stoker's *Dracula*, as Ronald R. Thomas says, "arrive in London at the same time," and the vampire's "supernatural powers are identified with the effects of that magical medium" (303–4). Thomas Alva Edison's invention and Méliès's and the Lumière Bros.' first moving pictures cap a century of experimentation in visual entertainments. Media in the 1790s—the magic lantern, panorama, phantasmagoria, and Eidophusikon—used light and sound effects to picture rural and metropolitan scenes. These early media awed, agitated, or alarmed spectators, as dead celebrities paraded across invisible screens, or living figures wasted to skeletons, as avalanches crashed, volcanoes spewed, or St. Paul's burned.[26] Like the phantasmagoria, early nineteenth-century media "moved entertainment a step closer to the cinema," and the diorama projected picturesque scenes through a "rudimentary camera shutter" (Altick 219, 170–72). These technologies of the visible shaped the spectatorial look by offering the body "virtual mobility." As the look became virtual, the observer became more immobile; only the diorama literally mobilized, by technologically turning, the observer's body, transforming him into "a component of the machine" (Friedenberg 28; Crary 113). The images produced by these technological entertainments thus anticipate moving pictures, as the eye's perceptual apparatus was amplified and extended outside the body. And, in 1922, F. W. Murnau would shoot Stoker's vampire as a "play of light and shadow" that "haunt[s] the human world" (Thomas 297).

These early media and cinematic figures anticipate the cyborg, the clone, and the ectogenous posthuman. The 1990s heritage vampire and monster exploit worries about twenty-first-century laboratory science, about biotechnology, genetic engineering, and the future of sexual reproduction, for at the millennium, many UK and U.S. citizens feared that new reproductive technologies (NRTs) could disrupt "natural" sexual and familial relations. Extending Shelley's worry about paternal electrical experiments and elaborating Stoker's anxious glee at technological modernity, Branagh's and Neil Jordan's 1990s heritage horror films arouse and allay anxieties about artificially produced beings. Taking the edge off techno-future shock, they manage worry with the period look, return spectators to numbness by reinforcing "natural" sexual and familial arrangements even as they parody ectogenesis or vogue queer sexual replication. Broadening the technological scope and range of heritage film, these movies take a parodic pleasure in dread.

Doing Kinship in Gothic Horror

Although the 1930s celluloid vampire hinted that vamping was somehow sexy, the Universal Studio Frankenstein series—*Frankenstein* (1931), *Bride of Frankenstein* (1935), and *Son of Frankenstein* (1939)—subsumes sex to the heterosexual reproductive imperative. In *Son of Frankenstein,* for example, not creating the couple but reproducing an heir is required. *Frankenstein* introduces, then drops, a love triangle among Henry Frankenstein, Elizabeth, and Victor Moritz, although Baron Frankenstein (Frederick Kerr) concurs that Henry's laboratory mania means "there must be another woman." Yet the film's teleology drives to produce (the hope of) an heir, a son to bear the name of the father (and the movies). Nevertheless, the film repeatedly defers a marital ceremony: the bride and the baron are "kept waiting" by the groom-son; despite the bride's dismissal of bridesmaids and fear that "something is come between" her and her fiancé, despite the monster's kidnapping of fiancée, the film aims to end with a wedding. Instead, the bridal gown goes unworn, the Frankenstein-family orange blossoms and best man's boutonniere dry out, and the baron drinks the celebratory brew alone. "A son to the House of Franken-stein," the baron toasts, as he hijacks the ancestral wine that a bevy of ser-vants meant for his son, now recuperating from monster bashing. Only in *Son of Frankenstein* does the scientist-son's bride bear the wished-for heir: it's the longest gestation in film history. Like the original film's bride, however, the boy exists only to be kidnapped by the monster, with whom he reports having played games and from whom he received gifts; the father is dead. At film's end, new mother, father, and son clinch, with Amelia, the nurse, looking on, just as at *Bride*'s end, scientist and wife embrace, he murmuring "darling, darling." These films provide audiences the desired happy ending—so sequels and sons may follow.

I have termed the reproductive imperative in *Frankenstein* and *Son of Frankenstein* has more than one such scion. Whereas Shelley's novel names the scientist the monster's figurative father, Rowland V. Lee's spoof of James Whale's film identifies the scientist-son as monster sibling; here, the scientist becomes genealogical brother to the monster his father "fathered." When Ygor (Bela Lugosi) insists to the new baron, Wolf Frankenstein (Basil Rathbone), that he must make the sick monster well, Frankenstein responds, "Do you mean to imply, he's my brother?" As he leaves the secret cellar sickroom, Frankenstein scratches out the inscription on his father's coffin: "Maker of Monsters" becomes "Maker of Men." The avuncular monster, stealing his figurative nephew's fairy-tale book, demonstrates that "doing kinship" has gone awry, as the generations metaphorically collapse around the creature. The heterosexual reproductive imperative at work in the Universal horror films produces monster as brother and uncle, as the fatherless alien finds a surreal, paro-died "home" in castle and town named for his "creator" and ultimately is murdered by his figurative sibling in the boiling sulfur springs that ener-gize the laboratory. This fantasmatic kinship structure parodies those at Universal Studios, where the son, Carl Laemmle Jr., who adopted his father's name as a young man, took over an independent production unit and relegated his father to his own old job.[27]

I have termed the reproductive imperative in *Frankenstein* and *Son of Frankenstein* "doing kinship," a term I borrow from anthropology. Whereas the concept of the family in sociology focuses on a social institution, detailing its members' psychological roles, legal responsibilities, and affec-tive ties, the concept of kinship in anthropology describes the structures of origin and descent that identify relationship through blood or by mar-riage. Kinship is thus a social network rather than a self-contained node.

Like the other terms I use in this chapter—"genre," "romance," and "monster"—the term "kinship" is malleable, is, as Sarah Franklin says, "a productively contestable episteme" ("Debate" 138). In nineteenth-century anthropology, as Stocking demonstrates, the concept of kinship denoted savagery and race and served to measure degrees of evolution toward civilization (*Victorian* 187–237). In the early twentieth century, kinship signified a universal linkage of humanity; under structuralism, it measured degrees of social order in traditional and modern cultures; in late twentieth-century anthropology, as Marilyn Strathern acknowledges, the concept may "belong to a world already passing." The term, "procreation," by contrast, refers to "the generative moment, to the act of begetting, to the effectiveness of a capacity" ("Regulation" 180; "Relational" 208).

Shelley's Frankenstein fears procreation, forestalls his wedding, and prefers work in the lab to sex with his wife. As though forecasting the "breathless horror and disgust" he will feel toward his progeny, the scientist's early enthusiasm is "checked by ... anxiety": oppressed by a "slow fever," he becomes painfully "nervous"; "doomed by slavery to toil," he feels guilty of a crime (33–34).[28] Figurative (and future) criminal, enslaved, industrial being, Frankenstein worries, loses sleep, falls ill. After the monster's birth, Victor imagines his creature as his "own vampire" (49). When his monster requests a "'companion'" of "'the same species,'" dread strikes the scientist. "'You must create a female for me, with whom I can live in the interchange of those sympathies necessary for my being'"—a "'creature of another sex,'" the monster demands (97–99). Although the monster mentions sex only as difference and reproduction not at all, Frankenstein interprets the demon's wish as sexual and so generative, indeed, as a projection of his own desire to "father" a new "species" (32). Should he make the monster a mate, the sympathy for which the demon "thirsted would be children, and a race of devils would be propagated upon the earth" (114). Frankenstein has (pro)created a "categorical problem" that the monster, in turn, "embodies" and threatens to reproduce (McLane 963). Despite critical debate about the monster's wishes, Frankenstein's interpretation remains a reasonable inference; as Victor destroys the monster's future mate, the bereaved being cries, "'Shall each man ... find a wife for his bosom, and each beast have his mate, and I be alone?'" (116). Although wives do not necessarily reproduce, they did so routinely, if often perilously, in 1818, as Mary Shelley knew all too well, for the turn-of-the-century debates about early maternal breastfeeding, the hire of wet nurses, the use of obstetric instruments, and the practices of abortion and infanticide were widely publicized in the medical press and formed a locus of anxieties about "natural" sexual bodies.[29] The embrace envisioned by monster, maker, and reader alike thus instigates the fantasy of companionate desire—and reproductive dread.

Frankenstein's procreative angst about "future ages" and "generations" maps a larger cultural anxiety onto his laboratory work of mediation. Although critics generally interpret Frankenstein's fear of birth as a figure for Shelley's dread of childbirth and maternity, Maureen McLane views the monster's hypothetical offspring as a potential mob or "mass," which "introduces a Malthusian calculus" into the novel, a species competition (979). In the novel's central worry, Frankenstein fears that the category "human" may be made malleable by laboratory procreation/mediation. Only geographical separation, he imagines, can prevent the pandemonium possible when different species reside together in Europe without sympathy. The danger of future species mixing and of multinational population flows haunts the scientist's early nineteenth-century story, anticipating Stoker's late-century anxiety about reverse colonization (Arata). His own vampire rises from the grave to suck the sustenance from his (pro)creator and all those for whom he cares; this undead quasi-object, like Stoker's later vampire, kills by leaving marks on the neck, is seemingly ubiquitous, and threatens the human species through his own possible replication.[30]

In Branagh's *Mary Shelley's Frankenstein,* nothing about reproduction is "natural." Remediating Shelley and incorporating James Whale, Branagh displaces his predecessors' electrical apparatus for reanimating morselized corpse with ectogenesis. Branagh's procreation scene mixes tropes for vulnerable flesh with scientific prowess: hacking off a cholera victim's limbs, Victor cries, "More direct power"; cut to a meat cleaver, whacking dead meat; cut to a woman's collecting amniotic fluid under birthing chair and handing the bucket to Frankenstein, while birthing mother screams. Close-up of dead frog in vitro; electric needles pierce frog flesh; current runs; frog eyes open; dolly in on beaker as it breaks and, now upside down, frog croaks in close-up. Music swells. Cut to iron tub being filled with amniotic fluid; hands sewing flesh; cut to scientist checking Leonardo's Renaissance anatomical figure of man. This articulation of science and art as procreation enhances the scientist's metaphorical power, and . . . cut to Branagh, whirling off his cape as he enters the laboratory: the scientist as celebrity, music rising and blaring as the virile "father" whirls around the laboratory, chest naked, to begin the work of mediation. Corpse rises to light, then, lowered, is fastened into autogenetic womb filled with amniotic fluid. Victor pricks needles into corpse's feet through valve in tub, pricks again and again. Electricity jumps, wheels turn. Victor joins an apparatus to tub, what looks like technologically gigantic "penis" and "testicles"; cut to eels—technosperm?—flowing from "penis" and into amniotic tub. The naked-torsoed scientist jumps on top of the tub, metaphorically impregnating the "womb," having technosex: "Live!" he screams at the "embryo" inside. Camera tracks in to a porthole in "womb," producing fetal images for spectator and scientific "sperm donor" alike; close-up on fetal hand; the sound track booms as the hand hits the glass: it "quickens." Victor turns toward the camera as it tracks in on his naked torso: "It's alive!" he whispers, echoing all other cinematic Frankensteins—but more flamboyant, sexy, and virile than they. The tub turns over, and the "embryo" escapes; Victor slaps, imitating birth. Branagh's parodied scene of procreation as laboratory experimentation separates sex from conception and reproduction to arouse—and spoof—spectatorial anxiety about perverse replication.

Frankenstein prepares to penetrate the womblike tub, where his monster awaits impregnation, "quickening," and "gestation." (Mary Shelley's Frankenstein, 1994)

Despite Branagh's parody of NRTs as metaphorical sexual organs, his procreation scene works because it knowingly represents the link between nature and culture that gets disrupted by the interventions of assisted conception. In the British parliamentary debates about the Human Fertilisation and Embryology Bill of 1989 and Act of 1990, which addressed the licensing of infertility services and regulation of future embryo research, the biotechnological domain was seen to guarantee the division between pre-embryo and embryo (Price 35–36). Whereas in 1818, "quickening" would have marked the embryo's viability, in the 1990s, the fourteen-day moment in which the primitive streak of tissue appears on a sonogram replaced quickening, granting biological science rather than maternal experience the authority to identify embryonic existence. In the 1994 Muller Report of the Human Embryo Research Panel in the United States, members distinguished between embryos intended for transfer to female wombs and those not so intended; a range of embryo researches were disallowed by the NIH report, primarily because, like the cultural vampire and electrically animated monster, they "shift and challenge the boundaries" of the human (Squier, "Boundaries" 103–4, 109). Yet, as Franklin demonstrates, once in place as guarantor, technology displaces the biological (since sight of the actual primitive streak is no longer necessary), and nature, assisted by machinery in the act of conception, "becomes *a mediated authority, a partial foundation*"; indeed, it becomes "doubly mediated," that is, "interpreted by . . . scientists" and "rendered arbitrary by the law" that regulates it (Franklin, "Debate" 135–36; emphasis in original).

In Branagh's film, the laboratory is such a doubly mediated place. Not "natural" but not "cultural" or "social" either, the laboratory—and its work of mediation—displaces the biological even as it procreates a biotechnological anomaly that produces anxiety and laughter. Moreover, this quasi-object knows itself reproduced, in the splicing institution and sutured medium of film, and the star-director flaunts his glamorous, pumped-up body, his capability to mock, mimic, and spoof a cultural problem mediated through a literary classic and a film genealogy. The celluloid monster is a remediated natural/cultural being produced by a mechanical apparatus; he embodies a categorical problem more profound than does Shelley's print-culture monster, as cinematic metaphors for assisted reproduction destabilize any simple equation of the biological with the natural by invoking its own technological activities, industrial relations, cultural belatedness, and capacity to produce pleasure.

The cultural anxieties created by NRTs involve this technologically produced disruption of nature/culture and so of the socially constituted kinship relations that govern biological facts. Is a procreative (paternal) or reproductive (maternal) act performed in the clinic a sexual act or not? Does it signify a kinship relation? Is Victor Frankenstein his monster's "father"? Mary Shelley's figurative answer is "yes," and the terms "father," "creator," and "author" name this metaphorical kinship relation throughout her novel. Branagh's answer, however, can only be "it depends upon what a father is or does." For under the regime of NRTs, distributed paternity vexes the definition of fatherhood: is the father he who donates the sperm? he who rears and/or adopts the child? Distributed maternity is more multiply vexed: is the mother she who donates the egg? she whose body and blood nurture the embryo in the womb? she who rears the child? Clearly, technologically assisted reproduction separates childbearing from childrearing and distributes acts of parenthood across biological, social, and cultural domains to "potentiate the divisibility" of parenthood (Farquhar 16). Branagh's mise-en-scène invokes NRT-produced distributed maternity, as a mother's amniotic fluid is separated from and embryo grows outside a literal womb. Paternity is likewise distributed among laboratory instruments that figure sexual penetration, sperm donation, and artificial insemination. Shelley's representation of and the Universal *Frankenstein*'s jokes about reproductive kinship relations get trumped by Branagh's doubly mediated late-century procreativity.

From the perspective of NRTs, then, the monster created by distributed parenthood might represent or anticipate an "orphaned embryo," one used to produce possible life but abandoned, never implanted, never cultivated or acculturated, except by himself and, accidentally, by his "surrogate" father, De Lacey (who, repeating his creator's paternity, also rejects him). In the late twentieth century, such orphaned embryos might remain frozen at infertility clinics for a possible five-year period, which could be extended an additional ten years by the embryo's or pre-embryo's legal owners.[31] The accumulation of "orphaned embryos" in clinical settings has become a "population" question—a "classically overdetermined reproductive dilemma"—not unlike Shelley's novel's Malthusian calculus (Franklin, "Orphaned" 167). Although her novel may anticipate the doubly mediated work of artificial reproduction, however, Shelley could never have dreamed of ectogenous life, of cloned sheep or IVF babies, especially in an age that invented new "natural" duties for mothers and sentimentalized maternity (Perry, *Novel* 227). This postindustrial, computer-age technology creates a new level of anxiety about whether assisted conception involves a natural, sexual act, whether kinship relations in North Atlantic cultures can be maintained under the regime of NRT, whether pre-embryos or embryos may be owned and stockpiled or systematically destroyed, whether "persons-yet-to-be" are being denied life (Franklin, "Debate" 145; see Gallagher 147).

Public debates about science's power to create life have become visible at nodal points, moments of extreme social and cultural dislocation, during the nineteenth and twentieth centuries. In the twentieth century, the debate about ectogenesis emerged in the 1920s and 1930s, within a matrix of discourses such as eugenics, public health, and sexual reform, and alongside fears of degeneration and postwar European reproductive decline. In the century's first decades, Jon Turney argues, a "mass reading public, a diversified and stratified press," and scientific researchers aware of their cultural visibility all conjoined to "evoke profound disquiet" about the possibility of creating life in the laboratory (90). In the 1920s and 1930s, Susan Squier notes, debate focused on the emergence of reproductive biotechnology and, specifically, on ectogenesis (*Babies* 69). The press publicized discussion about these cultural fears. Aldous Huxley (who penned screenplays for *Jane Eyre* and *Pride and Prejudice*) and his friends debated among themselves and in popular and scholarly journals about reproductive sex, contraception, the future of motherhood, and eugenics (Turney 99).[32] Huxley's story "The Tissue Culture King," which celebrated the (future) possibility of biological mutation and ectogenesis, recalls Frankenstein's worries a century after Mary Shelley told her Villa Diodati ghost story; reprinted in a pulp sci-fi magazine, "Tissue" reached a wide popular audience.[33] Ectogenesis secured its most powerful impact, however, in Huxley's *Brave New World* (1932), in which the separation of sexual reproduction from marriage and of childbearing from flesh terrified a nonetheless fascinated readership.

The ectogenesis debate reemerged in Britain after the birth of Louise Brown in 1978 (Squier, *Babies* 58, 13–15). Throughout the 1980s, Michael Mulkay suggests, the "rights and wrongs" of embryo research concerned members of Parliament, lobbyists, doctors, scientists, academics, the clergy, journalists, "interested organizations and pressure groups," and members of the public (2). During the 1990s parliamentary embryo debate, which I've discussed above, the public expressed its "longstanding cultural ambivalence about science" in general but about biotechnology in particular (117). In the popular press, nonscientists who condemned research on human embryos used the figure of Frankenstein (and other mad-scientist imagery) to argue that scientists were dangerous, that embryo research threatened the family, that the government must institute strict controls over it (118–21).[34] Practitioners and supporters of embryo research, however, justified NRTs in the popular press by evoking maternal joy at unexpected conception, touting the elimination of genetic risk in pregnancy, celebrating scientific gains to create "therapeutic advance" and "social benefit." Proresearch scientists "won the public debate" in the British press and in Parliament by fashioning an upbeat pronatalist story that "combined the authority of science with moving personal testimony" and with "conventional family values" (82). Ironically, this pronatalist tale identifies an ideological meaning occluded by the more-available rhetoric of anxiety, for the primary users of NRTs—infertile married couples, in particular; unmarried heterosexuals, usually women; and, rarely, homosexual couples who might otherwise, and often do, adopt—seek to succeed physiologically at what they cannot "naturally" achieve: childbirth.[35]

The late twentieth-century reproductive and kinship anxieties addressed in the parliamentary embryo debate seem to be widely shared. In her ethnographic inquiry in northwest England, Jeanette Edwards discovered that her research subjects held seemingly contradictory views of assisted conception: infertile couples should be helped to achieve pregnancy and birth, they believed, yet interference in the natural processes of reproduction is dangerous. They worried about whether egg or sperm donation between siblings or in-laws might constitute figurative or future literal incest; about whether biotechnological relatedness could constitute affective kinship ties—as emerged in the case of Baby M in the United States; that assisted conception and reproductive technologies might disrupt concepts of identity; about cloning—"'We'd just all be *zombies,'*" one informant feared (79; emphasis in original). Edwards classifies these sensed dangers as "biological, psychological, and relational": thus risks to future personhood, to genetic identity, and to affective family and social relations all threatened the "naturalness of the family" (82; quoted in Franklin, "Debate" 131). In his interviews in southeast England, Eric Hirsch discovered additional concerns about consumerism and NRTs, Brave-New-World-style governmental control of reproduction, and the maintenance of conjugality in the face of distributed parenthood and disrupted kinship relations (92–93). These informants worried, in particular, about genetic engineering, children as commodities, the future of gay parenting, the fragility of the conjugal couple—about the naturalness of companionate marriage and the nuclear family (97, 114, 101, 107).

In the twenty-first-century United States, the millennial debate focuses on cloning and embryonic stem-cell research. Despite Britain's 1990 Embryology Act, the U.S. Congress has passed no bill regulating human cloning or IVF procedures. In 2004, the President's Council on Bioethics recommended that professional societies and assisted-reproduction practitioners tighten self-regulation, improve data collection, and more actively aid patient decision making. Seeking to offer a "compromise on cloning," the report urges a ban on reproductive but not on therapeutic cloning; such a compromise might facilitate restoration of federal funding for embryonic stem-cell research. Yet one council member notes public fears about embryo research's "slippery slope": "stem cells today, cloned babies tomorrow." Only with ethical safeguards in place, he admits, will the ban on federal funding "no longer make . . . sense as a moral distinction" (Hall, "Panel"). These safeguards include bans on reproductive cloning, on embryo research after fourteen days following conception, and on transferal of human embryos to nonhuman species. In the early twenty-first century, however, the religious right seeks to set the terms of debate, for the council's initial draft-report included "ideological language," according to the American Infertility Association's director, that would protect "nascent human life" and demand bureaucratic reporting regulations impossible to carry out (Hall, "Panel").

Worries about cloning animated the 1990s film adaptations of *Frankenstein* and, as a new spate of clone novels, plays, and TV shows demonstrates, millennial pop culture as well. For cloning, which may well have been inconceivable in the 1930s, stimulated the 1990s cultural imaginary and continues to do so, in the millennium.[36] Whereas 1930s horror films pictured biotechnology as terrifying, if awesome, 1990s films tell cyborg stories, narrate posthuman lives of the future, and spoof the kinship and familial worries of spectators, making them laugh, making them take knowing pleasure, even glee, in future shock. Branagh's 1994 monster tells a cyborg story of "adolescence" and "sexual maturity," of hybrid self-education and self-regulation, of reproductive slippery slope. In Branagh's film, the monster leaps, in slow motion, onto a solitary figure, his maker, in a mountainous, snowbound landscape and drags him down an icy hole (birth canal?) into his lair; the monster asks "Who am I?" and "Of what materials am I made?" Expressing cyborg subjectivity, the monster feels like an alien, member of a different species, despite his humanoid, if gargantuan, shape. Told by a being who is simultaneously "entit[y] and metaphor," is "living being and narrative construction," the monster's tale represents the first cyborg story (Hayles, "Cyborg" 322). Corman's *Frankenstein Unbound* simply pictures the monster as cyborg. Whereas Branagh cast as his creature Robert De Niro, Corman cast a newcomer without tough-guy star image. Rather than imitate Jack Pierce's flat-topped, neck-bolted makeup for Boris Karloff, Corman's makeup department designed prosthetic molds for Nick Brimble's face that highlight the creature's status as biotechnological being. The creature's spaceshipoid neck protuberances, hard-body musculature, and Romantic, flowing red hair identify him as science-fiction, space-age cyborg trapped in a period costume drama.

Based on Brian Aldiss's savvy period/sci-fi rewriting of Shelley's novel, *Frankenstein Unbound* tells the story of scientist Joseph Buchanan (John Hurt), who stumbles into the Villa Diodati during a time-and-space slip, produced inadvertently as a side effect of his laser-technology weapons

Hoping to tell his cyborg story, the monster jumps his scientist-creator in the Alps. (Mary Shelley's Frankenstein, *1994*)

testing. When he meets Victor Frankenstein (Raul Julia) in 1817, Buchanan tells his precursor that twentieth-century "scientists have made far greater monsters than yours." Seeking to intervene in Shelley's story, Buchanan hopes to save Justine Moritz (Catherine Corman) by convincing Frankenstein or Mary Shelley to "tell the truth" about the monster's murder of William. Instead, Frankenstein bullies Buchanan into providing the electricity to enable a bridal birth, by tapping the power in his car's global positioning system (GPS). "Meet my monster," Buchanan intones, as he activates the car's laser-implosion capability. As the camera cranes out to the ceiling and the lighting/lightning turns the laboratory blue, Buchanan's "monster" blows up Frankenstein's Geneva, turning it into a snowbound, blasted landscape. Morphing to soot in Buchanan's nearly wrecked twentieth-century laboratory (another time-and-space slip), the cyborg booms, "You think you have killed me, but I am with you forever; I am unbound." Despite Buchanan's effort to "stop Dr. Frankenstein," he discovers the limit of his agency: the forces of biotechnology, laser technology, and artificial intelligence cannot be reversed or undone.

Unbinding these monstrous forces, Buchanan discovers the principles of mutation and emergence. As Hayles notes, mutation "names the bifurcation point at which the interplay of pattern and randomness" makes a system "evolve in a new direction"; emergence implies that properties or beings "appear on their own," developing characteristics neither planned nor anticipated by their (pro)creator (*Posthuman* 33, 225). During the film's time-and-space slips, systems evolve and morph, mixing different configurations of embodiment, technology, and culture. Corman links individualistic subjectivity, electric technology, and narrative in the historical moment, 1817; distributed cognition or agency (the scientist, the car's talking GPS), laser technology, and sci-fi film in 2013; and posthuman "subjectivity," various forms of artificial intelligence, and virtual reality in an as-yet unrepresented future. In *Frankenstein Unbound*, the monster promises that, being unfettered, he will continue to exist as a principle of emergence, in which recursivity and laboratory feedback loops allow deviations spontaneously to emerge. As Buchanan's GPS demonstrates, aliveness can be separated from embodied materiality, although not from all matter. Hayles notes, moreover, that the posthuman can be defined as a matrix of complex interactions among mutation, materiality, information, and hyperreality. In Corman's film, the posthuman may take a benign, indeed helpful form (Buchanan's GPS, complete with soothing female voice and caretaking urges) or develop into a malign, evil entity that obeys general but unknown, rules (the laser-produced monster). The former fails Buchanan in his hour of greatest need; the latter promises that it is eternal, ubiquitous, and infinitely malleable. Corman's film refuses to answer the question: will the posthuman annihilate or preserve the subject as we know it?[37] Complexly joined, these two force fields, when articulated with the principle of embodiment, may arouse in spectators strong exultation or anxiety—or both simultaneously.

Whereas cyborg subjectivity and posthuman generation animate Branagh's and Corman's *Frankensteins* respectively, anxieties about kinship and family, about nonsexual replication, energize Neil Jordan's *Interview with the Vampire*. As James R. Keller aptly notes, Anne Rice's vampire chronicles—and screenplay, which Rice herself wrote—parody embodied selfhood, companionate coupling, conventional procreation, and nuclear-family relations (15). This mass-cultural vampire story about mutational subjectivity represents vamping as figurative stalking, a sort of rape, and updates the aristocratic arranged-marital couple as a queer partnership. Like an unhappy heterosexual husband, Lestat (Tom Cruise) devises Claudia's (Kirsten Dunst's) vamping to prevent Louis from leaving him: "Now he's going to stay and make you happy," he tells Claudia after her first gluttonous feeding; "you're mine and Louis's daughter now." Yet this queer unit bears all the traces of the 1990s dysfunctional middle-class family so dear to millennial popular-cultural versions of nineteenth-century fiction (Gelder 113). In a queer parody of kinship networks, Rice's screenplay includes scenes of Claudia's childish greed, deceptiveness, and misbehavior. In montage: a seamstress falls dead at Claudia's feet, and Lestat, seeing her teeth smeared with blood, cries, "Who will we get to finish your dress?" Cut to Claudia's piano lesson, the teacher strikes her knuckles with a wand; "Beware the little digit," he cautions. Cut to Claudia prowling a doll maker's shop; the proprietor says his dolls are too expensive for a little girl; she leaves the shop, satisfied grin on face, miniature replica of herself in arms. Cut to the piano teacher, slumped over keyboard; "What did I tell you?" Lestat yells, seeing the corpse fall on the ivories; "Never in the house," Claudia recalls. "They finished off whole families," Louis voices over Claudia's little concert for a happy family audience; cut to a trail of coffins exiting a plantation house. Later, Lestat—himself a ghoulish undead corpse—tells Claudia, "You've been a very, very naughty little girl."[38]

Even as he spoofs Rice's novel's and screenplay's queer ectogenous family, Jordan vogues vampirism as a cavalcade of stage-and-screen costume drama. As Louis and Claudia become spectators at the Theatre des Vampires, Louis sneers, à la Merhige: they're "vampires who pretend to be humans, pretending to be vampires"; "how avant-garde," Claudia scoffs. Although Jordan's play invokes earlier *Draculas* and *Frankensteins*, it also represents them as media events, as staged scenarios for late-century viewing: onstage, Santiago (Stephen Rea) calls a soon-to-be vamped woman "my bride," tossing her naked body to black-clad vampires who slither on the proscenium floor, much as had 1930s brides in drawing room and lair, but with spectatorial figures for ourselves watching. "Monstrous," Louis laments, as the anxious audience files silently out of the amphitheater. When Louis torches the Theatre des Vampires in retaliation for Claudia's and Madeleine's murders, burning vampires hurl from windows and down stairs, not madwomen from the attic but mad queers from the catacombs, and so vogue both *Jane Eyre* and *Mary Shelley's Frankenstein.* Later, the vampire goes to the movies, as media technology supersedes the proscenium. A "mechanical wonder allowed me to see the sunrise for the first time in 200 years," Louis's voice-over explains, as he watches the final sequence of F. W. Murnau's *Nosferatu* and blockbuster sunrises from *Sunrise, Gone with the Wind,* and *Superman.* As the film ends, the interviewer as wannabe vampire ("You want a companion; make me like you") drives across the Golden Gate Bridge; Lestat leaps from the backseat, presumably sups, and, having hijacked the car and recovered his youthful looks, lip synchs the classic Rolling Stones tune "Sympathy for the Devil": "I'm a man of wealth and taste."[39]

Jordan's pun on "taste" mocks the heritage-film mode that adapts high culture for a middlebrow audience. As genre, gothic horror indulges the demand for even as it ridicules the pretensions of fidelity aesthetics, as the morph aesthetic, costume drama, and vogued vamping criticize or tart up the period look. Yet the "gothic" in gothic horror links the genre to romance, to female desire—and to anxiety about sexual vulnerability, bodily penetrability, and the perversity of sex. The gothic horror genre's conventions thus excite spectatorial vacillation between pleasure and pain, multiply sexual identifications and pleasures, inoculate against apathy, and produce thrills, chills, arousal, and laughter as quasi-affects. Hollywood's obsession with getting vampire and monster right, moreover, make the male and female spectator monstrous, for the need to consume cultural monsters both whets and stimulates that desire: incorporating the screen image, spreading the word, viewers metaphorically vamp others, and so produce and reproduce acts of spectatorial consumption (Fuss, "Homo-spectatorial" 730). Indeed, under the regime of new Hollywood cinema, horror has been franchised, as sequel, prequel, and monster-bash. A century after Stoker's novel, Stephen Sommers's *Van Helsing* (2004) pictures a digitally enhanced hero for a special- and visual-effects age: Van Helsing (Hugh Jackman) puts Frankenstein out of business, emerges from burning laboratory, and morphs from corpse to cowboy; joined by a beautiful princess (Kate Beckinsale), he battles CGI wives, Mr. Hyde, and Dracula, as Sommers puts special-effects connoisseurship at the center of the film-viewing experience. The millennial vampire/monster thus updates Dracula and Frankenstein for cultural consumers in an age of excess consumption, body-techno anxiety, and political apathy. "Vampires have an eternal place in American entertainment," Stanley says; "every generation has its bloodsuckers" ("Bites").

· CHAPTER 4 ·

Middlebrow Audiences, Cinematic Sex, and the Henry James Films

Popular culture does not ... attempt to reproduce the psychological depth and density of texture of a novel by Henry James (for which we should all be truly grateful).... "High" art ... naturalize[s] ... superior taste.... Artistic complexity is a class distinction: [it] excludes the masses.

—John Fiske, "Popular Culture"

Sex is the last taboo in film.

—Catherine Breillat, "Film Goes All the Way"

Today's "meat movie" is tomorrow's blockbuster.

—Carol J. Clover, *Men, Women, and Chain Saws*

NOT ALL FILMMAKERS AND CRITICS agree with John Fiske's assessment of Henry James's impossible—and unpalatable—availability for popularization. Nevertheless, moviegoers rejected three of the millennial films of James's novels, refusing to identify them as popular cultural texts. Whereas *The Wings of the Dove* garnered four Academy Award nominations, after which it opened nationally in multiplex theaters, *The Portrait of a Lady, Washington Square,* and *The Golden Bowl* opened in "selected cities," played for several weeks in university towns and large urban areas, and promptly disappeared from large-screen view.[1] All four films, however, earned remarkably mixed reviews. Stephen Holden called *The Golden Bowl* "handsome, faithful, and intelligent" yet "emotionally distanced" ("Sensibility"); Janet Maslin complained that Campion's *The Portrait of a Lady* "stripped" the "social observation and psychological texture" from James's story (B29); Cynthia Ozick, that it failed to capture

James's rendering of the "gossamer vibrations" of "inner life" (H1, H22). The closing sex scene of *The Wings of the Dove* excited special mention: Daphne Merkin found it "unsettling and unsexy" (122); Philip Horne, "daringly painful" and full of "crude gusto" (89); Dale M. Bauer, a betrayal of "James's sexual subtlety" (247). These comments reveal more about their writers than about the films' qualities, however, for they report largely subjective responses to the movies as measured against memories of the novels. Yet adaptations are never wholly faithful to their literary sources; they must be interpreted, too, as situated within particular cultural formations and historical situations, industrial production and distribution regimes, and new Hollywood filmmakers' careers.

Not the reviews, however, but the films' uneasy position as quality heritage product in a new Hollywood, multinational, coproducing industry accounts for their problematic reception. Moreover, the Henry James filmgoers, like the readers of the novels themselves, have never constituted a mass audience. When she filmed *The Portrait of a Lady*, she was not "trying to win a popularity prize," Jane Campion said. "It's not middle of the road cinema " (quoted in Feinstein 212). Agnieszka Holland filmed a story "impossible" to adapt, *Washington Square*, because she felt a "deeper connection" to James's tales than do "many American directors" (Crnkovic 4). Clearly the female filmmakers of *The Piano*—a surprise hit whose director did not think it "would be nearly that popular"—and of *Europa, Europa* (1990)—a major event in independent cinema due to its focus on a Jewish German soldier during the Holocaust—chose to make these films about nineteenth-century women not solely to further their careers. Indeed, directors know that a series of box-office flops can seriously damage their ability to choose projects, acquire funding in the blockbuster era, and garner the marketing and publicity moneys necessary to appeal to independent filmgoers. Campion explains the director's dilemma: "Don't get me wrong, there's a part of me that wants to be popular too" (*Interviews* 125). Yet popularity at the box office—at least in the 1990s—often eluded directors of heritage film, quality costume drama, or serious melodrama. Adapted for the screen, the films of Henry James's novels deploy these mixed and often feminized genres to entice a female, a bookish male, and a cultured gay spectator to the box office.

The links among literary film, popularity, and mass culture are vexed at best. In his work on popular culture, John Fiske disparages the mass-culture industry for seeking to "incorporate" the people's culture, even as the people "excorporate" the industry's products, for whereas "popular culture is never mass culture, it is always closely bound up with it" (331). Although Fiske idealizes the popular as a site of resistance, the history of mass culture's emergence is crucial to the study of film adaptation, as to popular culture. Late nineteenth-century growth and diversification in the North Atlantic publishing industries made fiction available for mass-cultural production and so for wide popularity. Yet given the demographic and appetitive diversity of the late nineteenth-century audience for books and short fiction and the late twentieth-century taste for films, given the decline in literary reading and independent film consumption at the millennium, popular culture has now virtually eclipsed the highbrow for the general reader (Romano). Whereas James's novels have entered the canon of high-modern, elite culture, their film adaptations' status within a segmented and increasingly transnational and global culture industry might more appropriately be characterized as middlebrow, a problematic cultural category whose industrial functions are unstable and whose institutions are still diversifying. The films of Henry James's novels are not unique in their search for a middlebrow heritage audience; rather, they highlight or foreground the problematic ways that elite culture may be remediated to serve a middlebrow audience in an industry that rigorously exploited niche markets in the 1990s. The films of Jane Austen's novels question whether a film can be faithful to its nineteenth-century original; the films of James's novels inquire whether a heritage film with a high-cultural source text can become popular. In a matrix of cultural forces and industrial relations, the problem of audience segmentation, the growth of commodity culture, and the cultural rage for popularity created a cross-over hit, a "comparative flop," and two modest successes.[2]

Heritage film continues to appropriate classic literary culture to secure a large crossover audience, and Henry James's vexed position as a high-cultural author who sought a general readership makes his work an apt case study for this chapter. Indeed, James's anxiety about his novels' salability attracted filmmakers themselves troubled by what constitutes popularity. James's narrators, moreover, inscribe their narratees as intimate observers of their stories' heroines, reader-voyeurs who spy on sexualized melo-dramas and on cosmopolitan scenarios played out by expatriates, trans-national citizens, and downwardly mobile hangers-on. These scenes entice readers to wonder who is sleeping with whom, whether pleasure accords with desire, whether evidence of the illicit remains hidden or is somehow traceable. James represents his own anxiety about cultural popularity as a heroine's desire for acculturation or consumption of tasteful objects; the films display these cultural goods, which demonstrate their directors' impeccable skill at controlling spectacle, and which flatter their audiences for having shown the good taste to purchase this cultural product. The filmmakers who shoot James's novels often, like their source author, feel anxious about their films' popularity; displaying their auteurism, Holland and Campion shoot films that index their status as art flicks even as they solicit a middlebrow spectator. Other directors in search of the crossover hit shoot James's hinted-at but undramatized sex scenes: James Ivory stages sex as quality costume drama; Iain Softley appropriates the codes of soft-core pornography to mainstream James for the middlebrow marketplace. As a group, these filmmakers have multiple strategies for sexing up James, as they shoot high-cultural novels for a middlebrow, but highly literate, audience.

Henry James and the Middlebrow

Henry James yearned for popularity even as he despised and despaired of achieving it. Although he craved recognition in the "public market of magazines, bookstores, and libraries," Michael Anesko suggests, James was contemptuous of popular-press celebrity. Despite his desire to print, distribute, and sell his books, James modeled "discretion" in his interactions with publishers; he manipulated his status as a transatlantic author so as to publish his tales simultaneously in British and North American periodicals and then, again, to control copyright through the timing of book publication. Knowing his books a commodity, he recommended to other artists that they produce "'vendible [and] *placeable*'" artistic objects; Edith Wharton suspected he had "secretly dreamed of being a 'best-seller'"—a term that had just entered the publishing lexicon (Anesko ix, quotes on 5, 11). James was destined "to affront a publicity" he had the "weakness to loathe," Richard Salmon avers; "if James refused to sever his links with the mass market," however, "equally he wished to maintain his distance from it" (2–13, 76). When *The Bostonians* and *The Princess Casamassima* flopped, he bemoaned to his friend William Dean Howells that after the promising receptions of *Daisy Miller* and *The Portrait of a Lady*, the two new novels had "reduced the desire, and the demand, for my productions to zero—as I judge from the fact that though I have for a good while past been writing a number of good short things, I remain irremediably un-published" (*Letters* 209). In the face of his apparent eclipse, James acted like a modern professional writer dependent on publication for his income: he hired an agent, a newly created cultural intermediary; sought the buzz and applause of a live theatrical audience—an endeavor at which he failed spectacularly; retreated to Rye as a "reclusive author," shrewdly sensing that "being unpopular . . . had a cachet of its own."[3] In the face of the "devouring *publicity* of life," James bemoaned that, for the modern author, both personal life and professional work were objects on display for public scrutiny.[4] James's struggle with the problem of publicity, of selling the products of a soon-to-be-residual elite culture, was not his individual problem. Historically situated at the moment when professionalism was booming, its discourse consolidating, and mass culture emerging, when the book business was diversifying and the author becoming a modern businessperson, when the institutionalization and "sacralization" of culture had begun to elevate once simultaneously popular and elite cultural forms (such as opera), James had to invent himself as author and in relation to his readership without historical precedent (Strychacz 5–22; Levine 85–168). Given his profound ambivalence about commodified culture and the "vulgarized" market for novels, James acknowledged, in *The Art of the Novel*, that he had sought to educate a "general reader." Yet his contemporaries—Joseph Conrad and E. M. Forster, Virginia Woolf and Gertrude Stein, Ezra Pound and T. S. Eliot—cared little for such readers, seeking to locate literature as the elite cultural product James himself paradoxically produced.

In the late nineteenth and early twentieth centuries, a general reader—an intelligent, well-educated book buyer seeking absorption, pleasure, and intellectual stimulation—was being fashioned by the bookselling industry. The significant growth in commercial publishing, Janice Radway maintains, occurred when "changes in manufacturing" and in the "organization of the market economy were consolidated" and when, in addition, "complex technologies and new transportation methods" enabled extension of markets and commercial enterprises (*Books* 130). After the advent of railroads and the development of machine-driven print technologies at midcentury, cheap book production and dissemination fueled the rise of newspapers in the United States, the emergence of the "employee-writer," the "proactive editor," and a "book readers could use"(133, 136); in Britain, the cheap periodical, part issue, triple-decker, and magazine serial (Feltes 57–64). As Radway and N. N. Feltes demonstrate, new definitions of book, author, and reader challenged notions of intellectual property and the functions of cultural work, as writers and publishers struggled over control of the new commodity-book's ownership. As the fiction market again exploded in the 1870s, Shumway claims that literature became the "bearer of class-identified taste, national tradition, and 'aesthetic' relief from increasingly rationalized labor" (35). In the twentieth century, institutions such as the Book-of-the-Month Club began to sell the "literary book" and to serve an educated generalist readership, Radway says, even as modern literary criticism developed to police and consolidate a "new high literary zone" (*Books* 137, 140). Despite critics' contentions that the club "promoted passivity and a decline in taste among the reading public," its advertising tapped "modern anxiety about the self" to create "'book enthusiasts'" and "'sell the reading idea'" even as the book-selecting experts created a "new *kind* of cultural commodity" for a growing mass-consumer society in which it was still nevertheless important to "become 'cultured'" (Rubin 97, 99, 104, 103, 104). Although James's novels and tales entered high culture, as an author he sought to serve the same "average intelligent" reader the Book-of-the-Month Club would later cultivate.

Middlebrow culture is an early twentieth-century invention aligned with the emergence of new cultural institutions and intermediaries. Radway and Lawrence Napper link the term's emergence to the rise of radio: the term came to prominence in Britain during the 1920s mass communications and media expansions; in 1925, *Punch* associated it with the BBC's 1922 remit to deliver high culture to the British middle classes (*Books* 219; Napper 111–12). As a "monopoly funded by licence fees," Napper notes, the newly constituted BBC "address[ed] the whole nation," was "answerable to the state," "protect[ed] the nation from the excesses of American market forces," and served a mission culturally to educate the British citizenry. This middlebrow media institution and its aesthetic "'divided the general educated audience from the high intelligentsia,'" Napper notes, members of whom consumed high culture rather than its bestseller cousins or remediated versions (111–13). Joan Rubin links the middlebrow's U.S. emergence with not only radio but also developments in book selling and advertising, the "higher journalism," and "great books" curricula. Emerging nineteenth-century notions of "genteel culture" sought to link elites with generalists in an effort to educate the masses, to instill a "taste for good reading" (10–13, 15–21). Culture had become simultaneously "accessible to anyone" and so vulgarized or standardized, as writers, reviewers, and other tastemakers sought to accommodate "a variety of needs" in a changing cultural climate (29–33, 143–44).

In the 1920s and 1930s, cultural gatekeepers, producers, and consumers debated the merits of the middlebrow. Balancing the cultural demands of critics and the government against those of a mass audience, 1920s British filmmakers chose to appeal to "the tastes of the new suburban middle classes" that had emerged as the service and knowledge sectors expanded to produce the professional-managerial middle class (Napper 115). During the 1930s, Sue Harper notes, popular and middlebrow reviewers and their readers debated the quality, verisimilitude, and pleasures of historical and costume film. The middlebrow debates were surely informed by the work of F. R. Leavis and the *Scrutiny* group, Harper argues, whose pronouncements about the "ennobling effects of high culture" and invectives against popular culture reached a wide audience of educated readers; in response, highbrow gatekeepers bashed costume drama as sentimental and historically anachronistic (63, 59, 72). Even as the middlebrow critical position consolidated in the mid- to late 1930s around the values of historical accuracy, realism, and "moral improvement of the masses," the mass audience continued to demand pictorial pleasure: hence the wild popularity of Gainsborough bodice rippers (Harper 56–63).

Aimed at a later generation of the middlebrow audience, the millennial adaptations of James's novels solicited a general yet intelligent cultural consumer as spectator. All sought to become popular, to cross over from the independent or art-house sector to mainstream box-office success. The crossover film, Higson argues, "plays a key role in broadening the appeal of the art-house sector" and thus enjoys a privileged position with independent producers (*Heritage* 102, 123–27). Whereas films made for discriminating audiences of educated, often urban, consumers do not make "big money," independent filmmakers can recover their costs and make modest profits through crossover success, even as they experiment with noncommercial products (Sklar 293–95). Heritage films appeal to an older, middle-class, professional audience, yet, in addition, they seek to attract the "relatively youthful audience that constitutes the mainstream core" (Higson, *Heritage* 105).

The James novels seem tailored to serve this upscale yet crossover middlebrow market. Full of eroticized perversity, innocent female victimage, and familial or marital distress, these stories seem culturally and historically transportable—as relevant to and usable by late twentieth-century as late nineteenth-century audiences, if updated and adapted for changing sexual mores and increasingly sophisticated tastes. Whereas James's readers' desires were aroused by the texts' highly nuanced and psychologically complex narratorial situations, the films' spectators' desires get gratified by mise-en-scène and montage, by visualized spectacles of masculine abuse, female ruination or manipulation, and sexual spoliation. In the decade of feel-good art-house blockbusters, even the educated cultural consumer might (and did) choose the upbeat, post-Thatcherite *The Full Monty* (1997) and, in the first decade of the new century, the sentimentalized *Amélie* (2001) over the ironic and only slightly perverse *Washington Square* or the heritage costume drama *The Golden Bowl.* The art-house filmgoer, once a member of a specialized but highly coherent audience, now had a range of options as consumer within a parallel media marketplace. As the "independent-supplier" segment of the industry—in video and cinema—sought to "adapt to shifting retailer buying patterns," the "higher-profile" art film competed not only with A-list films but also with B-movies, big box-office foreign films, and other genre titles (Wilson 1, 8). As a variety of products became available for a once-coherent market, competition for the intelligent generalist's cultural dollar intensified.

The social function of middlebrow culture continues to become more complex as print culture declines and new media of all kinds expand their market position. As I argued in chapter 1, Pierre Bourdieu's belief that a hierarchy of the arts corresponds to a class hierarchy of its consumers neglects that, despite the belief that the class standing and economic status of the family provide the situation and disposition to acquire legitimate taste, taste no longer functions necessarily as a marker of class (*Distinction* 1–17). Given the century-long expansion of the North Atlantic middle class and the increasingly diversified cultural menu of American baby boomers and their offspring, cultural consumption no longer may be mapped directly onto class (Cannadine, *Class* 190; Kammen 254; Rubin 101). Yet as Radway indicates, high-cultural critics still rank the middlebrow pleasures enjoyed by the ever-growing new middle class as, by definition, "suspect" (*Books* 321). Whereas high-culture consumers practice the skills of aesthetic detachment and interpretation, popular-culture consumers seek immediately usable and disposable material; the middlebrow consumer, however, seeks cultural knowledge even as she or he hopes to experience the pleasures of attentive absorption. If the text chosen is narrative, this consumer enjoys identifying with the character(s) and indulging a taste for romance or fidelity aesthetics, taking satisfaction in the process of consuming. Ironically, the middlebrow cultural consumer chooses primarily what has been widely consumed by others and so already popularized (*Books* 323–28).

The films of James's novels gratified middlebrow pleasures even as they sought to provide cultural expertise. The film adaptations of classic novels or dramas that crowded the 1990s cultural marketplace served much as did the popularized classics peddled by the Book-of-the-Month Club in the 1920s through 1940s: they nurtured "middle-class longings for the prestige conferred by familiarity with high culture," created around the consumer the "aura of art," and confirmed the "status of the cultured self" (Radway, *Books* 321). Like the readers of the Book-of-the-Month Club selections, the consumers of the James films might present themselves as educated individuals by showing that they knew—or seemed to know—classic literary texts renowned for their intellectual and motivational complexity and for the difficulty they posed to the reader. Yet millennial viewers of *The Portrait of a Lady, Washington Square, The Wings of the Dove,* or *The Golden Bowl* need not have read the books to know the classics. Heritage filmgoers might be specialist or nonspecialist consumers (readers or nonreaders); they did not need, as Holland suggested of American directors, to know much James, if any. Nevertheless, the Henry James heroines who themselves sought acculturation as a way to confirm their status, taste, and marriageability appealed to the middlebrow filmgoer in search of quality pleasures and cultural expertise.

Middlebrow acculturation, everywhere modeled in James's novels, educates taste even as it provides consumers relaxation, gratification, amusement, and entertainment. Seeking to reach a generally educated yet discriminating reader who bought books to acquire culture and enjoy the pleasure of immersion, James's novels fashioned themselves as cultural capital. These novels anticipated their own popularity, their remediation onstage, if not screen: calling attention to their marital scenes and their romance scenarios as mise-en-scènes, the James novels fashioned their reader as spectator. Shaping narratees as discriminating observers, the James narrator solicits his own remediation; it should not surprise us, then, that he later becomes embodied in Alistair Cooke who, narrating the BBC's *Golden Bowl,* talks to the spectator about the pleasures of watching and interpreting.

Discriminating Observers

James's novels insist upon the centrality to fiction of seeing, knowing, and spectatorship. His earliest narrators speak to narratees as, by analogy, the author speaks to his readers—as befits a writer eager to educate a generally intelligent reader into appreciating high-cultural fiction. In a book specifically about taste, acculturation, tourism, and culture as both business and prostitution, Christopher Newman, the gauche American, "'wants the biggest kind of entertainment a man can get'" (*The American* 24).[5] In *The Europeans,* an old-country woman sets out to "see the world," hoping to sell herself as a charming commodity on the new-world marriage market, as suitors become "entertainer[s]," Puritan mansions "museum[s], and "'queer Bostonian[s]'" sexual "'amuse[rs]'"(155, 107, 145). In these pendant novels, published in 1877 and 1878 respectively, narrators poke fun at their heroes' and heroines' bad taste in art and in sexual partners. Here, the narrator inscribes and determines his narratee's act of seeing and of judging character as a mode of educating the reader: "You would have perceived," he states, that "our hero . . . had not a high tone"; "you would not have pronounced" Gertrude Wentworth "especially pretty" (*The American* 65; *The Europeans* 46). While denigrating his protagonists, James's narrator hails the narratee, reader, and "observer" as "attentive," "discerning," or "discriminating" (*The Europeans* 33, 35; *The American* 3).

Ready for adaptation for the big and small screen, James's print-cultural products frame and construct seeing as a mode of knowing. So as better to present hero or heroine, the narrator presents them as looking through or being looked at through frames and windows or other characters' perceptions. The Sunday morning on which, the narrator remembers, he first saw her, Eugenia "stood at the window of her little drawing-room, watching the long arm of a rose tree" that she wished her own (*The Europeans* 151). Eugenia's long gaze around Robert Acton's house recalls Elizabeth Bennet's at Pemberley. "Looking about" in a mood of "curious contemplation," she admires the staircase landing, window with plants, afternoon light, endless hallway, and Oriental rug: *"Comme c'est bien!"* she murmurs, as James identifies seeing as a metaphoric desire to possess (168). Framed in the text, Eugenia presents herself for a spectator's look; looking herself, she makes the spectator look with her.

In this early fictional relay of looks, characters know themselves watched even as they watch others. When she strolls in Boston, Eugenia is "conscious of much admiring observation" by "nice-looking people" to whom, the narrator notes, a "distinguished" woman "could not be an object of indifference" (43). Gertrude and Eugenia imagine their social function as to-be-looked-at; unmarried females "'don't know who may be observing'" them and must thus be always "'on . . . guard'" (48). When Acton returns from Newport, the narrator constructs a complex relay of figural looks as an invitation to seduction:

> He stood in her little garden; the long window of her parlour was open, and he could see the white curtains, with the lamp-light shining through them. . . . There was a sort of excitement in the idea of seeing Madame Munster again; he became aware that his heart was beating rather faster than usual. . . . [He] went along the piazza and, approaching the open window, tapped upon its lintel with his stick. He could see the Baroness within; she was standing in the middle of the room. She came to the window and pulled aside the curtain; then she stood looking at him a moment. (141–42)

Ironically, Acton here stumbles into a sexual scenario that stages a threesome, as he hears but does not see another man stumble offstage. Yet "the *mise en scène*," the proscenium on which Eugenia shall perform her story of marital disgrace to solicit a proposal, fails to provide her a happy ending (45). Nevertheless, this scene of exchanged looks faithfully finds its way into Merchant Ivory's *The Europeans* (1979), a film that, like the other films of James's tales, exploits the structure of the look to depict eroticized scenarios.

James's narrator entices his discriminating-observer narratee and, by analogy, James's reader, into a dangerous high-cultural milieu: the emergent modern world of dysfunctional marriages and international cosmopolitanism. Ralph Touchett is perhaps the perfect "cosmopolite"— he's "'a little of everything and not much of any,'" Henrietta Stackpole slyly defines; Mrs. Touchett is the perfect "American absentee," the "amiable colonist" of Florentine and Parisian metropolitan cultures (*The Portrait of a Lady* 81, 183). Indeed, cosmopolitanism and acculturation are intimately linked in these mid- and late-career novels, for each portrays an American girl, fresh from provincial Albany, New York, or other eastern U.S. city, who is wooed by an authentically or inauthentically acculturated cosmopolitan, European, or Europeanized man. Although the American girl's marital choice may thus earn her the distinction and prestige of a highly cultured metropolitan husband, her destiny is sealed by her inability to distinguish the hanger-on expatriate from the legitimately cultured man—or by her national naiveté and refusal to care for the difference. Isabel Archer's rejection of Lord Warburton's marriage proposal horrifies her uncle and fascinates Ralph Touchett; Catherine Sloper's European tour doubles her value on the marriage market despite her desire to wed a man with "luxurious tastes [but] scanty resources" (*Washington Square* 151). Although Milly Theale's accidental and equivocal escape from the marital clutches of Kate Croy and Merton Densher produces the transcendent aura at which acculturation aims, the dove must die, leaving her memory to haunt Merton and incapacitate him for marriage to Kate. Already acculturated, cosmopolitan expatriates, Maggie Verver and her father, Adam, demonstrate the dangers and perversity of cosmopolitan marital speculation.

Still, James's narratorial stance toward his characters and their stories, his contact with his reader and his delegate, whether character or narratee, is vexed at best. James Buzard describes James's paradoxical disparaging of and imaginative participation in his characters' acculturational projects as demanding from the reader a "vacillation between irony and investment" (225). *The Portrait of a Lady*'s narrator's tone resembles Ralph Touchett's "loose-fitting urbanity," an attitude that covers over sinister wisdom with a kind of metropolitan hospitality (234). The narrator's insouciant take on Isabel's character—her theories, her imagination, her desire for knowledge, her belief in her own finer mind and sensitivity—imperceptibly slips, via free indirect discourse, into representations of Isabel's very theories, imaginings, and misreadings of herself and others; he elegantly invokes, enjoys, and pillories the high-class social buzz of perceptions and rumors about Isabel's learning and culture. The reader, charmed by Isabel's ambitions and seduced by the subtleties of free indirect discourse, soon neglects the insistent repetitions of the narrator's seemingly sympathetic yet judgment-ridden prose. *Washington Square*'s narrator, somewhat less sophisticated than the narrator of *The Portrait of a Lady*, repeatedly reminds us that he's telling a tale, acknowledging the "awkward confession[s]" he must "make about [his] heroine": she's a romp, a glutton, a "commonplace child" (34–35). Yet that last observation belongs, through indirect discourse, to Catherine's father, onto whom the narrator often displaces his disparagement. Sloper "almost never addressed his daughter save in the ironical form," the narrator admits, and when locked in combat with her over her choice of husband, Sloper—and the narrator—takes pleasure in the "prospect of entertainment" she provides (46, 126).

James's narrators seduce readers into desiring intimate figural knowledge precisely as a form of entertainment. Each American girl is "our heroine"; Isabel Archer or Catherine Sloper performs for us, as we idealize her innocence but come to disdain her unknowingly self-displayed ignorance. Addressing her as "poor girl," the narrator patronizingly portrays Catherine as helpless and victimized, Isabel as spoiled egoist. Ralph, our author's delegate in *The Portrait of a Lady*, sympathizes with Isabel's unhappiness even as he patronizes her: her masked and mechanical look; the serenity painted on her face; her function as "advertisement" for a happy marriage, as "representation" for Gilbert Osmond and his desires. Having coaxed and flattered us into admiration of and pity for our figural friends, however, the narrator next makes us participants in their suffering. Just as Ralph pities "'poor Isabel'" and Isabel "'poor Lord Warburton!'" our narrator condescends to "poor Ralph," whose role as the "humorous invalid" makes his "disabilities . . . part of the general joke." But "we, who know more about poor Ralph than his cousin," become accomplices in condescension, in desiring secret knowledge of who's slept with whom, who's slapped whom, who can't perform in the bedroom (*The Portrait of a Lady* 249, 285–86). As James's novel raises the question of intimacy's connection to deception, his complicit reader soon longs to know whether Isabel is as unhappy as all her friends think her; whether Osmond is really brutal; whether Madame Merle is his lover and Pansy's mother, as the reader suspects long before Isabel is told so.

In *The Wings of the Dove*, how we know and see, and so value and desire, others determines the complex and unstable quality of intimacy. Milly, who "work[s]" on her associates' sympathy, curiosity, and fancy, can only be known to us "by feeling their impression and sharing, if need be, their confusion" about her. Like Susan Stringham, we fall under the "spell of watching her": we track, pounce, spy, and scientifically inspect Milly; our watching, like Susan's, is a "way of clinging to the girl," of taking pleasure in her comeliness. As Susan looks into an Alpine view of great beauty, sees her friend sitting at ease on the dizzying edge (much as does Ivory's Catherine Sloper), a thousand thoughts roar in her ears, a commotion that "left our observer intensely still and holding her breath": it's a site and a sight of intimate solitude, of mortality (*The Wings of the Dove* 130–35). Moreover, we know our figural friends through sights we imagine others have seen of them. After her visit to Sir Luke Strett, Milly waits for Kate's visit; she watches from the balcony as Kate arrives, and "a mute exchange, but with smiles and nods, took place between them on what had occurred in the morning." Milly suddenly sees, moreover, that the splendid and handsome image Kate presents to her "was the peculiar property of somebody else's vision," that the "fine freedom" she shows Milly she has also shown Merton Densher; "it struck our young woman as absurd," the narrator notes, that "a girl's looking so to a man could possibly be without connexions." Like most events or dialogues in this novel, the narrator confesses, these scenes "lasted less than our account of them." Yet only the narrative stretch that James everywhere practices as narratorial strategy in *The Wings of the Dove* can represent the "vibration" of impression and intimacy (219–20).

As this discursive structure of impression and intimacy demonstrates, knowledge and desire are always mediated by a third in James's novels. *The Golden Bowl* articulates seeing and knowing through a discerning observer, through metaphors of seeing as revelation. Adam Verver and Maggie exchange looks at Fawns, when daughter realizes father is being pursued by the Miss Lutches and Mrs. Rance. Adam sees "the look in his daughter's eyes," a "look with which he *saw* her take in" the pursuit and his acquiescence (112–13). Fanny Assingham, the author's delegate, and the third, tells Adam that she "'*saw*'" the Misses' and Mrs.' "'consciousness'" and so understood their sense of Charlotte's womanly charm; "'I see, I see,'" Adam responds (143–44; emphasis in original). A "vast expanse of *discovery*," a "hallucination," a "vision" strangely revealed that, as a father, Adam had to marry Charlotte so Maggie would seem not to have forsaken him (153–54; emphasis in original). James's ironizing discourse presents Adam's knowledge as produced solely through the mediating observation of the third. After Amerigo's return from Matcham, he and Maggie act the part of a couple, but a third hovers, haunts. Suddenly, "light flashed" and "spread," as Maggie realizes that Amerigo's cue to act as husband comes not from her but from Charlotte. "They had a view of her [own] situation," she knows, the impression of which remains, a "witness" to their having "kept [her] in position so as not to *dis*arrange them" (328–31; emphasis in original). Later, "before her glass," "recognitions flash at her" as Maggie recognizes that Adam married for *her,* and that, to keep her husband, she must sacrifice her father without his knowing it (357–59). Here, father and daughter see and suddenly know about seduction, mimetic desire, mediation by the observation of a third. But a foursome demands a doubled third, and by novel's end, Maggie knows she has seen more than she bargained for.

The American girl's acculturation, then, occurs in metropolitan set-tings that invoke sexual predation, triangulation, and sadomasochistic pain—as though cosmopolitan culture were grounded on perversion. In each story, we see the American girl's manipulation by a friend, aunt, or parent; observe efforts to secure or transmit a dying girl's, father's, or uncle's inheritance; and watch sadistic sexual or marital relations. In *The Wings of the Dove,* Merton and Milly guard each other at the game of intimacy, "she knowing he tried to keep her in tune with his conception, and he knowing she thus knew it. Add that he again knew she knew, and yet that nothing was spoiled by it, and we get a fair impression of the line they found most completely workable" (412). Merton's displacement of female narratorial delegates distances Milly from Kate's, Susan's, and Maud's manipulations of her; suffused with Milly's sacrificial aura, they, like we, tolerate and enjoy her hurt and pain even as we, like Merton, excuse ourselves from responsibility for it. The third's figural authority but discursive invisibility exposes the structure of sadism in *Washington Square,* for masculine aggression is everywhere on display, even if denied or displaced. As Catherine is sacrificed by her father, the narrator exhibits and imaginatively enjoys her suffering, as do we: Sloper threatens to aban-don his daughter on an Alpine cliff; she denies that dad might choke her; feeling a "vicious" and "cruel" desire to "abuse somebody," Morris thrusts the figurative "sacrificial knife" into Lavinia's hand (154, 175, 157). (Toward the film's end, Catherine lies face down in the street, abjected.) In *The Golden Bowl,* Maggie's sad sense of her marriage's limitations, Char-lotte's desperate misery at her enslavement, Fanny Assingham's social sur-vival, all provide the reader knowing despair. Engaged by the narrator and secured within the narrative contract, the reader is full of desire to know more about these characters whose passions and perversions she's begun to fathom, wants to witness sadistic hurts even as she distances herself from her own complicity. This is high-cultural aesthetic pleasure at its best.

Yet James's characters' deceptions and manipulations, the narrators' condescension toward and pitying of their fragile virtues and inevitable missteps, may appear unattractive to the millennial reader. In *The Portrait of a Lady*, the narrator rhetorically generalizes Isabel's misfortunes by taking Ralph as his delegate. "Poor human-hearted Isabel, what perversity had bitten her?" he wonders ruefully, even as he "recognize[s]"— and identifies with, makes us a party to—Osmond's abuse (331). Isabel's portraitured happiness, moreover, represents marital unhappiness in general; "You could criticise any marriage," Isabel imagines Ralph imagining of her engagement and rationalizing her response; "it was the essence of marriage to be open to criticism" (286). Generalizing this criticism of marriage out of the novel and into the world, the narrator implicates the reader in this perverse structure, makes us aware of our own posed and sham happiness, our own complicity. We, too, have become condescending, patronizing, cynical cosmopolites; we, too, have been bitten by perversity. How bored and mildly entertained are we by these unhappy marriages! Appalled and fascinated, we can't put the novel down.

Spectatorship is the operative metaphor for this complex and complicitous, high-cultural narratorial contract. The Jamesian narrator has a "taste for the *mise-en-scène*," Buzard quips; viewing others as actors and himself as mere member of the audience, the narrator senses that "the job of director might suit him better" than does storytelling (264). In *The Wings of the Dove*, Merton finds himself reduced to "mere spectatorship" during Kate's "beautiful entrance": Maud's "managerial" look at her protégé, from head to foot; Kate's self-presentation as "distinguished actress" who can "dress," walk, look, speak, and in every way "express . . . the part"; his own "purchase of stall," all identify Kate as staged and presented—but as valuable, merchandised, commodified (271–72). In *The Portrait of a Lady*, the scene before Isabel's long meditative vigil inscribes her act of spectatorship: she receives "an impression," watches from the threshold a "sort of familiar silence," a "freedom" between old friends: "the thing made an image, lasting only a moment, like a sudden flicker of light. [Osmond's and Merle's] relative positions, their absorbed mutual gaze, struck her as something detected. But it was all over by the time she had fairly seen it" (342–43).

This scene of spectatorship is a cinematic moment that flickers, then cuts to another frame. It's a scenario: a staged show that accumulates significance and invokes sexualized, retrospectively reconstructed, knowledge. Although Isabel fails to read this scenario rightly, we are less "innocent[ly] ignorant" than she (*The Portrait of a Lady* 451). We, too, have been spectators, and—partially because we've witnessed other scenes of seduction—we immediately conclude that these two are lovers. Some readers may long to see more scenes of Isabel's misery. Some may wish to witness an explosion: physical violence, marital abuse, sadomasochistic acts to match the sexual asides, maneuverings, and manipulations. Some may yearn to see Isabel sleep with Lord Warburton, who hangs around Pansy because he's still smitten with her stepmother; or with Caspar Goodwood, who seems to have given up his exemplary American business out of passion for a woman who spurns him. Some readers may be disappointed when treated, instead, to the cold sneers and silent treatments of a merely unhappy marriage—even if it is a massively failed coupling between the American girl and a charismatic, narcissistic aesthete.

As millennial filmmakers intuitively knew, Henry James's novels seem made for the big screen. Their spectatorial narrations, layered structures of knowledge, and complicit readers enable the directors of *The Portrait of a Lady, Washington Square, The Wings of the Dove,* and *The Golden Bowl* to depict James's narratorial contract even as they hope to satisfy filmgoers accustomed to the middlebrow pleasures of absorption and identification. As films diversified and niche markets emerged, directors and advertisers alike adopted the single product/multiple market formula, which enabled films to reach wider audiences, including PG-13 and NC-17 viewers variously familiar with sexual content. Campion's and Holland's films about an American girl's acculturation mix middlebrow with quality pleasures, yet their films also index their directors' auteuristic and artistic appropriations of James, thus limiting their box-office popularity. As John Carlos Rowe notes, "advance publicity, celebrity casting and expensive production budgets" identify all the 1990s James films as "intended" to cross over to a mainstream audience (210). Campion, whose *The Portrait of a Lady* was a modest independent success, and Holland, whose art-house film was not, both repurpose nineteenth-century stories about women, marriage, and money to thematize the filmmaker's wish for box-office business and so popularity. These heroines' fascination with acculturation, then, identifies them with the professional middle class even as it aligns them with high-cultural aspirations and so separates them from middlebrow pleasures.

Cultured Spectators, Tasteful Objects

The American girl in Europe stands in for the middlebrow cultural consumer, who seeks expert guidance, knowledge, and culture but may not know authentic from inauthentic acculturation. She or he wants, with Isabel, desperately to "know something of human affairs"; with Catherine, to tour but not perversely to display her cultural ignorance to others; with Milly, to sate her starvation for art, and so to become an acculturated woman herself, capable of receiving impulses and impressions, becoming acquainted with the classics: to acquire cultural and social capital (*The Portrait of a Lady* 143; *Washington Square* 125; *The Wings of the Dove* 244). Unlike James's novels, which portray the narrator/narratee relationship as homosocial and clubby, these films solicit a female spectator and, thus, allow heroines to look. "Have you called me here to look at you?" Morris (Ben Chaplin) asks Catherine (Jennifer Jason Leigh) testily; "I did want to look at you," she confesses; "you're beautiful." When the woman looks, Linda Williams theorizes, she challenges her role as to-be-looked-at and threatens to become monstrous—as Sloper believes Catherine to be. Yet the spectator, too, looks at this gorgeous man, hoping, with her, that he wants not Catherine's fortune but her love. Although James's male protagonists appeal to book readers, Hollywood seems to say, only the American girl appeals to middlebrow movie consumers. Purchasing a ticket to *The Portrait of a Lady, The Wings of the Dove, The Golden Bowl,* or *Washington Square, Daisy Miller,* or *The Europeans,* the spectator buys a cultural product that portrays acculturation as a marital value for females. It is a critical commonplace that heritage film, costume drama, and melodrama address a feminine, although not necessarily female, audience, as gay men, bookish men, *and* women indulge in middlebrow quality pleasures (Vincendeau xx; Dyer, *Queers* 204–28).

For movie spectators, these films may indulge sadomasochistic desires. Campion's *The Portrait of a Lady,* in particular, pictures abusive sexual scenes of all kinds. After Lord Warburton leaves Florence, the spectator's wish to see a fight gets gratified, as Campion's mise-en-scène visualizes the marital violence James's novel refuses to show. Such scenes violate James's sexual restraint and so please late-century audiences accustomed, since the 1970s emergence of new Hollywood film, to seeing at least simulated sex on screen. Shot in the film's pervasive cold blue light, with a virtually chiaroscuro palette, the scene's style is gothic, complete with mansion, walls shot in canted frame. The action: a marital dispute in which a husband accuses his wife of humiliating him. As Osmond (John Malkovich) strides into the darkened drawing room, he grasps and piles pillows, then grabs and deposits Isabel (Nicole Kidman) on top of them, as though she were a bad daughter and he a chastising father. Isabel's figure is shot in parts, as an index of the violated, morselized body she might well become: the camera tilts up from her hands, corseted waist, and swinging handbag, over her slightly bared bosom and chokered throat to her face; zooms in on her torso, virtually slasher style, as Osmond forces her to stay put. Campion shoots his hand over hers and, as Osmond holds her black glove, cuts to Isabel's face and we hear, almost before we see, the glove slap her. Same shot/reverse shot structure of hand and face: close-up of Osmond and Isabel arguing; cut to a high-angle shot of Osmond's feet as he crosses an Oriental rug to his wife's figure—and trips her. The high-angle shot of her crouching on the black-and-white floor as he stands over her, the room seemingly lit through a draped and gauze-covered window fronted with a giant black candelabrum, portrays this visualized marital violence as virtually vampiristic, as a matter of power rather than sexuality. Indeed, this scene's metaphors and implicit thematics—paternal rage, fetishized and fragmented female body, corset and glove—articulate sex and violence. When Isabel stands, smoke rises behind her; Osmond grasps her arm again, and, aggressively nuzzling her cheek, moves slowly and malevolently toward a kiss, then disgustedly turns aside. This sadistic scene visually updates James for the 1990s, incorporating hints of slasher and vampire flicks into its scenario of female helplessness and masculine brutality. The viewer watches these acts with a certain Jamesian "unpleasant fascination," a feeling enhanced—if the spectator has read James—by knowing this scene is a result of updating and genre mixing (*The Portrait of a Lady* 449).

As a heroine who chooses her husband unwisely, yet, unlike millennial women, has few chances to leave him, James's Isabel is a representative modern wife. Although James wrote his novel well after the British Matrimonial Causes Act of 1857 and during the debate about the 1882 Married Women's Property Act, he understood that changes in the divorce law did not produce immediate social or ideological change. After midcentury, the separated or deserted woman, defined legally as *feme sole,* had equity rights over her property, but married women did not—and, in Henry James's awful irony, Isabel brought to her marriage a "fortune" to which she now has no right. "'He married me for the money,'" she confesses to Ralph, in the novel's most intimate scene (*The Portrait of a Lady* 478). The 1857 act, moreover, preserved the inequality of grounds on which to sue for divorce (Poovey, *Uneven* 84): men could sue for simple adultery, women only for "aggravated" adultery (which necessitated acts of incest, bigamy, desertion, or cruelty)—and, in another Jamesian irony, Gilbert Osmond has given up adultery and, in the novel, is not physically cruel. In the heterogeneous United States, however, divorce was less rigorously regulated—by church, civil, or judicial law—than it was in England. Protestant settlements had formulated divorce laws during the colonial period; some colonies and states allowed legislative divorce well into the nineteenth century; informal marriage had become an established legal institution. The western frontier states, moreover, took a laissez-faire approach to divorce; there, "by 1860, migratory divorce was already part of the American scene" (Glendon 34). Indeed, the western states' liberality caused a "divorce mill panic," which in the 1880s created increasing pressure for legal reform (Riley 108–29). All told, the U.S. divorce rate has been historically higher than that for other industrialized nations and has risen in every decade since the Civil War (Goode 16). Several decades into the twentieth century, England remained largely a "non-divorcing society," and, despite more liberal laws, divorce in the United States was still a "relatively uncommon event" (Stone 383–90; Glendon 198).

James would have known about the American divorce controversy personally: Henry James Sr., Horace Greeley, and the free love advocate Stephen Pearl Andrews had debated the question of indissoluble marriage in the *New York Tribune* between November 1852 and February 1853. James's father argued for the availability of divorce, which served the "'manifest public welfare'"; Andrews, against legal bonds; Greeley, for the indissolubility of marriage (Riley 72). But the controversy was international as well. As a self-consciously transatlantic writer, James locates *The Portrait of a Lady*'s unhappy couple in Italy—alienated Americans in a Roman Catholic country, parent and stepmother to a second-generation American expatriate girl who has been convent educated, brought up by Italian nuns rather than by the unknown-to-her Frenchified yet American expatriate mother. These wandering cosmopolites live as outsiders in a country that, because Catholic, confirms their own perverse yet permanent marital commitment. "'Leave your husband before . . . your character gets spoiled,'" the modern American journalist Henrietta implores. "'With the off-hand way in which you speak of a woman's leaving her husband,'" Isabel responds, "'it's easy to see you've never had one!'" (417–18).

Isabel's story, as culturally useful to 1990s as to 1880s wives, is transportable across historical periods, narrative media, and national boundaries to address altered social circumstances. Millennial anxiety about the failures of marriage and the family as social institutions, moreover, helped to mobilize filmmakers' appropriation of James's novels. Although set at English country houses and Italian Renaissance mansions, the film remediates a story about the unhappy but civilized Jamesian couple that comments on contemporary dysfunctional partnership and the perceived problem of women's right to marital property. James's novel demonstrates the shift in sexual, marital, and reproductive ideologies that made it historically possible to scrutinize the links among gender, marriage, and property ownership. And the debates about divorce and women's property in the British Parliament were nothing if not shrill. In 1857, conservative members worried that the possibility of divorce would make citizens think marriage no more valuable than "'connubial concubinage'"; in 1870, that a divorced woman's right to her property would "'subvert the principle on which the marriage relation had hitherto stood'" (quoted in Shanley, "Rights" 366; Shanley, *Feminism* 73). By 1882, when fears of unrestrained sexuality among women and the poor had largely subsided, the government joined in sponsoring the bill, which passed with little acrimonious exchange (Shanley, *Feminism* 115–30).

It is not surprising that filmmakers would repurpose this 1880s novel about a married woman's property to address the pervasive 1990s fear that marriage and the family were in crisis. This sense of peril created shrill cries from across the political spectrum: that "deadbeat dads" who failed to pay alimony or child support should be jailed (they still are, in Michigan), that kids demonized or overidealized stepparents, that divorce irrevocably harmed children and should be made more difficult to attain (Chambers; Wallerstein and Kelly). David R. Shumway's otherwise thoughtful analysis of the rhetorics and ideologies of romance and intimacy takes as a given that there is, in fact, a "crisis in marriage," since between 1867 and 1929 the U.S. population increased by 300 percent, the number of marriages by 400 percent, and the divorce rate by 2000 percent (23). These seem like alarming numbers, yet they must be historically and demographically contextualized to be meaningful.

The sense of doom that surrounded divorce in the 1990s was exacerbated by gender and economic anxieties. Female economic independence and new legal definitions of marital property—such as pensions, medical insurance, career assets, and entitlements to company goods and services—seemed to endanger previously stable middle-class property-holding patterns. The 1970s invention of no-fault divorce in California, moreover, made divorce available to the masses; some states' adoption of "community property" as defining ownership of marital goods and most courts' practice of "equitable" distribution of such properties at dissolution has made divorce thinkable, especially for wives (Weitzman 110–42). Nevertheless, social historians who balance the divorce rate against statistics of marital longevity have contextualized the 1990s sense of crisis with demographic and mortality statistics. "Among currently marrying cohorts," only 40 to 50 percent will remain married after they've reached the age of fifty; given lengthened human longevity, however, marriages are neither more perishable nor of shorter duration at the millennium than they were in the nineteenth century (Goode 16; Glendon 194–95; Sweet and Bumpass 172–210). As Andrew Cherlin says, "For the first time in our nation's history, more marriages [now end] every year in divorce than in death" (309). Whereas a 1990s wife might find ending an abusive marriage as difficult as would have Isabel, her access to legal options, economic rights, and institutional supports would have made separation infinitely more likely.

Campion's film thus addresses the millennial problem of marriage and divorce, introducing into James's story the middlebrow pleasures that enable spectators to identify more fully with his characters. While the opening credits roll, unseen Australian women talk in voice-over about their sexual pleasure: the addiction to "being entwined with each other" that, at first fulfilling, becomes "negative"; the seeking a "mirror" so "loyal" that it reflects one's own image. A sequence of shots in both color and in black and white then portrays women of many ages and races, dressed in 1970s and 1980s fashions, presenting themselves to be looked at, looking back at the camera as though self-aware of their status as portraiture, as advertising for the film that follows. Soliciting an audience of baby boomer and younger women, domestic and transnational viewers, the film here displays its willingness to be read not only as a feminist comment on divorce but as an endorsement of the 1970s discourse of female self-assertion, or as a parodic 1990s pop-psychology of dysfunctional coupling. As the film ends, Campion problematizes James's conclusion; as Isabel turns from the door of the well-lit room and looks away from Gardencourt—the house of fiction?—she faces an unknown future rather than an almost certain return to her abusive husband.[6] Although James's 1880s Isabel sees her destiny as necessarily living out the consequences of her badly made and manipulated marital choice, Campion's 1990s heroine need hardly be "poor Isabel."

Despite its middlebrow pleasures, Campion's film did not reach a mass audience nor was it as popular as had been *The Piano* (1993). Although it solicited as spectator an educated and intelligent female (or feminine) consumer, *The Portrait of a Lady* encodes its commodity status and market niche as art flick. A film about art and commodification, it calls attention to its aesthetic through indexical figures, lighting, and mise-en-scène. Ralph's understanding that Isabel will be "caught" and "put in a cage" by her marriage to Osmond is everywhere represented by the film's repertory of images. Here is a short catalog. Spiderwebs: Isabel's parasol, which Osmond twirls before her face; chandeliers, through which an overhead shot portrays a dinner party; patterns on rotunda and loggia floors; Busby Berkeley–style dancers, via a crane shot. Bars: multiple shots through balustrades as figures ascend stairs, or the camera tilts up, through, and over balustrades into gardens; the portico through which Ned Rosier (Christian Bale) banefully cries, "Pansy"; the foregrounded bars through which Ralph (Martin Donovan) warns Isabel of her impending doom. Shots of hands, virtually always in close-up: "Don't touch," a guard intones as Henrietta (Mary-Louise Parker) strokes a recumbent effigy outside the Victoria and Albert Museum; Isabel clasps her hands by her face as she listens to a new friend play Schubert at Gardencourt; Madame Merle (Barbara Hershey) and Pansy (Valentina Cervi) entwine their gloved hands—one in black, one white—as they converse about (maternal) gift giving; Osmond's hands, in detail shot, stroke his daughter's, while she sits, embraced and visually eroticized, on his lap, and he talks of their life together; Madame Merle clutches a gift-wrapped doll for the convented Pansy; Gilbert slaps.

Campion's mise-en-scène also indexes its status as art film. The director includes statuary: catacombs; morselized and gargantuan hands and feet, of sculptures outside the Capitoline in Rome; a life-sized statue stands beside Isabel, as Osmond drones his love and the camera zooms alongside a catacomb wall with a death's head on it, the sound track gasping. Osmond, Ned, and Merle collect paintings, "bibelots," and "precious objects." Architecture serves to establish shots, often in canted frame or shot as the camera pans, tilts, or rolls; classical music plays on the sound track (Campion, *Interviews* 184). As a sign of taste, Campion's mise-en-scène depicts embroidered and beaded gowns with trains and bustles, high-bourgeois drawing room decor—perfectly arranged objects on mantles; candelabra in the frame plane as the camera tracks past; accumulated

Victoriana that hints at kitsch; the orientalized lace collar-and-cuffed dressing gown Madame Merle wears to welcome Ned Rosier; the velvet, satin,
and silk fabric everywhere so resplendent and textured it makes the viewer
want to touch; the omnipresent mirrors that represent self-reflection and
its failures. The film's mise-en-scène, then, inscribes art and aesthetics into
its scenario in part to signal its commodity status as art-house film, in part,
as product of independent filmmaking. Announcing itself as highbrow
culture, Campion's film separates itself from mainstream Hollywood fare,
naturalizing the superior taste of the filmgoer who has selected this film as
cultural product. Yet its status as art film and its encoding of its artfulness
as tasteful beauty made the film seem incoherent to a middlebrow audience of cultural consumers used to the suspect pleasures of spectatorial
absorption, viewing for the story, and identifying with a romance heroine.

Like Campion's *The Portrait of a Lady*, Holland's *Washington Square*
sought but failed to secure a middlebrow but discriminating spectator.
Although it scrutinized the middle-class question of a woman's marital
choice and its consequences, Holland's mise-en-scène and montage identify *Washington Square* as thoroughly highbrow. The opening sequence's
establishing shots of Washington Square betray the film's bid for an art-
house audience. After an overhead shot of the square, the camera tracks
down through the trees, dollies toward the house, tilts up and then down,
and tracks through an opened window into the parlor, dollies around the
room—cataloging the perfect Victoriana of furniture and decor—into
the dining room. On the sound track, a woman shrieks, and the camera
quickly pans to the stairway, tracks up, up, and up several flights of stairs,
pauses on a weeping servant girl, dollies into a bedroom, across a mirror,
and up a woman's bloody body to picture death by childbirth. "Your
daughter, sir," a nurse says, handing a baby to a black-garbed man. This
breathtaking sequence shot finds a visual equivalent for James's narratorial technique as it identifies and ironizes this infant's destiny. Bereft of
mother at her birth, Catherine Sloper first adores and then is locked in
combat with her sadistic and punishing Victorian father. (In the book,
Sloper declares that he is "'not a father in an old-fashioned novel,'" to
the narrator's—and reader's—sardonic amusement [83]). Throughout
the film, repeated high- and low-angle shots depict the power struggle in
which this father and daughter are "stuck like glue," as she seeks to marry
the man of her choice and he attempts to prevent her—even after his
death—from falling prey to scheming adventurers.

Throughout Holland's film, the moving camera and lengthy sequence shots enable the director to eschew cuts and edits as she portrays the flow of life at Mrs. Elizabeth Almond's (Jennifer Garner) home and the refusal of it in Washington Square. When Sloper (Albert Finney) seeks Mrs. Almond's advice about his daughter's engagement, the mise-en-scène includes a room adjacent to and behind the parlor from which a little girl walks, moving through the depth plane into the frame plane; she whispers to her mother, who gives her permission to indulge in some unnamed activity. When Sloper stands, walking to the window on the right, the camera displays a hallway behind him, leading to the front door, through which a young woman walks, pauses, and then retreats. Seemingly extraneous spectatorial information is crucial here, for the newborn Sloper examined in the sequence's beginning—and declared healthy—seems, figuratively, to grow, first to girlhood, then young womanhood, moving through the house and into her adult life. As Holland introduces this scene, the infant's young parents give the baby to grandmother (how differently from the servant's handing over of Catherine to her father at her birth!) and leave through the front door. Mixing the effects of mise-en-scène and montage, Holland shoots their departure around doors, into halls, and seemingly through walls. When Morris Townsend (Ben Chaplin) courts Catherine (Jennifer Jason Leigh) in her father's parlor, on the contrary, the mise-en-scène is posed, composed, and formalized, the frame closed and the action static. When Morris and Catherine discuss her father's decision to disinherit her should they marry, the two lovers sit, hands in lap, with a closed secretary between them. In conventional two-shot and shot/reverse shot, Holland's stationary camera shoots Catherine in purple dress, perfectly posed against the perfect Victorian parlor's dark green damask wallpaper, the mahogany furnishings gleaming. Here, Holland's shot selection pictures the staid and stolid scene of Victorian courtship. Taken together, these two camera styles indicate Holland's maturity as a filmmaker, her knowledge of film conventions, and her high-cultural aspirations.

Like Campion's *The Portrait of a Lady,* Holland's *Washington Square* deploys the arts as an index of acculturation. First, the woman is framed, portrayed as portrait or representation. Three times, Catherine watches out her window, framed by its frame, with caged bird by her side, looking for her father (or, ironically, lover), then runs down the stairs, screaming "Father's home!" (or murmuring, "I've been missed"). In these scenes,

Catherine's face dissolves into different stages of her girlhood: the crying girl becomes an older (though still bumbling) girl, then a poised young woman. Catherine's mother, dead in the opening shot sequence, appears throughout the film, hanging as a picture alongside other ornately framed women on the green and crimson damask walls. Later, Catherine is mirrored: she enters the mise-en-scène from outside the frame, reflected first in an ornately framed mirror near Morris; when she feeds her dying father, her face is echoed in another such mirror; trying out love, she kisses her image in a pier glass, laughing innocently as she thinks her first sexual thoughts. Rather than standing for female vanity, self-reflection, or beauty, these images represent the framed woman as trapped: Catherine, like these portraits of women, is stuck with her father and destined never to leave Washington Square, although she does not yet know it.

As does the sound track in *The Portrait of a Lady*, *Washington Square*'s sound track uses music as an index of acculturation. The young and nervous Catherine pees in her pants at a party when trying to sing Jan A. P. Kaczmarek's faux art song; later, she sings the song beautifully with her lover, at the piano, as a foolish Lavinia (Maggie Smith) joins in ("la, la, la, la, la, la," while rack focus highlights Sloper's sneer, in the background);

Catherine Sloper peers out the window of her father's house on Washington Square, where, like her pet bird, she is caged. (Washington Square, 1997)

on her Grand Tour, a soprano performs it in Europe, as gathering con-
certgoers dissolve into the frame, and Catherine, becoming cultured, listens, weeping over sheet music; Catherine plays it perfectly, at the film's
end, while the camera shoots her smiling, sardonically and knowingly,
after she commands Morris never to see her again. In *The Portrait of a
Lady,* the woman Isabel emulates, Madame Merle, plays Schubert's impromptus on the piano, as the newly arrived New York girl listens, hand
over mouth, in admiration. Throughout the film, Schubert's string quar-
tets sound the threat of sadism, the emergence of monstrosity; the quartet
in D minor (D. 810, 1824), "Death and the Maiden," articulates the American girl with acculturation's paradoxical outcome, with the link between
intimacy and mortality that Susan experiences in *The Wings of the Dove.*[7]
The sound track's music represents culture with a capital C, and learning
culture, the heiress increases her value as commodified object, as suitable
for acquisition in marriage, and as bearer and disseminator of Culture. Yet
these films ironically depict her acculturation as fitting her only for life as
a spinster and surrogate nurturer rather than wife.[8]

Unlike Campion and Holland, James Ivory and Iain Softley sought a
wide audience for literary film by adding kinky sex to their mise-en-scènes.
Softley's strategy to mainstream soft-core porn for middlebrow culture hit
big, as *The Wings of the Dove* grossed $1.3 million on the first weekend
of its U.S. release.[9] Whereas this film crossed over to multiplex exhibition, audience acclaim, and Academy Award nominations, however, *The
Golden Bowl* failed to excite art-house or alternative-cinema audiences, at
least in part because the sex seemed tame and the codes of costume drama
stagey. As these filmmakers repurposed for the 1990s stories about female
acculturation and independence, linking intimate relations to cultural
value and monetary worth, only one told a tale suitable for popularity in
the dot-com-boom decade.

Middlebrow Sex: Soft-Core Pornography and Costume Drama

Softley's *The Wings of the Dove* and Merchant Ivory's *The Golden Bowl*
more successfully delivered what Radway calls the suspect pleasures of the
middlebrow than did Holland's *Washington Square* or Campion's *The Portrait of a Lady.* Both films deploy mainstream discourses of sex to portray
the American girl's imbroglios and entanglements in Europe. Whether
depicted with "crude gusto" or as degraded and perverse, the sex in these

scenarios updates James for the millennium. Displaying the sex scenes only implicit in James's novels, exhibiting the female body, employing fetish, costume, or masquerade, these films solicit a mainstream moviegoing public as audience. The middlebrow consumer who enjoys identifying with the characters, indulging a taste for romance, and taking pleasure in the process of consuming is gratified by viewing; imagining herself acquiring the cultural capital of canonical fiction, she relishes the heroine's sexy savvy. Not acculturation, however, but conspicuous consumption excites these films' American girls. Lavish sets, opulent objects, sexy fashions, and extravagant furnishings surround our heroine and eroticize her for the spectator who purchases her moving-picture image. These films also solicit a consumer who enjoys voyeurism, exhibitionism, fetishism, or transvestism, for titillation and arousal are always at stake on screen—and fantasmatically, in the darkened theater. Whereas Merchant Ivory's sexy multinational costume drama looked outdated at millennium's end, Softley's tarting up of James, by contrast, attracted an audience accustomed to the mainstreaming of soft-core porn.

Softley's *The Wings of the Dove* tells a story about the heterosexual couple's erotic adventures. The opening credits roll over a sequence that identifies the look as inviting a sexual encounter with a stranger, a hard-core narrative device that highlights pleasure without complication (Krzywinska 223). Merton (Linus Roache) follows Kate (Helena Bonham Carter) through a newly opened Underground station; they get on a train; in shot/reverse shot, they watch each other; she exits and, in shot/reverse shot, he follows her up stairs, into an elevator; the camera tracks up through floors as the elevator rises, each barred shot frames the couple kissing and finally, under cover of his hat, Merton feels her buttocks. "Kate," he whispers; "no," she says, as the spectator discovers the sex play just that. Spectator absorption is guaranteed by this structure of the look, by the thrill of watching public sexual acts. As this enticement begins, our identification with Kate is tinged with arousal. Bonham Carter, already a heritage-flick, Merchant Ivory star, was an image recognizable as herself, bearing more aura than the character she played: as type, the good-girl sexpot discovering her erotic potential while on a European adventure or at a domestic cricket match. A high-quality actor, Bonham Carter's celebrity can open a picture, mobilize the market, and help ensure the investment of backers and the profits to production units. Despite her move out of the heritage sector—in, for example, *Fight Club* (1999), *Planet of the Apes* (2001), and *Harry Potter and the Order of the Phoenix* (2007)—she is herself a "form of capital" in the movie business (Dyer, *Stars* 9–22; see Vincendeau, "Memories" 30–32).

Softley's canny James adaptation exploits mainstream cinema's current appropriation of pornography's codes and conventions. But Softley's film merely hints at porno's "stock heroes, its story lines, its low-budget lighting and motel-room sets" (Hamilton B9). *The Wings of the Dove* invokes but outclasses hard-core porn by exaggerating its heritage mise-en-scène and high production values: gorgeous costumes—complete with remarkable hats!—that verge on the modern but recall the Victorian; chic blue or orange lighting that highlights cool or Mediterranean moods; a heritage-chick star who had then not yet disrobed on screen. By playing elegant lighting, costumes, and sets against porn codes and story lines, Softley's film goes distinctly middlebrow. Whereas porn became feature length by "imitating other Hollywood genres with a vengeance," Linda Williams argues, by attaching to other genres an "X-rated difference," Softley links his parodied porn flick to other mainstream genres (Williams, "Sisters" 108). The arousing heroine, the story line, and the sex scenes all recall melodramatized thriller chic. Many erotic scenes begin as one character follows another, in look-over-the-shoulder shot/reverse shot or steamy two-shot, through city alleys or up or down staircases; the staircase scenes recall Hitchcock's *Vertigo*—with spirals shot from overhead or from below, female feet leaving the frame and enticing the climbing (rising?) male up ladders—complete with Bernard Herrmann sound-alike music. When Merton and Kate have sex by a canal in Venice, Softley shoots them from behind, in medium long-shot, mid-cult *Fatal Attraction* fashion or soft-core *Last Tango in Paris* style, he standing while penetrating her (his shirttail out), she held up during intercourse by his hands, while he thrusts, and she wraps her legs around him. This sequence starts with a shot of gondolas and blued window frame; heavy breathing heaves on the sound track. To top it off, Kate is cross-dressed as a matador, for she and Merton have sex at the end of a carnival sequence, complete with orientalizing gypsy music and exotic street spectacle. The masquerading Kate returns home disheveled, tie undone and shirt open, and apologizes to the bedded Milly (Alison Elliot), just as a slumming husband might; "Don't lie to me," Milly retorts, playing cuckolded wife.

As in this scene, the sex in *The Wings of the Dove* always suggests a threesome, for the third enhances a couple's pleasure. Softley intercuts scenes of Milly's seduction of Merton ("I'm going to make a fool of myself tonight, I know it," she confesses) with shots of Kate looking at herself in a mirror and, in voice-over, speaking her love letters to the man who's kissing another woman. "I see you touch her and I'm scared," she says, as Softley cuts back to Milly and Merton. "Every time she looks at you and smiles," Kate voices over, as Milly smiles and the camera cuts back to Kate's reflected image, "don't forget that I love you more." In chic porn style, a little S&M adds spice to the mix. When Merton follows Kate up a staircase and into a blue-lit billiards room at Lord Mark's party, she drills him about the "older woman" he has just kissed, a kiss shot from Kate's perspective. "Did it hurt?" Kate asks of her refusal to marry him; "Is that what you wanted?" he returns; "I hurt so much you can't imagine," she murmurs. They kiss on the billiard table; "I want you to go back and kiss *her*," Kate says afterward, "with that mouth." This middlebrow appropriation of a soft-core porn motif suggests, moreover, that threesomes always involve not only same-sex rivalry but homoeroticism as well. When Kate positions Milly and Merton in one gondola, herself in another, the sequence ends with a long shot of the girls, drunken and giddy, leaning over and touching across the barely lit, nighttime canal; "come closer," Milly giggles as Merton presumably watches. After Lord Mark drunkenly gropes the sleeping Kate in her darkened guest chamber, Kate visits Milly's room; the camera tracks up from the foot to the head of the bed, over Milly's blanketed body, to her face; a door closes on the sound track, and Milly wakes and invites Kate to join her. "What's wrong?" Milly asks; the two girls cuddle, as Milly puts her arm around Kate's back and they clasp hands over her breasts.

These girl–girl erotic scenes seem to demand a male spectator. The "'lesbian' number" in pornography, Williams maintains, appeals to the male fantasy of making a third with two women (*Hard Core* 140–41). While indulging soft-core male fantasy, *The Wings of the Dove* inoculates the female spectator against the possibility—the fear?—of lesbian desire by representing women as appropriate viewers of explicitly sexual art of all erotic kinds. Softley rewrites Milly's National Gallery visit as an accidental stumble on a Gustav Klimt exhibit. Here, Milly encounters both Kate and Densher, as the lesbian number gets suggested. The camera tilts up *The Kiss*, cutting to Milly as she looks at it; she spies Merton through a series of arches, then Kate arrives: they're together. "I want to show you something," Kate says, drawing Milly to Klimt's *The Danaë*. Merton leaves the girls to look at the dazzling display of breast, mouth, and touch; the huge,

gilded, and fetishized buttocks and thighs. "It's not what you think," Kate
denies, clinching the implication that the couple's erotic looking necessitates heterosexual touch; spectatorship, the scene seems to suggest, may
also involve girl–girl identification when sexual arousal is linked to the look.

When Kate follows Milly into a bookstore, she again draws her friend to
erotic art, as they look at an etching of libertine cunnilingus *a tergo*. That
part of the bookstore's "reserved for men," Lord Mark (Alex Jennings)
later threatens; "I saw them," the still innocent Milly objects; "have I suddenly become corrupt?" Shot in the film's pervasive blue light, this scene
of revelry, drunkenness, and smoking mimics fun in a twenties cabaret;
the girls, dressed in shimmering blue gowns with one-feathered head-
bands, resemble flappers. The film announces itself as set in "London,
1910" (although the novel was published in 1902); its costumes suggest a
historically unstable but definitely modern milieu, as women began to lib-
erate themselves from the taboos that surrounded sex. It's okay for women
to watch—to take pleasure in—soft core, Softley suggests, activating the
metaphor that mobilizes his own appropriation of James. Indeed, as the
markets for adult films and porn video rentals expanded in the 1980s and
1990s, women, lesbians, gay men, and homosexual and heterosexual couples began to consume a mainstreamed, well-marketed, even feminist,
hard-core pornography (Williams, *Hard Core* 229–64).

Celebrity sex guaranteed *The Wings of the Dove* the middlebrow audience and big box office the other James films lacked. Whereas the eroticized scenes in *The Portrait of a Lady* endow Isabel with sexual fantasy, the
high-profile, heritage-chick star of *The Wings of the Dove* has sex with her
screen lover. Campion shoots Isabel in autoerotic multiple-partner fantasy:
she lies down, and the hands of two lovers appear, touching her breast,
stomach, and thigh; Ralph Touchett lies beside her, watching, spectator
to Isabel's pleasure in the threesome, then stands; standing too, Goodwood (Viggo Mortensen) attacks him; the lovers dissolve one by one
from Isabel's fantasied ménage à trois. Isabel's home-movie travels across
Europe—shot in grainy black and white, with the conventions of early
twentieth-century silent film and surrealist cinema, with a background of
exoticized pyramids and women in veils—picture her as "nude," as a high-
cultural image of the body made artful. But Softley brilliantly climaxes his
film with a nude sex scene that, like the novel, portrays love as expenditure, sex as exchange, and arousal as commodity. After the grieving Kate
burns Milly's bequest letter, she enters Merton's tiny bedchamber, sits on

his bed, and removes her black corset. Naked, she poses for his look in the Klimt nude's position; "I'll never take her money," he claims, sitting on the bed. They kiss; "I love you, Kate," he says; she removes his suspenders, then his shirt. Softley shoots the lovers in medium long shot, emphasizing whole body relations; Kate climbs on top, stretches her fully naked body on her lover's, her buttocks softly curving; "I love you, too." She sits, seemingly moving up and down on his penis; in shot/reverse shot, he watches as she moves; she throws her head back, in porn iconography's sign of female orgasm—but, instead, she stops, and weeps: "You're still in love with her." "She wanted us to be together," Merton assures her, in medium long shot through the brass bed's headboard, as the camera . . . withdraws. Cut to the two lovers lying beside each other; to her white face, in close-up, emphasizing expression and thus emotion. Merton says, "I want to marry you without her money." "Give me your word," Kate responds, "that you're not in love with her memory." In extreme close-up, tears mark her white face. Cut to retrospective montage of Milly, laughing, then the girls touching in gondolas—"come closer!"—then fade to black. In extreme close-up, Merton's wide eyes silently weep.

This culminating scene of failed sexual climax deploys the conventions of soft-core porn to secure a middlebrow audience. We watch the modern London girl climb on top of her lover, breasts bobbing; assume the active role during intercourse, taking control of the sex act and so breaking the taboo of female passivity. We hear of the third in the film's threesome, the American dove who haunts this bedchamber and prevents orgasm. We see her ghost in montage, reminding us of the girl–girl numbers. But the final scene is a "money shot" gone wrong: the male does not ejaculate and so visually prove his pleasure; the female, whose pleasure is central to this version of postmodern pornography, doesn't come; the emphasis on whole bodies and facial reactions highlights this money shot's difference from soft-core conventions. Although the spectator knows this sex scene is simulated, she or he has yearned to see Helena Bonham Carter naked, takes pleasure in viewing her fleshy body. Softley shoots Bonham Carter's breasts and face, buttocks and body, her whole body, so as to seem to deny the possibility of body double. The entire number, in which sex is enacted and money discussed, visualizes the novel's obsession with the intricate linkage of love with gain and loss. Merton steadfastly refuses to participate in a financial exchange through the hallucinated third, Milly, even as the dialogue reminds us that intimacy in *The Wings of the Dove* is always a matter of exchange, use, gain or loss, of working opportunities to enrich one's presentation, prestige, or pocketbook. The fetishization of Milly— her fortune, her beauty, her magnificence—characterizes a hallucinated intimacy in which sex is a commodity, but the consumer never gets the goods. Through the iconography of the money shot, this final scene in *The Wings of the Dove* foregrounds the problematic nature of heterosexual relations and sexual pleasure at the beginning—and end—of the twentieth century.

This cross between soft-core porn and independent film, finally, recalls the history of pornography's emergence at the box office and its eventual move into the mainstream. Modern popular pornography appeared concomitantly with the first anti-obscenity legislation, which seemed to produce rather than regulate printed sexual material (Williams, *Hard Core* 12, 87). It exploded after passage in 1857 of the British Obscene Publications Act, which enabled seizure and banning of books, and began to be consolidated in 1873, when the Comstock Act prohibited use of the U.S. mail to disseminate obscene or indecent materials or information that might promote abortion (Lewis, *Hard Core* 232). Linked to the emerging mass market for books, newspapers, and periodicals, this new attempt to censor sex when women could first legally use or refuse it identifies pornography's cultural function to problematize sexual relations even as it endorses heterosexual pleasure. In the 1950s United States, art cinema's growing popularity "led to the demise" of the Production Code in the next decade and to liberal Supreme Court rulings on censorship; the UK Obscene Publications Act of 1959, under which Penguin Books was tried for having

Merton Densher and Kate Croy mourn, after Iain Softley's final, failed "money shot" in The Wings of the Dove *(1997).*

published D. H. Lawrence's *Lady Chatterley's Lover,* strengthened protection against prosecution for serious literature (Gomery, *Pleasures* 191; Balio, "Art Film" 63).

By the 1970s, a more liberal marketplace helped create a niche for art-house erotica. With the 1972 debut of *Deep Throat* (Gerard Damiano), *Behind the Green Door* (Mitchell Bros.), and *The Devil in Miss Jones* (Damiano), porn became big box office, competing successfully with mainstream movies; indeed, *Deep Throat* was the first "crossover adults-only hit" and "the largest-grossing independent film of all time" (Lewis, *Hard Core* 208–12; Williams, *Screening Sex* 141). Yet these new porn films, which followed a group of supposed documentaries, such as *I Am Curious (Yellow)* (Sjöman, 1967), aimed not simply to celebrate the permissiveness associated with the 1960s sexual revolution, Williams maintains, but to depict the desire for greater knowledge about sex and sexuality. The 1970s porn films, too, first pictured the problem of female pleasure: what was female orgasm? could women take pleasure without it? who was responsible for its success or failure? They thus appealed to a mixed-sex audience, often of couples, as had mass-marketed, popular sexual self-help books, such as *The Joy of Sex,* which likewise affirmed the need for heterosexual partners' sexual knowledge and right to pleasure. As a popular genre, the new 1970s soft-core "sexual fairytales" and self-help books addressed the felt needs and experiences of a sexually adventurous audience.[10]

This sexually oriented audience had necessitated the shift from the Production Code to the new ratings system, a turning point, Jon Lewis says, in the creation of the new Hollywood (*Hard Core* 150). As films began to show nudity and violence before the ratings system went into effect, studios moved to release controversial films by their non-MPAA subsidiaries, anticipating the industry's millennial reliance on specialty divisions for distribution of mature-themed films. During the 1950s, the "process of divorcement" caused by the Paramount decision had made theaters more independent and enabled the newly popular art houses to show films without the MPAA production seal (Wilinsky 69). The emergence in the late 1960s of the new ratings system offered the studios the opportunity to update, diversify, differentiate, and effectively advertise their products and, perhaps more important, "precisely [to] target audiences" in an increasingly segmented cultural milieu (Lewis, *Hard Core* 141; Schatz, "New Hollywood" 15). As pictures were diversified and market niches identified, the single product/multiple market formula broke down. As art houses promoted their mission to support high culture for mature adults, some began to cater to a "specialized, segmented audience"; by the 1960s and 1970s, these exhibitors had stopped showing avant-garde and begun to run adult sex flicks, for profit motives (Wilinsky 72–73).

Changing sexual mores helped produce a new "frankness" in sixties and seventies cinema. As the blockbuster strategy "stalled" in the late 1960s, a new generation of filmmakers, who resembled the auteurs of "European art cinema," brought a new aesthetic into the mainstream (Schatz, "New Hollywood" 14). Soft core became acceptable to a wide audience with the *Emmanuelle* films, and porn crossed over into art film in *Last Tango in Paris* (Bernardo Bertolucci, 1972) and *In the Realm of the Senses* (Nagisa Ōshima, 1976), where it tested the "notion of obscenity" (Williams, *Screening Sex* 183). This renaissance caused a concomitant crisis in the art-house market, as art cinema entered a period of rapid decline coupled, nevertheless, with the sustenance of a "vigorous alternative cinema" (Schatz, "New Hollywood" 20–21). Post-1970s market volatility and unpredictability, however, has hindered art film's expansion of market share since its seventies boom (Balio, "Art Film" 63–64).

By the 1990s, mainstream cinema had appropriated the codes, story lines, and look of porn. It had also thematized that appropriation as nostalgia for the porn industry's 1970s popularity. *Boogie Nights* (Paul Thomas Anderson, 1997), for example, proposed 1970s casual, group, and orgiastic sex as a form of cultural retro. In *Eyes Wide Shut* (1999), a remediation of Arthur Schnitzler's ritual sex classic *Traumnovelle,* Stanley Kubrick brought mainstream porn full circle by casting Hollywood's then power couple, Tom Cruise and Nicole Kidman, as bored marrieds seeking sexual adventure. Invoking 1970s stylized sex even as he repurposed a high-cultural tale for a sex-hooked, mainstream audience, Kubrick commented on the impossibility of intimacy and fidelity in an era of financial speculation and excessive consumption. The fanzines' obsession with the Cruise-Kidman breakup—and with the later dating habits, engagements, and possible remarriages of both—proved his casting prescience and marketing savvy. Today's "meat movie," as Carol J. Clover says in my epigraph, may be tomorrow's blockbuster, even Oscar-nominated, picture.

Merchant Ivory's *The Golden Bowl* tarts up Henry James not by appropriating the codes and conventions of soft-core porn but by crossing them with costume drama and melodrama. As genre, the melodrama proliferates plots and subplots; involves a rapid series of scene changes; makes use of visual and aural stimuli produced by costume, lighting, elaborate scene setting, and music and noise effects. Like pornography or horror, a successful melodrama produces bodily sensations—here, tears, gasps, shouts, and sweat rather than shock or sexual arousal. The "mysteries of traditional melodrama," Martin Meisel argues, eventually produce revelations of "concealed identities" or "hidden crime" (65, 79, 66). In James's modern melodrama—which exhibits and suppresses its relations with that popular nineteenth-century genre—the mystery produces an enigma: are the Prince and Charlotte having an affair? The novel's entire project of "perceptual vigilance"—Maggie's, the author's, his delegate's, and ours—hangs on this question and on what constitutes evidence for its answer (*The Golden Bowl* 66). The telegram Adam declines to read? Our couple's appearances in public and the traces they leave behind for decoding (their photograph is one)? The golden bowl and its context of story, imagination, witness, and documentation? The melodramatic plot, its invocation of aristocratic misalliance and setting amid luxury and consumption, its arousal of bodily sensations and affects, its dedication to the regime of voyeurism, all identify the novel as available for melodramatic remediation.

Metaphors of seeing and excess also structure the costume drama, a genre, like melodrama, that has historically been linked to the female spectator. In the 1940s, Gainsborough bodice rippers eroticized melodrama, as the spectacle of libidinous women acting on their sexual desires transgressed forties notions of film realism and British moral consensus. Rather than record and celebrate "national heritage," Pam Cook argues, costume drama "mobilize[s] history as a site of sexual fantasy," subverting a coherent notion of historical or literary period to present "history as masquerade." A focus on fashion, coiffeur, and set decoration constitutes costume melodrama's audience appeal, as "decorative excess" and "spectacular display" capture and lure the feminized look (74–79). Costume drama flouts notions of authenticity as well as of the period look. Gainsborough took its spectator's historical knowledge for granted, Sue Harper argues, by expunging "conventional signs of authenticity"; the studio thus pictured the past as a site of "physical pleasure" and play for melodrama (129, 127). For Andy Medhurst, costume drama discards "a genteel commitment to period verisimilitude" for "the romping joys of frocking about" (11–12). In *The Golden Bowl*, Merchant Ivory deployed costume melodrama's feminized and decorative aesthetic, violation of period authenticity, and concomitant fascination with pictorial anachronism to provide a spectacular form of middlebrow pleasure. Yet the production team's product failed sufficiently to wink at its joys of frocking about and so alienated its core audience of acculturated or aspirant women, gays, and cosmopolites alike.

Merchant Ivory's extravagant mise-en-scène displays with little wit costume drama's highly decorative aesthetic. Shot in a palette of oranges, ochres, and golds, the sets are crammed with luxury goods: at the Prince and Maggie's mansion, the settees upholstered in gold silk, adorned with damask pillows, and festooned with wool and silken throws; the walls, covered in gold damask or red silk; the fireplaces, embellished with Italian tiles and the mantels with ornate gilt mirrors, the mantelpieces with vases, paintings, and the golden bowl. In one highly decorated set, the infant Principino bathes in a silver claw-footed tub before a marble fireplace, in a room whose walls bear European masterpieces, with busts and vases placed decoratively on the floor. At Fawns, Adam Verver's (Nick Nolte) "rented castle," the mise-en-scène is perhaps more lavish: marble floors and crystal lights meet wide wrought-iron and gilt staircases, where murals of cherubs embracing and lords clashing bedeck the walls; grand pianos furnish the intimate rooms; the walls are covered with portraits that—hilariously—"came with the house" and whose painters shall remain "nameless." The production team knows—and shows—that this decor is fabricated, as gentle irony produces spectatorial smirk. Yet failing sufficiently to play with authenticity, the film's quality pleasure in looking seemed corny.

The costumes likewise failed sufficiently to play the period look for laughs. Charlotte (Uma Thurman) and Maggie (Kate Beckinsale) frock about as though perpetually decorated for dinner: bustled, silkened and satined, bedecked with exquisite and expensive jewelry, hair elegantly coiffed, and makeup resplendent but tasteful. Such excessive display of costume serves the costume drama's ideological project to prioritize desire rather than period accuracy, to map, Stella Bruzzi says, a "genderised territory that centres on the erotic" (36). Freud's term "fetishized" signifies for Bruzzi, Cook, and Harper that the eroticism operated by costume drama exists "on the cusp between display and denial"; the costumes, which exhibit and disavow the availability of female flesh, "simultaneously obstruct" and "substitute" for the "'normal' sexual act" (Bruzzi 38–39). Despite Bruzzi's feminist slam at costume drama's political insufficiency, she nevertheless identifies the link between pleasure and perversity as costume melodrama's ideological project. The perverse signifies a swerving from normative sexual object choice and, as category, it articulates fetishism, transvestitism, voyeurism, and exhibitionism—all evoked by Merchant Ivory's mix of modes in *The Golden Bowl*.[11]

Merchant Ivory allegorizes costume drama as mode, for Charlotte and Amerigo (Jeremy Northam) attend, sans *sposi,* a *costume* ball. Dressed as a Renaissance prince, Amerigo figuratively becomes his ancestors, their title now degraded by the late nineteenth-century "proliferation of hereditary titles" (Cannadine, *Decline* 25); as Cleopatra, Charlotte exhibits her lure and allure, her barely exposed sexual desire for Amerigo, and her bespangled body, complete with glittering breast cups, with feathers and jeweled asp as headdress. Ironically, Fanny (Angelica Huston) dresses as the powerful yet sacrificed "Mary Queen of Scots" and Bob (James Fox) as hatchet man; on screen, only the latter couple goes home to couple, as Bob jumps Fanny, growling, while she giggles—a departure from James's portrayal of them as bound solely by "exhausted patience" (*The Golden Bowl* 206). Ivory also pictures a technology of exhibition within the costume ball's "drama," as a photographer watches the lovers "compose" themselves before he "exposes" the photographic plate, accompanied by a burst of light, with fade to white. Arms outstretched to display her glittering body and breasts, Charlotte's image is "fixed" on the photographic plate; Amerigo poses alone as conqueror; the two also pose together, much like man and wife, she sitting, he behind her, proprietary arm outstretched to her chair. Later, when the shopkeeper identifies their portraits as those of the golden bowl's near-buyers, these photographs mark Charlotte and Amerigo as lovers. This embedded masquerade and its allegorized picture call the spectator's attention to the fact that she watches a costume drama, that gowns and masks obstruct and substitute for the sexual act even as they exhibit and expose it. The costume as fetish thus performs its fetishization, playing its role as dress that claims to flaunt illicit even as it flouts licit sexuality.

Merchant Ivory allegorizes as well the novel's thematic of adulterous and intergenerational desire by staging its foursome, twosomes, and cross-couple threesomes in masquerades. At a massive and luxurious dinner, exotic dancers perform as a fastidious Maggie withdraws and an eager Charlotte watches. This scene of exposed and fleshy female bodies, bare-chested and beautiful young man, and bearded elder replays as performance an orientalized version of the Ugolino legend. As cuckolded ancient interrupts the dance of sexual touching and recumbent figures at orgy, the play portrays the violent murder of "son" and suicide of "stepmother." To depict the submerged thematic of ancestry and genealogy, Ivory shoots under the credits and cuts in during the film a fictionalized story of Amerigo's ancestors, one of whom slept with his stepmother while still an adolescent; her doom is fixed, as she's dragged from her sex-drenched bed by soldiers, on order from her husband, who explicitly calls her "a whore." This story reemerges as the opening sequence to Maggie and Fanny's talk about the "awfulness" Maggie imagines between her husband and her father's wife, and this time, Maggie must watch. Here, slides of Italy—complete with multiple shots of the now-antique projector and its operator—accompany the spoken Ugolino story: duke's wife caught in flagrante, his heirs' luring of beautiful women, and the fifth duke's taking the name, Amerigo, in honor of his discoverer cousins. When Charlotte and Amerigo later meet on the sly in London, they whisper at Madame Tussaude's, a lowbrow museum filled with waxed forms of historical lovers, criminals, and aristocrats, forever enacting their atrocities. The scene ends with Charlotte's delighted posturing before a fun-house mirror: their forms distorted, she and her reluctant lover look at their stretched, headless, and

Charlotte Stant, dressed as Cleopatra, poses for the photographer at a costume ball. (The Golden Bowl, *2000*)

disembodied reflections while anachronistic carnival music plays on the sound track. Merchant Ivory's technologies of exhibition stage sex, eroticism, and the fetishized image as on the cusp of desire and denial yet fail to deliver the frisson of James's self-conscious narratorial situation.

Via its costumes, masquerades, and performances, Merchant Ivory's *The Golden Bowl* shows the sex acts that Henry James leaves unreadable. In James's novel, the author's delegate, Fanny, displays and denies the lovers' affair.[12] When Bob Assingham asks her what happened between our couple, his wife responds, "'nothing'" because "'nothing *could*'"; "'she might have been his—,'" well, "'anything she liked—except his wife'" (*The Golden Bowl* 53–54). When Maggie asks what "awfulness" happened between her husband and her father's wife, Fanny claims ignorance. The reader knows, through spousal dialogue, that Fanny has herself "entertained" such a notion; when Bob later accuses his wife of procuring for the Prince the "'enjoyment'" of "'*two* beautiful women,'" Fanny unblushingly admits she has kept Charlotte within Amerigo's "'reach'" (382, 387, 394; emphasis in original). Deploying this delegate as spy, eyewitness, gossip, and liar, James suggests that her perfidy prevents us from trusting Fanny's judgments; Bob, Fanny's narratee, himself remains skeptical. In a brilliant adaptational move in the 1972 filming of the novel, the director James Cellan Jones pictures Bob as the author's delegate and Fanny as the ludicrous sharer of the surname that could be nothing but a sodomitic joke. Speaking directly to the audience before each episode, Bob (Cyril Cusack) speaks the narrator's words, providing the viewer seemingly trustworthy evidence.

Merchant Ivory does not, however, keep our couple's affair a mystery, for to James's enigma the film adds a sex scene only suggested by the novel. During the couple's tryst at an inn, Amerigo looks out a window, clad only in tweed jacket (and, as we will later see, underwear), smoking; cut to Charlotte, raising her torso from the slept-in bed, her camisole unbuttoned. Track Charlotte walking to Amerigo; she sits on his lap, and they kiss passionately, as she draws Amerigo's look to her suggested but never exposed breasts. "We might not make it home for dinner," she whispers. Cut to Charlotte's back to the camera, as Amerigo grabs her nightgowned buttocks and pushes her to the floor, her leg raised and lingerie pushed up to her crotch; he clasps her hands over her head, on the floor, suggesting his dominance and her submission; she giggles. Cut to a maid, overhearing, from the hall. Cut to Amerigo, touching Charlotte's breast.

In a two shot, Charlotte rolls on top and, as camisole separates from petti-coat, he puts his hand under the waistband, on her skin; she clasps *his* hands over his head. Cut to Maggie, modeled after a painting by John Singer Sargent and seated by the fire, her body elegantly dressed, recum-bent against an upholstered chair, waiting for her philandering husband.[13]

Although this sex scene might on first glance seem to be a bodice rip-per, there's nothing nasty about its dominance and submission, its re-spectable romps in S&M. In her nightdress, Charlotte looks as though posed for a fantasmatic "Victoria's Secret" catalog ad, a romantic interior shot for a popular millennial magazine, such as *Victoria, Victorian, Vogue,* or *Interior Design,* many of which featured stories on costume drama dur-ing the 1990s (see Yaeger; Edie Cohen; Van Meter). Charlotte's camisole, a feature of late-1890s underwear and of 1990s nostalgia, arouses spec-tator's desires and *looks* authentic; Amerigo's historically appropriate English country tweed jacket—but cut in contemporary style—meets anachronistic underwear, for men's drawers ended just above or below the knee during the period, and only later would such "knicker drawers" be-come "trunks" (Cunnington and Cunnington 137–38, 132). Because such male attire could hardly have looked romantic in 2001, costume designer John Bright dresses Northam in contemporary jockey shorts; cinematog-rapher Tony Pierce-Roberts, moreover, fails to shoot a corset unlacing (a required item of 1904 female underclothes) as prelude to the sexual act.[14] In Merchant Ivory's sex scene, the camisole and petticoat, and the tweed jacket sans shirt, update illicit sexual relations for the 1990s. Yet this hybrid-ized period look in underwear signifies a millennial anxiety about sex-uality's privacy, its ability to please and provide intimacy. The maid who overhears Charlotte's giggle in the inn's hall, like the spectator-voyeur, is unsatisfied with heavy breathing and wishes to, and does, see more.[15]

This sex scene is hardly explicit by early twenty-first-century standards. Kristin Hohenadel argues that whereas penetrative, sadomasochistic, and non-body-doubled sex scenes are increasingly on view in international art cinema, audiences nevertheless remain anxious and ambivalent about the graphic depiction of sex on screen. Despite the entrance of sex into main-stream movies, Hohenadel maintains, Hollywood's "glossy" and "saccha-rine" version of sex—"gauzy and backlit," choreographed and performed— may break more records at the box office than hard-core shots of sado-masochistic or penetrative pleasures. Independent filmmakers who want to shoot "real" sex must cope with actors' reticence, spectators' resistance, and the industry's self-censorship. Virginie Despentes and Coralie Trinh Thi hired hard-core actresses to star in their road-movie about a pornographic actress and prostitute on a murder spree, *Baise-Moi* (2000); although Chen Kaige shot British heritage star Ralph Fiennes and innocent-but-sexy chick Heather Graham in *Killing Me Softly* (2002) completely naked—and without body doubles—in scenes that suggested sadomasochism, he refused to "'show the things that nobody wants to see,'" he said, including full-frontal male nudity: "'I want the sex to have a very beautiful look'" (Hohenadel 20).

Sex, as Catherine Breillat says in my epigraph, is the "last taboo" in cinema. Art films that show the "messy truths about sex," Hohenadel claims, are generally produced outside the Hollywood system (20). Breillat's coproduced, transnational *Romance* (1999), which played only in selected cities and university towns, pictures sadomasochistic sexual acts from a woman's perspective. Appealing to a female audience, this film about a woman who pursues perverse sex as a potentially liberating act was hardly acceptable to contemporary feminist spectators. Due to the explicit and exploitative sex scenes, Breillat claims, critics and female fans judged *Romance* harshly (Hohenadel 20). Perhaps this criticism motivated Breillat to adapt *The Last Mistress* (2008), an erotic costume drama with very beautiful sex scenes that generate little heat. The long lines on *Eyes Wide Shut*'s opening night, moreover, may have been generated by curiosity about the orgy scene, about what was censored and what was not. Kubrick, who specialized in pictures that travestied their genres' codes and conventions, shot his porn flick to invoke and transgress the boundary in mainstream cinema between simulated sex and voyeuristic, nonchalant, but also frighteningly banal "real" sex, whether licit or illicit. Deploying mainstream production values, massive budgets, and celebrity stars, Kubrick sought a heterosexual and coupled audience by arousing male sexual desire even as he portrayed female pleasure. Unlike "real sex" or porn-genre filmmakers, Merchant and Ivory shot a glossy, gauzy, and sentimentalized big sex scene with a very beautiful but decidedly old-fashioned look.

The box-office failure of *The Golden Bowl,* the crossover and art-house success of *The Wings of the Dove* and *The Portrait of a Lady,* respectively, can be accounted for, at least in part, by industry exigencies, for securing the right production company and financial arrangements, distribution networks, and exhibition outlets inevitably enables or hampers a film's success. To become box-office hits, independent and art-house films must earn good reviews, especially in top venues such as the *New York Times* and the *New Yorker*, and good word of mouth, which may help make or break box office. Directors of heritage and literary films also depend, often early in a career, upon public-service television or government funding. For indie filmmakers, impressive film-festival screenings, award nominations, and cinephile enthusiasm may move a film into the mainstream, creating breakout or crossover success. Good casting, too, can open a film or dampen audience eagerness. In *The Golden Bowl*, narrow casting of both heritage and Hollywood stars sought to seduce a mainstream spectator accustomed to consuming soft-core porn. Designed as a "pre-sold" spectacle based on a classic novel, with "top stars, an excessive budget, a sprawling story, and state-of-the-art production values," *The Golden Bowl* nevertheless did not cross over.[16] Despite a multiplex platform release and an "art-house run," this saucy costume drama failed at the box office (Higson, *Heritage* 144).

Movies and Markets at the Millennium

The late-century multinational circulation of British national cinema and heritage film depends upon the global industrial and financial structures that enable filmmakers to produce, distribute, and exhibit their product in a consolidated entertainment environment. With the Reagan-era explosion of North American multi- and megaplexes and upgrading and expansion of European theatrical sites, enhanced practices of saturation booking, and multimedia advertising for potential blockbusters, the conditions had been created for a vertically reintegrated entertainment industry. Spectacular growth in the entertainment markets, moreover, fueled creation of more media product; between 1984 and 1989, Richard Maltby maintains, "the total world market for filmed entertainment doubled in size," and revenues at the majors grew "9 percent per annum" ("Post-Classical" 35, 37). In the 1980s, mergers and leveraged buyouts facilitated blockbuster marketing and saturation booking; in the 1990s, popularity of the high-concept, global event movie made independent production and international distribution more expensive (39); and at century's end, independents began to imitate the majors' preselling and profit-splitting strategies (Schamus 95–96). According to producer James Schamus, indie films now must be modest successes at the box office to make even a small profit, since they, like foreign, ancillary-resistant art films, are rarely carried by rental chains, get free-TV deals, or figure significantly in "large television syndication packages" (95). During independent film's moments of box-office triumph—in, say, 2002–3, when a dozen high-profile indies competed head-to-head for audience dollars, critical praise, and award nominations, or 2005–7, when a market glut forced a new generation of DIY directors to self-distribute—periods of overproduction and so falling profits occur, followed by those of underproduction. As Shamus asserts, "'Independent' cinema has quickly become a victim of its own success" (103).

In the new Hollywood environment, the "'software product'" marketed for multiple hardware delivery includes not just feature films but video and computer games, TV shows, recorded music, book and magazine publications, and Web-based images (Balio, "Presence" 61). In these circumstances, independent production becomes a risky business. The small independents and mini-majors have mostly gone out of business; the big independents have been gobbled up by the major studios and are now being sold or shuttered. The relationship between Disney and Miramax may serve as a case study. In 1993, Disney bought the Weinstein brothers' award-winning company, which had once depended for success on its founders' innovative marketing skills, on the ability to buy movie rights at film festivals, on developing art-house films with the "potential to cross over," and on cultivating niche markets and "targeting upper-class, discerning, and intellectual audiences."[17] In 1992, "'determined to become the largest producer of intellectual property in the world,'" Disney had formed a partnership with Merchant Ivory that "provided partial financing in exchange for domestic distribution rights" (Balio, "Presence" 65, 66). Having acquired two successful independents, Disney became the most profitable company in the business, as Miramax captured the "largest market share five times" during the decade (Balio, "Trends" 181). Distributor of *The Wings of the Dove* and *The Golden Bowl*, Miramax continued to dominate the prestige, high-culture end of the market even as it added midcult films to its roster (Balio, "Presence" 66; "Trends" 170). But Harvey and Bob Weinstein, who founded Miramax in 1979 and later became Disney specialty-division employees at Buena Vista Pictures, grew disenchanted with the studio; they divorced their company from Disney in 2005 (Disney retained the Miramax name and library) and are now releasing films at the Weinstein Company (Balio, "Art Film" 66). The major independents—"hybrid" kinds of companies—have "fragmented the marketplace for independent film," according to Justin Wyatt, by producing faux "mainstream" and crossover pictures, creating an "increasingly competitive market" as independent film production contracts (86–87).

As production shrinks and the major independents fuel periods of boom and bust, alternative funding is essential to the making of small movies. Although it is notoriously difficult to generalize about independent and art-house filmmakers' careers, a number of the directors I examine in this chapter began with the help of public television funding. The New South Wales Film Corporation, New Zealand Film Commission, Television New Zealand, and Channel Four Films (UK) helped finance Jane Campion's quirky, autobiographical *Sweetie* (1989); the biopic about the New Zealand writer Janet Frame, *An Angel at My Table* (1990); and *The Piano*. In the United States, memory of the Production Code of America's ties to the Catholic Church and to state censorship boards and, in the UK, distrust of Thatcher's culture-wars propaganda and heritage-culture legislation made critics skeptical of the public-service sector as feature-film funder. Yet John Hill invokes the long tradition of public service in British media and culture, calling on the government to restore and increase its grants programs for British cinema ("National" 17). The "modern successor" to "private patrons of the past," government funding guarantees that independent filmmakers may choose to shoot innovative scripts (Appleyard 306). Colin MacCabe links this tradition clearly to TV, urging that additional funding from public-service television, much like that awarded to commercial-free Channel 4, is necessary to secure British cinema's future ("Subsidies" 27). In the 1970s and 1980s, Mike Leigh hyperbolized, "'all serious [British] filmmaking'" was "'done for television'" (quoted in Giles 70). It continues to be the case that, on any given day in the UK, the cultural consumer may tune in to BBC-4 radio to hear excerpts from *Wuthering Heights* or may catch a new Austen serial on BBC-2, since public-service broadcasters believe that quality costume dramas, period dramas, and literary adaptations constitute their "ideal material" (Higson, *Heritage* 113).

Not only shifts in independent ownership and exhibition practices but also the increasing importance of advertising shapes the kind of film producers can fund and filmmakers make. The high cost of prime-time TV advertising commodifies film, making it "as readily available for immediate consumption as any other nationally advertised product" (Paul 82). Independent and crossover films, moreover, require more promotional work and publicity than do blockbusters, and distributors of such product work with "specialist public relations firms" as limited-release films roll out slowly and increasingly depend on a core audience's positive word of mouth, on free publicity, good critical reviews, and prestigious award nominations (Higson, *Heritage* 134). The 1990s dominance of the "'teen and pre-teen bubble'" and the "'boomers with kids'" theatrical-market segment necessitated that national advertising campaigns serve simultaneous releases; and during the decade, the independent market suffered a one-third fall in profits. In the millennium's first decade, independent cinema is entering a period of crisis resembling that of the late 1970s. In 2000, the art-house box office suffered a 15 percent drop from the previous year, with a saturated market in which too many distributors handled too many films and too few films had "staying power in theaters" (Balio, "Trends" 181; Higson, *Heritage* 139). As the ancillary or aftermarket rather than the theatrical box office generates Hollywood's profits, as a film's video "gameability" determines its saleability, as the rental store drops VHS for DVD and DVD for Blu-ray, film has become software, a multimedia commodity that advertises tie-ins, video games, hamburger joints, and media hardware (Paul 83–84). Even with a strong first week or weekend, films become "product" in a parallel media marketplace.

Independent cinema nevertheless performs crucial cultural work at the millennium. Public-service television and national and heritage cinemas routinely accomplish "cultural transfers" for a globalized cinema (O'Regan 111). Whether on Masterpiece Theatre, as Merchant Ivory production, or international coproduction, heritage film serves a transnational, cosmopolitan, even diasporic audience seeking cultural information about the world at large. Merchant Ivory peoples its heritage films and adaptations with foreigners of various ethnic backgrounds: American girls, upwardly mobile usurpers, impoverished aristocrats, and shabby hangers-on. Whereas such period drama is generally associated with British national culture, Merchant Ivory produced and filmed its movies in New York, London, Paris, and India; its films attracted viewers not only in domestic and export markets but also in multicultural communities around the globe. Bonded in a "deep emotional" way, according to actress-chef Madhur Jaffrey, the "Merchant Ivory family" lived, worked, and partied together for more than thirty-five years.[18] Members of the Merchant Ivory group were also transnationals, for each fell in love early in life with a culture other than his or her own: the Indian Merchant with Paris's food and cosmopolitan culture; the American Ivory with India's art; and Ruth Prawer Jhabvala, a Polish German Jew whose family migrated to Britain during World War II, with India, where she lived for many years with her husband, C. S. H. Jhabvala. This international, high-culture, and gourmet-foodie group was drawn to the metropolitan and expatriate writings of Jean Rhys, Kazuo Ishiguro, Jhabvala herself, and, most often, of E. M. Forster and Henry James.[19] Forster's *Howards End* epigraph—"Only connect"—articulates the cultural, class, and sexual-orientation boundary crossings that the team engineered, delivering cosmopolitan pleasure to a mainstream, middlebrow, and global audience.

As the independents and the hybrid major-independents produce more crossover, middlebrow product, the market continues to fragment, and the audience for heritage and literary film stays home with Netflix. Whereas in the 1980s and early 1990s, industrial conditions—multinational coproduction, hardware/software synergy, and multimedia windows for exhibition—enabled the Jane Austen movies to explode onto multiplex, art-house, and television screens, increasing market segmentation and audience fragmentation made modest box-office success difficult for the millennial independent product. Despite Merchant Ivory's mixing of melodrama and period costume drama—genres traditionally viewed as attractive to a female audience—their casting of upmarket, international heritage-star celebrities, and their films' distribution by Miramax, their last heritage adaptations could not compete globally with testosterone action pictures and their male megastars.[20]

· CHAPTER 5 ·

Styles of Queer Heritage

Wilde stands now as the Crown Prince of Bohemia: an almost mes-
sianic figure [of] Art and Beauty; a saint to [gays who need] heroes
and martyrs; a role model. . . . [Yet] to picture him primarily as a
gay martyr avant la lettre is, I think, to play into the hands of those
who brought him down a hundred years ago.

—Stephen Fry, "Playing Oscar"

It has come to seem . . . an obligation for non-gays to understand
gay sensibility . . . [yet] with [a] fascination and anxious . . . toler-
ance. . . . Our turn-of-the-century Wilde is not just a gay martyr but
a postmodern one, too—a pomo homo.

—Adam Gopnik, "Invention of Oscar Wilde"

"I am one of the stately homos of Britain."

—Quentin Crisp

PERHAPS IT IS INEVITABLE THAT THIS BOOK on remediations of
nineteenth-century British fiction should end with Oscar Wilde and
those who invent, imitate, or appropriate him, for Wilde has one of the
century's most powerful afterlives. In her groundbreaking work on Wilde
and on queer theory, Eve Kosofsky Sedgwick argues that gay male culture
has undertaken, during the last century, a "rehabilitation of 'the sentimental'" that shapes gay culture and encourages "the larger culture" to appropriate a sentimental male homosexuality as "spectacle" (*Closet* 144–45).
She reminds us, too, of sentimentality's rhetorical history: its function
as term of "high ethical and aesthetic praise" in the eighteenth century;
as "derogatory code name" for the feminine in the nineteenth century;
its twentieth-century fixation on a locus of emotions "stereotyped as

feminine" (150, 144–46). Yet sentimentality has a much more complex literary history than Sedgwick acknowledges, for as Claudia L. Johnson notes, "sentimentality is politics made intimate" (*Austen* 2). In the late eighteenth century, she argues, women writers adopted the mode to blur, unsettle, or disrupt gender norms and codes, to drive a "wedge between sex and gender" so as to "open out some thrilling possibilities for women" (*Austen* 78, 160, 11, 17). Early eighteenth-century male writers deployed the sentimental for class politics, whether to defend aristocratic privilege in an age of "uncertain relationships between aristocratic and bourgeois," Robert Markley notes, or to occlude class difference "by tacitly offering to admit [to the gentry] those of demonstrated virtue" (212, 216). For both Johnson and Markley, the sentimental mode may enhance the prospects for recognition of marginal groups by members of dominant ones. In the twentieth century, gay cinematic projects appropriate the sentimental to create queer visibility and to win heterosexual sympathy—if a fascinated, anxious, and envious one, as Adam Gopnik notes (78).

The sentimental mode, when appropriated by gay culture, also intersects with issues of class and status, the body and its image, and spectatorial relations. Sedgwick theorizes spectatorial relations as always already abjecting the queer, yet when implicated with the sentimental, such identificatory networks perform a double move. Audrey Jaffe notes that "scenes of sympathy," in which an observing subject feels sympathy for a suffering object, evoke fears of contamination, anxieties of becoming the other, as the other is "displaced into representation" through fantasy and projection (7). Lynn Festa suggests that the sentimental as an eighteenth-century literary form "locates" emotion and "designat[es] who possesses affect and who elicits it"; sympathetic identification thus differentiates subjects, "sorts" spectator from suffering victim, and constitutes "communities of sociability grounded in shared economic, moral, aesthetic, or class-based interests" (3–5). Although Jaffe examines the ways sentimentality serves a consolidating capitalism, and Festa, the ways it humanizes colonized others yet differentiates them from metropolitan subjects, in 1980s and 1990s gay heritage film, sentimental spectatorial relations sort queers from straight others to create communities of sociability, acknowledge heterosexual anxiety about queer cultural styles, and mobilize heterosexual identification with and sympathy for the gay other. The word "other" also makes clear that this ghostly fear—fascinated, anxious, and envious—provides coverture for the sympathizing subject, who may use representation to sort the self from those with whom he or she identified in the scene of sympathy. This concealment haunts the nineteenth- and early twentieth-century texts appropriated by gay projects.

Gay cultural projects deploy heritage as cinematic mode to address and resolve differences of rank, ownership, and nation in the private sphere's homosocial spaces. As Sedgwick argues, no element of the nineteenth-century continuum of male homosocial desire can be understood outside of its "intimate and shifting relation to class"; this is no less true of the 1990s than of the 1890s (*Men* 1). Thus 1980s and 1990s heritage film appropriates 1890s and early twentieth-century narratives to investigate melodramatic Oxbridge male homosociality, sentimental suffragist sisterhood, camp drawing-room performance, gothic connoisseurship, and doomed portraiture. The country house is now home to homos as well as heteros, and the closet has become the attic schoolroom, the childhood bedchamber, or the gothic boathouse. Social restraint, deference due to rank, and paternal benevolence may be sentimentalized or interrogated, for even as sentiment's politics of intimacy consolidates homoerotic relations in gay heritage, the mode opens a space, as Johnson and Markley maintain, for political contestation, for class or sex mobility. Heritage also quizzes primogeniture, which produced historically a "psychologically and socially subversive" experience of status inconsistency. Gay sentimental heritage represents and nurtures the anxieties, worries, and fears those contradictions induced (McKeon 171–73).

Queer heritage also displays the gay male body as spectacle. As Steve Neale notes, mainstream cinema's "male norm, perspective and look" investigates woman and the female image while seeking "to repress or disavow any erotic ... relations between the [male] spectator and the male image," yet in Hollywood films, "male homosexuality is constantly present as an undercurrent" ("Masculinity" 19). The queer heritage look, unlike mainstream Hollywood's, offers itself to the same-sex or heterosexual spectator and solicits from both a homospectatorial look via the mirrored-image scene, POV shot, or glance/object cut. The erotic male body is on display here, often as visual representation, and the period look centers not on women but on men, on costumed dandies, "aunties," dons and students, white-flannelled boys playing cricket, and beautiful portraits. Quality pleasures are queered, as affect becomes central to the mode. Queer heritage also rewrites the romance genre and courtship plot to speak the unspeakable, to produce a same-sex couple capable of living, if only fantasmatically, in the greenwood. Gay heritage cinema promotes the sentimental project to make gay men visible in history, for heritage takes a "broadly positive view of homosexuality," Richard Dyer notes, while "depicting pasts that did not" ("Heritage" 43–45). Despite a two-decades-long critical debate about its values and status as a cinematic mode, Dyer has been nearly alone in identifying heritage as a privileged formation for gay cultural projects.[1]

Oscar Wilde as icon retrospectively originates, centers, and focuses these projects. Although this chapter assembles a wide range of novels about homosexuality and homoeroticism (by Henry James, Virginia Woolf, and E. M. Forster, for example) and film remediations of their work (by Merchant Ivory, Bill Condon, and Sally Potter), I argue that Wilde serves as model for imitation as well as for divergence. As Stephen Fry notes in my epigraph, Wilde is what we, looking back, imagine him; worshiping him as "messiah" or "saint," identifying with him as model, or pitying him as martyr, we somehow, too, make him ours, make him modern. Indeed, Wilde's trials for "gross indecency" precipitated a historically crucial scene of sympathy that demanded a spectatorial look, constituted homosexual sociality, and mobilized heterosexual rage, anxiety, and empathy. Oscar Wilde's figure positions the homosexual in a modern cultural, literary, and cinematic history.

Picturing Oscar Wilde as Icon

By the mid-1990s the second Wilde fin de siècle was in full swing. In Brian Gilbert's sentimental heritage biopic, Oscar Wilde becomes, as Shelton Waldrep writes, not quite "a poster boy for gay liberation" but something close to it (51): a gay bourgeois gentleman, unbesmirched by his homosexuality, a sentimental hero.[2] *Wilde* (1997) pictures the playwright (brilliantly played by out-gay look-alike Stephen Fry) as caught in a tragic love story, as wishing only for something like a Boston marriage with Bosie (Jude Law) but trammeled with the responsibilities of wife, children, earning a paycheck. The plot inscribes Wilde as having lived a "double life": it layers fairy-tale domestic life for Wilde, "the selfish giant," with Constance (Jennifer Ehle), Cyril (Jackson Leach), and Vyvyan (Laurence Owen), on the one hand, with seductions by renters, buggers, and Bosie, on the other. In *De Profundis*, Wilde viewed his own life story as performative, as a kind of play he could not imagine having starred in.[3] In Julian

Mitchell's screenplay, the "real" story is an open secret: Wilde's sodden passion for the selfish boy who did not deserve him, the boy who, bored with the country cottage his lover has rented for the couple, runs off in a snit because Wilde writes rather than plays with his Oxford friends. "You're so mean and penny-pinching and middle-class, all you can think about is your *bank* balance," Bosie sneers (Mitchell, *Wilde* 113). Later, when an ill Wilde pitifully requests a glass of water, Bosie responds, "You'll be wanting me to empty your chamber pot next. . . . You're just a boring middle-class man" (140). In ever-tighter shot/reverse shot close-ups, Bosie regards himself in gilt-edged mirror as he throws a temper tantrum. "You *like* me, you lust after me, you go about with me, because I've got a title, that's all. . . . You're the biggest snob I've ever met. And you think you're so daring because you fuck the occasional boy" (140). Although the film solicits the spectator's identification with and sympathy for Wilde during Bosie's histrionics, his accusations expose the film's sentimental reading of Wilde. Director Brian Gilbert's Oscar *is* middle-class; he *is* a snob; he *does* envy Bosie's birth and fortune. The sympathetic spectator squirms, knowing that Bosie is an aristocratic snot and Wilde a patsy; he or she nevertheless perseveres in taking pleasure from looking at the sentimental scenario of beautiful boy, his reflection, and that of saddened lover, all shot over Law's shapely shoulder.

Gilbert paradoxically identifies Wilde as gay culture's mediator, as historical origin and as model for imitation. On the opening night of *The Importance of Being Earnest,* a dozen young men emulate Wilde, wearing his signal green carnation. Yet the gay-passion plot obscures the film's obsession with mediation.[4] Despite his protestations, the vanity-sodden boy desires the playwright precisely because everyone else does, which precipitates all the rivalrous, enraged, and envious affects associated with triangular desire: the jealous John Gray (Bob Sessions) wants to kill Bosie, Robbie (Michael Sheen) tells him, because Wilde loves Bosie; Douglas later echoes this, accusing Robbie of hating him because *he* was not Oscar's only boy. The sympathetic viewer wonders why Wilde finds his young lover so attractive and his renter friends so appealing; although wowed by the sweaty, lubricated lad in the sex scenes with a very beautiful look, his genitals hidden by a jacquard throw (no male frontal nudity mars the film's upscale tastefulness), the spectator clearly sees Bosie as an over-valued love object unworthy of Wilde's lust.[5] Perhaps because Gilbert knows that the youth so little warrants the great writer's attention, his

Wilde excuses Bosie's antics. Mitchell's screenplay represents the beautiful boy, so "hurt" and so little loved, as "ashamed of loving men"; his
family made him that way: his mother who spoils yet spurns; his father
who "bullies" and whom, in his fits, he "becomes exactly like" (142). Yet
Bosie loves Wilde as much as he *can* love, Oscar claims. Bosie is transfig-
ured not by desire but by Wilde's role as mediator, as a queer model with
whom Bosie identifies, whom he sometimes emulates, sometimes desires.
Here, the scene willfully muddles and misrepresents affect, as the sentimental spectator identifies and sympathizes with Wilde yet separates himself from his humbled, abjected, tragic, and blinded figure, safely placing
Oscar in heritage scenario, as tears verge on sneers.

Gilbert's film obscures even as it exposes Wilde's role as mediator.
Despite his tragic abjection, Wilde appears as a monumental subjectivity,
an autonomous and nearly messianic figure. Unlike Bosie, Robbie, Gray,
and the Taylor-circle lads who mimic and mock him, Wilde refuses to
be anyone's disciple. Constance betrays the paradox of such divine originality: no one understands the "courage he needed to be himself," she
maintains, yet he "needs disciples" (174, 96). Gilbert represents Wilde's
same-sex desire as entirely spontaneous and utterly original; his homosexual identity differs fundamentally from that of the buggering Bosie,
whom Gilbert shoots (over Fry's shoulder) rutting, while Wilde watches
(147). In *Wilde,* the model homosexual thus refuses to heed his disciples'
advice to leave England: he will not run away, for throughout his life
he "fought the English vice. . . . Hypocrisy"; if he doesn't stop Queensberry (Tom Wilkinson), "who will he harm next?" "Where your life leads
you," he tells the pleading Robbie, "you must go" (162). Borrowing from
Richard Ellmann's "magisterial biography," even as he "sometimes dis-
agreed with [Ellmann] profoundly," Mitchell represents Wilde's megalo-
maniacal self-destructiveness as heroic, exemplary, and without historical
precedent. From this perspective, Wilde appears a brilliant innovator, a
gay saint (Fry, "There Never Was" 11).

Gilbert's sentimental heritage film posits a congenital theory of homosexual causation that creates spectatorial identification and sympathy
even as it constitutes a certain distant hesitancy.[6] Mitchell's Constance
blames herself for Oscar's abandonment of the family: she spent too
much time with the children, she tells Ada (Zoë Wanamaker); she was
"too silent"—if she had "known," if she had only "spoken up" (96, 174).[7]
Robbie, too, blames himself; "if I hadn't—pushed him," he worries; yet

Ada responds, "Oscar was very lucky to meet you, Robbie. Think who else it might have been" (197). Nevertheless, Wilde blames himself for failing to "command" his feelings for Bosie. "I shall never forgive myself. If we could choose our natures," Wilde mourns to Constance, who visits him in prison. "But it's no use. Whatever our natures are, we must fulfill them. . . . I didn't know myself, I didn't know" (192–93). But Constance refuses to seek a divorce, tells her jailed husband that the children love him; cut to close-up of their hands clasping. Although these scenes of sympathy locate others as responsible even as they disavow accountability, Wilde believes that his "congenital homosexuality," as Mr. Lasker Jones would later diagnose Forster's Maurice Hall, made him do it. Affirming Wilde's role in his own tragedy, his in-court performance of "extravagant deniability" and "flamboyant display," his insistence on pursuing Queensberry's accusation of sodomy, *Wilde* confirms the historical precipitation of gay identity. Inviting late twentieth-century knowing gay spectators to admire and emulate Wilde's self-staging, seeking straight sentimental spectators to sympathize with yet differentiate themselves from him, Gilbert displays Wilde as historic origin, as icon in heritage scenario. As Neil Barrett discovers, however, Wilde is one of many origins of homosexual history, the traces of which appear in gay scandals well before 1895.[8]

Although historians of gay culture have quibbled about exactly when homosexual identity emerged and about its relationship to historically earlier sexual practices of, for example, sodomy and molly-house visit, Oscar Wilde has not been displaced as, somehow, its originator. Linda Dowling argues that, before 1895, a "new system of values and attitudes," often about art with a common relation to "the inchoate counterdiscourse of 'homosexuality,'" gradually emerged into visibility, yet the "Wilde catastrophe" nevertheless "precipitated" a "radical condensation of sexual categories" (133). Our view of Wilde's trials, she continues, as a moment of founding "is a modern construction, a myth produced in our own cultural moment" that "project[s] an as-yet-unthought of polarization of 'homosexual' versus 'heterosexual' . . . backward upon an indeterminate welter of late-Victorian psychosocial categories" (133). Yet we seem to need and demand that moment of founding, as does she; our postmodern need for clarity of vision, for certainty about gay identity, encourages us retrospectively to reconstruct Wilde as icon, to display him as representation. We thus locate our affect, sympathy; project abjection onto Wilde, the once-suffering other; and sort ourselves from him, if we are heterosexual, or, whether gay or straight, identify ourselves with his suffering. As paradoxical founder of gay identity, Wilde helps his followers invent a heritage.

Wilde's performance as iconoclastic originator of homosexual identity also serves, in gay history, to occlude his role as mediator. The "process of mediation," René Girard maintains, creates a "vivid impression of autonomy and spontaneity" when subjects are "no longer autonomous and spontaneous"; in recapturing the past original, the modern subject hides the fact that he has "always copied Others" so as "to seem original in [his] eyes" and in his own (38). Casting Wilde as originator, then, occludes the modern gay subject's role as disciple: imitating Oscar, he, too, is granted spontaneity, originality, and autonomy. Stephen Fry well understands the paradox of Wilde's position: we "ask ourselves if we have the courage to be like him," Fry writes, "by which we mean the courage to be like ourselves" ("Playing" 88). In gay culture, then, impersonation paradoxically enacts both originality and discipleship. As Alan Sinfield notes, younger users need not be aware that camp mimics the "effeminate leisure-class dandy": "they are camp because other gay boys are camp" (156). Wildean discipleship serves as the subcultural glue of post-Stonewall U.S. and post-1967 British gay communities, and Wilde as a figure for originality both incites and covers over such emulation. Heterosexual anxiety about homosexuality in the 1990s, moreover—exacerbated by the Clinton-era "don't ask, don't tell" policy, by the millennial emergence of gay civil unions, and by the juridical and congressional debates about gay marriage—has sustained and supported the discourse of homosexual founding.[9]

Gay heritage film wins sympathy from heterosexual viewers and consolidates a homosexual community by queering the period look. Gilbert's film revels in the pleasures of heritage spectacle, including in its mise-en-scène gorgeous male costume, antique furniture, and Oxbridge architectural landscapes. Country cottages, gardens, picturesque streams, and seaside sands provide quality pleasures with no postmodern edge. The heritage aesthetic of the image serves this cultural project well, for the beautiful boy may thus be attired in white flannels, costumed and coiffed, or tastefully disrobed. Rather than investigate the dynamics of homosexual relationship, one reviewer sneered, Gilbert's film "settles for 'heritage' soap opera with a muck-raking spin," its "*Masterpiece Theater*" aesthetic, "impossibly dated" (Rayns 187). Yet this reviewer fundamentally misunderstands Gilbert's cultural project. This 1990s gay male sentimental project to picture Wilde as martyr to late-Victorian sexual mores arouses sympathy, even pity, and the occasional spectatorial tear, even as it enables spectators to separate themselves from the suffering pictorial icon. Soliciting an international, middlebrow, new-professional as well as a gay audience, Gilbert joins heritage and sentiment to picture queer mediation, as Wilde is framed (both legally and on screen) and so displaced into representation as figure of sympathy and abjection, mobilizing multiple desires and identifications. Faithful to Ellmann's tragic biographical tale yet retrospectively rewritten from a contemporary perspective, *Wilde* mobilizes sentiment's double move to constitute multiple audiences.

Sentimental Queer Heritage

Merchant Ivory's gay sentimental heritage films, unlike Gilbert's, implicitly argue that gays need not imitate Oscar Wilde. Although written nearly thirty years apart, James's *The Bostonians* (1886) and Forster's *Maurice* (1914, 1971) queer the English novel's dedication to country ideology— paternal benevolence, deference due to rank, and social restraint—to represent status inconsistency and anxiety about class as central to the history of homosexual culture. Both narratives question notions of rank and national culture, and both transmute the courtship or romance plot by imagining wooer and beloved as members of the same sex. Filming two homosocial communities—the suffragists in Boston, the Socratic circle at Oxford—Merchant Ivory's James and Forster adaptations (1984, 1987) present a fluid, permeable, and multiple sexual scenario that destabilizes hierarchical status and class-based identity, that traces the historical decline of country house, gentry rank, and the British Empire. Ivory shoots heritage landscapes, country and suburban scenes, and Magdalen College architectural views (as did Gilbert in *Wilde*) to produce spectatorial pleasure appropriate to period drama. Remediating novels about sentimental homosociality, Merchant Ivory mobilizes the spectatorial relations of identification and desire to constitute gay subcultures, to arouse heterosexual sympathy, and to allay straight anxiety.[10] These films' "restrained and even dour" aesthetic, Claire Monk says, makes "gay men seem 'just like everyone else'" ("Sexuality" 9–10).

In *Maurice*, Forster's unstable hierarchy of classes exposes status inconsistency and anxiety, inscribing the gentry's historical decline. Forster acknowledges in his "Terminal Note" that Clive Durham represents

Cambridge; Maurice Hall, Suburbia (*Maurice* 251). Yet Clive is also a member of a once powerful aristocracy that must confront its modern political limits. Once Wiltshire's squires and now its lawyers and politicians, Clive's family wishes him not to "depart from their tradition" of land annexation, estate improvement, and county politics (70). Marked not by "decay" but "immobility," however, the country house displays its "bad repair," improper management, and "dilapidation" (89, 166). By novel's end, the suburban Maurice deems the "derelict" country house "unfit to set standards" or "control the future" of England (239). Maurice's and Clive's national yet oedipal narratives—the two are sons of symmetrical fatherless families—pose the question: shall each representative young man step into "the niche that England had prepared for him" (55)? Shall Clive, as his mother dreams, "take his place in the countryside," manage the "game" and the "tenants," and enter "politics" (95)? Shall Maurice fulfill his "promis[e]" as "suburban tyrant," enter his father's old firm, and "stiffen" into a "pillar of [the] church" (101, 46)? Nevertheless, Clive canvasses for reform, vaguely hoping to help the poor even as he condescends to his servants, tenants, and neighbors at cricket (167). Seeing his mirror image in a shop, Maurice recognizes "a solid young citizen": "Quiet, honourable, prosperous without vulgarity" (154). Whereas Clive assumes the paternal mantle, the middle-class Maurice rejects deference due to rank and paternal benevolence and, in his affair with the gamekeeper, exuberantly undermines social restraint, even as status inconsistency feeds queer arousal.

Whereas Forster sets suburban against gentry ranks, James's U.S. novel sets national region against region. Forster gently ridicules the masculine culture of English public school, Cambridge, the country house, the sporting green, and the office, but James scoffs at the American culture of suffragism, spiritualism, and the Boston marriage. James positions Brahmin, cultured Boston against pretentious, metropolitan New York and both northeast cities against the Deep South's failed "old slave-holding oligarchy" (*The Bostonians* 12). The Civil War between North and South also serves as metaphor for the war between the sexes, via Basil Ransom's and Olive Chancellor's cross-regional and erotically rivalrous cousinship, a relation that appears alongside the sibling thematic that, in Oscar Wilde, covertly represents homosexuality. Just as Forster mocks the class relations of heritage culture, James parodies regional conflict, destabilizes gender arrangements, and bemoans the decay of paternal benevolence.

Writing a "check for a considerable amount," a phallicized Olive buys Verena from her father, who pockets the check into "some queer place on his queer person" (168). As she "bargain[s]" with Olive, Mrs. Burrage hopes to "buy" the Boston girl for her feminized, piano-playing son (311). In James's postgentrified American culture, an emasculated paternalism exchanges aristocratic or gentry benevolence for crass but pragmatic capitalism, and deference due to rank for phony chivalry.

James deploys the courtship plot to depict late-century paternalism in crisis and heterosexual masculinity under siege. Ransom thinks female public speaking resembles a "stage" show, with Verena as "singer," "trapeze" artist, or "actress before the footlights" (269–70). Yet Verena preaches liberation from the "'comfortable, cozy, convenient box, with nice glass sides,'" a confinement in which women "'have been kept for centuries'" (274). Verena's domestic "glass box" resembles nothing so much as Sedgwick's "glass closet" (*Closet* 164), in which secrecy and threat deform the imprisoned figure, from which escape seems impossible, and in which forced self-exhibition solicits an antifeminist or homophobic gaze. Olive's and Verena's Boston marriage, which describes a common New England female erotic arrangement, topically coincides with a sentimentalized homosexuality; less socially constrained than homosexual men, these women nonetheless submit equally to homophobic threat—in the figure of Basil Ransom and in their fear of publicity, pilloried so well by the character Matthew Pardon. Ransom rants to his prey:

> "The whole generation is womanized; the masculine tone is passing out of the world; it's a feminine, a nervous, hysterical, chattering, canting age, an age of hollow phrases and false delicacy and exaggerated solicitudes and coddled sensibilities, which, if we don't soon look out, will usher in the reign of mediocrity. . . . The masculine character, the ability to dare and endure . . . that is what I want to preserve." (343)

As Verena capitulates to his "siege" and Ransom "palpitat[es] with his victory," the narrative concludes with James's narratorial ambivalence about the heteronormative outcome he so devoutly wishes yet so thoroughly reviles: "It is to be feared that, with the union, so far from brilliant, into which she was about to enter, these were not the last [tears] she was destined to shed" (399, 464). Soliciting his reader's tears *and* outrage, James portrays the struggle to resist homophobic threat even as his courtship plot creates the heterosexual couple.[11]

If James queers the courtship plot by triangulating two homoerotically linked females and a hypermasculinized, heterosexual man, *Maurice* queers narrative courtship by seeking to couple two gay men in the face of homophobic threat. Forster's unprecedented cultural project—to portray a sentimental seduction involving gay sexual acts—produces uncertainty about how to plot. What major cardinal functions or narrative kernels, for example, structure stories of gay sex? Clive's sudden illness (he faints when dining with the Halls) indexes hysterical effeminacy (he can't stop sobbing) and signals his emerging antihomosexual disgust. "Against my will I have become normal," he writes Maurice, while recuperating in, ironically, Greece (116). After a later "row," Maurice weeps: "'What's going to happen?'" "'What an ending!'" (130). The tear as sign marks these events as major cardinal functions, but to characters ignorant about Clive's and Maurice's desire—as to the knowing reader—they seem strangely unmotivated. Forster's plot is full of narrative illogic. Maurice's grandfather—a supernumerary character—falls ill and dies, anointing Ada as his heir and expunging paternalism from the novel; Maurice's self-induced "rivalry" with Ada over Clive ends with her engagement to Chapman (141); Maurice falls for a schoolboy—but knows it's just "lust" (150). Next, Maurice seeks a hypnotist who treats inverts, but the countrified Alec Scudder sabotages his psychic treatment (192). After gamekeeper and professional have sex, introducing a moment of risk into the narrative, homophobic threat looms, as Alec subsequently bullies and blackmails Maurice. Nevertheless, the two male lovers couple—and Forster insists on his ending's credibility. "A happy end was imperative," he says, for it allows two men to "fall in love and remain in it for the ever and ever that fiction allows"; if it "ended unhappily, with a lad dangling from a noose or with a suicide pact, all would be well" for homophobic readers intent on witnessing suffering and punishment. Forster's sentimental rural England, a fantasied and projected scene of sympathy without spectators, imagines sexually gratified ghosts "roam[ing] the greenwood" (250, 254).

Forster believes that his "ever and ever" can be achieved only in a story with "period interest" (254). Although he means by this phrase historically anachronistic and narratively trivial, Forster's interest in what is now period detail makes *Maurice* apt for queer heritage appropriation. John Hill and Andrew Higson argue that, in heritage film, spectacle subverts narrative trajectory and that this focus on display trivializes a source novel's socially progressive thematics. For Hill, heritage deploys a "pictorial rather than dramatic" style, and the pleasure of looking necessarily "undercut[s]" spectatorial comprehension of a narrative's "social criticism" (Hill, *1980s* 80, 86). For Higson, heritage stages "a space for display of heritage properties rather than for the enactment of dramas" and eschews "emotional engagement" in favor of a "fascination" with "period artefacts," "splendid" costumes, and scenes of "landscape properties conserved by the National Trust"; heritage spectacle "undermines" plots characterized by "liberal or 'progressive' sentiments" (*Heritage* 39–40). Quality pleasure demands a different libidinal economy of narrative, of the look, and of emotional tone or attitude, however, when associated with gay cultural projects. *Maurice* and *The Bostonians*, for example, solicit audience affect by dramatizing filiative and affiliative encounters; the tears, goose bumps, and fears appropriate to closeted or constrained figural emotions constitute their mood, or tone. Gay heritage plots thus devalue "fast pace and narrative energy," exploring instead "character, place, atmosphere, and milieu."[12] Merchant Ivory's heritage aesthetic eschews rapid cutting and close-ups to create scenes of seduction differently, while providing the emotional pleasures of sympathy and identification.

Maurice and *The Bostonians* foreground the *culture* in heritage to attract a professional middle-class spectator. In *The Bostonians*, Olive (Vanessa Redgrave) reads to Verena (Madeleine Potter) in a Victorian drawing room; they browse in the library, touch artifacts at a museum, and frolic in Harvard Yard in the rain; dissolve to Olive's scrapbooks, as the suffragist crosses frame left to show the pictures to Verena; the two embrace; in flashback, females gather for the photograph Verena later looks at—close-up of lens, flash; laughing, Olive reads a letter to Verena: should women cook or attend Harvard with their fellows? Here, Merchant Ivory's heritage mise-en-scène visualizes cultural exchange as sentimental; the pictured homosocial, homoerotic bond elicits spectatorial identification and sympathy and provides tasteful quality pleasures. In *Maurice*, scenes of sympathy picture male homosocial and homoerotic companionship. The first sequence—intertitle: "Cambridge, 1909"—opens with a panorama of King's College, Cambridge (Long, *Films* 151); cut to shot through windows, pan into and across Dean's room, to men chatting about culture over tea; cut to close-up of three feet tapping, tilt up legs, as students translate Plato, hesitating over passages about "the beloved." Later, a spire pierces a Gothic arch; Maurice (James Wilby) looks for Risley (Mark Tandy); cut to Clive (Hugh Grant), reading pianola scores of Tchaikovsky. In these sequences, metaphors for heritage culture (literary, political, and musical), for homosocial relations (conversation, dining, reading, frolicking), and for closeted homoeroticism (spatial piercing, doors opening, window being penetrated) produce period interest and gay quality pleasures.

To solicit sentimental heritage spectators, Ivory shoots English landscapes, seascapes, and suburban scenes; Magdalen College architectural views; and interior decor as tasteful settings for same-sex passion. Although for Higson, the Cambridge scenes simply "follow the views," functioning minimally as establishing shots, in fact, these scenes picture homoerotic desire and sexual arousal for a sentimental spectator.[13] Three crane shots of colleges; intertitle: "Summer term, 1909"; cut to close-up of Clive; slow track out, he leans against a white-flannel-clad thigh; a hand creeps into upper-right frame, caresses Clive's hair; cut to embrace with Maurice. In Cambridge and country house scenes, Ivory has said, window entry represents the "desire to penetrate to the innermost parts of certain places" (Long, *Conversation* 216). Two establishing shots surround a close-up of Clive, thinking in bed; cut to window, Maurice climbs in, announces "I love you," hugs, kisses, and climbs out the window. Cut to the two men on motorcycle and sidecar; to a close-up of two hands, joining; to two men lying in a field, touching, fondling, and kissing: Clive's "no." Later, Scudder (Rupert Graves) climbs through another window into Maurice's room at Pendersleigh: "Lie down," he insists, kissing Maurice's bare chest. Cut to Maurice entering the boathouse, rousing a sleeping Alec, and, in close-up, the two kiss; in shot/reverse shot: "Now, we shan't never be parted," Alec announces. In the morning, the men talk, shot fully nude, about sex and money. Reserving the public "gaze" for a different kind of "romance," contrary to what Higson suggests, *Maurice* depicts quality pleasures of looking, desiring, and hoping for a happy ending for homosexual lovers (*Heritage* 39, 38).

In *The Bostonians*, an 1880s and 1890s American painterly aesthetic pictures female same-sex desire. Two women, costumed entirely in white cotton, frolic on a rocky New England coast: Verena hugs Olive and sings Poe—it's their "kingdom by the sea"—as the two begin slowly to dance. This sequence associates shore, virginal attire, and female embrace to depict the women's pleasures as aesthetic, bodily, and regional: as Boston marriage or protolesbian coupling. Later, the two women in white talk on the shore; Olive lies on the sand on her side, a fully clothed odalisque, and Verena lies aslant atop her, facing the camera. Still later, the seaside serves as a backdrop for the battle between same-sex and heterosexual passion that gets played out on Cape Cod. Low-angle shots of a phallic Basil Ransom (Christopher Reeve), striding atop the dunes or cliffs as he appears to the beached ladies; drum roll on sound track. Miss Birdseye (Jessica Tandy), in long shot, pictorially arranged under umbrella, watches, thinking of death. Here, the horizon is high on the frame, flattening out heritage mise-en-scène as though it were a Long Island landscape by William Merritt Chase or a peopled nocturne by James McNeill Whistler.[14] In these scenarios of protolesbian desire and of hypermasculinized threat, seascapes girdle a homosocial community or provide a boundary between the sexes. This pictorial aesthetic, like the cultured mise-en-scène, behooves Ivory's sentimental project to make gay and lesbians visible to the culture at large in 1984, the year the bathhouse scandal broke in San Francisco.

The gay heritage scene of sympathy moves the spectator to sentimental identification by making visible the look upon which it depends. As Ransom emerges the victor for Verena's affections, Ivory intercuts scenes

Maurice Hall and Clive Durham have their first, surprised embrace. (Maurice, 1987)

of a lonely, silent Olive with those of Ransom's successful seduction. The camera tilts slowly from a close-up of stacked handwritten letters (signifying time's passing), up Olive's neck, to an extreme close-up of her sad face; cut to Olive alone, on the widow's walk, looking; to the shore, where Olive stands still in a pictorial long shot, looking; to the drawing room, as the maid wonders why Verena has not returned; cut to Ransom and Verena on shore, she exiting right rear, stopping, returning, he rising from the boat, as the two embrace, kiss; cut to Olive onshore at dusk, still looking, in long shot; running into frame plane, she holds her side as though in pain; she dashes across sunset-lit dunes to the left; she kneels by the inlet, weeping, in long shot; dissolve to shot/reverse shot of Olive looking at sea, Verena's fantasied corpse washing ashore. In this remarkable sequence, Olive's movements, whether frenzied or immobile, drawn against a nocturnal, almost Whistlerian landscape, depict her desiring search for Verena and her desperation over her friend's desertion. Stage-and-heritage star Vanessa Redgrave—with subdued British accent, careful diction, sober timbre of voice, mobile face, and expressive eyes—enhances Olive's affective power, feminist point, and narrative functionality.[15]

Olive Chancellor and Verena Tarrant, all in white, by the rocks and sea of Cape Cod. (The Bostonians, *1984*)

At *Maurice*'s end, Clive's likewise sad look suggests his yearning for Maurice and his marriage's failure. Embracing Anne (Phoebe Nicholls) from behind, reflected in her dressing mirror, Clive looks melancholy; she, anxious. Clive closes the bedroom shutters; cut to his look out the window; cut to a montage of a remembered Maurice, shouting joyfully at Cambridge; Clive and Anne, shot from the garden, look worriedly out the window; fade to credits. In an earlier bedroom scene, Anne twice looks covertly at her husband's naked buttocks, then away, squeezing her eyes closed; Clive, close-up on pillow, looks mournfully into the darkened room, perhaps thinking of the absent beloved. As Clive, Hugh Grant, in his first feature film, emerged into heritage stardom; as Maurice, James Wilby quietly glamorized the to-be-looked-at suburbanite desired by gentry and country youths alike. Edits that foreground Grant's and Wilby's looks—and looks—structure these long, silent scenes that create sentimental identification and sympathy for the protogay figure and acknowledge the anxiety that subtends that figure's silence. Making the look visible, these scenes identify the beloved's function as to-be-looked-at, even as they frustrate the looker's looking to arouse spectatorial sympathy.

Merchant Ivory's pictorial aesthetic appropriates James's. In an 1883 notebook entry, James sketched his desire to write a novel with a "*pictorial* quality" (Howe x; emphasis in original). He chose to write "a very American tale," a tale about the "situation of women, the decline of the sentiment of sex, the agitation on [women's] behalf" that, as Irving Howe suggests, produced *The Bostonians*' "undisciplined pictorial looseness" (xi). Yet James's pictorialism is hardly undisciplined, and he mobilizes it as both scene painting and inclusive social scenario. Indeed, James paints his social pictures by enabling the narrator to move flexibly among the consciousnesses of his characters rather than to see only through the eyes of one. In the novel's first third, Ransom serves as focalizer, thereby facilitating James's scathing portrait of woman suffrage and its adherents— shown to be fools, egoists, and old maids all. Ransom judges the harmless Miss Birdseye, for example, "a confused, entangled, inconsequent, discursive old woman, whose charity began at home and ended nowhere" (27). Rant follows. Later, the reader sees events from Olive's perspective and so feels sympathy for the woman Ransom at first views as "a signal old maid" (18). Nevertheless, our narrator calls Olive martyr, hysteric, and spinster, whereas he embraces a qualified version of Ransom's radically skeptical conservatism. "I shall not attempt a complete description of Ransom's ill-starred views," he notes, "being convinced that the reader will guess them as he goes"; yet, he worries, "I betray him a little," for Ransom "never mentioned such feelings"; "he liked to talk as well as anyone; but he could hold his tongue" (194–95). In this narratorial situation, the narrator bonds with Ransom, whom he seems to know, and with the reader, whom he identifies as male. This clubby masculinist narratorial stance, complicit with homophobic anxiety, threatens the female and suffragist community otherwise represented in the novel.[16] This male homosociality also facilitates the novel's pictorial method, enabling its wide-ranging portrait of nineteenth-century New England's social movements, cultural crazes, gender debates, and emergent public discourses.

Merchant Ivory's queer heritage adaptations remain largely "faithful" to their source narratives' *"purpose"* (Long, *Conversation* 158). Jhabvala says of *The Bostonians* that the "great scenes" are "all there," so she faithfully transfers major cardinal functions and narrative kernels from one narrative medium to another (DVD). Jhabvala's and Hesketh-Harvey's screenplays nevertheless crucially change narrative chronology and logic. Jhabvala suggested that Hesketh-Harvey strengthen her screenplay for *Maurice* by inserting a narrative sequence that rationalizes Clive's conversion: Lord Risley accosts a soldier, is arrested, sent to court, and sentenced to hard labor for "taking advantage of a man of the lower orders."[17] Here, Jhabvala's proposed sequence historicizes the narrative's context, for in England, the Criminal Law Amendment Act of 1885—which sought to moralize male sexuality by raising the age of consent for girls, to prevent child prostitution and female slavery—also outlawed, via the Labouchere Amendment, "acts of gross indecency"—private homosexual bodily contacts of undetermined nature and kind—between men.[18] Risley's fate thus recalls Oscar Wilde's, as the legal penalties for practicing homosexual acts reduce to ruin one aristocratic male and cause another to go straight. This added narrative kernel also reduces the plot's courtship muddle and makes heteronormativity appear doubly functional, if deadly dull. Jhabvala's adaptation of *The Bostonians,* on the contrary, alters not a narrative kernel or cardinal function but the story's conclusion. The novel's end, she says, was "good for James" but not for Verena, the film, or modern consciousness (DVD). As a hooded Verena elopes with her penniless lover, Olive takes her place and delivers a resounding oration that wins enthusiastic applause; fade to credits. Jhabvala's narrative additions and changes to both films depict the terroristic effects of homophobic blackmail, the homosexual panic of a sympathetic gay character, and the power of speaking out in public. Released during the time of Thatcher's antigay funding legislation, of AIDS crisis and homophobic backlash, *Maurice*'s "coming out" narrative defines the sentimental gay cultural project.[19]

Jhabvala and Ivory submit James's characters, atmosphere, tone, and perspective to adaptation proper, enhancing heritage spectacle to represent feminist politics as patriotic. Fourth of July fireworks serve as a backdrop for Miss Birdseye's birthday, and parallel editing of fireworks, applauding audiences, and singing women link feminist's celebration to the nation's; as Miss Birdseye blows out her cake's candles, her comrades chorus about "one big army, marching on" as "Stars and Stripes" plays on the sound track. Jhabvala's screenplay expunges the novel's multiple centers of consciousness, altering James's conservative gender politics and celebrating same-sex passion. During James's time, the Boston marriage, a culturally sanctioned and publicly accepted long-term monogamous relationship between women, was commonplace in New England literary circles and perhaps in James's own family, yet, Martha Vicinus notes, the protolesbian couple appeared as well in Northern Europe, where educated, professional women lived outside the heterosexual marital unit (246). Whereas, Jhabvala notes, James could only suggest, via the protolesbian couple, how "crazy" Olive is about Verena, the 1980s film could show lesbian sexual fascination. Verena tells Olive about her correspondence with Ransom while the two women undress, then dress one another, in their Lower East Side lodgings; as the gong rings for lunch, the women kiss and make up.

In James's and Forster's narratives, homosexuality is "unspeakable," for both tell stories of the closet. Although Miss Birdseye says of Olive and Verena as a couple, "'It's a very close and very beautiful tie, and we think everything of it here,'" James never mentions the women's erotic connection (*The Bostonians* 223).[20] The relationship makes narrative sense, however, only if the Olive-Verena-Ransom triangle is doubly erotic—both heterosexual and lesbian. Here, James's novel anticipates and Merchant Ivory's film confirms the centrality of the secrecy/disclosure binary to queer narrative and spectacle. Whereas James's novel is complicit with the closet, Forster's novel—when published—interrogates it. Forster portrays the hypocrisy of Maurice's Oxford don, for example, in whose translation class "the unspeakable vice of the Greeks" is omitted yet who is later revealed by his nephew, Lord Risley, to be himself heterosexually confused and perhaps impotent (*Maurice* 51). To erase the Greeks' "'inclin[ation],'" Clive avers, "'omit[s] the mainstay of Athenian society'"; Maurice, who "hadn't known [the unspeakable] could be mentioned" felt "a breath of liberty" touch him (51). Yet *Maurice* everywhere emphasizes the legal and social unacceptablity of gay male sex in early twentieth-century Britain; in novel and film, Mr. Lasker Jones advises Maurice to live outside England, where homosexuality "is no longer criminal" (211). Nevertheless, the Labouchere Amendment remained in effect, for although the Wolfenden Committee's 1957 Report produced legislation that tightened restrictions on prostitution, its recommendations that private, consensual sex between homosexuals be decriminalized were not enacted until the 1967 Sexual Offenses Act.[21] As a result, Forster's novel, as his "Terminal Note" suggests, "remain[ed] in manuscript" and was published only posthumously (250). Merchant Ivory brings *Maurice*'s moment of liberty to the screen and, in doing so, restores the love that dare not speak its name to its central place in heritage film.

As published novel and gay heritage film, *Maurice* appropriates and revises Oscar Wilde for the twentieth century. Indeed, Maurice can only name his sexual preference to Dr. Barry by identifying himself as "'an unspeakable of the Oscar Wilde sort'" (159). Forster's self-censored novel reconsiders the public-school and Cambridge culture that manipulated male homosociality and tolerated homoerotic (if not homosexual) friendships, that instilled in students the Hellenic cultural tradition that, Dowling suggests, historically preceded and shaped Oscar Wilde's aesthetic, imbibed under Walter Pater's tutelage (113–27). Yet "Maurice doesn't have to be like Oscar Wilde," the film and novel show (Sinfield 140). Forster's project masculinizes Maurice, thereby revising the post-1895 notion that the man who practiced gross indecency was an effeminate dandy and would-be aristocrat.[22] In this sentimental heritage film, Ivory provides Maurice the "sympathy" for which he "yearns," moving his audience to the same sadness they see displayed on Clive's face at the film's end. Paradoxically, however, Forster's self-censorship of his homosexual novel facilitated the Wildean stereotype's emergence as a gay North Atlantic cultural type: the effeminate, dandified, high-cultural connoisseur of opera, ballet, and celebrity (Bronski 92–143). Although Wilde erupted into print (biography, memoir, trial transcript, complete works, letters, and literary-critical studies) and onto the screen in the mid-1940s, by the 1990s, the Wildean icon had become synonymous with queering culture.

The Queer Gothic Look

Wilde's allegory of closeted representation, *The Picture of Dorian Gray*, queers the already curious gothic to solicit readers who, like Dorian, become spectators of "Dorian." For Sedgwick, Wilde's gothic novel "condenses" triangular male desire for and rivalry over the beautiful boy into a plot about "the mysterious bond of figural likeness and figural expiation between Dorian Gray and his own portrait" (*Closet* 164, 160). That expiation, moreover, culminates and concludes the gothic plot: painting a tableau in which two men, "transparent" to one another, "chase *a deux*" across an evacuated landscape "toward a climax that tends to condense the amorous with the murderous in a representation of male rape" (*Men* 91; *Closet* 163). Although Sedgwick does not define "transparent," it stands for, I believe, the gothic gay narrative's investment in specularity, a making visible of the sentimental look under the regime of unspeakability. Creating multiple scenes of figural looking at the portrait, Wilde stimulates not scenes of sympathy but identification with and introjection of the picture's youthful beauty. A site of displaced affect in the sentimental scenario, the picture also mobilizes the rivalrous, envious affects of mimetic desire; as representation, it offers replication as metaphor for closeted homosexual reproduction through spectatorial relations. The figures that gather to look at the semblance of Dorian debate that spectatorship: is it aesthetic or immoral? The narratorial situation stages the reader's look as allied to and relayed with Dorian's, making queer specularity perverse, a swerving from heteronormativity.

Wilde's matrix for queer gothic's reproduction of "life" as art may be mapped onto Mary Shelley's monstrous scene of creativity, in which, as she describes it in her 1831 "Introduction" to *Frankenstein,* her imagined scientist and she exchange looks with her hallucinated monster through a veiling curtain: a "thrill of fear" ran through her (172). When Basil Hallward's eyes first meet Dorian's, a "curious sensation of terror" "came over" the painter, a sense that Dorian might "absorb" or "dominat[e]" his "whole nature [or] soul" (*The Picture of Dorian Gray* 6). As Shelley's scientist creates monstrous life in the attic laboratory, so Basil Hallward "'recreate[s] life'" as a beautiful portrait that grows monstrous in the attic schoolroom (10). Dorian takes "real pleasure in watching" this "most magical of mirrors," as, mocking Narcissus, he kisses those "painted lips" (103). "Was it to become a monstrous and loathsome thing[?]" Dorian wonders about the portrait that specularizes his body and soul, takes on his looks, and makes him spectator of a semblance of himself, makes him semblance to himself (103). The look inscribes the technology of specular discipleship; serving as artist's model, the beautiful boy is replicated as picture, later hung high in the attic, framed and covered by curtain. Come to a kind of life, which registers on the framed face, the painting allegorizes the displacement of affect into representation. As moral index, it looks on and knowingly judges Dorian's dandyism.

This matrix of specularity, dispersed across the narrative, figures the queer aesthetic as a form of monstrous mediation. First seeing Dorian at Hallward's studio, Lord Henry Wotton begins vampirically to "influence" Basil's sitter: "'All influence is immoral,'" he croons; "'to influence a person is to give him one's own soul'" (16–17). Dorian has had, he insists, "'thoughts that have filled [him] with terror, day-dreams and sleeping dreams whose mere memory might stain [his] cheek with shame—'" (18). The older man had "touched some secret chord that had never been touched before," our narrator avers, that was now "vibrating and throbbing to curious pulses" (18). "'There is no such thing as a good influence,'" Wotton says, for the tutelary subject "'does not think his natural thoughts, or burn with his natural passions. . . . His sins, if there are such things as sins, are borrowed. He becomes an echo of some one else's music, an actor of a part that has not been written for him'" (16–17). The look between two men morphs into the vanitous, rivalrous triangle of mimetic desire, for the relations among Lord Henry, Basil, and Dorian make sense only if they represent homoerotic as well as homosocial desire and identification. Aghast at Dorian's heartless response to Sybil Vane's death, Basil Hallward cries, "'You look exactly the same wonderful boy'" who served as his model; the transformation to cad "'is all Harry's influence'" (105, 18). Here, Wilde identifies the scene of specular mediation as the primary mode of closeted gay cultural projects; whether poisoned by vampiric word, decadent book, or the pathological connoisseurship of chapter 11, the vamped boy sorts himself from suffering, locating affects of moral anguish in his semblance.[23] Himself model, displaced into representation, and pictorial spectator, Dorian is a figure for the multiplied knowledge produced by spectatorial relations.

Dorian also enters into spectatorial relations with his ancestors' portraits, becoming thereby subject and other, spectator of their figures and displaced through them into representation as well as filial (re)semblance.

As Dorian strolls through his country house's "gaunt cold picture-gallery," looking at the "portraits of those whose blood flowed in his veins," Wilde posits pederastic mentorship as genealogical aristocratic transmission (139). Unlike Elizabeth Bennet, who, as aroused spectator of Darcy's and his ancestors' portraits, practiced acculturation to enhance her worth for upper-gentry marriage, Dorian, already a spectator of his own semblance, becomes, through spectatorship of his ancestral portraits, both aristocratic descendant and monstrous specter. "Was it young Herbert's life that he sometimes led," he wonders; "had some strange poisonous germ crept from body to body till it had reached his own" (139)? Perhaps his "macaroni" forebear's sensuality, or the Prince Regent's companion's delight in orgies: "How curious it all seemed!" (140).[24] The ancestral gallery leads, we think, to Dorian's own attic-bound portrait, but, no, to his mother's picture: as Dorian looks at it, his painted mother laughs, her carnation withers, the wine spills from her cup, her eyes seem "to follow him wherever he went" (140). Just as Dorian's portrait's face displays his hidden immorality, his mother's image betrays her once-lived decadence. In a curious reversal, the painted figure becomes her son's spectator and, as her look follows his body, the reader recalls another attic-bound semblance, that of Dorian himself. That picture has by reversal become the "real" or original Dorian, whose innocent face bears no trace of his sins, and the painting has become his own precursor. Indeed, Ellmann notes that Wilde treated his mother "almost as though he were her precursor rather than she his" (5). In *The Picture of Dorian Gray,* Wilde scripts the novel's open secret as a closeted inheritance from sodomite, dandy, alcoholic, and sinful pre-selves, for, Dorian imagines, these ancestors simply multiply his personality, and, as their lives become his own, they are subsumed by and end in him. Dorian, like Wilde, is subject/other, model/picture, and spectator/specter of his destiny, strange amalgam of substance, spectacle, and spectatorship: the tragic position necessarily occupied by the queer in the 1890s, Wilde insists.

Dorian's ancestral portraits anticipate the novel's staging of identification or introjection, the displacement of the suffering other into representation, and self-sorting, into which the reader as figurative spectator is seduced. "'It has all the terrible beauty of a Greek tragedy,'" Dorian says of Sybil Vane's death, "'a tragedy in which I took a great part, but by which I have not been wounded'" (98). Lord Henry explains this paradox: "'Suddenly, we find that we are no longer the actors, but the spectators of the play. Or rather, we are both. We watch ourselves, and the mere wonder of the spectacle enthralls us'" (98). Just as Dorian is spectator of, spectacle in, and semblance of his portrait, so he watches and participates in the tragedy of Sybil's death—without himself being deeply affected. The genre he names, tragedy, also identifies murder, suicide, and displacement as central to this drama, for, becoming sentimental spectator, Dorian, who implicitly "performs" as Sybil's lover yet sits with Lord Henry in the audience, thus enjoys the coverture afforded by the drama's acted scene of sympathy. Sedgwick's "subcategories of the sentimental" swirl around this performative yet spectatorial setting: "the prurient; the morbid; the wishful; the snobbish; the knowing; the arch" (*Closet* 151). Each term describes Dorian's identification with and incorporation of Lord Henry's scornful judgment of Sybil's artistic failure, her sentimental and sacramental self-sacrifice. Lord Henry's participation in this dramatic scene of sympathy mobilizes Sybil's displacement into representation: his location as second spectating other, at his aristocratic ease, empties her acting of substance, making art into artifice, as Dorian's love is transmuted into "exquisite disdain" (90). Once Desdemona, Ophelia, Juliet, and Imogen— "'all the heroines of romance,'" Wotton says—Sybil, displaced into drama, has "'never really lived, and so she has never really died'" (99).

Dorian's position as participant and spectator echoes the "double strategy" by which Wilde constitutes his 1890s spectators as both knowing and distanced. This Wildean move, Regenia Gagnier argues, operates on the uses of class or rank for a derisive yet comic culture. Putting on stage characters who represent the old "ineffectual nobility" and gentry, at whom "the new administrative and enterprising classes could laugh, even while they prided themselves on having usurped their power," Wilde reflects to his spectators, in a mediated form, their own conspicuous consumption yet enables them to laugh at the farce. Seducing a coterie, an "audience of intimates," by contrast, Wilde enables members of his circle to read his homosexual subtexts, which please his disciples and multiply their number (106, 46). Wilde constructed himself as late-century celebrity precisely through spectatorship; "to a great extent," Gagnier claims, "*Dorian Gray* is about *spectators*" (57). This mode of spectatorship is historically and culturally possible only in an emergent mass society of the spectacle, ruled by dependence on the image and on advertising (8–10). Although this spectator is theatrical and self-fashioning, Wilde likewise constitutes spectatorship in his narrative. An implicit narratee watches the spectacle alongside the narrator, even as figural and narratorial discourse constitutes him as participant in the play. "It was the passions about whose origin we deceived ourselves that tyrannized most strongly over us," Lord Henry thinks to himself; in this scenario, "we" refers to himself and his other self, himself and his contemporaries, the narrator and narratee, the implied author and implied reader (95). Later, Dorian ruminates: "Nay, without thought or conscious desire, might not things external to ourselves vibrate in unison with our moods and passions?" (103). Here, our narrator's free indirect discourse implicitly identifies his narratee—and Wilde, his reader—as member of a coterie, which enables the reader vicariously to participate in the Dorian camaraderie and to watch it at the same time: he, too, plays a part without being wounded.

During the novel's own historical moment—a decade in which the aristocracy was visibly losing its normative social force—shifting class tensions among rising groups such as dandies, gentlemen, and new women precipitated a crisis of masculinity (Gagnier 51). In the wake of World War II, when Albert Lewin released his film adaptation of *The Picture of Dorian Gray*, the first in thirty years, Britain was likewise confronting new class and gender tensions and postwar problems: the need to rebuild bombed-out cities and suburbs, to jump-start a stalled economy, to equalize wealth through creation of the welfare state, to ensure that Britain's population growth sustained its national position and influence, and to restore moral masculine virility so as to enhance the family's stability (Weeks 232–39). In the postwar United States, masculine anxiety served the social need to move factory-employed women back to the private sphere; the lack of suitable housing for returning GIs caused the explosion of suburbs; and an emergent baby boom necessarily moved women into the new home (May 37–91, 135–61). These 1950s gender anxieties, subtended by worry about the nation's future role in the world and the postwar economy, eclipsed gay culture and returned gays and lesbians to the closet. In response to these social imperatives and to the strictures of Hollywood's Production Code, Lewin's *The Picture of Dorian Gray* (1945) heterosexualizes its hero. Rewriting the plot to create the marital couple, the film entices North Atlantic women into marital happiness and fidelity. Suppressing Wilde's novel's homosexual subtext, Lewin soothes injured postwar masculinity during a decade of anxiety about gender, nationalism, and economics.

Lewin's and Dan Curtis Productions' adaptations of *The Picture of Dorian Gray* rewrite Wilde's tale about the closet as heterosexual romance.

In Lewin's film, Dorian's (Hurd Hatfield) trips to London's underworld portray his sins as drinking, drugging, and heterosexual whoring; the trapped Sybil Vane (Angela Lansbury) trills the nationalistic anthem, "liberty can't be sold." The film thus solicits a postwar middle-class spectator who, if female, sympathizes with Sybil's desire to escape the barroom and marry; who, if male, excoriates Dorian's lust even as he enjoys Dorian's sexual triumphs. The figure of Gladys, Basil Hallward's niece (Donna Reed, before her eponymous TV show for 1950s U.S. housewives), who appears at one witty dinner party in Wilde's novel, provides Hallward an upper-middle-class home with child and nanny. The girlish Gladys lisps her intention to wed Dorian; when grown up, she will propose marriage, if he fails to do so. At film's end, Gladys's eavesdropping wannabe boyfriend, David (Peter Lawford), bribes a servant and so enters the attic schoolroom, thus preparing for Dorian's portrait's unmasking before an audience of intimates, an unmasking that will unite the heterosexual couple following its destruction—and Dorian's.

Remaking Lewin's film, Dan Curtis's teleplay, *The Picture of Dorian Gray* (1973), recaps the protagonist's sins of slumming, drug-and-alcohol dependence, and heterosexual whoring. Once more, Hallward's niece, here Beatrice (Linda Kelsey), falls in love while a child with her uncle Dory, and this time she marries him, in a saccharine wedding tableau. Dorian's (Shane Briant) extensive voice-over, like Lord Henry's (by George Sanders) in Lewin's film, narrates his own disloyalty, (unspecified acts of) debauchery, and efforts to go straight with Beatrice. Scribbling in his diary, Dorian sends Beatrice to bed without him, then takes one last look at the portrait he hopes will prove his heterosexual love, his "new life," worthy. After his self-penetration, skeletal hand on corpse chest, Dorian's voice-over continues its narration, speaking the film's moral after his death. Who speaks? Who writes? The teleplay neither asks nor answers, as schlock gothic eschews any overt reference to homosexuality, any hint of the closet. Despite the demise of the Production Code and the emergence, in 1968, of the ratings system, Curtis's *Dorian* went straighter than ever, perhaps because Dan Curtis Productions (originators and remakers of *Dark Shadows* [ABC 1966–71]) specialized in soap-opera horror for the small screen during a decade in which the U.S. audience demanded escape yet sought out covert representation of their class, gender, and fiscal fears and woes. Beleaguered by oil shortages, price controls, double-digit inflation, and high interest rates, North American cultural consumers purchased

Curtis's schlock gothic because it sentimentalized and melodramatized an unspoken conversion narrative: to marriage and fidelity.

John Gorrie's queer teleplay, *The Picture of Dorian Gray* (1965, 1976), dramatized by John Osborne during the sexual revolution, rehabilitates the sentimental queer for TV, later for theatrical, audiences. Osborne prettifies Dorian (Peter Firth) almost to girlishness, as he swishes and minces across sound stages and drops onto chaises longues. When he first appears in Basil Hallward's studio, dressed in white, and Basil (Jeremy Brett) introduces him to Lord Henry (John Gielgud), Dorian rustles across the room and puts out his hand; when he wishes himself eternally young, he dashes to the garden window, throws himself in a chair, and, turning away from the audience, weeps hysterically. Here, the beautiful boy projects his readiness for portraiture, for framing and hanging, for displacement into sentimental representation. Lord Henry and Dorian "hold hands" on knees; later, Hallward confesses his jealousy, as he, too, touches; later still, Dorian takes Basil's hand before he jumps him in the attic, as the two go down together in a clinch, before Dorian knifes his friend. Finally, Dorian seduces Alan Campbell (Nicholas Clay); while disposing of Basil's corpse, he croons, "I've waited to hear you call me Dorian" (in highfalutin English, it sounds like "Darling"): track in to two shot; the two nearly kiss. Dorian's head rests on Alan's shoulder, and he embraces his friend-victim. Although these scenes thematize the homosexual touch, homosocial blackmail, and sodomitic penetration, they also perform Dorian camaraderie as queer sentimental send-up, mainstreamed as the "BBC Play of the Month."

Why, given its popularity with filmmakers at midcentury, was *The Picture of Dorian Gray* not remade during the heritage-crazed 1990s?[25] The narrative itself provides some answers. Because no causally logical plot structures the story, transferring the novel to film requires plot clarification and elaboration. Adapting character, atmosphere, tone, and point of view creates another challenge. Scenarios of spectatorial triangulation—in which Dorian is displaced into spectacle by Basil, practices antiquary connoisseurship under the watchful influence of Lord Henry, and introjects the undead pictures of his ancestors—provide little cinematic material. Lewin's morph of Dorian from black-and-white figure to Technicolor corpse could have little appeal for millennial special-effects and CGI junkies: witness Van Helsing's self-creation in the eponymous wannabe blockbuster.[26] Oliver Parker calls Wilde "too theatrical" for screen adaptation; although, he says, shooting a "period piece" paradoxically allows the director to comment on contemporary events, *The Picture of Dorian Gray*'s representation of decadent connoisseurship and tasteful acculturation comments on no 1990s scandals and only covertly arouses anxieties or fears (Sterngold). Yet the nineties mainstream emergence of gay male culture opened a space in which to picture male homosexuality for an "intimate" audience of knowing Wildeans and for the heterosexual culture at large. *The Picture of Dorian Gray* may no longer appeal to either audience, however, since to be gay is no longer gothic.

From this perspective, Bill Condon's *Gods and Monsters* (1998) seems a curious rewriting of Wilde's novel that links the gothic as genre with sentimental queer heritage. The film tracks Frankenstein in Hollywood, imagining Mary Shelley's monster as a precursor of a hideous lineage: James Whale and his *Frankensteins*, Christopher Bram and his gay-pulp fictional *Father of Frankenstein* (1995), Condon and his "second monster." As did Oscar Wilde, Condon portrays an artist who seeks a subject for portraiture: here, an old man and a hunky sitter who can be moved either to love or to murder. Not an aristocrat, connoisseur, or dandy, this portraitist is an effeminate, working-class boy become Hollywood gent. Shooting a pulp-fictional biopic of Whale, Condon casts an openly gay English stage actor, Ian McKellan, as an out homosexual British filmmaker in 1950s Hollywood; mixing the Wildean modes of gothic horror and camp, Condon extends the parodic pouf subtext of Whale's horror classic, *Bride of Frankenstein,* even as he appropriates and revises Wilde's story of the dandy whose portrait becomes grotesque as he remains beautiful. In telling the story of a gay filmmaker's fall, obsession with memory and career, and suicide, Condon pictures the gothic's monstrous male modeling and rehabilitates the sentimental for 1990s heritage film. Although not itself a gothic horror film, *Gods and Monsters* is nevertheless the most self-reflexive film about horror's aesthetic since Michael Powell's metahorror masterpiece, *Peeping Tom* (1963).

Condon positions not portrait poser but portraitist, James Whale, at his gay male project's center. Art copyist and Hollywood icon, Jimmy created the Frankenstein image that his flaming gay fan, Mr. Kay (brilliantly played by Jack Plotnick), calls "one of the great images of the twentieth century"; "Don't be daft," Whale spits, when Kay links the monster image with Mona Lisa (Condon, *Gods and Monsters* 15). The biopic's narrative centers on the portrait's status and nature: will Clayton Boone (Brendan Fraser) serve as painter's model? If so, will he display the naked male body so desired by the portraitist's gaze? Is the posing situation a front for homosexual seduction? As story becomes striptease, Jimmy manipulates Boone into gradual stages of undress, as Whale pretends to paint and spills his childhood and Hollywood stories. The portrait-sitting situation foregrounds the former director's look, edited into the scenario with glance/object cuts. Shot first through a window, a naked-to-the-waist Boone mows grass in an upscale, mid-1950s Hollywood garden; cut to Jimmy, shot looking through the window; shot/reverse shot of Jimmy watching Boone work, via a glance/object cut that suggests, but does not depict, Whale's point of view. Later, the glance/object cut pictures Jimmy's solicitation, as he invites Boone into his studio; framed in the studio's screened doorway, Clayton's torso, although not yet bared, is eroticized. In a later sitting, glance/object cuts replace Boone with a memorialized bare-chested boy, who poses seductively in the door's frame, requesting that Jimmy watch him dive. Intercut with increasingly tight, even extreme, close-ups of Whale's face—with a slight smile and a far-away look in his eyes—the remembered scene unfolds; cut to naked boys with "bare buttocks" and "hard arrogant pricks," as Jimmy recounts frolicking in his swimming pool in voice-over. Through parallel editing, Condon stitches the spectator into the look's structure, as the relay of looks suggested by glance/object cutting forces him (or her) to assume the homospectatorial look.

Although Diana Fuss theorizes the homospectatorial look for female fashion photography, her theories likewise suit motion-picture spectatorship. The homospectatorial look functions through a "network of identificatory processes," including narcissism, misrecognition, and self-objectification, that seeks to recover pre-mirror-stage fantasies and to introject in the subject the "(m)other's imago" or image ("Homospectatorial" 716, 718). Specular images of faces or of the body in pieces picture infantile experiences of fragmentation—of "'castration, mutilation, dismemberment, [and] devouring'"—that invoke maternal plenitude (718, quoting Lacan). The female spectator's look at the overly invested close-up of (maternal) face initiates same-sex fascination, hostility, and uncertainty (722–27). This look at fashion photography's representation of face, morselized body, or bared neck, Fuss says, invites the spectator to incorporate the other as image and to view the self as reproduced or reproducible. Defining this look as vampiristic transmutes introjection into incorporation, for the desire to be the other "draws its very sustenance" from the desire to have the other (730). As a form of "screen memory," this look's images are likewise "manufactured and mapped onto the past in order to disguise a present anxiety" (734).

Likewise, the glance/object cut in Condon's film about an out gay 1930s Hollywood filmmaker's reveries, daydreams, and memories at mid-century invites the homospectatorial look. Condon directs that look at framed displays of the beautiful male body, at close-ups of a dreaming male face, at flashes back to fantasies of lost love, and at hallucinated moments of homoerotic approach through mirror-image reflection. In *Gods and Monsters,* the look incorporates the other even as it reproduces the self as other: Whale becomes an image, a hallucinated reflection, a Hollywood icon who created not a beautiful but a grotesque (moving) picture. Retrospectively ascribing Jimmy's homoerotic wishes to the Great War period, projecting the 1990s spectator's hope for Jimmy's fulfillment back onto the 1950s even as it displays 1930s gay desire, conceals the contemporary anxiety that sentimental gay male culture may reactivate homophobic terror and threat, the possibility of the closet. Hollywood biopic thus sorts gays from others, consolidates homosexual socialities, and yet seeks sympathy for Whale from straight and gay spectators alike. It locates the oedipal family in the remembered past and, displacing it into multiple scenes of identification and desire, creates a new genealogy of sons and monsters.

In gay male gothic, not the repetition of maternal-imago introjection but the foreclosure of the paternal metaphor facilitates the son's incorporation of the same-sex other, the model's reproducibility. When Whale explodes at Boone after having told war tales, he hallucinates his father's lower-class face in the place where Boone sits for his portrait, the place where other young men presumably sat, in the past, for theirs. Jimmy himself here fantasmatically occupies the position of beautiful boy as well as homospectatorial viewer; his boy lovers displace the "poor, dumb father" to undo the boy's childish rage at a father's failure to see his son's artistic talent. In a later mirror-image scene, Clayton positions himself as the beautiful boy, ready for reproducibility. An over-the-shoulder shot of Whale at the window; as we see his reflection in the glass, a reflected figure moves in behind Whale, stripping his shirt off; it's Clayton, statuesque, dropping the clothing that covers his genitals, off-frame. "You wanted to draw me," Clayton challenges; "it's going to happen," Whale murmurs. After Whale forces him to don a World War I gas mask, Boone's doubly irised, jumpy, and anxious POV shots match his panicked pants on the sound track; Jimmy touches Boone's naked, well-muscled torso from behind, kisses his neck, grabs his "prick" under the gardener's draped towel. Jimmy: "I want you to kill me, break my neck; come on, strangle me; . . . You could be my second monster." Boone: "I am *not* your monster." Here, Jimmy is paternal imago, demanding sonly murder, activating homospectatorial incorporation, and soliciting symbolic sodomitic rape. The hallucinated paternal face, the mirror shot of beautiful male body, and the model's POV shot stage this spectatorial relation.

As Dorian Gray becomes spectator of his own portrait, so Jimmy Whale becomes spectator of his own images. Looking like an ancient suburban married couple, Hanna (Lynn Redgrave) and Mr. Jimmy watch Whale's old movie on TV, drinking milk and munching cookies. Condon intercuts with this couple's spectatorship scenes of Boone, his buddies, and girlfriend watching at a bar. Intercut, too, are scenes from *Bride of Frankenstein,* in a complex triangular version of filmic consumption or introjection and media reproducibility. The embedded, appropriated clip also stages for the spectator his or her appropriate response to the picture. Cut to the filmed bride, screaming, as the monster croaks "friend." "She is horrible," the good Christian Hanna declares; "She is beautiful," Jimmy the monster-maker demurs; Betty, the back-talking barmaid, croons, "All right! You don't want him" (38–39), as Elsa Lanchester screams; cut to the monster's hand, pulling the phallic lever that blows up the laboratory tower; the happy heterosexual couple (Colin Clive, Valerie Hobson) cuddles as the scene ends.[27] Hanna likes the "happy ending": the "bad people are dead and the good people live"; it's "corny," a "hoot," Betty (Lolita Davidovich) whoops: "Scary is scary and funny is funny," she quips, "you don't mix them" (39, 36–37). Yet Jimmy's comedy about death does just that, mixes genres to create a metahorror flick about the look, cinematic spectatorship, and filmic consumption or incorporation. When Whale and Boone smoke cigars after lunch, miming the parodic scene in which De Lacey teaches the monster to smoke, drink, and talk, Whale wants to know whether Clayton's bar pals laughed; "no," Boone fibs (56). Here, the film provides its spectator with contradictory affective instructions: is it horrible or beautiful? scary or funny? It's both, but, above all, it's sentimental.

As Condon's film pictures the sentimental, the characters' tears instruct the spectator to weep. Sentimentalizing the amorous and aggressive gothic scenario in which Whale begs Boone to kill him, Condon ends the scene with Boone's sobs and Whale's penitence. When Jimmy longs for his lost lover Barnett (Todd Babcock), when Jimmy repeatedly apologizes to Boone for having offended him, when Hanna and Clayton look, in tightening close-ups and two shot, at the dead, waterlogged Jimmy in his swimming pool, the mise-en-scène displays choked-back tears. No wonder that after a fantasized and projected Jimmy lies down to his death in the trenches with his hallucinated lover, Condon cuts to another appropriated clip from *Bride of Frankenstein*—as Franz Waxman's musical theme for the monster sighs from De Lacey's violin. It's the same sad music that, during the flashbacks, haunted Condon's viewer; whether background to flashback of remembered childhood, fantasied erotic, or dreamed post-coupling scenes, this melancholy, nostalgic tone signifies sentimental excess. "I cannot see you," De Lacey tells the intruding monster, as the tune moans; "I cannot see anything at all; I am blind." As Condon appropriates *Bride of Frankenstein*'s parodic impulse, he also superadds pity and pathos. Deploying the homospectatorial look through glance/object cutting, Condon seduces the spectator into the sentimental world of gay spectatorial relations, of identification, incorporation, and self-reproducibility.

This spectatorship produces a scenario of filmic (re)production. After Hanna and Jimmy watch *Bride of Frankenstein,* remembered applause rings

Jimmy Whale floats in the swimming pool after his suicide. (Gods and Monsters, *1998*)

on the sound track, as a glance/object cut from a close-up of McKellan's face segues into Jimmy's memories of life on the set. Costumed to resemble their 1935 actor-counterparts, Condon's Ernest Thesinger (Arthur Dignam [uncredited]), Colin Clive (Matt McKenzie), and Elsa Lanchester (Rosalind Ayres) assemble on the sound stage for the take. "Is the audience to presume that Colin and I have done her hair?" Thesinger queries; "not only did her hair but dressed her? What a couple of queens we are, Colin." Jimmy responds, "Yes, a couple of flaming queens. And Pretorius is a little in love with Dr. Frankenstein, you know" (47). As the cameras roll, the present-day Whale, in close-up, sighs with satisfaction, and the scene uncannily reproduces the black-and-white classic: "the Bride of Frankenstein," Pretorius announces. Afterward, Jimmy goes to bed and dreams: monster voice-over, "We are friends"; cut to a pajama-wearing Jimmy, backlit, on the original's set; cut to the laboratory, to Clayton playing Frankenstein and carrying Jimmy down the tower's stairs. Clay pokes Jimmy, acting as the monster, on a surgical table, trepans the skull, takes out the brain and replaces it with another; in close-up, he threads a needle and sews the skull, turns instrument dials; cut quickly between Jimmy's face and flashing lights. But wait: Whale wakes in his color-drenched bedroom. This parodic movie-dream substitutes the gardener for the scientist; the filmmaker for the monster. The look's reversibility and cinema's morph aesthetics campily reproduce the original (with canted shots on replicas of sets). Here, the filmmaker participates in his own productions, acting the role of monster, via a network of identificatory processes that hallucinate fantasies of and anxieties about self-alienation and mutilation, fragmentation and dismemberment, and castration, as the skull stands in for the reproductive power of the filmmaker as bearer of the monstrous phallic look.

Later, Condon intercuts clips from *Bride of Frankenstein* as Boone and his son watch the film on TV, in a narrative coda not present in Bram's source novel. "If you're in trouble," De Lacey says, "perhaps I can help you"; monster and De Lacey smoke; cut to Boone, smoking. De Lacey: "Before you came, I was all alone"; monster: "Alone, bad. Friend, good." "Pretty cool," says the kid (Jesse James), who lies on the living room floor, watching; "better than most monster movies." Boone shows his son Whale's sketch (a portrait?) of the monster, inscribed to Clayton: "FRIEND?" (109–11). As he takes the trash out, Clayton goose-steps in the rain, arms extended, masquerading as the monster; the hunk who once sat for his "portrait"—a squiggle, Whale reveals after the sodomitic rape scene—is himself entangled in spectatorial relations as he belatedly acknowledges to his son his identification with Whale's first monster. In this scene, Boone is also transformed from son-monster to patriarch; Boone outgrows the role of "big, fun, irresponsible kid," to which Betty assigned him, to become the father who looks after, gives comfort to, and teaches his son (43). Thus the boy-become-progenitor, himself producing a son, undoes a displaced version of Jimmy's childish rage at his remembered, hallucinated, punishing father and so subverts, sentimentally, the collapse of generations Lee shot in his spoof of Whale, *Son of Frankenstein*.

Set in the decade of Whale's suicide, Condon's film about 1950s Hollywood solicits a doubly fashioned 1990s audience of straight *Frankenstein* fans and a gay coterie. Whale sums up his Hollywood career to Clayton: "Making movies is the most wonderful thing in the world. Working with friends. Entertaining people" (62). Yet Condon's Hollywood is a semi-closeted scene in which homosexuals struggle with secrecy and disclosure. Gay fandom: Mr. Kay chortles, "Tell me everything you remember about making 'Frankenstein'"; "it's the monster movies you'll be remembered for"; Jimmy makes him strip for each revelation (14, 11). Gay celebrity: Jimmy introduces Clayton as "my—ahem—gardener" at George Cukor's reception for Princess Margaret, itself a parody of fifties Hollywood Anglophilia and a figure for nineties Anglofilmia. Gay sentiment and homosexual panic: David Lewis (David Dukes) cautions Jimmy that his flamboyant transgressivity endangers all Hollywood homosexuals. Condon's "portrait" of a filmmaker whose homosexuality was well known in Hollywood tells all to sympathetic spectator-members of 1990s gay subcultures and to the middlebrow heritage audience at large. Christopher Bram's crossover source novel, which opens as gay pulp (Clayton's "back muscles tens[ed] beneath his T-shirt, thighs and buttocks flexing in his fatigue pants" [3]), instead represents Boone as the protagonist and focalizer who increasingly admires, pities, and sympathizes with the aging film director. Focusing on Clayton's relationship with Whale, *Father of Frankenstein* tells the tale of a hunk heterosexual's fascinated attraction to gay Hollywood culture, as the novel appeals to both gay and straight readers.[28]

As self-reflexive and self-reproducing gay sentimental gothic, *Gods and Monsters* verges on camp. Susan Sontag identifies the "origins" of camp taste in eighteenth-century connoisseurship, in consumption or incorporation of the pleasures provided by "Gothic novels, Chinoiserie, caricature, artificial ruins, and so forth"; moreover, the "relation of [contemporary] Camp taste to the past," she notes, is "extremely sentimental" (282). Seizing the pouf subtext of *Bride of Frankenstein,* the 1990s gay filmmaker makes Whale's monsters camp, for their "out of date" status provides a "necessary detachment" and "arouses a necessary sympathy" to produce camp style (286). For Sontag, as for critics who follow her, Oscar Wilde is a "transitional figure" in the history of camp, an image on which tradition turns and from which legacies flow (290). Wilde inherited from his precursors and, in turn, models for his followers the aesthetics of connoisseurship, taste, and sensibility that, in the 1990s, made camp hip.

Heritage Camp

Despite unconfirmed reports of its demise, camp continues to constitute its audience through what we now recognize as a Wildean move. Camp, Sontag says, "is a mode of seduction"; it "employs flamboyant mannerisms susceptible of a double interpretation; gestures full of duplicity, with a witty meaning for cognoscenti and another, more impersonal, for outsiders" (283). Contemporary camp thus constitutes socialities and sorts others much as did Wilde's campy comedies. Like nineteenth-century structures of homosocial desire, like late twentieth-century sentimental gay heritage, camp also mobilizes an intimate and shifting relationship to class and rank, to fashion or style as aesthetic, and to social mobility of all kinds. Thus the "modern dandy" historically displaced the aristocrat as the iconic cultural connoisseur; just so, the postmodern "connoisseur of Camp" historically replaces yet replicates the dandy, as a "self-elected class" of gays constitute themselves "aristocrats of taste" (Sontag 288–90). Camp taste consumes and incorporates high culture by mimicking and mocking its upper-class pretensions. "Posh culture," Sinfield insists, is a "leisured preserve" to be vogued and laughed at (156). In camp, Andrew Ross notes, the "class aspirations and upward mobility of a middlebrow audience" become the "in" taste of a minority elite (319).[29] For the campy spectator, the look at sentimental heritage spectacles of rank, nation, and country house may expose aunties, queer sex acts, and curious crossdressers; metaphors for heritage social restraint may morph into not unspeakability but skit. The quality pleasures of looking at period costumes, at decorative art and furniture, and at heritage estate also indulge the gay glance at beautiful men in white flannels—figures such as Alec Scudder who, when dressed for cricket, looks "like a gentleman" (Dyer, *Queers* 201). If camp makes good taste of kitsch, heritage camp makes tasteful drag of high culture.

Oliver Parker's 1990s films of Wilde's comedies play period costume drama as high camp, borrowing Wilde's double move for constituting his audience. In the 1890s, Wilde's madcap plays mocked the old nobility, inviting the new enterprising, administrative classes to laugh at gentry dupes and to celebrate their own rank usurpation; in the 1990s, Parker's camp scenarios encourage the professional middle class to laugh at extinct elite style even as it celebrates its taste for cultural consumption. In *An Ideal Husband,* Parker enhances audience pleasure in the spectacle by fashioning locations merely suggested or unimagined by Wilde: a suffragist meeting of the Women's Liberal Association, a friendly fencing match, a female game of charades, a masculine conversation in the sauna, a marital sex scene, a meeting of Parliament—complete with female spectators in the women's gallery. Parodying staged spectatorship, Parker shoots in the film a theatrical performance of *The Importance of Being Earnest,* as Mrs. Cheveley (Julianne Moore) looks through opera glasses, in POV shot, at the proscenium, then scans the audience, its members, in turn, peeking at her. Parker pictures film's power to represent, to project and reproduce, and constitutes an audience of distanced yet intimate spectators who, looking, enact spectatorial relations. Watching Parker's reproduced play, we, like Mrs. Cheveley, look at the spectacle and see that, figuratively, we ourselves are being looked at even as we look.

Parker's films spoof Wilde's already theatricalized aesthetic. Parker mixes modes and genres to demonstrate cinema's incorporative reproduction of earlier hybrid styles that are, nevertheless, historically anachronistic to Wilde's comedies. In *An Ideal Husband* and *The Importance of Being Earnest,* he riffs on 1930s and 1940s spy flicks. *Husband*: Sir Robert Chiltern (Jeremy Northam) tells Lord Goring (Rupert Everett), in black-and-white, low-contrast, shadowy flashback, about Baron Arnheim's financial and power-crazed pedagogy and his own sale to the Jew of a cabinet secret that netted himself a small fortune. *Earnest*: under the credits and in two additional scenes, bailiffs chase Algernon (Rupert Everett, again) down black-and-white, low-contrast, shadowy streets, scenes that culminate in the bailiffs' confrontation with Jack (Colin Firth, again) in which they demand that he pay "Ernest Worthing's" (not his—he has refused to pay—but Algy's) Savoy Hotel bill; Miss Prism (Anna Massey) recounts

Jack's history in black-and-white flashbacks of babies in prams, streets shot from an infant's POV through handbag handles that, snapping shut, wipe to black. Chase-scene music spoofs spectatorial anxiety about origins, wealth, and inheritance.

In *The Importance of Being Earnest*, Parker adds visual sex jokes to subvert and ironize class and gender politics. Under the credits, Algy and Jack watch costumed music-hall girls can-can; all turn, flip skirts over bottoms, as members of the audience—Algy, Jack, other men, and we spectators—view slits in underwear that ambiguously suggest vaginal or anal penetration, followed by a short, short drag scene. Lady Bracknell (Judi Dench) flashes back to her maiden lack of fortune and past as a music-hall girl, showing her suddenly big belly to the astonished (soon-to-be-father) aristocrat. To prove her loyalty to her "Ernest," Gwendolen Fairfax (Frances O'Connor), in black-and-white, visits an Asian artist, in color, whose tattoo gun—intercut with curlicued letters that spell "Ernest"—moves slowly up her bare leg; cut to a very modern Gwendolen in a motor car, gingerly sitting on newly tattooed (penetrated?) bum. Under final credits: Gwendolen sympathizes with a recumbent Jack, about to be tattooed on buttocks with "Gwendolen." Parker's jokes about outmoded three-volume novels, lowbrow music halls, orientalized tattoo artists, and anal penetration parody Wilde's texts' spoofs of the urge to gain gentry power or power over the gentry—yet go slumming, too.

Wilde's plays pillory nineteenth-century signifiers of rank, genealogy, and inheritance and substitute a queer connoisseurship that spoofs cultural consumption as crass incorporation. In Parker's country house interiors, period-costumed women and men frock about, enabling spectators to take pleasure in, even as they laugh at, their (own) luxurious tastes and commitment to commodity culture. Stuffed with aesthetic objects, hung with self-referential pictorial and illustrative artifacts, draped in fabrics with sensuous surfaces and textures, the mise-en-scène is shot in flashy period palettes. As Jack approaches Lady Bracknell's manorial country house, he is ushered into a foyer adorned with lavish tapestries, walled in ochre marble, with staircases on each side; he is escorted through anteroom after room, his picture snapped (in stop action, face askew) several times (for purposes of blackmail?); and shown into the grand lady's presence. Costumed in a lavender gown, Lady Bracknell plays the powerful "auntie," a figure Sedgwick glosses as, in late nineteenth-century slang, the "passive sodomist" or "man who displays a queenly demeanour" (*Tendencies* 59);

she wears a lavender garland (seemingly her favorite color) on her left shoulder, lace at the décolleté neckline and on the cuffs, a multiple-strand pearl choker, one long strand extending down her aristocratic heritage bosom. She and her black-clad minions take notes, as Jack responds to her impertinent questions. On period chairs with gilt frames, upholstered in red velvet, the women sit before red damask wall coverings, gold-and-white Louis Seize paneling, ornate gold-framed mirrors, floor-length scarlet satin curtains with gold-tasseled tie-backs; ornate glassware decorates the tables, and flowers are everywhere. Cut to close-up of Lady Bracknell's elegantly ringed hand, seizing a gold-gilded goblet, pouring water from a glass decanter, and (track to face) she drinks: Jack's house, number 149, she intones, is on "the unfashionable side" of Belgrave Square; her daughter may not "marry into a cloak-room and form an alliance with a parcel." Exaggerated fashion and sensuality provide the spectator visual and tactile pleasure (you just itch to touch the velvet), as Parker shoots Wilde's dandified aestheticism as tasteful heritage drag.

Parker likewise spoofs as drag Wilde's tongue-in-cheek heterosexual coupling. In a sequence without precedent in the play, silly Cecily Cardew (Reese Witherspoon) parodies intimate self-disclosure as she records in her diary invented scenes of courtship, proposal, engagement, broken engagement, and so forth. Later, having quarreled over "Ernest," Cecily and Gwendolen make up, as Algy romps about the garden with piano and banjo-player, crooning to his sweetheart lowbrow music-hall tunes. In response, Cecily fantasizes pre–Raphaelite Brotherhood sexual scenarios: in diaphanous gown, long hair curled and flowing, she stands, tied to a stake; she watches a black-clad knight (being a poor student, she gets it wrong) as he rides to her rescue; and, surrounded by viol players clad in costumes with William Morris leaf-and-flower motif, she caresses her armor-clad knight—aha! it's Algy—and babbles about love. These medievalized fantasies—appropriations of PRB appropriation—parody heterosexual courtship as chivalrous, yet also as the perverse figures familiar to PRB followers of youths languorously outstretched, waiting to receive Janey Morris mouths on whatever body part is nearest. Here, the doubly constituted camp spectatorship enables cognoscenti readings of heterosexual romance as cover for homosexual oral sex, for Parker's camp appropriation of the courtship plot's seemingly "straight" yet perverse narrative exposes the male "sibling" story as the comedies' "real" sexually arousing tale (Sedgwick, *Tendencies* 64–65, 67).

The Wilde comedies could hardly have succeeded at the St. James, at the Theatre Royal, except during an age of excess expenditure, extravagant luxury, and highly confident consumerism. Nor could the Parker pictures have succeeded at the box office. Parker remediates Wilde's plays for a film audience drenched, like the 1890s theatrical spectator, in the society of the spectacle and committed to the pleasures of cultural consumption. Wilde's historically residual aristocrats living off their titles and reputations, upper-gentry gentlemen selling state secrets for cash, effete bachelors overcoming their handbag genealogies; silly girls fantasizing their romantic futures and rivaling one another for men likely to fall into the bourgeoisie; socially climbing mothers hoping to ensure their daughters' financial futures: these farcical figures resemble ourselves, during a late-century boom decade a hundred years later. Although Parker deleted Lady Bracknell's historically situated reference to the already residual gentry dilemma about landed estates ("What between the duties expected of one during one's lifetime, and the duties exacted from one after one's death, land has ceased to be either a profit or a pleasure. It gives one position, and prevents one from keeping it up" [*The Importance of Being Earnest* 493]), her inquisition about Worthing's "worth" is nonetheless clearly comprehensible to the postmodern spectators who consume it. The camp take on the gilded-age wealth effect produced a cultural moment in which audiences accustomed to luxury could laugh at others in such ruthless yet parodic pursuit of it. That laughter suppresses even as it expresses contemporary anxiety about wealth's instability and luxury's ephemera, and allows the spectator to feel secure in his or her own financial and class position even as he or she fears losing it. The prescient Parker seized on Wilde's plays as apt vehicles for remediation in a heritage decade of economic boom, extravagant taste, posh culture, and gay camp connoisseurship.

The emergence of gay culture in cosmopolitan centers and the mainstreaming of gay figures in middlebrow media such as television make the queer visible in the 1990s as he or she was not in the 1890s. Although Wilde rehabilitates his stagy conventions from Restoration comedy, he nevertheless insists that his plays represent a modern connoisseurship. For Wilde, the dandy represents the collective life of the race and so becomes "absolutely modern, in the true meaning of the word modernity"; for Sontag, looking back half a century later, Wilde's homosexual followers pioneer a "modern sensibility"; later still, camp solves the problem of "how to be a dandy in the age of mass culture" (*The Critic as Artist* 382;

"Camp" 292, 290). During his trials for gross indecency, Moisés Kaufman argues, Wilde posed as the modern dandy, constituting his courtroom audience as coterie/cognoscenti and himself as spectator of, commentator upon, and participant in the spectacle of his crime. Postmodern Wildean appropriations such as Kaufman's *Gross Indecency* (1998) and Will Self's *Dorian* (2002) reconstruct the Old Bailey trials as though they were modern; or imagine Baz Hallward as living with, but Henry Wotton dying from, AIDS, Baz writing fey trash about it. And in "Dorian Gray" (2001, black-and-white print), Yinka Shonibare pictures himself, the photographer, as black Victorian dandy, as "Dorian" (McRobbie). As Tony Kushner quips, Kaufman's play captured the "flaming" contradictions of Wilde's passion, a contradiction that enables the long Wilde "legacy" (143; Bristow, *Legend*).

Virginia Woolf's modernist *Orlando* seems a curious send-up of Oscar Wilde, yet it too participates in the Wilde legacy. When Dorian Gray strolls through his picture-gallery, he anticipates Orlando, who ambles through the fictionalized Knole's marvelous galleries, looking, with the reader, at figures for himself; Dorian's forebears' portraits and *Orlando*'s appropriated pictures of Vita Sackville-West and her family represent the subject's own reproducibility, the spectacle of inheritance or legacy. As Dorian incorporates his ancestors, Orlando embodies Sackville-West's pictured genealogy, as s/he moves from early modern to modern moment. Sally Potter's avant-garde *Orlando* incorporates these portraits as high camp even as it participates in the sentimental project to make the queer visible to a professional, middle-class heritage audience and to a coterie. For Potter as for Sedgwick, camp is a "different name" for the sentimental (*Epistemology* 144).

Avant-Garde Queer Heritage

"*Orlando* is to me the most cinematic of Virginia Woolf's books," Sally Potter has said (Ehrenstein 5). Even as she spectacularizes heritage's sites, sights, and mise-en-scènes for the 1990s, Potter restages Woolf's cavalcade of English literary culture to interrogate 1980s heritage film's focus on the thematics of rank and inheritance, its adherence to fidelity aesthetics, and its sentimental notions of Englishness (Brunsdon 167).[30] Although her film earned critical praise and did good mainstream box office, Potter views *Orlando*'s art-cinema aesthetic as part of her "avant-garde inheritance": her use of nonclassical and fractured narration that eschews romance closure; of characters that resist spectatorial identification; of style that foregrounds artifice.[31] Despite Potter's "ruthless changes" to Woolf's narrative, however, the film everywhere depends upon its intertextual relation with its source novel, for Woolf's satire of biography, fictional character, and gender/sexual identity enabled Potter's spoof, likewise, to "suggest . . . Sapphism" (Potter, *Orlando* ix; Woolf, *Diary* 3: 177). Potter's circumspection about sex acts and sexual orientation positions her *Orlando* outside "the lesbian and gay cinema movement" of the 1990s, much as Woolf's protected her *Orlando* from censorship, from the kind of legal battle that ultimately banned Radclyffe Hall's contemporaneous *The Well of Loneliness* (1928).[32] Like Woolf, Potter yokes a sentimental Sapphic literary culture with the avant-garde to queer English literary heritage.

Appropriating heritage's reliance on gesture, look, and mise-en-scène, Potter transmutes its aesthetic of the image to depict historical periods as a series of color-coded tableaux. "'The England of Elizabeth is gold and red, that of James grey and silver,'" she says; the lighting "'brings it all to life'" (Glaessner 54–55). The film's longest sequence fashions *Orlando*'s early-modern courtly adventures as pageant. Shot largely at night, the Elizabethan festivals on ice and in manor hall use glittering lighting, exaggerated tracking, and frame-within-a-frame mise-en-scène to emphasize plenty, languor, and luxury: the early-modern psychopathology of affluence. A castrato (the gay pop star Jimmy Somerville) sings, as Elizabeth I (a campy Quentin Crisp) is rowed upriver; as the camera tilts up to a tardy Orlando's slowly lifting face, the intertitle, "1600 DEATH," announces a new tableau, which deploys a processional aesthetic. Elizabeth and Orlando (Tilda Swinton) stroll down a double rank of trees, sleek designer dogs in tow; cut, as they exit to a meadow and the Queen sits, measures Orlando's leg, designating him her "son," her "limb"; in the next scene, the Queen coaxes Orlando's face into her lap (which cognoscenti would have known concealed a penis), then "kisses his forehead sensuously"; close-up on his "handsome leg" (Potter, *Orlando* 8–9). "The house," the Queen whispers, "For you [and] your heirs," placing the deed in his garter. Orlando thus becomes the Queen's metaphorically homosexually reproduced son and so "inherits" the country house that serves as the film's visual spine. In the tableau's second processional, a file of black-clad men, headed by Orlando, follows a casket, with mourning women trailing behind: first the Queen's death, then Orlando's father's, they whisper. In these opening scenarios, the limb represents aristocratic inheritance and pageant figures heritage, as queer reproduction displaces paternal inheritance.

Recalling *The Picture of Dorian Gray*, Potter anchors her film with Orlando's portrait, which she links with England's cultural heritage. The opening text is voiced over a close-up of the beautiful boy: "because this is England, Orlando [is] destined to have his portrait on the wall and his name in the history books" as "heir to a name that meant land and property." Potter's heritage "son," like Dorian, incorporates ancestral portraits: the early-modern Orlando and Euphrosyne (Anna Healy) stand before a painting of his parents, the Great House in the background, and, turning toward and looking at the camera, striking the portrait's poses, they figuratively become Orlando's ancestors who've stepped out of the picture, the postmodern version of a Renaissance couple and Dorian genealogy. As the film ends, a modern Orlando returns to the house and enters the Great Hall, where Japanese tourists ogle the likeness of Orlando as a young man. Orlando and her daughter (Jessica Swinton) likewise look, becoming tourists of their own past and genealogy, as Orlando's voice-over echoes: "She's lived for four hundred years and hardly aged

Orlando, the beautiful boy, strolls with Queen Elizabeth I, played by camp pop star Quentin Crisp. (Orlando, 1992)

a day"; "because this is England, everyone pretends not to notice" (Potter, *Orlando* 61). The English country house morphs into stately home, as the Great Hall opens to heritage tourists in the modern age of publishing, the electronic age of videotape, the postmodern age of avant-garde cinema.

In this avant-garde heritage flick, the country house is home to the modern androgyne but not to the dispossessed postmodern transgendered queer. "You are a party to several major lawsuits," two black-clad men announce in Knole's eighteenth-century courtyard, for as either corpse or woman, Orlando cannot own the "family seat" (Potter, *Orlando* 47). Refusing Archduke Harry's (John Wood) marriage proposal and offer of "respectability"—he promises to tolerate her "ambiguous sexuality"—an angered Orlando exits frame left, then reenters, complaining to the spectator: "Spinster!" Exit, return, to camera: "Alone!" (49). Shot from behind, she sprints into a hedge maze via POV shots and quick cuts, and, as she exits, her costume morphs; she enters fog—and the nineteenth century. Earlier, in the famous sex-change scene, Potter shoots Orlando in bed and then slipping out of the sheets *and* her man's wig. Cut to a close-up of hands in water, in a golden bowl, the black background gold-spangled; cut to Orlando's profile in close-up; she washes, turns toward the camera; cut to a long shot of her body, naked, from behind, reflected in a keyhole-shaped pier glass; voice-over, then address to the spectator: "Same person. No difference at all. Just a different sex" (40). Cut to England: Orlando looks at her reflection in a handheld mirror, as she corsets before a pier glass; tracking around her torso, the camera tilts up to Orlando's face; cut: she walks through a furniture-shrouded gallery, learning to manage her gown's huge panniers; a peacock cries on the sound track. Body is not destiny; character is not essence; gender identity is costume.

In the film's twentieth century, Potter sentimentalizes queer heritage, turning Orlando's story into sappy new-age tale. When Orlando visits the house she has lost, a mother and child motorcycle into the courtyard, shrubs shrouded; cut to a close-up of Orlando, one tear on her cheek. Meanwhile, Orlando's daughter frolics in the uncut meadow, shoots the country house and estate with a camcorder, and looks at her mother, in handheld close-up POV shot. Here, Potter rewrites *Orlando* as a postmodern *A Room of One's Own* (1929). In that work, a genealogy of female precursors—aristocratic women "shut up in their parks among their folios" who "wrote without audience or criticism" (Woolf, *Room* 66)—

historically enabled the nineteenth-century middle-class woman to write novels. In Potter's *Orlando,* those foremothers (and androgynous fathers) produce an electronic-age daughter. At film's end, female filiation displaces heterosexual romance. "'There will be another generation of daughters'" to ensure continuity and inheritance, Potter says; she's "'me, or our futures,'" she's "'all of our daughters'" (Florence 281–82). The film's final maternal scene, presided over by an angel, returns Orlando, four hundred years after her inheritance, to the oak tree, in extreme close-up of "open, radiant, steady gaze," recalling but refusing to repeat the tear (63).

In the film's conclusion, Potter links sentimental postmodernism with queer cultural tropes and jokes. A gay pop-icon angel hovers in the sky, trilling new-age ditties that sentimentalize historical loss: letting go the past, life's beginning, human joining, being born and dying. Casting Quentin Crisp, the "Queen of Queens," the self-identified "stately homo," as Elizabeth I; Jimmy Somerville as countertenor castrato-angel; androgynes Billy Zane as Shelmerdine (who arrives on horseback, spoofing Rochester) and Tilda Swinton as Orlando, Potter threads a queer subtext through her film. As David Ehrenstein notes, *Orlando* "touches on such

In the twentieth century, Orlando and her daughter motorcycle into the Great House's park, preparing to become heritage tourists. (Orlando, 1992)

hot-button issues as feminism, imperialism, and gender and gay/lesbian politics, all the while seducing audiences that would be loathe to deal with such topics head-on" (2). For Potter, this "'gay/lesbian/queer sensibility'" represents the "'connectedness between beings'" (MacDonald 219). Although Potter self-censors her film's sex scenes and is circumspect about her sexual orientation in postproduction interviews, she nevertheless participates in the sentimental gay cultural project to make the queer visible to the culture at large, to insert a transgendered him/her into a history of culture.

In Potter's avant-garde sentimental heritage, as in Wilde's aesthetic, spectatorial engagement is doubly constituted. Sequences end with Orlando's framed face, displaying a knowing look that addresses the spectator. These close-ups—whether full face, profile, or half shadowed—invoke the homospectatorial look. Orlando's direct address masks even as it enables spectatorial identification with and desire for her. Although Potter calls this repeated close-up "a golden thread" that "connect[s] the audience, through the lens, with Orlando," this tactic to fuse the "spectacle and the spectator [into] one" is another figure for the queer subject's reproducibility, for the homospectatorial look as incorporative and self-reproducing (Potter, *Orlando* xiii). Refusing stable points of identification with a gendered same and encouraging desire for a transsexed and gendered other, Potter's close-ups render the spectator, likewise, a spectacle and Orlando, a spectator of her spectator. Potter, like Wilde and Woolf before her, constitutes her audience as comprising distanced others as well as intimates: hailed by Orlando's address and produced by identification with the hero/ine's close-up, the spectator becomes a member of a queer coterie, yet sorting him- or herself from the scene of identificatory sympathy, projects Orlando's face into representation. Enjoying the sentimental pleasures of sympathy, the spectator nevertheless distances him- or herself from campy new-age heritage.

Potter's *Orlando* refuses to bring "'a reverential attitude'" to British history and heritage (Florence 276). Funded, coproduced, and created by Russian, British, Italian, Dutch, and French companies and technicians, the film casts "'European eyes on an English story'"; it contends against England's "'addiction'" to cultural "'mythologies of the past'" as rooted in a "'national identity'" created during Elizabeth I's reign (Florence 276; Glaessner 53–55).[33] Instead, *Orlando* depicts the emergence and decline of the British country house, the empire, and the nation, identifying country ideology, class deference and submission, and paternal benevolence as outdated. Shot on location in St. Petersburg and Uzbekistan, Potter's European coproduction competes strategically with Hollywood. Art cinema has been coproduced since Italy's Andreotti Law (1949) reduced American film imports and mandated coproduction with France, even with Britain, in an effort to enliven postwar national film production (Neale, "Art Cinema" 26–28). Coproduction boomed when a postwar decline in moviegoing reduced profits; as the suburbs exploded, families grew, television became dominant, and the drive-in theater as an exhibition sector expanded (Schatz, "New Hollywood" 12–13). After Thatcher privatized the National Film Finance Corporation, British cinema increasingly sought international cofunding and transnational audiences; by the 1960s, coproduction was a "fact of moviemaking" (Gomery, *Pleasures* 183). The 1990s, when new media outlets and markets threatened the health of avant-garde, art-house, and queer cinema, necessitated a new round of transnational deal making.[34] Representing the international in and as though Britain, Potter's *Orlando* is what Colin MacCabe calls "post-national European cinema" ("Post-National").

Potter's postnational film stages, she says, a "biting and satirical view of the English class system and the colonial attitudes arising from it" (Potter, *Orlando* xi). Orlando's stint as Royal Ambassador to Turkey reminds the spectator, as does Sir Thomas Bertram's journey to oversee his failing Antiguan plantations in Patricia Rozema's *Mansfield Park,* that England's wealth depended upon early-modern global exploration and nineteenth-century colonial exploitation. Orlando's ritualized encounter with the Khan of Khiva spoofs the British "*manly* virtues" of "Loyalty!" and "Courage!" as the Khan toasts "*brotherly* love" with vaguely homoerotic overtones; "You, an Englishman, are not *afraid*?" he queries his sworn ally (34, 38; emphasis in original). Yet when Orlando walks away from the battleground, shot with a handheld camera, Potter's invention of a setting, characters, and narrative kernels without precedent in the novel "opens up an ironic gap between the monuments of the national culture and the colonialism on which they are built."[35] Although Woolf's novel likewise circulated a transsexual subject in oriental cultures as an emissary of British rule, Potter deploys her hero/ine to expose England's imperial mythology from the perspective of postnational European cinema.

Thus *Orlando* posits postnational cinema as one of heritage film's possible future modes. As Julian Jarrold's most recent films demonstrate, heritage may remain period costume drama, recycling locations, readapting old scripts, reinscribing sentimental spectatorial relations as central to Britain's cultural past—and, in the case of *Brideshead Revisited* (2008), heterosexualizing a homoerotic tale. It may, as this chapter demonstrates, curiously sentimentalize, queer, or make campy heritage space and spectacle. Or it may travel beyond the North Atlantic community, into English-speaking communities around the globe, reimagining the sentimental project for global citizens. Those potential heritage consumers—women, girls, and bookish men from India, Saudi Arabia, Taiwan, Hong Kong, and other locations—live in postcolonial societies, nations in which culture, film, and aesthetics have been influenced by a colonial past.[36] As populations emigrate, heritage film also appeals to diasporic and exilic communities, picturing their colonial pasts for use in postnational futures. Cultural consumption is shaped by these global forces, as populations become hybridized and expatriate minorities become national majorities. Locating the transsexed protagonist into a "designed, framed, constructed, [and] imagined whoosh of [British imperial] history," Potter prophesies a postnational, queered yet sentimental heritage. And just as there is no monolithic ideological bias in heritage film, there is no one future for representations of the British national past on screen.

Mass Culture and
Global Heritage

We are living in an increasingly global media environment. Access to
multiple channels and types of transnational media is problematiz-
ing ... questions of national cultures and identities, national cine-
mas and genres.

—Hamid Naficy, *Accented Cinema*

The BBC will continue to [make classic-novel adaptations] because
it is one of the things that people expect the BBC to do.

—Andrew Davies, "Conversations"

T HERE WILL ALWAYS BE AN AUDIENCE for classic serials and film adaptations of nineteenth-century British fiction and, Andrew Davies
cheekily suggests, a production company or television network eager to
provide them. As a new spate of Austen adaptations and spin-offs hit the
theaters in 2007, Marty Moss-Cowane, host of Philadelphia's *Radio Times,*
announced, "Jane Austen Mania" is "back"; indeed, "it never went away."
Not just Austen fandom but advertising and marketing, cinema spaces,
and exhibition practices created such cultural frenzy. Although a multiple-
movie deal or sequels to, prequels to, and remakes of a property, all generally owned by one studio or its corporate parent, constitute what critics
now call a "franchise," the "Austen franchise," broadly defined, has shaped
the production, reception, and marketing of heritage film. Despite having
been produced by various studios, specialty divisions, and independents,
as well as by Bollywood and Tamil cinema, the 1990s films of Jane Austen's
novels might be called a "product brand" (King 69) that, mixing styles
and modes, can be exploited to sell a product, whether high-cultural, middlebrow, popular, or mass-cultural, to a largely female audience across a
wide range of exhibition windows. Julian Jarrold's faux biopic *Becoming*

Jane (2007), a recent entry in the Austen sweepstakes, alters the fidelity aesthetics within which the 1990s films (but for Amy Heckerling's *Clueless*) operated to entice a new generation of teen-aged girls—and a crossover, multigenerational, mixed-sex audience—to the theater. The BBC's retooled *Masterpiece Classics* appeals to girls, their elders, and hardcore Janeites in the North Atlantic world. And Hindi cinema submits Austen to the song-and-dance Bollywood aesthetic to woo national and diasporic citizens to the movie-palace box office or small screen. The heritage boom is hardly over.

Becoming Jane confirms the two-decades-long megaplexing of Jane Austen. In its first weekend, the film opened in suburban New Jersey in two independent cinemas (one in a strip mall, the other freestanding), one multiplex, and one megaplex, exhibition sectors that clearly shape consumption of film products. Each exhibition venue serves a different niche audience and so they rarely share bookings; each has a different cultural history as well. Although it currently enjoys an ever-smaller share of exhibition revenues, independent moviemaking emerged with the "'little cinema' movement of the 1920s" and began to coalesce around independent producers and rivals Samuel Goldwyn and David O. Selznick during the studio era (Wilinsky 67 and passim), consolidated and expanded as a niche market during the 1950s and 1960s art-house movement, largely devolved into the repertory or X-rated "adult" movie house in the 1970s (Gomery, *Pleasures* 172–96), and became culturally prominent in the 1980s United States by riding on the "first wave of capital" that funded the home video business after a boom in the "healthy public TV market in Europe" (Schamus 94; Higson, *Heritage* 124–25). In 1981, the first group of heritage films hit the independent theaters and the televisual airwaves: Peter Weir's *Gallipoli*, Hugh Hudson's *Chariots of Fire*, and on television, Charles Sturridge's *Brideshead Revisited*. In 2008, Jarrold's *Brideshead Revisited* recycled Evelyn Waugh's Catholic country-house nostalgia for millennial viewers, using the same locations but putting heterosexual romance at the story's center. Yet *Brideshead Revisited*, a specialty-division film that had a slow-rollout release and was distributed by Miramax, as was Jarrold's *Becoming Jane*, did not cross over to the multiplex. Independent theater owners and producers, moreover, have seen their profits slowly squeezed since the Reagan administration re-allowed the industry's vertical integration, made illegal by the 1948 Paramount decision's demand for separation of the film industry's distribution and exhibition sectors.

Becoming Jane opened not only at independent theaters but at the multiplex and megaplex as well. At the ten- or twelve-screen multiplex, usually built in the 1980s and located at a suburban shopping mall (often tucked away in a corner and so necessitating a trek past upscale stores), fans generally see the current blockbuster, the testosterone megapic, and the global event movie (Paul 83; Hirschberg; King 49–59). The same fare is on display at the 1990s and twenty-first-century megaplex, a freestanding space with between sixteen and thirty "supersized" auditoriums outfitted with stadium seating, cup holders, curved screens, digital sound, an entertainment center, video and virtual reality games, a food court, and an upscale playground (Acland 107–8, 113, 123; Paul 84; Edgerton). Since it must compete with all other shopping mall and freestanding exhibition outlets, the megaplex—an "all-inclusive family-oriented entertainment park" (Acland 108)—may itself contain an art cinema or an IMAX theater as well as screens with conventional technological delivery systems. These theatrical spaces exhibit different cultural products, serving niche markets and audiences within a segmented cultural field: intellectual, high-cultural, or cineaste seekers of cultural capital; blockbuster addicts, thrills; family groups, PG fare; and horror fans, the new gornography. In the twenty-first century, the multi- and megaplex function spatially as did the Hays Office's censorship in the 1930s through 1960s: to make film product available for a wide range of movie consumers, all in one proximal space and at times flexible enough to serve consumer desires and exhibitor profits.

Film became a postindustrial commodity at the 1980s multiplex, which emphasized the immediate availability of "mass-market pictures at the expense of specialty films" (Acland 103). Heavily advertised on television, in newspapers, and on the Internet, movies became a "mass produced item" and the moviegoing experience, a kind of shopping; after theatrical release, film was "merchandized like [and as] wares" in a big-box store and later sold on DVD (Hark 15; Paul 81). Saturation booking—opening on as many screens as possible, which necessitates strong first-week box-office numbers—emerged to serve these late-century movie palaces, which contributed to a fragmented cultural scene and necessitated massive expenditures on marketing (Acland 150–62). *Becoming Jane* took in just under $1 million at one hundred U.S. screens in its first weekend—nothing to compare, in the following weekend, with *Superbad*'s opening of $31.2 million (McElroy)—but a highly respectable showing for a heritage biopic and sufficient to justify a ten-week run, with nearly $19 million gross; *Brideshead Revisited,* on the contrary, opened on thirty-three U.S. screens and earned \$340,000 during its first weekend.[1] Eager to hop on the lucrative Austen bandwagon, exhibitors of *Becoming Jane* ignored clearances (agreed-to zones around viewing regions) and distributors saturation-booked, turning the Regency writer into full-blown mass-cultural commodity.

Becoming Jane will also enjoy a long and productive afterlife in ancillary markets. The aftermarket—DVD rental store or sales outlet, pay-per-view cable TV, or the Internet—increasingly makes of film not just a commodity but "content" in a converged, synergistic multimedia entertainment environment (Miller et al. 147–49). In an era of "*postcelluloid* cinema culture," the motion-picture theater no longer dominates "moving-image culture," and vertical reintegration of the industry demands profitability "from a wide spectrum of mass-media enterprises" (Acland 46, emphasis in original; Gomery, "Corporate" 53). In the new Hollywood, as in the global marketplace, the "'software product'" designated for multiple hardware delivery includes not just feature films but video and computer games, TV shows, recorded music, book and magazine publications, and Web-based moving images, as film becomes advertisement for ancillary marketing (Balio, "Presence" 61). Print spin-offs likewise proliferate, including novels such as Paula Marantz Cohen's *Jane Austen in Boca* or *Jane Austen in Scarsdale,* Helen Fielding's *Bridget Jones's Diary,* and Karen Joy Fowler's *The Jane Austen Book Club*—all mass-market paperbacks the bestsellers of which became movies. Tie-ins such as the "Jane Austen Action Figure" enter the toy market; whereas the other superheroes pose for battle and victory over millennial bad guys, on the Austen box, the ad copy reads, "Weapon of Choice: Character Study." Although these merchandising tricks have been with us at least since Stephen Spielberg's *Jaws* (1975) and George Lucas's *Star Wars* (1977) and no doubt longer, the Jane Austen franchise—plus tie-ins, spin-offs, toys, and costumes—appeals primarily to audiences that consume mass-market or heritage romance.[2]

The Austen franchise thus selects as its purchasers female or "feminine" cultural consumers. The global event movie, jammed with visual and laboratory-based special effects, appeals to male viewers, primarily to those in the highly valued fourteen-to-twenty-four-year-old market segment (Miller et al. 158). Yet the female spectator is member of a highly prized demographic as well. Although Hollywood genre flicks (horror, the western, road pictures) attract teenaged male viewers, the woman's film (the melodrama or romance) woos female spectators to the theater and, later, to the ancillary market and its various exhibition windows. This has been true historically. Melvyn Stokes concludes that, however limited geographically and by education, age, and sex, 1920s and 1930s spectators were "predominantly female" and Hollywood believed women its "primary market" (43–44); although he notes that pre-Code audience composition can only roughly be approximated, Thomas Doherty agrees that, by "common consent," women comprised the prewar moviegoing majority and Hollywood "catered to" their interest in melodrama, romance, and sex pictures (126). Although at midcentury, studio heads viewed adolescent males as their primary audience, in the late twentieth century, women and men were going to the movies at about the same rate. The megaplex emerged as Hollywood producers and theater owners sought to serve both male and female audiences, both action and romance fans.

Although the material conditions of cinemagoing at today's multiple, indeed, transnational and global, exhibition sites are still difficult to codify, Hollywood's need to solicit a female audience has not changed. The new, increasingly multiply marketed movies of Jane Austen's novels attract discriminating female viewers across niches, theater venues, and national locations, as well as their partners, husbands, and daughters. Heritage film still sells product in the service of social distinction: the disposition to acquire legitimate taste, to appreciate and take pleasure in canonical literary texts adapted for the screen. This tasteful consumer might view *Becoming Jane* at the local freestanding indie house or upscale multiplex; her preteen daughter, at a local Regal Entertainment Group megaplex, the country's top theater chain with 4,472 screens at 413 sites ("Fabulous Fifty"). In the millennial suburban Northeast, exhibitors sought both demographics: the adolescent fan of teen romance; the Austen enthusiast and her bookish husband; the gay purchaser of period pleasures. The Jane Austen franchise also meets a new corporate goal of cinema owners: enticing baby boomers to the box office. With the "'graying' of the cinemagoing population," quality control of product and enhanced "bourgeois civility" of amenities please audiences who practice "tasteful spectatorship" and who purchase at the concession stand not Coke and popcorn but Starbucks coffee and petit fours (Acland 118).

The presold product—central to the phenomenon in which Regency novels about courtship and class mobility become fodder for Hollywood and BBC remakes, spin-offs, prequels, and fake biopics—supports and sustains the heritage franchise. As classic fiction with a large and global fan base, the Jane Austen novels are "already familiar to a potential audience" (King 50); the well-organized, transnational Jane Austen Society of North America (JASNA) provides a ready-made mass audience of dedicated consumers of presold Austen product. Although canonical literature is always presold at a number of sites and is regularly taught by educators to cultivate the tastes of young consumers, new organizations have emerged to enhance audience appeal, prevent print's disappearance, and sell additional cultural product. The contemporary book club, whether in the neighborhood, at the local public library, or attached to Oprah Winfrey's nationally syndicated TV show, constitutes a new, albeit revivified, organ of cultural consumption. The "Staff Favorites" advertising at independent and chain bookstores also increases sales of featured novels, and rental schemes, such as Netflix, drive revenues by encouraging excess consumption. Like other twenty-first-century cultural products—upscale food, National Trust properties, English gardens, national and regional parks, heritage theme parks—the book and film must be sold as an "intangible" experience attractive to always-changing consumer groups, for cultural products must compete with experiences available to shoppers across the "spectrum of consumable commodities" (Hark 15). The Jane Austen franchise results when preplanned marketability creates profits from purchases by female spectators across consumption locations and market segments.

The new Austen mania, produced and directed by Hollywood's and Britain's younger generation, serves a different group of female moviegoers. Joe Wright's *Pride and Prejudice* (2005), also saturation-booked at multiple venues, opened during the all-important Christmas holiday season and grossed $38.5 million on U.S. screens, repurposing Austen's stories of status anxiety, estate envy, and luxury cultural goods for the adult fan but picturing a romantic marriage proposal and "post-coital clinch" for the increasingly global teenaged set (Stanley, "Yes"). In the millennium, a new breed of actress updates the Austen star image. Not Greer Garson's Lizzie as the uppity broad of 1930s screwball comedy, whose skill and drive gain her power and admiration, whose snappish responses to gentlemanly snobbery subdues Laurence Olivier's Darcy in every sexual battle; not Jennifer Ehle's Lizzie, walking Pemberley's picture gallery and admiring its owner's "regard," or tastefully flirting with upper-gentry, partially disrobed gentleman; no, Keira Knightley and Anne Hathaway instead bring millennial girlhood to the megaplex. Veteran of Gurinder Chadha's *Bend It Like Beckham* (2002) and Gore Verbinski's adventure-romance *Pirates of the Caribbean* (2003), Knightley brought swashbuckler girlfriend sex appeal and postfeminist wit to Wright's Lizzie; Hathaway, star of *The Devil Wears Prada* (2006) and *The Princess Diaries* (2001), attributed to Jane drive, ambition, and professional mobility. Both films linked the heroine with a mother figure: naive career girl faces off against bitchy boss, and anxious teenager gets soothed by wannabe aristocratic grandmother (Holden, "Devil"). These and other star images, Richard Dyer notes, may manage, expose, or oppose dominant ideologies. Although he fails to consider significant differences among female spectators as a group, he suggests—perhaps simplistically—that "particularly intense star-audience relationships occur amongst adolescents and women," who share an "intense degree of role/identity conflict and pressure" and "partial" exclusion from adult, male cultures (*Stars* 38, 37). Knightley's and Hathaway's star images exploit the contradictions between teenaged female sexual anxiety and millennial desire for independence. If Ehle's Lizzie is every forty- or fifty-something's favorite independent, even "mature," Austen heroine ("Jane Austen Mania"), Knightley is every twenty-something's sexpot good girl.

Knightley and Hathaway also update the Austen body for the millennial teenaged set. Like Gwyneth Paltrow's, Knightley's and Hathaway's collarbones grace bared chests and swelling cleavage above Regency gown décolletage, their curled and coiffed hair haloed by glamour lighting. Yet the millennial Austen face goes Paltrow one better, as the heroine looks out of the frame in close-up, exuding self-satisfied to-be-looked-at-ness, as "wide-eyed intensity" and botoxed pout excite teen girl envy and arouse boy alike (Holden, "Wit-Lit"). Knightley and Hathaway bring to Lizzie and Jane the svelte young-adult body that Paltrow likewise disrobed a decade ago in Alfonso Cuarón's *Great Expectations* (1998), tastefully morselized by tilt and close-up, pictured via soft-core look of female arousal. Nothing so shocking need grace the Austen franchise now, which is targeted at a younger and more knowing female demographic. Although Paltrow's Emma won her Mr. Knightley's hand, and Ehle's Lizzie, her Darcy's, both Paltrow and Ehle have aged into roles as wife and mother (Ehle, in *Wilde*) or older professional woman (Paltrow in *Possession* [2000] and *Iron Man* [2008]). Heritage hunk Jeremy Northam and male pin-up Colin Firth, too senior now to play the Austen mate, get superseded by James McAvoy,

fresh from the rakish exploits of *The Chronicles of Narnia* (2005), the political intrigue and sexual shenanigans of *The Last King of Scotland* (2006)—
and cast next, opposite Knightley, in Joe Wright's genre-mixing Great War
romance adaptation of Ian McEwen's *Atonement* (2007).

In *Becoming Jane*, girlish romance takes precedence over Austen's professional life as an author. Jarrold borrows freely from Jon Spence's biography *Becoming Jane Austen: A Life*, which speculates that Tom Lefroy, an
Irish law student, was Austen's first and most important love and that she
longed for him throughout her life. "It is unclear," however, John Halperin
notes, whether "this was a pleasant flirtation or a serious affair of the
heart," since Austen mentions Lefroy playfully only in letters of January 1796 and, more seriously, in November 1798 (61); Deirdre Le Faye
judiciously reports the surviving evidence, including niece Caroline's
skeptical, perhaps anxious letters about "'that old story,'" rumors told
and retold but without substance (Austin-Leigh 277–78). *Becoming Jane*
claims to be a fictional prequel to the novels and is a faux remake of
other Austen adaptations, including Patricia Rozema's *Mansfield Park*
(1999). Yet Rozema's remediation, which likewise charts the emergence
of the modern woman novelist, fabricates a mix of source novel, biography, and edited letters rather than films an ersatz first novel as a period
costume drama. Nevertheless, in Jarrold's film, Jane also writes: "What's
she doing?" Lady Gresham (Maggie Smith) asks; "Writing," her mother
(Julie Walters) sighs. Here, Jane inks out text that resembles Austen's,
but isn't quite, in favor of overheated prose. After she elopes with her
lover then changes her mind, Jane sits down at her domestic desk, quill
in hand; cut to close-up of blank paper, quill dripping, as she inscribes
the title, "First Impressions," with a flourish as underline: "It is a truth uni-
versally acknowledged, that a single man in possession of a good fortune,
must be in want of a wife," she has written, suggesting that the justly
famous first sentence of *Pride and Prejudice* originated in frustrated and
lost love.

Jarrold's romanticized budding writer differs from Jeremy Lovering's
mature, already famous Austen. In the BBC *Masterpiece Classics Miss
Austen Regrets* (2008), Austen worries about her publisher and pens her
later novels, *Emma* and *Persuasion*. Romance centers not in Aunt Jane's
youthful flirtations but her niece Fanny's questions about courtship and
marriage. In fitting conclusion, Cassandra burns Austen's letters, leaving
behind those that screenwriter Gwyneth Hughes has used to "imagine"

Austen's biography, as host Gillian Anderson explains. The new *Master-piece Classics* updates the thirty-seven-year-old series, which was admittedly "beginning to look antiquated." "We're not tarting it up or dumbing it down," producer Rebecca Eaton avers, hoping to please loyal BBC fans yet seeking younger viewers (Jensen). Andrew Davies pens four of the six fast-paced teleplays: opening *Sense and Sensibility* with a seduction scene that Austen only reported, late in the novel, as consequential backstory; inventing "little scenes" of kidnapping and B&D that Catherine Morland "makes up for herself" in *Northanger Abbey,* Davies adds the suppressed scenes Austen "couldn't write" ("PBS to Air"). These postclassic serials eschew faithful transcription of Austen dialogue and narratorial discourse; although Davies admits he sometimes does "just copy it out" of her novels, he is no Fay Weldon (Cartmell and Whelehan, "Conversations" 244). Updating romance for the millennial spectator, Davies confesses he likes a "bit of bodice ripping" ("PBS to Air").

Not just Austen but other classic British novelists join the heritage franchise's marketing for new female and feminine audiences. Whereas Mira Nair exoticizes William Makepeace Thackeray's *Vanity Fair* to solicit the middlebrow heritage spectator, Gurinder Chadha and Rajiv Menon incorporate and indigenize Jane Austen, respectively, for the national, diasporic, and global markets (Mishra 51). Nair, born in India and now living in New York, shoots a goody-goody heritage flick that sprinkles Thackeray's novel with Indian exoticism: Becky (Reese Witherspoon) eats a really hot chili curry with aplomb; Jos Sedley (Tony Maudsley) gifts his seductress with an Asian parrot; Major Dobbin (Rhys Ifans) gets transferred to Bombay; like all expendable younger sons, Rawdon Crawley (James Purefoy) dies in an unnamed desert outpost that resembles India; Becky dances an updated *murja* as postcourtesan culture bump-and-grind for Lord Steyne (Gabriel Byrne); and Becky marries Jos at film's end in India, as the reunited lovers ride on an elephant amid a festive procession, with Becky's oft-muddied trunk securely affixed to its behind. Nevertheless, Nair's adaptation flopped at the box office because her exoticized heritage film portrays the India-loving, upwardly striving Becky Sharp as a good woman.[3] Becky bids Rawdon to war with tears and embraces, crying, "I am a woman in love, aren't I?" "You are a woman who has been truly loved," he responds, kissing her pregnant belly through her diaphanous red gown. She sells her horses to the Brussels-fleeing Bareacres, denying herself a seat in their carriage so she may remain with likewise pregnant Amelia in the war-torn city. She feeds an angry Rawdon substandard meat and refuses to pay the butcher, but regrets both. When Steyne sends Rawdy Jr. away to school, Becky's hand meets her boy's on the carriage glass, as they bid a loving adieu. Nair's Becky dallies with Steyne, sends her son away, submits herself to social snubbing, all because she had to, to support her beloved husband and family, as, without irony, Nair depicts Becky's claim that she could be a good woman on £5,000 a year.

With the millennial release of Chadha's *Bride and Prejudice* (2004) and Menon's *Kandukondain Kandukondain* (2000), the Austen franchise has gone global.[4] Although at first sight a mismatch, English heritage and Bollywood films share a hybrid aesthetic and manage audience affects by mixing genres, manipulating star images, and spectacularizing mise-en-scènes. The former Miss World Aishwarya Rai plays two Austen characters—as Helena Bonham Carter played two by Henry James—updating the sari-clad South Asian female body and face for the global millennium. Amalgamating realism and fabulism, Hindi cinema pictures an Indian girl at home who breaks into song and dance, magically journeys to an exotic location, and dons costumes in a ravishing palette of garish yellows, greens, or reds. Bollywood addresses a culturally and racially heterogeneous postcolonial nation; with its many regions, multiple religious affiliations (Hindu, Muslim, Sikh), castes, and mixed-race peoples, the postcolonial Indian nation is among the most complex and heterogeneous of millennial communities. Yet Bollywood's contemporary audience is no longer solely national, as the South Asian diaspora extends the Indian community beyond India's boundaries. Hamid Naficy notes that diasporic access to a "global media environment" problematizes notions of national cultures and cinemas, genres, filmmaking styles, and audience reception (203). Bollywood's mise-en-scène—manufactured through "heterogeneous production practices" from "prefabricated parts" rather than a drafted screenplay—produces a *masala* genre, which Vijay Mishra calls "sentimental melodramatic romance" (Desai 57; Mishra 13). For Rajeswari Sunder Rajan, this "postmodern hybrid culture"—the "product of the new [South Asian] middle classes and, specifically, of their consumerism"—allies spectators with a "global metropolitan" and English-speaking world ("English" 18; Desai 62).

Chadha incorporates the English *Pride and Prejudice* into a transnational crossover film, remediating Austen's hierarchies of rank as racial and national difference. A Hollywood hotel heir accompanies an Anglo-Indian friend to Amritsa to find a shy bride and meets instead matchmaker mother, businessman father, and marriageable daughters; meanwhile, the nonresident Indian (NRI) cousin comes courting and, rejected by Lalita (Aishwarya Rai, playing the Lizzie character), marries instead her best friend, Chandra (Sonali Kulkarni, playing Charlotte); after rejecting the arrogant American, Will Darcy (Martin Henderson), Lalita falls for Wickham (Daniel Gillies), himself toying with and seduced by Lahki (Peeya Rai Chowdhary). And so on. This heritage-Hindi genre mixer fuses East and West, Broadway and Bollywood. The Bakshi girls' number, "I Just Want a Man Who Loves Romance," for example, plays like a song from *Grease,* the girls in white nighties bouncing around their mansion, dissing Kholi for his love of LA, his dislike of American women—"too outspoken and career-oriented," he complains, especially "the lesbian." Paying tribute to the musicals she grew up with, Chadha positions her film for crossover success, as her diasporic politics target a multiple audience of hip second-generation migrant teens, first-generation fans seeking shots of the homeland, and European and U.S. heritage consumers who, like Kholi, "prefer hip hop" to tambour.[5]

Paul Mayeda Berges's screenplay endorses even as it critiques diasporic Westernization. "Don't turn India into a theme park," Lalita chides Darcy, poolside, while enjoying the hotel his already wealthy mother hopes to acquire. At film's end, Darcy takes Lalita on a whirlwind multicultural helicopter tour, from the Gehry Theater to the Grand Canyon to an LA beach, complete with robed, gospel-singing choir and surfer dudes; as the song ends, the lovers caress, backlit. Berges spoofs Mr. Collins as the foolish and westernized Mr. Kholi (the scene-stealing Nitin Ganatra), whom the Bakshi girls imagine clumsily working out, ineptly jumping a girl's bones, and living in the Valley (a West Coast diasporic in-joke); meanwhile, Kholi and Chandra live happily in a McMansion, with a mammoth SUV in the driveway, and, after her Pemberley epiphany in a Beverly Hills hotel, Lalita delightedly chooses Darcy, "the most eligible bachelor in LA."

Whereas Chadha incorporates Austen's novel about English courtship, Menon indigenizes *Sense and Sensibility* for a regional South Indian and a national audience. Self-consciously parodying the Bollywood aesthetic by shooting Tamils trying to shoot a Tamil film, Menon differentiates his cultural product from those of Mumbai even as he situates his film within a reformulated all-India cinema (Tyrrell 269–70). Adding action scenes to the traditional sentimental melodramatic romance, *Kandukondain*'s song-and-dance sequences display a new form of multicultural global culture. Shot in increasingly exotic locations, the sequences borrow from and indigenize other national cinemas as though to triumph over them, to incorporate into Hindi cinema the desert-sheik, gothic horror, Hollywood musical, and global video and MTV aesthetics of its competitors. In the sixth song sequence, for example, Manohar (Ajith, as Edward Ferrars), protagonist, star, and filmmaker, performs on a ship's-deck set and in sailor costumes that resemble those of 1940s Hollywood musicals. He dances with the action heroine who stars in his first film, as Menon's scenario incorporates its star's; magically, the heroine morphs into a more modestly costumed Sowmya (Tabu, as Elinor) as the dancers perform the desired but delayed love match that Mano's—and Menon's—completed films will finally picture. At this sequence's center, the 1940s Fred Astaire–style musical embeds a Britney Spears dance video look-alike. Here, Menon celebrates Indian stardom and fandom ("I'm an action heroine," Mano's star whines; "What about my fans?"), even as he questions Hindi film's Westernization. The nondiegetic nature of all but the final song foregrounds Bollywood codes and conventions, yet all the numbers are love songs, shot in settings that function like Jane Austen's balls, bringing together men and women, allowing them to transgress the censor's injunction against sexual touch in Indian cinema (Mishra 101).

Menon's movie about moviemaking knowingly mixes cinematic with "real" scenes as a postmodern ploy. Immediately after the credits: a shot of female feet, tilt up to red hem; cut to close-up of face, to skirt blowing up over body, displaying legs; "cut," a man yells out of frame, as the costume manager complains about the star's bad lip-synching, and the scenario becomes film set. Alluding to the famous Marilyn Monroe publicity shot, Menon exhibits the female body as to-be-looked-at in a westernized structure of global video culture even as the reference to lip-synching refers to conventional Hindi cinematic codes. When the girls' grandfather dies late in the film and they leave the family mansion (sparing them the early eviction their Austen originals suffer), they trudge through the house, shot overhead through a glass ceiling, then through the city's streets, bearing luggage, as a filmmaker enters frame right: they're in a movie. The Pemberley moment: a gopher scouts locations; what Sowmya and her matchmaking mother think is a marriage proposal is, in fact, a movie deal.

"Stars don't scout locations," a crew member tells Mano. "A Tamil movie with a court scene?" another queries, joking about traditional courtesan culture; another thinks Mano's courtship "sounds like a better love story than our movie." Cut to the sheik number, set among Egypt's pyramids, shot on decommissioned railroad—or sound stage?—tracks.

Menon's movie pictures a technologized, global visual culture that appeals to a middle-class, well-educated, domestic or diasporic audience even as it solicits the home crowd that wants a *masala* film with a twist. Shrika, Meena's mistaken love (the Willoughby figure), addresses the camera; cut to pictures of him on magazine covers, in advertisements; a TV interview with shots of the set and multiple TV screens displaying the stock market "hero." Shrika is pure star image: created by the interpenetration of entrepreneurship with communication and computer technologies, he plays in multiple media windows even as he spouts to Meena traditional Hindi love poetry. Although Sowmya learns by reading the newspaper that Mano has been sacked from his first film, *Speed,* she watches on TV as he romances his action-heroine star at an awards ceremony. When Meena becomes a music star, Major Bala (Mammootty, as Colonel Brandon)

*Manohar—protagonist, filmmaker, and star of the movie-within-a-movie—sings and dances on a Fred Astaire–style set. (*Kandukondain Kandukondain, *2000)*

watches shoppers purchase her CD, as her poster graces the walls. Meanwhile, Sowmya's computer program is a success in America; Mano's movie, a hit at the palace. Situating technologies of reproduction and circulation within his film's diegetic space, Menon gets behind the scenes of Bollywood spectacle, displaying its conspicuous visuality as an aspect of postmodern, postcolonial *masala* culture.

Hindi-heritage's *masala* aesthetic—which makes it so popular at home—also helps it travel. Already an international cultural industry, Indian cinema is increasingly reaching Western theaters and ancillary markets. An audience of cinephiles committed to multiculturalism already exists in Western English-speaking countries. Yet given the cultural stress surrounding an international migrancy well under way, Indian cinema may also serve a postnationalist project to negotiate the cleavages between national migrant populations and those of their host nation-states. Paul Gilroy argues that twentieth-century American models for managing cultural pluralism are now breaking down and that an emerging multicultural majority threatens neoconservative notions of a stable national identity, even as racial and economic segregation fixes and reinvigorates "the most tired racial archetypes and imagery" (B10). In the UK, a melancholic romance with the lost Empire and the contemporary presence of migrants (whether Muslim, African, or Eastern European) create anxiety about "the integrity of Britain's national culture and national identity," about whether Britain might become a "minor adjunct" to U.S. global power in the years ahead, about British-born Muslim terrorism (B8–9). The Hindi-heritage crossover may also tap what Gilroy calls a "porous and fluid conception of national community" to assuage an anxious British national traditionalism, and an "unavoidable exposure to otherness" may support a "convivial culture" that reaches across racial and ethnic boundaries (B10). As a popular (although critically reviled) film such as *Bride and Prejudice* indicates, it may well become unremarkable in the twenty-first century that a Hollywood hotel heir romances a newly impoverished Indian beauty through the medium of a nineteenth-century English literary classic.

Hindi-heritage film, in general, woos a female spectator familiar with the English literary classics and seeking cultural capital. Austen's novels, studied in Indian college courses "virtually indistinguishable" from those of the "metropolitan university in the west," suit contemporary India, Chadha says, with its arranged marital system (Sunder Rajan, "English" 7; DVD).[6] Ruth Vanita's Indian English-literature university students, she

reports, misread and appropriate Austen's endorsement of "love marriage" as a critique of the South Asian tradition of "arranged marriages"
(93). Yet other South Asian and Middle-Eastern girls like Jane Austen as
well. "It's a bit like our society," a teenaged Saudi Arabian says of Georgian
England, "dignified, and a bit strict"; Joe Wright's *Pride and Prejudice* is
her "favorite DVD" (Zoepf). In Azar Nafisi's secret 1990s literature seminar, seven Iranian girls read Austen and recount their own tales of sexual
fantasy, marital abuse, and proper courtship, under a regime where "love
was forbidden, banished from the public sphere" and sex was "suppress[ed]
violently." Austen's novels feature "rebels who say no to the choices" of
"silly mothers, incompetent fathers," and a "rigidly orthodox society,"
Nafisi notes; as one student says, "We're *way* behind Jane Austen's times"
(302–4, 307, 259).

On *Radio Times,* a JASNA blogger and an American academic who
writes Austen spin-off novels talked with readers and moviegoers from
the United States and Asia. An Iranian woman, who discovered Austen
through her daughter's reading in an American high school, focused during her on-air time on Austen's relevance for her culture, which disallowed
dating; a Chinese woman, who read *Pride and Prejudice* in Chinese translation while at college after the Cultural Revolution, likewise stressed
Austen's universal appeal across cultures and in different historical periods. Cross-cultural, transnational, or transhistorical, Jane Austen mania *is*
back and has never gone away; a new adaptation is playing on a big or
small screen near you as heritage film in all its forms—feature-length film,
classic serial, and ninety-minute or two-hour teleplay—complexly depicts
the North Atlantic historical and cultural imaginary in global contexts.
Commanding a wide-ranging sense of the literary, visual, and social contexts in which it is always already embedded, heritage film raises questions
about the future of culture even as it transmits and disseminates literary
culture for a postnational, globalized, postmodern age.

Notes

Introduction

1. See Leitch, *Film Adaptation*, chap. 1; and Whelehan, "Adaptations: The Contemporary Dilemmas."

1. Heritage Film, Classic Serial, and England's Jane

1. See Bourdieu, *Distinction* (5–8 passim) and "Forms" (46–48), for distinctions among economic, cultural, and social capitals. According to Harold Perkin, this class emerged in the 1870s, with the rise of professionalism and as the middle class defined its relationship to rank; Daniel Bell's 1970s new service class is its twentieth-century descendant (Urry, *Gaze* 87–91).

2. Urry's high-cultural examples are attendance at operas, drama, museums, classical concerts, dance, and environmentally sensitive activities such as yoga and hiking and climbing; middlebrow examples are fishing, bowling, vodka and whiskey drinking, golf, rock concerts, and Spanish holidays (*Consuming* 225). The definition of "middle class" as constituting certain occupations, which the researcher could list and characterize and which, in successive census documents, could accrete, is itself a Victorian conceptualization; see Ed Cohen 20.

3. For instance, Bourdieu draws upon preindustrial, feudal, and Enlightenment models without distinguishing among them; see "Forms" and "Marriage Strategies."

4. John Hill makes some of these same points (*1980s* 74–76).

5. Hipsky makes some of these points; unlike him, however, I do not disdain this viewer's values.

6. Giddings and Selby cheekily report that *Radio Times* featured a tie-in pin-up of Colin Firth as Darcy (117). On Darcy's body, see Hopkins; on Pemberley's landscape as commodity and aesthetic, see Ellington.

7. As one gentleman's tutor said, "The possession of such rarities, by reason of their deadly costliness, doth properly belong to princes, . . . [s]uch as are skilled in them" (quoted in Tinniswood 56). By the seventeenth century, the gentleman virtuoso's private collections of curiosities confirmed his prestige, power, and dominion; by the eighteenth, members of the cultivated elite displayed their taste

and cultural accomplishments in their estates' portrait galleries, which exhibited family portraits alongside Old Italian Masters, continental statuary, and antique marbles (Girouard 164–80; Colley 173–75).

8. Tinniswood 91–96. Given the volume of visitors by the 1820s, country house owners began to reform visiting arrangements: some fixed a day of admission, others issued tickets, all vetted visitors and their servants for suitability (Tinniswood 63, 96, 102; Mandler, *Stately* 9).

9. Marrying up within the gentry, however, hardly represented a revolutionary change in this rank's purity; due to primogeniture, downwardly mobile younger sons (and daughters) never fell terribly far in Regency England (Ginger Frost, personal communication, spring 2002).

10. Sonnet argues against Jameson's notion that a sense of historicity waned in the 1980s by claiming that historical literary adaptations "rehistoricize" nineteenth-century meanings for the contemporary spectator (54).

11. Galperin notes that the "novel's social allegory, involves a transfer of stewardship from the aristocracy to the professional classes" and that its heroine ultimately marries "a representative of the new order" (*Historical* 219). Pidduck notes that the sailing ship as "movement-image" in the films of Austen's novels represents, on screen, "imagined mobility" and that Wentworth portrays a "robust worldly masculinity" (35).

12. Poovey calls women the "crucial pawns in the struggle for landed wealth, upon which both political power and social prestige ultimately depended" (*Proper* 11).

13. Although she drew my attention to this shot, Favret did not so interpret it.

14. Perry calls Lady Russell, Anne's aunt and mother surrogate, a "placeholder for a kind of maternal power"; a "ghostly presence," she is historically residual, the "last trace of an independent woman—on her way to extinction in the nineteenth century" (*Novel* 348).

15. The location is the garish, even ostentatious Chatsworth (Holden, "Looker" B12).

16. According to Fabricant, however, Elizabeth's having been asked to marry the master makes her identification less gauche and naive than it would otherwise have been (256).

17. Galperin argues that Darcy's "resemblance," having been "taken in his father's life time," identifies Pemberley's current owner as contained by and subject to "the ordinances of patriarchy and entailment," as "flatten[ed] rather than enlarg[ed]" by representation (*Historical* 130). Yet surely a novel so fully about representation, aesthetics, and cultural acquisition and consumption less fully condemns this female look in the estate's portrait gallery.

18. Such visiting began in the 1580s, with dissolution of the monasteries and countryside royal progresses to them; by the 1690s, travelers were welcomed at

the country house—stuffed, after the collecting mania of seventeenth-century virtuosi, with cultural objects ready for viewing. Despite the waning of aristocratic hospitality and generosity, modernized conventions governed the visit: writing in advance, being vetted by the housekeeper or butler, and offering her or him a financial reward in turn for seeing the house's saloons, galleries, and cultural treasures (Tinniswood 94–100; Mandler, *Stately* 10–17).

19. Williams, *Marxism and Literature* 46–54. The picturesque depended on rugged disproportion and variety, detail and novelty, and viewing landscape from vantage points on property owned by members of the landed establishment but now accessible to middle-class travelers (Andrews 36).

20. Copley and Garside 8, quoting John Barrell; Williams, *Marxism and Literature* 49.

21. Andrews 81; Bermingham 87; Galperin, *Historical* 46–59.

22. I've condensed a great deal of history here; see Cannadine, *Aspects* 10–34, and Colley 159–61.

23. 84; see also Tuite, *Romantic* 130–31; Sales 105–6.

24. See Perry's balanced and sophisticated take on Austen's colonial/imperial position, given her class, gender, and family connections ("Imperialism"), and Wiltshire's strident demystification of postcolonial embarrassments ("Decolonising").

25. My argument in this paragraph has been influenced by Urry, *Gaze* 16–39. Duckworth notes that Austen's final fragmentary novel, *Sanditon,* confirms the future decline of estate and emergence of seaside resort (xi).

26. Brosh notes that Leonard's film represents its heroines as possessing the "tastes of a consumer culture that the novels long predate" (44).

27. During the 1930s, studio publicity departments used fashion to draw female spectators to the box office, and women often adopted star costume to blur class distinctions (Herzog and Gaines 84).

28. Brosh argues that *Pride and Prejudice* "has it both ways": "it satisfies the female audience's desire to compensate for Depression-era deprivations while also allaying male anxieties by asserting that women do not really want money, only love" (35).

29. *Pride and Prejudice* was released in the year *Gone with the Wind* became the first blockbuster, with the biggest-ever tie-in "merchandising blitz" (Balio, *Enterprise* 171).

30. Hill, "Relationship" 151–52; quoted in Giles 70. Caughie notes that, in the 1980s, "British film [was] alive and well and living in television," that British film's dependence on TV, on national and international film festivals—and on literary adaptation, I would add—was "symptomatic of a British art cinema emerging in the 1980s and 1990s: an art cinema, balanced precariously between a European sensibility and the North American market, which is economically dependent on television" ("Convergence" 217); see Appleyard 306 and MacCabe, "Subsidies."

31. Giddings and Selby 2–16; Giles 71; Cardwell, "Small Screen" 187–88. The BBC's dramatization of Anthony Trollope's *The Warden* in 1951 and of *Emma* in 1973 mark the historical span of classic serial's "Sunday teatime" TV dominance in Britain. During that time, all of Austen's novels but *Northanger Abbey* were serialized (that novel was dramatized in 1987), although many of these are now unavailable for viewing (Giddings and Selby 21, 19–20; see Marilyn Roberts).

32. See Jarvik 168–97; Bommes and Wright 276–88.

33. Kerr 6; see Kammen 56, 61.

34. Giles 87. For an excellent discussion of government policy toward and funding of film in the Thatcher years, see Hill, *1980s* 31–52; on Channel 4, see Hill, *1980s* 54–59 and Hill, "Relationship" 156–62.

35. As Frank Miller says, "In 1980, the nation took a turn to the right that made the Nixon years seem tame by comparison" (232).

36. Howkins 80, 75. Here, Howkins misreads country ideology as produced through nineteenth-century retrospective. Thomas Hardy will, nearly a century after Austen, exploit this rural ideal in his Wessex novels; Davies knew this, and conceived of his ending as "like [those] in Hardy's or Tolstoy's novels" (Birtwistle and Conklin 57).

37. Kerr 11. Caughie notes that "behind the disdain for the classic serial, literary adaptation, and the costume drama lurks a resistance to the feminine" (*Television* 207).

38. *Revisited* 106, 82–98. Like Pidduck, Cardwell neglects these adaptations' relationship with their literary sources, primarily because she argues that they may be more productively understood as intertextual with other TV serials.

39. Lowenthal notes that the Commons Preservation Society was founded in 1865; the Society for the Protection of Ancient Buildings, in 1877 (with William Morris at its head); the National Footpaths Preservation Society (which sought to enshrine as heritage icon the rural English landscape, already identified as existing in a national-cultural tradition), in 1884 (278–82). On the Victorians' notion of the stately house and its ruin in "Olden Time," see Mandler, *Fall* 21–69; on Thatcher's support of "Victorian values," see Joyce 111–39.

40. Bommes and Wright 274. See also Wright 50–52; Miele 17–23; Wiener 67–72; Mandler, *Stately* 184–87, 338–48.

41. Heritage tourism's high local multiplier kept roughly half of tourist expenditure in a locality, although it was always unevenly distributed among the new service workforce. The Lake District, with its National Trust properties and National Park landscapes, sustained continuous growth (Urry, *Gaze* 107–9, 116).

42. Bommes and Wright (269) write this, paradoxically, in the early 1980s, prior to Wright's mid-1980s agitation.

43. Tuite somewhat overstates the case when she notes that the "British agrarian Romantic canon" to which Austen is central "refashion[s] as national culture" that of "the ruling classes" ("Domestic" 111).

44. On the distinctions I list, see Urry, *Gaze* 84.

45. Balio, "Major Presence" 58. Mazdon discusses the GATT context in which French critics deplored U.S. cultural imperialism and notes, as well, the ways the concept ignores the "heterogeneity of . . . cultural formations and the dialectical nature of struggles over [cultural] power" (12).

2. Being True to Nineteenth-Century Narrative

1. Although I use the term "normative" as though it were stable, its meaning and significance change, under different modes of production and exhibition and as the cultural notions and social constructions of the couple shift.

2. Perry calls Charlotte Collins a "vestigial character, left over from an era of pragmatic rather than romantic matches" (*Novel* 255).

3. Pidduck notes that Ang Lee shoots Margaret as a "dynamic, moving detail in the otherwise posed, still shots," to suggest female potentiality among the film's symbols of "social constraint and repression" (33).

4. Perry notes, however, that the competition between new wives and sisters is characteristic of fiction written during the historical shift from consanguineal to conjugal families, as women's power increasingly resided in their position as wives rather than as sisters or daughters (*Novel* 141–42).

5. *Letters* 208 (emphasis in original); see Sales 65–69; Laudermilk and Hamlin 75, 93–94.

6. Historians have moved the "origins" of this shift ever earlier, as they examine pre-nineteenth-century documents.

7. See also Marx 263–64; Freedland 157–58.

8. In the novel, Cathy reassures Heathcliff; if he washes "it will be all right" (65).

9. Dunaway 174–75; Clark 51; Leaming 257–61; Thomson, *Rosebud* 239–43.

10. "To Samuel Goldwyn, prestige was a screenplay by a New York playwright," Mordden notes; "to David Selznick an adaptation from Dickens" (11).

11. Selznick marketed *Gone with the Wind* by giving Loew's New York theaters exclusive rights, charging exhibitors and audiences exorbitant prices, and attaching trailers for *Rebecca* to those for *Gone with the Wind,* for example (Schatz, *System* 291–92).

12. Solomon 220, 241; Schatz, *System* 331; quoted in Balio, *Grand Design* 207.

13. Nemesvari notes that the British TV version of *Tess* uses this same figure for authenticity, and it is likewise linked to voice-over (172).

14. Despite an intertitle's claim that *Abismos de Pasión* "remain[s] true to the spirit of Emily Brontë's novel" by showing that "love can only be fulfilled through death," that "instincts and passions" are timeless, Buñuel's film violates all notions of fidelity to his source novel (Buñuel 205).

15. http.rogerebert.suntimes.com/apps/pbsc.dll (6 August 2006); Holden "Jane."

16. Michael Nyman's heroic music announces this narrative event (the bypass) as the film's primary cardinal function; it may also be a synecdoche for narrative deferral.

17. Nemesvari notes that the London Weekend Television *Tess*, despite its representation of Alec as rapist, nevertheless imagines, without precedent in the novel, that he loves Tess: he is thus "killed for love" (177).

18. Niemeyer notes that prerelease publicity for *Titanic* heralded Winslet's "first nude scene," a year prior to her "celebrated foray into onscreen nudity" (182).

19. Cuarón, like Karel Reisz in *The French Lieutenant's Woman* (1981), remediates print culture not by picturing books in mise-en-scène but fine art (for Reisz, theater), an embedded metaphor for film as visual-cultural medium.

20. De Niro in Martin Scorsese's 1970s films (*Mean Streets, Taxi Driver,* and *Raging Bull*); *The Godfather* films, *Goodfellas* (1990), and the *Cape Fear* remake (1991); *The Deer Hunter* (1978); and, later, *Mary Shelley's Frankenstein* (1994). Internet Movie Database, 20 February 2005, http://www.imdb.com.

21. Bancroft in *The Graduate* (1967), *The Miracle Worker* (1962). Internet Movie Database, 20 February 2005, http://www.imdb.com.

22. For discussion of the ways anxiety about the "Self-Made Man" subsumes masculinity in the twentieth-century United States, see Kimmel; of the ways society has "betrayed" postwar men, see Faludi. Jeffords declares 1991 "the year of the transformed U.S. man" from tough guy to "sensitive, loving, nurturing, protective family m[a]n" (197).

3. Reproducing Monsters, Vampires, and Cyborgs

1. Barron; Gillis; Franklin, *Embodied* 188. For the early story of cloning, see Kolata and see Wilmut, Campbell, and Tudge.

2. G. Jones 292, 281–314; Nye 64–65. Charles Dickens's and E. M. Forster's novels address these fears, for their respective historical moments.

3. Leitch suggests that the "update" takes an "overtly revisionary stance toward an original text" to "criticize [it] as dated, outmoded, or irrelevant," due to changed audience expectations ("Tales" 142, 143). For Leitch, only the "true remake"—as though there could be an authentic as opposed to inauthentic remake—paradoxically "emphasizes the problematic, contingent nature of its

own meanings" (145). Interestingly enough, most work on remakes is about French film remade by Hollywood; see Mazdon.

4. Mellor 288; Butler 306. For Rauch, electricity as technology differentiates the immoral scientist, Victor Frankenstein, from moral figures, who seek, as did Aldini, to "restore" life to the just dead rather than to "create" life from dead matter (106–9, 117–18). For Graham, the 1832 revision's increasing focus on the excesses of scientific experiment moralized the text—perhaps inviting Mellor's and Rauch's readings—and its use of electricity parodies the notion that material "life is animated by metaphysical spirit or soul" (75).

5. See Mellor 303–5; Rauch 106–7, 112, 232n.; Golinski 212–14; Butler 304–7.

6. *Modern* 10–11, 20–31, 24, 37, 39–43.

7. Butler argues that Lawrence's notoriety between 1819 and 1822 caused Shelley to remove the details of Frankenstein's scientific education and of the incestuous Frankenstein marriages, which "touch on genetic concerns" (312–13); Clayton, that in 1831, Shelley "dramatizes scientific overreaching" and adds rhetoric "to lay bare the dangers of Romantic egotism," which muddies her Enlightenment critique of science (128–31). Clayton's project, which traces postmodern anxieties about cyborgs and cloning back to Shelley's novel, resembles my own, although our theories of cultural appropriation differ greatly.

8. My thinking about the laboratory mise-en-scènes has been influenced by Brunas, Brunas, and Weaver (24–26) and by Sevastakis (96–98).

9. See Kittler, "Legacy"; Sadoff, *Sciences* chap. 4; and Clayton.

10. Pick 2, 235. Pick portrays the degeneracy discourse as powerfully addressing perceived political and social crises across Europe. Thus in Italy, Lombroso's focus on the "constitutional inheritance of the criminal" addressed the northern intelligensia's worries after unification, about the Peninsula's population, widely thought to consist of brigands, anarchists, revolutionaries, and racial primitives; in France, Benedict-Augustin Morel's notion that degenerate inheritance of acquired characteristics across generations would worsen until a kinship line became extinct explained fears about immigration, population explosion, poverty, and a declining birthrate in post-1848 Paris; and in Britain, fears about the "casual residuum," geopolitical class separation, the status of the body in London's slums, and the growth of mass democracy (110–20, 50–59; Nye 59–64). By the 1890s, fears of urban degeneracy served the emergent eugenics movement, which would later prove popular in fiction.

11. Halberstam calls Stoker's novel a "machine-text" that productively creates and interedits texts, examines the "activities of reading and writing," and "generates myriad interpretive narratives" (90–91).

12. According to Benshoff, the term "strangest," represents a subterranean address to homosexual spectators (46). Such a reading, I would suggest, depends

upon an overly generalized reading of all minoritization as homosexual or queer.

13. As Skal notes, these shots were introduced during reediting, since Universal demanded changes in the original cut (*Monster* 124–25).

14. Due to its mass audience, reformers argued, cinema could corrupt more viewers than books did readers, for a book's impact depended "'on the keenness of the reader's imagination,'" whereas film's depended on "'the vividness of presentation'" (Lewis, *Hard Core* 120). Krzywinska notes that "censorship is always embedded within a mélange of cultural, legal, governmental, media and industrial investments" (85). For a condensed overview of the history of film censorship in Britain and the United States, see Krzywinska 87–105.

15. Black recounts the engrossing story of bowdlerization, plot alteration, and thematic moral regeneration exercised on these novels (84–106).

16. Shumway notes that screwball comedy "emerged on the cusp of the newly restrictive production code of 1934, which forced films to become much less explicit"; these comedies "depict[ed] a sexual relationship without showing it" (88). As a result, dialogue and sexy banter displaced foreplay, and marriage or remarriage inevitably occurred at story's end (Krzywinska 96).

17. Skal lists only the censoring countries; my inference (*Monster* 125, 138). Berenstein reports that as the late-decade commitment to prestige pictures emerged, a "growing international disdain for horror" and its anti-Christian "perverse representations of sex" intensified (15). Curtis notes that, given the PCA's objections to *Bride of Frankenstein*'s "'excessive brutality and gruesomeness,'" Whale eliminated ten minutes from the film, including a scene of "grim comedy in which Dwight Frye murders his uncle and pins the job on the Monster" (249–51).

18. After the 1950s, when Hammer rediscovered him, Dracula again went underground until adoption of the ratings code in 1968, which acknowledged audience segmentation and brought explicit sex to the screen (Hutchings). Lewis tells the story of the code's demise: a "new production code became necessary because the studios had given up adhering to the old one" (*Hard Core* 105–35); on audience differentiation and the ratings system, see Mazdon 17.

19. Joslin argues that Coppola may have borrowed the "reincarnation romance" from the 1932 Universal pic *The Mummy*, with Boris Karloff, or the Kharis movies of the 1940s; in 1960, he says, the Italian film *L'Ultima Preda del Vampiro* (*The Playgirls and the Vampire* in the United States) also portrayed a reincarnation romance; 1972's *Blackula* shoots Dracula alongside a reincarnation romance, but Dracula is not the film's hero (69–70).

20. Given the difficulty of audience-reception study, Cherry identified survey respondents through "memberships of horror fan groups and fantasy societies," through horror magazine readerships, and from among "attendees at horror film

festivals and conventions." Respondents included dedicated and casual horror fans, viewers with wide-ranging tastes, and a wide cross section of the population in terms of age, education, employment, marital status, and geographical location (189). Williamson tells us little about the demographics behind her study or about the scope of her interaction with her interviewees. Austin's highly unsystematic study of horror spectators corroborates Cherry's formulations specifically for Coppola's film (302–5).

21. After the 1948 Paramount decision, the move to remake European, specifically French, film coincided with the emergence of a segmented, multiple audience in the United States, including those for art-house cinema, youth-oriented film, and mainstream movies (Mazdon 13–17, 21–23).

22. This notion was, of course, pioneered by Fredric Jameson, in his mapping of the disjunctions between the "capacities of the individual human body to locate itself" in time and space under postmodernism (*Postmodernism* 44).

23. Pierson differentiates "visual" from "special effects"; the former are design features, whereas the latter are post-production effects (50, 103).

24. I borrow the phrase "morph aesthetics" from its early 1990s coinage, with *Terminator 2* (Wasko 31). Kavka calls a similar mode "gothic mutability" (212). Skal, moreover, calls Coppola's claims to authenticity "misleading" (*Gothic* 278–79).

25. For the screenplay's text of this montage, including its various points of view, intercuts, medium shots, and close-ups, see Coppola and Hart 107–12.

26. Altick 125–36, 217–18; Friedenberg 20–29. Coppola replicates some of these effects in the cinematograph scene.

27. Industry insiders joked that German-immigrant Laemmle relations staffed the studio's minor positions (Brunas, Brunas, and Weaver 114–15; Skal, *Gothic* 210). James Whale, too, practiced Hollywood nepotism, hiring when possible members of his companion, David Lewis's, family: "It was in the middle of the Depression and work was tough to come by," Lewis's niece, Julie, told James Curtis (238).

28. Shelley added the phrase "guilty of a crime" to her second edition of *Frankenstein* (1831).

29. See Kipp 21–52. Perry calculates from demographic data that, in the eighteenth century, "at least 10 percent of fertile, married (sexually active) women died in childbirth" (*Novel* 366).

30. Armstrong argues that Stoker's text "render[s] intolerable all social groupings hostile to the family." Thus the "novel begins by proposing an ideal family and concludes with a family that has incorporated certain qualities of the vampire"; "vampire practices," she says, "represent precisely that notion of kinship as one that reproduces itself at the expense of humanity" (*Novels* 147). Not Stoker's novel, however, but our postmodern perspective on it—by virtue of our

embeddedness in the culture of NRTs, clones, and artificial life—constitutes this interpretation.

31. Franklin details the media coverage when the first five-year period elapsed in 1996, "fuelled by the drama of a countdown to locate thousands of couples, in Britain and elsewhere, whose written consent was required to prevent a thawing of would-be progeny" ("Orphaned" 167). The *New York Times* covered the story in the United States, after the next five-year period ended (Greenhouse). See also Gallagher.

32. The Huxley circle included writers such as J. B. S. Haldane; his wife Charlotte, a feminist journalist; his sister, the novelist Naomi Mitchison; as well as their friends Julian and Aldous Huxley (Turney 100–109).

33. The story appeared first in *Cornhill Magazine* and the *Yale Review* and was reprinted in a 1927 issue of *Amazing Stories* (Turney 107; Squier, *Babies* 40–42).

34. "One doesn't expect Dr. Frankenstein to show up in a wool sweater, baggy parka, [with a] soft British accent, and the face of a bank clerk," one early news story began. "But there in all banal benignity he was: Dr. Ian Wilmut" (Wilmut, Campbell, and Tudge 222).

35. On the difficulties of defining the family in the wake of assisted reproduction by same-sex couples, see Belluck and Liptak.

36. See, for example, these clone, vampire, zombie, and alien texts. Novels: *Cast of Shadows,* by Kevin Guilfoile; *Never Let Me Go,* by Kazuo Ishiguro; films: *Clonus,* directed by Robert S. Fiveson; *Godsend,* directed by Nick Hamm; *The Island,* directed by Michael Bay; plays: *A Number,* by Caryl Churchill; TV: *Buffy the Vampire Slayer,* of course, and *True Blood;* in production: *Pride and Prejudice and Zombies* and *Pride and Predator.*

37. My reading in this paragraph has been influenced by Hayles, *Posthuman.*

38. Despite the author's denial, it is a commonplace in Rice criticism that she, like Mary Shelley, wrote her first novel after the death of a child, a five-year-old daughter, Michelle, from leukemia: "I never consciously thought about the death of my daughter while I was writing it," Rice claims; "it was like dreaming" (B. Roberts 7; Ramsland 58).

39. Coppola also mobilizes this pun, when Dracula sees Harker's locket-portrait of Mina, his own reincarnated love.

4. Middlebrow Audiences, Cinematic Sex, and the Henry James Films

1. Internet Movie Database, 19 December 2005, http://uk.imdb.com/title; Internet Movie Database, 7 January 2006, http://uk.imdb.com/title.

2. Higson notes that *The Golden Bowl* took less than £1 million at the UK box office (*Heritage* 144, 107).

3. Anesko 127–30, 143.

4. *Notebooks* 82 (emphasis in original); Salmon 78–79.

5. My thinking about acculturation in James's novels has been shaped by Buzard.

6. Pidduck also notes this connection between James's final image and his theory of fiction (76–79).

7. Kramer also identifies Schubert's music as central to the story: the A-flat and G-flat impromptus of Opus 90 to interpellate Isabel and her mirrored, doubled, and fragmented subjectivity; the string quartet to constitute her fate, her "doomed, alienated, sexually tormented subjectivity" (29–30, 34, 48).

8. Critics often view Holland's film's end as feminist, but consigning Catherine to a role as spinster child-care provider hardly seems progressive; see Rowe 194, 208; Pidduck 66.

9. Internet Movie Database, 12 January 2006, http://uk.imdb.com/title.

10. Williams, *Hard Core* 98, 154; Sklar 294–95; Gomery, *Pleasures* 183–96; Krzywinska 220; Williams, *Screening Sex* 112–43, on *Last Tango in Paris* (1972) and *Deep Throat*.

11. An example of the fetish: an object or nongenital region of the body produces sexual pleasure, or "certain extrinsic conditions" bring it about (Laplanche and Pontalis 306).

12. I borrow the term "delegate" from Rivkin.

13. Ivory notes that John Singer Sargent was an "obvious influence" in *The Golden Bowl* (Long, *Conversation* 247).

14. See Steele. Neil LaBute shoots the corset unlacing scene brilliantly in his adaptation of A. S. Byatt's *Possession* (2002).

15. Polanski's landlady spectator-voyeur, in *Tess*, whose eye to the keyhole irises onto a scene of murder, is the postmodern type of this spectatorial-titillation strategy.

16. Schatz's terminology—about the independent mogul, David Selznick, who invented saturation booking for the premiere of *Duel in the Sun* (1946) ("New Hollywood" 11)— suits Merchant Ivory's comparative flop no less than King Vidor's.

17. Balio, "Art Film" 66, 71; Wyatt 76; Higson, *Heritage* 128–32.

18. Long, *Films* 16, 32. All three lived in the same East Side apartment building, prior to Merchant's death, and Merchant and Ivory shared a manor house or owned neighboring houses (the details here are contradictory)—one, an 1805 Federal-style mansion that resembled "a cross between an English country house and a small informal film colony"—two hours north of New York City (Hoge B2; Pym 27). Merchant was the "patriarch of the clan," said one adopted family member (Long, *Films* 16).

19. Long, *Films* 12–32. As Hoge says, Merchant Ivory's "cultural disinheritance . . . give[s] them a particular appreciation of James's Americans in Europe or Forster's Englishmen in India" (B2).

20. See Staiger 242; Balio, "Trends" 169, 173, 174.

5. Styles of Queer Heritage

1. Monk also notes heritage's focus on gender and queerness in *A Room with a View*, in particular ("Sexuality").

2. Finch and Kwietniowski argue that *Maurice* is a melodrama full of "absent fathers, denial, alteration, illness, hysteria, tears, unrequited love, idolation, paranoia, entrapment, duplicity, and false closure" (73). A similar argument might be made about *Wilde*.

3. I'm indebted for this point to Kerry Powell (personal communication).

4. I take my terms, of course, from René Girard's *Deceit, Desire, and the Novel*.

5. Monk notes the absence of male frontal nudity in *Wilde*; she notes, too, that the often-derided *A Room with a View* shoots a "display of penises" and so represents "something of a cinematic landmark," since in mainstream "hetero sex scenes," "extravagant measures will be taken to conceal the male organ at all times" ("Sexuality" 9).

6. Jagose notes that neither essentialist (what I call "congenital") nor constructivist views about gay causation are necessarily equivalent to political positions, whether homophobic or homophilic (10–29).

7. The casting of Ehle—the never-to-be-forgotten Elizabeth Bennet in the 1995 A&E *Pride and Prejudice*—as Constance serves to solicit heritage-fan sympathy with the poor neglected wife.

8. See *Who Was That Man?*

9. As David Halperin suggests, the creation of gay subcultures has historically been aided by homosexual panic, whether the late nineteenth- or late twentieth-century versions; see *One Hundred Years of Homosexuality*.

10. As Pidduck notes, "*Maurice* fulfills a gay liberation agenda of visibility and positive images" (144).

11. As Person notes, the casting of post-*Superman* Christopher Reeve slightly ironizes Basil's stiffest conservative rants.

12. Higson, *Heritage* 37. Interestingly enough, these terms mirror McFarlane's in his structural theory of film adaptation.

13. Ibid. 38. As Bristow maintains, Forster invariably returned—literally and thematically—to Cambridge, where Apostolic brotherhood provided homosexual iconography ("*Fratrum*").

14. This pictorial aesthetic permeates Merchant Ivory's films, and, for example, the nude male bathing scene in *A Room with a View* (1986) closely resembles

Eakins. Ivory notes Sargent's influence, as I noted in chapter 4. Rowe likewise discusses this pictorialism.

15. Ivory told Long that, after Redgrave turned the picture down, and Glenn Close withdrew, Redgrave "suddenly agreed to take the part" (*Conversation* 167).

16. As Terry Castle notes, the narrator's innuendo constructs a "*hypocrite lecteur* who enjoys extemporizing on female homosexuality (and freely abominating it) while also pretending not to recognize it" (170)

17. See Long, *Films* 150; *Conversation* 210–11.

18. According to Powell, few in the courtroom during Wilde's trials knew what constituted "gross indecency" (personal communication). As Ed Cohen notes, the Hyde trial transcripts are constructed out of newspaper stories, yet "at no point did the newspapers describe or even explicitly refer to the sexual charges made against Wilde" (4, see also 69–93). As Kaufman claims, "There were as many versions of what had occurred at the trials as there were people involved" (xiv).

19. I borrow the term "coming out" from Pidduck (144).

20. Castle argues that, via subterranean references to Émile Zola's scandalous novel *Nana,* James creates lesbianism as a "ghost" in the novel, a "spectral effect rather than something lavishly embodied" (170).

21. In *Sex, Politics, and Society,* Weeks argues that the Wolfenden Report represents both an expression of postwar anxieties (about the Cold War, the decline of moral values, the population question) and a blueprint for the "permissive" legislation of the 1960s (239–44, 267–69).

22. Bristow notes that Forster "loathed" the effeminate aesthetic associated with the cultural icon Oscar Wilde, yet he experienced "anxiety about the status of the effeminate man of letters" and felt the need to "masculinize" him (*Effeminate* 12, 57).

23. As Paglia notes, this scene portrays "homosexual generation," a vampiristic implanting of unnatural passions that homoerotically infuses into the other a passive, semblant subject (518).

24. White says Wilde substituted the term "curious" for "the more explicit 'queer'" (111, vii). The term, of course, permeates *The Picture of Dorian Gray.*

25. *The Picture of Dorian Gray* was shot three times during the silent era but not remade during the 1930s, the decade of prestige adaptations. New versions by David Rosenbaum (2004) and Duncan Roy (2006) have not been widely exhibited, and few if any horror fans have seen them. Oliver Parker's adaptation of the novel, *Dorian Gray,* had not been released in the United States prior to this book's publication. Internet Movie Database, 7 September 2006 and 9 November 2009, http://imdb.com.

26. Although color film stock was available in the 1930s and 1940s, color had not yet become the standard feature-film format.

27. Young makes some of these same points.

28. Bram, an openly gay writer, wrote the novel as a potential story for a "possible documentary," a hoped-for movie deal: perhaps *Gods and Monsters* (276).

29. Some additional ways to theorize camp: for Dollimore, camp invades, subverts, and hollows out notions of identity; for Babuscio, it transmutes depth (of content, identity, authenticity) into surface, aestheticism, irony, humor, and theatricality through mimicry, parody, pastiche, and exaggeration (311, 41).

30. Potter positions herself outside the popular-comedic traditions deployed by John Madden in *Shakespeare in Love* (1999) and *Mrs. Brown* (1997) and costume-drama camp (Parker), but alongside the high-cultural remediations of Jarman (*The Tempest* [1979]) and Greenaway (*Prospero's Books* [1991]).

31. Florence 277; I borrow several countercinema strategies here from Street (*British* 173).

32. Florence 283. Ouditt makes some of these same points.

33. Companies and funds involved included LenFilm, an innovative Russian studio, and British Screen; the European Co-production Fund and the European Script Fund also participated (Glaessner 53; Potter, *Orlando* 68).

34. See Hill, "Future" 66; Hirschberg 91; Gertner 109.

35. Caughie said this of another avant-garde heritage film, Derek Jarman's *The Tempest*, but it applies as well to *Orlando* ("European" 41).

36. For example, Hindi cinema inherited the "erotic economy of the look and the counterlook," once created between Indian performer and spectator, by the "colonial space" from the British proscenium arch (Mishra 9).

Epilogue

1. See Box Office Essentials and Internet Movie Database, respectively, for these box-office details. Thanks to Ken Eisen, of Shadow Distribution and Railroad Square Cinema, for providing me access to the former.

2. Selwyn may have invented such merchandizing; at its release in 1939 he marketed *Gone with the Wind* by attaching trailers for the upcoming *Rebecca* (Schatz, *System* 291–92).

3. See Internet Movie Database, 5 August 2005, www.uk.imdb.com.

4. Miller et al. note that the megaplex has likewise gone global, as an increasing number of films are screened in these mammoth movie palaces around the world (159–60).

5. Mishra identifies the different audiences that consume Hindi cinema as cultural product: the "home crowd" that chooses a *masala* film "in the current style with a twist"; the "diasporic home video set (largely homemakers and children)," for whom viewing is "habitual" rather than "spectatorial"; the "theorist," who "fix[es]" the homeland in diasporic consciousness; and the "diasporic spectator"

who seeks an "ideal homeland" story (if first generation) or a host-nation critique (if second generation) (13–15). Hoping to combine Bollywood and Hollywood, all "tied up with a British sensibility," Chadha mixes a dash of *Fiddler on the Roof*, *Oliver*, and *West Side Story* with Austen (DVD).

6. For an analysis of the nineteenth-century imposition of English literary studies on Indian subjects, see Viswanathan.

Bibliography

Acland, Charles R. *Screen Traffic: Movies Multiplexes, and Global Culture.* Durham N.C.: Duke University Press, 2003.

Altick, Richard D. *The Shows of London.* Cambridge, Mass.: Belknap Press, 1978.

Altman, Rick. *Film/Genre.* London: BFI, 1999.

Amis, Martin. "Jane's World." *New Yorker,* 8 January 1996, 31–35.

Andrews, Malcolm. *The Search for the Picturesque: Landscape Aesthetics and Tourism in Britain, 1760–1800.* Stanford, Calif.: Stanford University Press, 1989.

Anesko, Michael. *"Friction with the Market": Henry James and the Profession of Authorship.* New York: Oxford University Press, 1986.

Annas, Alicia. "The Photogenic Formula: Hairstyles and Makeup in Historical Films." In Maeder, *Hollywood and History,* 52–77.

Appleyard, Brian. "The Arts." In *The Thatcher Effect,* edited by Dennis Kavanagh and Anthony Seldon, 305–15. Oxford: Clarendon Press, 1989.

Arata, Stephen. "The Occidental Tourist: *Dracula* and the Anxiety of Reverse Colonization." *Victorian Studies* (Summer 1990): 627–34.

Armstrong, Nancy. *Fiction in the Age of Photography: The Legacy of British Realism.* Cambridge, Mass.: Harvard University Press, 1999.

———. *How Novels Think: The Limits of British Individualism from 1719–1900.* New York: Columbia University Press, 2005.

Austen, Jane. *Emma.* Introduction by Penelope Fitzgerald. Oxford: Oxford University Press, 1999.

———. *Jane Austen's Letters.* Collected and edited by Deirdre Le Faye. 3rd ed. New York: Oxford University Press, 1995.

———. *Mansfield Park.* Edited by R. W. Chapman. *The Novels of Jane Austen,* 3rd ed. 6 vols. Oxford: Oxford University Press, 1934.

———. *Persuasion.* Edited by Patricia Meyer Spacks. Norton Critical Edition. New York: W. W. Norton, 1995.

———. *Pride and Prejudice.* Introduction by William Trevor. Oxford: Oxford University Press, 1999.

———. *Sense and Sensibility.* Edited by R. W. Chapman. *The Novels of Jane Austen,* 3rd ed. 6 vols. Oxford: Oxford University Press, 1934.

Austen-Leigh, William, and Richard Arthur Austen-Leigh. *Jane Austen: A Family Record.* Revised and enlarged by Deirdre Le Faye. London: British Library, 1989.

Austin, Thomas. "'*Gone with the Wind* Plus Fangs': Genre, Taste and Distinction in the Assembly, Marketing and Reception of Bram Stoker's *Dracula*." In Neale, *Genre and Contemporary Hollywood,* 294–308.

Babuscio, Jack. "Camp and the Gay Sensibility." In *Gays and Film,* edited by Richard Dyer, vol. 1, 40–57. London: BFI, 1977.

Bailey, Beth L. *From Front Porch to Back Seat: Courtship in Twentieth-Century America.* Baltimore: Johns Hopkins University Press, 1988.

Baker, Dean. *Plunder and Blunder: The Rise and Fall of the Bubble Economy.* Sausalito, Calif.: PoliPoint Press, 2009.

Balio, Tino. "The Art Film Market in the New Hollywood." In *Hollywood and Europe: Economics, Culture, National Identity: 1945–95,* edited by Geoffrey Nowell-Smith and Steven Ricci, 63–73. UCLA Film and Television Archive Studies in History, Criticism and Theory. London: BFI, 1998.

———. *Grand Design: Hollywood as a Modern Business Enterprise, 1930–1939.* History of the American Cinema. Vol. 5. Gen. ed. Charles Harpole. New York: Charles Scribner's Sons, 1993.

———. "Hollywood Production Trends in the Era of Globalisation, 1990–99." In Neale, *Genre and Contemporary Hollywood,* 165–84.

———. "'A Major Presence in All of the World's Important Markets': The Globalization of Hollywood in the 1990s." In Neale and Smith, *Contemporary Hollywood Cinema,* 58–73.

Barron, James. "New Breed of Cat: A Clone." *New York Times,* 8 October 2004, national ed., A24.

Barthes, Roland. *S/Z.* Translated by Richard Miller. Preface by Richard Howard. New York: Hill and Wang, 1974.

Bartlett, Neil. *Who Was That Man? A Present for Mr. Oscar Wilde.* London: Serpent's Tail, 1988.

Bauer, Dale M. "Content or Costume? James as Cultural Capital." In Griffin, *Henry James Goes to the Movies,* 240–53.

Beck, Aaron T. *Love Is Never Enough: How Couples Can Overcome Misunderstandings, Resolve Conflicts, and Solve Relationship Problems Through Cognitive Therapy.* New York: Harper and Row, 1988.

"Becoming Jane." Box Office Essentials. Ken Eisen, Shadow Distribution, personal correspondence.

Belluck, Pam, and Adam Liptak. "Gay Parents Find Big Legal Hurdles in Custody Cases." *New York Times,* 24 March 2004, national ed., A1, A14.

Belton, Ellen. "Reimagining Jane Austen: The 1940 and 1995 Film Versions of *Pride and Prejudice*." In *Jane Austen on Screen,* edited by Gina Macdonald and

Andrew F. Macdonald, 175–96. Cambridge: Cambridge University Press, 2003.

Benshoff, Harry M. *Monsters in the Closet: Homosexuality and the Horror Film.* Inside Popular Film Series. Manchester: Manchester University Press, 1997.

Berenstein, Rhona J. *Attack of the Leading Ladies: Gender, Sexuality, and Spectatorship in Classic Horror Cinema.* New York: Columbia University Press, 1996.

Berg, A. Scott. *Goldwyn: A Biography.* New York: Alfred A. Knopf, 1989.

Bermingham, Ann. *Landscape and Ideology: The English Rustic Tradition, 1740–1850.* Berkeley: University of California Press, 1986.

Birtwistle, Sue, and Susie Conklin. *The Making of Jane Austen's "Emma."* London: Penguin Books, 1996.

Black, Gregory D. *Hollywood Censored: Morality Codes, Catholics, and the Movies.* Cambridge: Cambridge University Press, 1994.

Bolter, J. David, and Richard Grusin. *Remediation: Understanding New Media.* Cambridge, Mass.: MIT Press, 1999.

Bommes, Michael, and Patrick Wright. "'Charms of Residence': The Public and the Past." In *Making Histories: Studies in History-Writing and Politics,* edited by Richard Johnson et al., 253–301. Minneapolis: University of Minnesota Press, 1982.

Bordwell, David, Janet Staiger, and Kristin Thompson. *The Classical Hollywood Cinema: Film Style and Mode of Production to 1960.* New York: Columbia University Press, 1985.

Bourdieu, Pierre. *Distinction: A Social Critique of the Judgement of Taste.* Translated by Richard Nice. Cambridge, Mass.: Harvard University Press, 1984.

———. "The Forms of Capital." Translated by Richard Nice. In *Education: Culture, Economy, and Society,* edited by A. H. Halsey et al., 46–58. Oxford: Oxford University Press, 1997.

———. "Marriage Strategies as Strategies of Social Reproduction." *Family and Society: Selections from the Annales: Economies, Sociéties, Civilisations,* edited by Robert Forster and Orest Ranum; translated by Elborg Forster and Patricia M. Ranum. Baltimore: Johns Hopkins University Press, 1976.

Bram, Christopher. *Father of Frankenstein.* New York: Plume/Penguin Books, 1995.

Braudy, Leo. "Afterword: Rethinking Remakes." In *Play It Again, Sam: Retakes on Remakes,* edited by Andrew Horton and Stuart Y. McDougal, 327–34. Berkeley: University of California Press, 1998.

———. "The Genre of Nature: Ceremonies of Innocence." In Browne, *Refiguring American Film Genres,* 278–309.

Brennan, Timothy. "Masterpiece Theatre and the Uses of Tradition." In *American Media and Mass Culture: Left Perspectives,* edited by Donald Lazere, 373–83. Berkeley: University of California Press, 1987.

Bristow, Joseph. *Effeminate England: Homoerotic Writing after 1885.* New York: Columbia University Press, 1995.

———. *"Fratrum Societati:* Forster's Apostolic Dedications." In *Queer Forster,* edited by Robert K. Martin and George Piggford, 113–36. Chicago: University of Chicago Press, 1997.

———, ed. *Oscar Wilde and Modern Culture: The Making of a Legend.* Athens: Ohio University Press, 2008.

"British Women Lose Court Fight Over Possessing Frozen Embryos." *New York Times,* 2 October 2003, national ed., A5.

Broder, John M. "UCLA Suspends Donations of Cadavers, Pending Inquiry." *New York Times,* 10 March 2004, national ed., A1, A18.

Bronski, Michael. *Culture Clash: The Making of Gay Sensibility.* Boston: South End Press, 1984.

Brontë, Charlotte. *Jane Eyre.* Edited by Richard J. Dunn. 3rd ed. Norton Critical Edition. New York: W. W. Norton, 2001.

Brontë, Emily. *Wuthering Heights.* Edited by Linda H. Peterson. Case Studies in Contemporary Criticism. Boston: Bedford Books, 1992.

Brooke, James. "Korean Leaves Cloning Center in Ethics Furor." *New York Times,* 25 November 2005, national ed., A1, A8.

Brosh, Liora. *Screening Novel Women: From British Domestic Fiction to Film.* Houndmills: Palgrave Macmillan, 2008.

Browne, Joy. *Dating for Dummies.* Foster City, Calif.: IDG Books Worldwide, 1997.

———. *It's a Jungle Out There, Jane: Understanding the Male Animal.* New York: Crown, 1999.

Browne, Nick, ed. *Refiguring American Film Genres: History and Theory.* Berkeley: University of California Press, 1998.

Brunas, Michael, John Brunas, and Tom Weaver. *Universal Horrors: The Studio's Classic Films, 1931–1946.* Jefferson, N.C.: McFarland and Co., 1990.

Brunsdon, Charlotte. "Not Having It All: Women and Film in the 1990s." In *British Cinema of the 90s,* edited by Robert Murphy, 167–77. London: BFI Publishing, 2000.

Bruzzi, Stella. *Undressing Cinema: Clothing and Identity in the Movies.* London: Routledge, 1997.

Bukatman, Scott. *Terminal Identity: The Virtual Subject in Postmodern Science Fiction.* Durham, N.C.: Duke University Press, 1993.

Buñuel, Luis. *My Last Sigh.* Translated by Abigail Israel. New York: Alfred A. Knopf, 1983.

Butler, Marilyn. *"Frankenstein* and Radical Science." In *Frankenstein,* edited by J. Paul Hunter, 302–13. New York: W. W. Norton, 1996.

Buzard, James. *The Beaten Track: European Tourism, Literature, and the Ways to Culture, 1800–1918.* Oxford: Clarendon Press, 1993.

Campion, Jane. *Jane Campion: Interviews.* Edited by Virginia Wright Wexman. Conversations with Filmmakers. Jackson: University Press of Mississippi, 1999.

Cannadine, David. *Aspects of Aristocracy: Grandeur and Decline in Modern Britain.* New Haven, Conn.: Yale University Press, 1994.

———. *The Decline and Fall of the British Aristocracy.* New Haven, Conn.: Yale University Press, 1990.

———. *The Rise and Fall of Class in Britain.* New York: Columbia University Press, 1999.

Cardwell, Sarah. *Adaptation Revisited: Television and the Classic Novel.* Manchester: Manchester University Press, 2002.

———. *Andrew Davies.* The Television Series. Manchester: Manchester University Press, 2005.

———. "Literature on the Small Screen: Television Adaptations." In Cartmell and Whelehan, *The Cambridge Companion to Literature on Screen,* 181–95.

Carroll, Noël. *The Philosophy of Horror, or Paradoxes of the Heart.* New York: Routledge, 1990.

Cartmell, Deborah, and Imelda Whelehan, eds. *Adaptations: From Text to Screen, Screen to Text.* London: Routledge, 1999.

———. *The Cambridge Companion to Literature on Screen.* Cambridge: Cambridge University Press, 2007.

———. "A Practical Understanding of Literature on Screen: Two Conversations with Andrew Davies." In Cartmell and Whelehan, *The Cambridge Companion to Literature on Screen,* 239–51.

Castle, Terry. *The Apparitional Lesbian: Female Homosexuality and Modern Culture.* New York: Columbia University Press, 1993.

Caughie, John. "Becoming European: Art Cinema, Irony and Identity." In Petrie, *Screening Europe,* 32–44.

———. "The Logic of Convergence." In Hill and McLoone, *Big Picture, Small Screen,* 215–23.

———. *Television Drama: Realism, Modernism, and British Culture.* Oxford: Oxford University Press, 2000.

Chamberlin, J. Edward, and Sander L. Gilman, eds. *Degeneration: The Dark Side of Progress.* New York: Columbia University Press, 1985.

Chambers, David L. *Making Fathers Pay: The Enforcement of Child Support.* Chicago: University of Chicago Press, 1979.

Chatman, Seymour. *Story and Discourse: Narrative Structure in Fiction and Film.* Ithaca, N.Y.: Cornell University Press, 1978.

Cherlin, Andrew J. "Marital Dissolution and Remarriage." In *Diversity and Change in Families: Patterns, Prospects, and Policies,* edited by Mark Robert Rank and Edward L. Kain, 305–29. Englewood Cliffs, N.J.: Prentice Hall, 1995.

Cherry, Brigid. "Refusing to Refuse to Look: Female Viewers of the Horror Film." In Jancovitch, ed., *Horror, The Film Reader,* 169–78.

Clark, Virginia M. *Aldous Huxley and Film.* Metuchen, N.J.: Scarecrow Press, 1987.

Clayton, Jay. *Charles Dickens in Cyberspace: The Afterlife of the Nineteenth Century in Postmodern Culture.* New York: Oxford University Press, 2003.

Cleto, Fabio, ed. *Camp: Queer Aesthetics and the Performing Subject: A Reader.* Ann Arbor: University of Michigan Press, 1999.

Clover, Carol J. *Men, Women, and Chain Saws: Gender in the Modern Horror Film.* Princeton, N.J.: Princeton University Press, 1992.

Cohen, Ed. *Talk on the Wilde Side: Towards a Genealogy of a Discourse on Male Sexualities.* New York: Routledge, 1992.

Cohen, Edie. "Costume Drama." *Interior Design* (July 2000): 156–61.

Colley, Linda. *Britons: Forging the Nation, 1707–1837.* New Haven, Conn.: Yale University Press, 1992.

Collins, Jim, Hilary Radner, and Ava Preacher Collins, eds. *Film Theory Goes to the Movies.* New York: Routledge, 1993.

Condon, Bill. *Gods and Monsters: The Shooting Script.* Based on the novel *Father of Frankenstein,* by Christopher Bram. Introduction by Ian McKellen. Foreword by Clive Barker. A Newmarket Shooting Script Series Book. New York: Newmarket Press, 2005.

Cook, Pam. *Fashioning the Nation: Costume and Identity in British Cinema.* London: BFI, 1996.

Coontz, Stephanie. *Marriage, A History: From Obedience to Intimacy, or How Love Conquered Marriage.* New York: Viking, 2005.

Copley, Stephen, and Peter Garside, eds. *The Politics of the Picturesque: Literature, Landscape, and Aesthetics since 1770.* Cambridge: Cambridge University Press, 1994.

Coppola, Francis Ford, and James V. Hart. *Bram Stoker's "Dracula": The Film and the Legend.* New York: Newmarket Press, 1992.

Craft, Christopher. *Another Kind of Love: Male Homosexual Desire in English Discourse, 1850–1920.* Berkeley: University of California Press, 1994.

Craig, Cairns. "Rooms without a View." *Sight and Sound* n.s. 1, no. 2 (June 1991): 10–13.

Crary, Jonathan. *Suspensions of Perception: Attention, Spectacle, and Modern Culture.* Cambridge, Mass.: MIT Press, 1999.

Crnkovic, Gordana P. "Interview with Agnieszka Holland." *Film Quarterly* 52, no. 2 (Winter 1998–99): 2–9.

Cunnington, C. Willett, and Phillis Cunnington. *The History of Underclothes.* London: Michael Joseph, 1951.

Curtis, James. *James Whale: A New World of Gods and Monsters.* Boston: Faber and Faber, 1998.

Desai, Jigna. "Planet Bollywood: Indian Cinema Abroad." In *East Main Street: Asian American Popular Culture*, edited by Shilpa Davé, LeiLani Nishime, and Tasha G. Oren, 55–71. New York: New York University Press, 2005.

Doane, Mary Ann. *The Desire to Desire: The Woman's Film of the 1940s*. Bloomington: Indiana University Press, 1987.

Doherty, Thomas. *Pre-Code Hollywood: Sex, Immorality, and Insurrection in American Cinema, 1930–1934*. New York: Columbia University Press, 1999.

Dollimore, Jonathan. *Sexual Dissidence: Augustine to Wilde, Freud to Foucault*. Oxford: Clarendon Press, 1991.

Dowling, Linda. *Hellenism and Homosexuality in Victorian Oxford*. Ithaca, N.Y.: Cornell University Press, 1994.

Duckworth, Alistair. *The Improvement of the Estate: A Study of Jane Austen's Novels*. Baltimore: Johns Hopkins University Press, 1971.

Dunaway, David King. *Huxley in Hollywood*. London: Bloomsbury Publishing, 1989.

Dyer, Richard. *The Culture of Queers*. London: Routledge, 2002.

———. "It's Being So Camp as Keeps Us Going." In Cleto, *Camp*, 110–16.

———. "Nice Young Men Who Sell Antiques—Gay Men in Heritage Cinema." In Vincendeau, *Film/Literature/Heritage*, 43–48.

———. *Stars*. London: BFI, 1979.

Edgerton, Gary. "The Multiplex: The Modern American Motion Picture Theater as Message." In Hark, *Exhibition*, 155–59.

Edwards, Jeanette. "Explicit Connections: Ethnographic Enquiry in North-West England." In Edwards, et al., *Technologies of Procreation*, 60–85.

Edwards, Jeanette, et al. *Technologies of Procreation: Kinship in the Age of Assisted Conception*. 2nd ed. London: Routledge, 1999.

Ehrenstein, David. "Out of the Wilderness: An Interview with Sally Potter." *Film Quarterly* 47, no. 1 (1993): 2–7.

Ellington, H. Elisabeth. "'A Correct Taste in Landscape': Pemberley as Fetish and Commodity." In Troost and Greenfield, *Jane Austen in Hollywood*, 90–110.

Ellmann, Richard. *Oscar Wilde*. New York: Alfred A. Knopf, 1988.

Elsaesser, Thomas. "Tales of Sound and Fury: Observations on the Family Melodrama." In *Home Is Where the Heart Is: Studies in Melodrama and the Woman's Film*, edited by Christine Gledhill, 43–69. London: BFI, 1987.

English, Richard, and Michael Kenny, eds. *Rethinking British Decline*. Houndmills: Macmillan Press, 2000.

Fabricant, Carole. "The Literature of Domestic Tourism and the Public Consumption of Private Property." In *The New Eighteenth Century: Theory, Politics, English Literature*, edited by Felicity Nussbaum and Laura Brown, 254–75. New York: Methuen, 1987.

"Fabulous Fifty." *Boxoffice,* January 2001, 40.

Faludi, Susan. *Stiffed: The Betrayal of the American Man.* New York: William Morrow, 1999.

Farquhar, Dion. *The Other Machine: Discourse and Reproductive Technologies.* New York: Routledge, 1996.

Farrell, Warren. *Women Can't Hear What Men Don't Say: Destroying Myths, Creating Love.* New York: Penguin Putnam, 1999.

Favret, Mary A. "Being True to Jane Austen." In Kucich and Sadoff, *Victorian Afterlife,* 64–82.

Fein, Ellen, and Sherrie Schneider. *The Rules: Time-Tested Secrets for Capturing the Heart of Mr. Right.* New York: Warner Books, 1995.

Feinstein, Howard. "Heroine Chic." *Vanity Fair,* December 1996, 212–14.

Feltes, N. N. *Modes of Production of Victorian Novels.* Chicago: University of Chicago Press, 1986.

Festa, Lynn. *Sentimental Figures of Empire in Eighteenth-Century Britain and France.* Baltimore: Johns Hopkins University Press, 2006.

Finch, Mark, and Richard Kwietniowski. "Melodrama and 'Maurice': Homo Is Where the Het Is." *Screen* 29, no. 3 (Summer 1988): 72–80.

Fiske, John. "Popular Culture." In Lentricchia and McLaughlin, *Critical Terms for Literary Study,* 321–35.

Flinn, Caryl. "The Deaths of Camp." In Cleto, *Camp,* 433–57.

Florence, Penny. "A Conversation with Sally Potter." *Screen* 34, no. 3 (1993): 275–84.

Foldy, Michael S. *The Trials of Oscar Wilde: Deviance, Morality, and Late-Victorian Society.* New Haven, Conn.: Yale University Press, 1997.

Forster, E. M. *Maurice.* New York: W. W. Norton, 1993.

Fowler, Bridget. *The Alienated Reader: Women and Romantic Literature in the Twentieth Century.* New York: Harvester Wheatsheaf, 1991.

Franklin, Sarah. *Embodied Progress: A Cultural Account of Assisted Conception.* London: Routledge, 1997.

———. "Making Representations: The Parliamentary Debate on the Human Fertilisation and Embyology Act." In Edwards et al., *Technologies of Procreation,* 127–65.

———. "'Orphaned' Embryos." In Edwards et al., *Technologies of Procreation,* 166–70.

Freedland, Michael. *The Goldwyn Touch: A Biography of Sam Goldwyn.* London: Harrap, 1986.

Friedenberg, Anne. *Window Shopping: Cinema and the Postmodern.* Berkeley: University of California Press, 1993.

Friedman, Lester, ed. *Fires Were Started: British Cinema and Thatcherism.* Minneapolis: University of Minnesota Press, 1993.

Fry, Stephen. "Playing Oscar." *New Yorker,* 16 June 1997, 82–88.

———. "There Never Was Such a Man." Introduction to *Wilde.* Screenplay and afterword by Julian Mitchell, 7–23. London: Dove Books, 1997.

Fuss, Diana. "Fashion and the Homospectatorial Look." *Critical Inquiry* 18, no. 4 (Summer 1992): 713–37.

———. "Monsters of Perversion: Jeffrey Dahmer and *The Silence of the Lambs.*" In *Media Spectacles,* edited by Marjorie Garber, Jann Matlock, and Rebecca L. Walkowitz, 181–205. New York: Routledge, 1993.

Gagnier, Regenia. *Idylls of the Marketplace: Oscar Wilde and the Victorian Public.* Stanford, Calif.: Stanford University Press, 1986.

Galbraith, James K. *Unbearable Cost: Bush, Greenspan, and the Economics of Empire.* Houndmills: Palgrave Macmillan, 2006.

Gallagher, Janet. "Eggs, Embryos and Foetuses: Anxiety and the Law." In *Reproductive Technologies: Gender, Motherhood and Medicine,* edited by Michelle Stanworth, 139–50. Minneapolis: University of Minnesota Press, 1987.

Galperin, William H. "Austen's Earliest Readers and the Rise of the Janeites." In Lynch, *Janeites,* 87–114.

———. *The Historical Jane Austen.* Philadelphia: University of Pennsylvania Press, 2003.

Gamble, Andrew. "Theories and Explanations of British Decline." In English and Kenny, *Rethinking British Decline,* 1–22.

Gardner, Gerald C. *The Censorship Papers: Movie Censorship Letters from the Hays Office, 1934–1968.* New York: Dodd, Mead, 1987.

Gelder, Ken. *Reading the Vampire.* London: Routledge, 1994.

Gertner, Jon. "Box Office in Box." *New York Times,* 14 November 2004, sec. 6, 104–9, 124, 130, 132.

Giddens, Anthony. *The Transformation of Intimacy: Sexuality, Love, and Eroticism in Modern Societies.* Stanford, Calif.: Stanford University Press, 1992.

Giddings, Robert, and Keith Selby. *The Classic Serial on Television and Radio.* Basingstoke: Palgrave, 2001.

Giles, Paul. "History with Holes: Channel Four Television Films of the 1980s." In Friedman, *Fires Were Started,* 70–91.

Gillis, Justin. "Ailing Dolly, First Cloned Animal, Is Euthanized." *Washington Post,* 15 February 2003, A2.

Gilroy, Paul. "From a Colonial Past to a New Multiculturalism." *Chronicle of Higher Education,* 7 January 2005, B7–10.

Girard, René. *Deceit, Desire, and the Novel: Self and Other in Literary Structure.* Translated by Yvonne Freccero. Baltimore: Johns Hopkins University Press, 1965.

Girouard, Mark. *Life in the English Country House: A Social and Architectural History.* New Haven, Conn.: Yale University Press, 1978.

Glaessner, Verina. "*Orlando:* Fire and Ice." In Vincendeau, *Film/Literature/
Heritage,* 53–57.

Glavin, John. Introduction to *Dickens on Screen,* 1–8. Cambridge: Cambridge
University Press, 2003.

Glazer, Mitchell. "On the Lam with Roman Polanski." Interview with Roman
Polanski. *Rolling Stone,* 2 April 1981, 40–45.

Glendon, Mary Ann. *The Transformation of Family Law: State, Law, and Family in
the United States and Western Europe.* Chicago: University of Chicago Press,
1989.

Golinski, Jan. *Science as Public Culture: Chemistry and Enlightenment in Britain,
1760–1820.* Cambridge: Cambridge University Press, 1992.

Gomery, Douglas. "Hollywood Corporate Business Practice and Periodizing
Contemporary Film History." In Neale and Smith, *Contemporary Hollywood
Cinema,* 47–57.

———. *Shared Pleasures: A History of Movie Presentation in the United States.*
Madison: University of Wisconsin Press, 1992.

Goode, William. "World Changes in Divorce Patterns." *Economic Consequences of
Divorce: The International Perspective,* edited by Lenore J. Weitzman and Mavis
Maclean, 11–49. Oxford: Clarendon Press, 1992.

Gopnik, Adam. "The Invention of Oscar Wilde." *New Yorker,* 18 May, 1998, 78–88.

Grady, Denise. "Thawed Ovary Tissue Yields Healthy Embryo." *New York Times,*
9 March 2004, national ed., D7.

Graham, Elaine L. *Representations of the Post/Human: Monsters, Aliens, and
Others in Popular Culture.* New Brunswick, N.J.: Rutgers University Press, 2002.

Greenhouse, Linda. "Twenty-Year Extension of Existing Copyrights Is Upheld."
New York Times, 16 January 2003, national ed., A22.

Griffin, Susan M., ed. *Henry James Goes to the Movies.* Lexington: University of
Kentucky Press, 2002.

Guillory, John. "Canon." In Lentricchia and McLaughlin, *Critical Terms for Literary Study,* 233–49.

Gunning, Tom. "An Aesthetic of Astonishment: Early Film and the (In)Credulous
Spectator." In *Viewing Positions: Ways of Seeing Film,* edited and introduction by
Linda Williams, 114–33. New Brunswick, N.J.: Rutgers University Press, 1995.

Halberstam, Judith. *Skin Shows: Gothic Horror and the Technology of Monsters.*
Durham, N. C.: Duke University Press, 1995.

Hall, Donald. Afterword to Thomas Hardy, *Tess of the D'Urbervilles: A Pure
Woman,* 421–30. New York: Signet, 1964.

Hall, Stephen S. "U.S. Panel about to Weigh In on Rules for Assisted Fertility."
New York Times, 9 March 2004, national ed., D1, D4.

Halperin, David M. *One Hundred Years of Homosexuality and Other Essays on
Greek Love.* New York: Routledge, 1990.

Halperin, John. *The Life of Jane Austen.* Baltimore: Johns Hopkins University Press, 1996 [1984].

Hamilton, William L. "The Mainstream Flirts with Pornographic Chic." *New York Times,* 22 March 1999, national ed., B9.

Hansen, Miriam. *Babel and Babylon: Spectatorship in American Silent Film.* Cambridge, Mass.: Harvard University Press, 1991.

Haraway, Donna J. "A Cyborg Manifesto: Science, Technology, and Socialist-Feminism in the Late Twentieth Century." In *Posthumanism,* edited by Neil Badmington, 69–84. London: Palgrave, 2000.

Hardy, Thomas. *The Collected Letters of Thomas Hardy.* Edited by Richard Little Purdy and Michael Millgate. 7 vols. Oxford: Clarendon Press, 1978–88.

———. *Tess of the D'Urbervilles: A Pure Woman.* New York: Signet, 1964.

Hark, Ina Rae, ed. *Exhibition, the "Film" Reader.* London: Routledge, 2002.

———. "General Introduction." In Hark, *Exhibition,* 1–16.

"Harlequin Books Seek a Younger Audience." Narrated by Karen Michel. *Weekend Edition Saturday.* National Public Radio. WVXU, Cincinnati, 12 February 2005.

Harlow, John. "Jane Austen's Bennet Girls Go Zombie Slaying." *Timesonline,* 8 February 2009. http://entertainment.timesonline.co.uk/tol/arts_and_enter tainment. 17 June 2009.

Harper, Sue. *Picturing the Past: The Rise and Fall of the British Costume Film.* London: BFI Publishing, 1994.

Hayles, N. Katherine. *How We Became Posthuman: Virtual Bodies in Cybernetics, Literature, and Informatics.* Chicago: University of Chicago Press, 1999.

———. "The Life Cycle of Cyborgs: Writing the Posthuman." In *The Cyborg Handbook,* edited by Chris Habels Gray, with the assistance of Heidi J. Figueroa-Sarriera and Steven Mentor, 321–35. New York: Routledge, 1995.

Hayward, Susan. "Framing National Cinemas." In *Cinema and Nation,* edited by Mette Hjort and Scott MacKenzie, 82–102. London: Routledge, 2000.

Henry James Letters. Edited by Leon Edel. Vol. 3. Cambridge, Mass: Harvard University Press, 1980.

Herzog, Charlotte Cornelia, and Jane Marie Gaines. "'Puffed Sleeves before Tea-Time': Joan Crawford, Adrian and Women Audiences." In *Stardom: Industry of Desire,* edited by Christine Gledhill, 74–91. London: Routledge, 1991.

Hewison, Robert. *The Heritage Industry: Britain in a Climate of Decline.* London: Methuen, 1987.

Higson, Andrew. *English Heritage, English Cinema: Costume Drama since 1980.* Oxford: Oxford University Press, 2003.

———. "Re-Presenting the National Past: Nostalgia and Pastiche in the Heritage Film." In Friedman, *Fires Were Started,* 109–29.

Hill, John. *British Cinema in the 1980s: Issues and Themes.* Oxford: Clarendon Press, 1999.

———. "British Television and Film: The Making of a Relationship." In Hill and McLoone, *Big Picture, Small Screen,* 151–76.

———. "The Future of European Cinema: The Economics and Culture of Pan-European Strategies." In *Border Crossing: Film in Ireland, Britain and Europe,* edited by John Hill, Martin McLoone, and Paul Hainsworth, 53–80. Belfast: Institute of Irish Studies in association with the University of Ulster and BFI, 1994.

———. "The Issue of National Cinema and British Film Production." In *New Questions of British Cinema,* edited by Duncan Petrie, 10–21. BFI Working Papers. London: BFI, 1992.

Hill, John, and Martin McLoone, eds. *Big Picture, Small Screen: The Relations between Film and Television.* Acamedia Research Monograph 16. Luton: University of Luton Press, 1996.

Hipsky, Martin A. "Anglophil(m)ia: Why Does America Watch Merchant-Ivory Movies?" *Journal of Popular Film and Television* 22, no. 3 (Fall 1994): 98–107.

Hirsch, E. D. *Cultural Literacy: What Every American Needs to Know.* Boston: Houghton Mifflin, 1987.

Hirsch, Eric. "Negotiated Limits: Interviews in South-East England." In Edwards et al., *Technologies of Procreation,* 91–121.

Hirschberg, Lynn. "What Is an American Movie Now?" *New York Times,* 14 November 2004, sec. 6, 88–94.

Hoge, Warren. "Celebrating the Capture of Another Glorious Space: Merchant Ivory Know What They Like." *New York Times,* 9 November 1999, national ed., B1, B2.

Hohenadel, Kristin. "Film Goes All the Way (In the Name of Art)." *New York Times,* 1 July 2001, national ed., sec. 2, 1, 20.

Holden, Anthony. *Laurence Olivier.* New York: Atheneum, 1988.

Holden, Stephen. "All the Sensibility That Money Can Buy." *New York Times,* 27 April 2001, national ed., E10.

———. "The Devil Wears Down her Nanny." *New York Times,* 24 August 2007, late ed., E1+.

———. "Jane Eyre." *New York Times,* 12 April 1996. *New York Times Online.* 25 May 2005 http://www.newyorktimes.com/movies.

———. "Marrying Off Those Bennet Sisters Again, but This Time Elizabeth Is a Looker." *New York Times,* 11 November 2005, national ed., B12.

———. "Our Wit-Lit Heroine Avoids Marrying a Juiceless Man." *New York Times,* 3 August 2007, late ed., E4.

Hopkins, Lisa. "Mr. Darcy's Body: Privileging the Female Gaze." In Troost and Greenfield, *Jane Austen in Hollywood,* 111–21.

Horne, Philip. "The James Gang." In Vincendeau, *Film/Literature/Heritage*, 85–91.

Howe, Irving. Introduction to *The Bostonians*, by Henry James, v–xxviii. New York: Modern Library, 1956.

Howkins, Alun. "The Discovery of Rural England." In *Englishness, Politics, and Culture, 1880–1920*, edited by Robert Colls and Phillip Dodd, 62–88. London: Croom Helm, 1986.

Hunter, Michael, ed. *Preserving the Past: The Rise of Heritage in Modern Britain*. Gloucestershire: Alan Sutton, 1996.

Hutcheon, Linda. *A Theory of Adaptation*. New York: Routledge, 2006.

Hutchings, Peter. "The Problem of British Horror." In Jancovich, *Horror*, 115–23.

Interview with Stuart Hall. In English and Kenny, *Rethinking British Decline*, 106–16.

Jaffe, Audrey. *Scenes of Sympathy: Identity and Representation in Victorian Fiction*. Ithaca, N.Y.: Cornell University Press, 2000.

Jagose, Annamarie. *Queer Theory: An Introduction*. New York: New York University Press, 1996.

James, Henry. *The American*. Edited by Roy Harvey Pearce and Matthew J. Bruccoli. Riverside Editions. Boston: Houghton Mifflin, 1962.

———. *The Bostonians.* Introduction by Irving Howe. New York: Modern Library, 1956.

———. *The Europeans: A Sketch*. Introduction by Tony Tanner. Harmondsworth: Penguin, 1964.

———. *Henry James Letters*. Edited by Leon Edel. Vol. 3. Cambridge, Mass: Harvard University Press, 1980.

———. *The Notebooks of Henry James*. Edited by F. O. Matthiessen and Kenneth B. Murdock. New York: Oxford University Press, 1961.

———. *The Portrait of a Lady*. Edited by Robert D. Bamberg. Norton Critical Edition. New York: W. W. Norton, 1995.

———. *The Wings of the Dove*. Edited by John Bayley. New York: Penguin, 1986.

———. *Washington Square*. Edited by Brian Lee. New York: Penguin, 1980.

Jameson, Fredric. *The Political Unconscious: Narrative as a Socially Symbolic Act*. Ithaca, N.Y.: Cornell University Press, 1981.

———. *Postmodernism, or, the Cultural Logic of Late Capitalism*. Durham, N.C.: Duke University Press, 1991.

Jancovich, Mark, ed. *Horror, The Film Reader*. London: Routledge, 2002.

"Jane Austen Mania." Host Marty Moss-Cowane. *Radio Times*. National Public Radio. WHYY, Philadelphia, 20 August 2007.

Jarvik, Laurence A. *"Masterpiece Theatre" and the Politics of Quality*. Lanham, Md.: Scarecrow, 1999.

Jeffords, Susan. "The Big Switch: Hollywood Masculinity in the Nineties." In Collins et al., *Film Theory Goes to the Movies*, 196–208.

Jensen, Elizabeth. "'Masterpiece Theater,' Now in 3 Flavors: Classic, Mystery, Contemporary." *New York Times*, 10 December 2007, late ed., E3.

Jhabvala, Ruth Prawer. "Conversations with the Filmmakers, Screenwriter: Ruth Prawer Jhabvala." Special feature on *The Bostonians* DVD.

Johnson, Claudia L. "The Divine Miss Jane: Jane Austen, Janeites, and the Discipline of Novel Studies." In Lynch, *Janeites*, 25–44.

———. *Jane Austen: Women, Politics, and the Novel.* Chicago: Chicago University Press, 1988.

Jones, Arthur. *Britain's Heritage: The Creation of the National Heritage Memorial Fund.* London: Weidenfeld and Nicholson, 1985.

Jones, Gareth Stedman. *Outcast London: A Study in the Relationship between Classes in Victorian Society.* New York: Pantheon, 1984.

Jones, Vivian. "'The Coquetry of Nature': Politics and the Picturesque in Women's Fiction." In *The Politics of the Picturesque*, edited by Stephen Copley and Peter Garside, 120–44. Cambridge: Cambridge University Press, 1994.

Joslin, Lyndon W. *Count Dracula Goes to the Movies: Stoker's Novel Adapted, 1922–1995.* Jefferson, N. C.: McFarland and Company, 1999.

Joyce, Simon. *The Victorians in the Rearview Mirror.* Athens: Ohio University Press, 2007.

Kammen, Michael. *American Culture, American Tastes: Social Change and the Twentieth Century.* New York: Alfred A. Knopf, 1999.

Kaplan, Carla. *The Erotics of Talk: Women's Writing and Feminist Paradigms.* New York: Oxford University Press, 1996.

Kaufman, Moisés. *Gross Indecency: The Three Trials of Oscar Wilde.* New York: Vintage, 1998.

Kavka, Misha. "The Gothic on Screen." In *The Cambridge Companion to Gothic Fiction*, edited by Jerrold E. Hogle, 209–28. Cambridge: Cambridge University Press, 2002.

Keathley, Christian. "Trapped in the Affection Image: Hollywood's Post-Traumatic Cycle (1970–1976)." In *The Last Great American Picture Show: New Hollywood Cinema in the 1970s*, edited by Thomas Elsaesser, Alexander Horwath, and Noel King, 293–308. Amsterdam: Amsterdam University Press, 2004.

Keller, James R. *Anne Rice and Sexual Politics: The Early Novels.* Jefferson, N.C.: McFarland and Company, 2000.

Kerr, Paul. "Classic Serials—To Be Continued." *Screen* 23 (1982): 6–19.

Kimmel, Michael S. *Manhood in America: A Cultural History.* New York: Free Press, 1996.

King, Geoff. *New Hollywood Cinema: An Introduction.* New York: Columbia University Press, 2002.

Kipp, Julie. *Romanticism, Maternity, and the Body Politic.* Cambridge: Cambridge University Press, 2003.

Kittler, Friedrich A. "Dracula's Legacy." *Stanford Humanities Review* 1, no. 1 (Spring 1989): 14–73.

———. *Gramophone, Film, Typewriter.* Translated and introduced by Geoffrey Winthrop-Young and Michael Wutz. Stanford, Calif.: Stanford University Press, 1999.

Kolata, Gina. *Clone: The Road to Dolly, and the Path Ahead.* New York: William Morrow, 1998.

Kramer, Lawrence. "Recognizing Schubert: Musical Subjectivity, Cultural Change, and Jane Campion's *Portrait of a Lady.*" *Critical Inquiry* 29, no. 1 (Autumn 2002): 25–52.

Krzywinska, Tanya. *Sex and the Cinema.* London: Wallflower Press, 2006.

Kucich, John, and Dianne F. Sadoff, eds. *Victorian Afterlife: Postmodern Culture Rewrites the Nineteenth Century.* Minneapolis: University of Minnesota Press, 2000.

Kushner, Tony. Afterword. In Kaufman, *Gross Indecency,* 135–43.

Lant, Antonia. *Blackout: Reinventing Women for Wartime British Cinema.* Princeton, N.J.: Princeton University Press, 1991.

Laplanche, Jean, and J.-B. Pontalis. *The Language of Psycho-Analysis.* Translated by Donald Nicholson-Smith. New York: W. W. Norton, 1973.

Latour, Bruno. *We Have Never Been Modern.* Translated by Catherine Porter. Cambridge, Mass.: Harvard University Press, 1993.

Laudermilk, Sharon H., and Teresa L. Hamlin. *The Regency Companion.* New York: Garland Publishing, 1989.

Lauritzen, Monica. *Jane Austen's "Emma" on Television: A Study of a BBC Classic Serial.* Gothenburg Studies in English 48. Göteborg: Acta Universitatis Gothoburgensis, 1980.

Laver, James. *Costume and Fashion: A Concise History.* Rev. ed. London: Thames and Hudson, 1996 [1969].

Leaming, Barbara. *Orson Welles: A Biography.* New York: Viking, 1985 [1983].

Leavis, F. R. *The Great Tradition: George Eliot, Henry James, Joseph Conrad.* New York: New York University Press, 1964 [1948].

Leavis, Q. D. *Fiction and the Reading Public.* London: Chatto and Windus, 1968 [1932].

Leitch, Thomas. *Film Adaptation and Its Discontents: From "Gone with the Wind" to "The Passion of the Christ."* Baltimore: Johns Hopkins University Press, 2007.

———. "Twice-Told Tales: The Rhetoric of the Remake." *Literature/Film Quarterly* 18, no. 3 (Fall 1990): 138–49.

Lentricchia, Frank, and Thomas McLaughlin, eds. *Critical Terms for Literary Study.* 2nd ed. Chicago: University of Chicago Press, 1995.

Levine, Lawrence W. *Highbrow/Lowbrow: The Emergence of Cultural Hierarchy in America.* Cambridge, Mass.: Harvard University Press, 1988.

Lewis, Jon. *Hollywood v. Hard Core: How the Struggle over Censorship Saved the Modern Film Industry.* New York: New York University Press, 2000.

Lewis, Judith Schneid. *In the Family Way: Childbearing in the British Aristocracy, 1760–1860.* New Brunswick, N.J.: Rutgers University Press, 1986.

Light, Alison. *Forever England: Femininity, Literature, and Conservatism between the Wars.* New York: Routledge, 1991.

Litvak, Joseph. *Strange Gourmets: Sophistication, Theory, and the Novel.* Durham, N.C.: Duke University Press, 1997.

Long, Robert Emmet. *The Films of Merchant Ivory.* New York: Harry N. Abrams, 1997 [1991].

———. *James Ivory in Conversation: How Merchant Ivory Makes Its Movies.* Berkeley: University of California Press, 2005.

Lowenthal, David. *The Past Is a Foreign Country.* Cambridge: Cambridge University Press, 1985.

Lupack, Barbara Tepa, ed. *Nineteenth-Century Women at the Movies: Adapting Classic Women's Fiction to Film.* Bowling Green, Ohio: Bowling Green University Popular Press, 1999.

Lyall, Sarah. "Inquiry Shows British Scientists Took Brains without Families' Consent." *New York Times,* 13 May 2004, national ed., A8.

Lynch, Deidre. "At Home with Jane Austen." In *Cultural Institutions of the Novel,* edited by Deidre Lynch and William B. Warner, 159–92. Durham, N.C.: Duke University Press, 1996.

———, ed. *Janeites: Austen's Disciples and Devotees.* Princeton, N.J.: Princeton University Press, 2000.

MacCabe, Colin. "A Post-National European Cinema: A Consideration of Derek Jarman's *The Tempest* and *Edward II.*" In Petrie, *Screening Europe,* 9–18.

———. "Subsidies, Audiences, Producers." In Petrie, *Screening Europe,* 22–28.

MacDonald, Scott. "Interview with Sally Potter." *Camera Obscura* 35 (May 1995): 187–220.

Madigan, Nick. "Inquiry Widens after Two Arrests in Cadaver Case at UCLA." *New York Times,* 9 March 2004, national ed., A19.

Maeder, Edward, ed. *Hollywood and History: Costume Design in Film.* London: Thames and Hudson, 1987.

Maltby, Richard. "'Nobody Knows Everything': Post-Classical Historiographies and Consolidated Entertainment." In Neale and Smith, *Contemporary Hollywood Cinema,* 21–44.

———. "The Production Code and the Hays Office." In Balio, *Grand Design,* 37–72.

Mandler, Peter. *The Fall and Rise of the Stately Home.* New Haven, Conn.: Yale University Press, 1997.

———. "Nationalising the Country House." In Hunter, *Preserving the Past,* 99–114.

Markley, Robert. "Sentimentality as Performance: Shaftesbury, Sterne, and the Theatrics of Virtue." In Nussbaum and Brown, *The New English Century,* 210–30.

Marx, Arthur. *Goldwyn: A Biography of the Man behind the Myth.* New York: W. W. Norton, 1976.

Maslin, Janet. "'Portrait of a Lady': It's Henry James, but not Literally." *New York Times,* 27 December 1996, national ed., B29.

May, Elaine Tyler. *Homeward Bound: American Families in the Cold War Era.* New York: Basic Books, 1988.

Mazdon, Lucy. *Encore Hollywood: Remaking French Cinema.* London: BFI, 2000.

McElroy, Steven. "'Superbad' Aces It." Arts, Briefly. *New York Times,* 20 August 2007, late ed., E2.

McFarlane, Brian. *Novel to Film: An Introduction to the Theory of Adaptation.* Oxford: Clarendon Press, 1996.

McGee, Micki. *Self-Help, Inc.: Makeover Culture in American Life.* New York: Oxford University Press, 2005.

McKeon, Michael. "The Secret History of Domesticity: Private, Public, and the Division of Knowledge." In *The Age of Cultural Revolutions: Britain and France, 1750–1820,* edited by Colin Jones and Dror Wahrman, 171–89. Berkeley: University of California Press, 2002.

McLane, Maureen Noelle. "Literate Species: Populations, 'Humanities,' and *Frankenstein.*" *ELH* 63, no. 4 (Winter 1996): 959–88.

McLemee, Scott. "Americans Found to Read Less Literature Than Ever." *Chronicle of Higher Education,* 16 July 2004, A1, 16.

McLuhan, Marshall. *Understanding Media: The Extensions of Man.* New York: McGraw-Hill, 1964.

McMaster, Juliet. "Class." In *The Cambridge Companion to Jane Austen,* edited by Edward Copeland and Juliet McMaster, 115–30. Cambridge: Cambridge University Press, 1997.

McRobbie, Angela. "The African Dandy." In *Yinka Shonibare: Double Dutch,* edited by Hugo Bangers and Gerald Matt. Rotterdam: NAi: publishers, 2004.

Medhurst, Andy. "Dressing the Part." In Vincendeau, *Film/Literature/Heritage,* 11–14.

Meisel, Martin. "Scattered Chiaroscuro: Melodrama as a Matter of Seeing." In *Melodrama: Stage, Picture, Screen,* edited by Jacky Bratton, Jim Cook, and Christine Gledhill, 65–81. London: BFI, 1994.

Mellor, Anne K. "*Frankenstein*: A Feminist Critique of Science." In *One Culture: Essays in Science and Literature,* edited by George Levine, 287–312. Madison: University of Wisconsin Press, 1987.

Merkin, Daphne. "The Escape Artist: Henry James's Unfilmable Passion for Renunciation." Review of *The Wings of the Dove,* directed by Iain Softley. *New Yorker,* 10 November 1977, 122.

Miele, Chris. "The First Conservation Militants: William Morris and the Society for the Protection of Ancient Buildings." In Hunter, *Preserving the Past,* 17–37.

Miller, Frank. *Censored Hollywood: Sex, Sin, and Violence on Screen.* Atlanta: Turner Publishing, 1994.

Miller, J. Hillis. *Thomas Hardy: Distance and Desire.* Cambridge, Mass.: Harvard University Press, 1970.

Miller, Nancy K. *The Heroine's Text: Readings in the French and English Novel, 1722–1782.* New York: Columbia University Press, 1980.

Miller, Toby, Nitlin Govil, John McMurria, and Richard Maxwell. *Global Hollywood.* London: BFI, 2001.

Mishra, Vijay. *Bollywood Cinema: Temples of Desire.* New York: Routledge, 2002.

Mitchell, Julian. *Wilde.* Screenplay and afterword. London: Dove Books, 1997.

Modell, John. "Dating Becomes the Way of American Youth." In *Essays on the Family and Historical Change,* edited by David Levine, Leslie Page Moch, Louise A. Tilly, John Modell, and Elizabeth Pleck, 91–126. College Station: Texas A & M University Press, 1983.

Modleski, Tania. *Loving with a Vengeance: Mass-Produced Fantasies for Women.* Hamden, Conn.: Archon Books, 1982.

———. *Old Wives' Tales and Other Women's Stories.* New York: New York University Press, 1998.

Monk, Claire. "The British Heritage-Film Debate Revisited." In *British Historical Cinema: The History, Heritage and Costume Film,* edited by Claire Monk and Amy Sargeant, 176–98. London: Routledge, 2002.

———. "Sexuality and Heritage." In Vincendeau, *Film/Literature/Heritage,* 6–11.

Mordden, Ethan. *The Hollywood Studios: House Style in the Golden Age of Movies.* New York: Alfred A. Knopf, 1988.

Moreton, Cole. "World's First Test-Tube Baby Celebrates Her 25th Birthday as One in a Million." *Independent on Sunday* (London), 27 July 2003, Home 5.

Mulhauser, Dana. "Dating among College Students Is All But Dead, Survey Finds." *Chronicle of Higher Education,* 10 August 2001, A51–52.

Mulhern, Francis. "English Reading." *Nation and Narration,* edited by Homi K. Bhabha, 250–64. London: Routledge, 1990.

Mulkay, Michael. *The Embryo Research Debate: Science and the Politics of Reproduction.* Cambridge: Cambridge University Press, 1997.

Naficy, Hamid. *An Accented Cinema: Exilic and Diasporic Filmmaking.* Princeton, N.J.: Princeton University Press, 2001.

Nafisi, Azar. *Reading Lolita in Tehran: A Memoir in Books.* New York: Random House, 2003.

Nairn, Tom. *The Break-Up of Britain: Crisis and Neo-Nationalism.* London: NLB, 1977.

Napper, Lawrence. "British Cinema and the Middlebrow." In *British Cinema, Past and Present,* edited by Justine Ashby and Andrew Higson, 110–23. London: Routledge, 2000.

Naremore, James. "Introduction: Film and the Reign of Adaptation." In *Film Adaptation,* edited by James Naremore, 1–16. New Brunswick, N.J.: Rutgers University Press, 2000.

Neale, Steve. "Art Cinema as Institution." *Screen* 22, no. 1 (1981): 11–39.

———, ed. *Genre and Contemporary Hollywood.* London: BFI, 2002.

———. "Prologue: Masculinity as Spectacle: Reflections on Men and Mainstream Cinema." In *Screening the Male: Exploring Masculinities in Hollywood Cinema,* edited by Steven Cohan and Ina Rae Hark, 9–20. London: Routledge, 1993.

———. "Westerns and Gangster Films since the 1970s." In Neale, *Genre and Contemporary Hollywood,* 27–47.

Neale, Steve, and Murray Smith, eds. *Contemporary Hollywood Cinema.* London: Routledge, 1998.

Nemesvari, Richard. "Romancing the Text: Genre, Indeterminacy, and Televising *Tess of the D'Urbervilles.*" In *Thomas Hardy on Screen,* edited by T. R. Wright, 170–82. Cambridge: Cambridge University Press, 2005.

Niemeyer, Paul. J. *Seeing Hardy: Film and Television Adaptations of the Fiction of Thomas Hardy.* Jefferson, N.C.: McFarland and Company, 2003.

Nussbaum, Felicity, and Laura Brown, eds. *The New Eighteenth Century: Theory, Politics, English Literature.* London: Methuen, 1987.

Nye, Robert A. "Sociology and Degeneration: The Irony of Progress." In Chamberlin and Gilman, *Degeneration,* 49–71.

O'Flinn, Paul. "Production and Reproduction: The Case of *Frankenstein.*" *Literature and History* 2 (Autumn 1983): 194–213.

O'Regan, Tom. *Australian National Cinema.* London: Routledge, 1996.

Ouditt, Sharon. "*Orlando:* Coming across the Divide." In Cartmell and Whelehan, *Adaptations,* 146–56.

Ozick, Cynthia. "What Only Words, Not Film, Can Portray." Review of *Portrait of a Lady,* directed by Jane Campion. *New York Times,* 5 January 1997, national ed., sec. H1, H22.

Paglia, Camille. *Sexual Personae: Art and Decadence from Nefertiti to Emily Dickinson.* London: Yale University Press, 1990.

Paul, William. "The K-Mart Audience at the Movies." In Hark, *Exhibition,* 77–88.

"PBS to Air Adaptations of Jane Austen Novels." Narrated by Lynn Neary. *Morning Edition.* National Public Radio. WHYY, Philadelphia, 18 January 2008.

Pells, Richard H. *Radical Visions and American Dreams: Culture and Social Thought in the Depression Years.* New York: Harper and Row, 1973.

Perkin, Harold. *The Rise of Professional Society: England since 1880.* London: Routledge, 1989.

Perkin, Joan. *Women and Marriage in Nineteenth-Century England.* London: Routledge, 1989.

Perry, Ruth. "Jane Austen and British Imperialism." In *Monstrous Dreams of Reason: Body, Self, and Other in the Enlightenment,* edited by Laura J. Rosenthal and Mita Choudhury, 231–54. Lewisburg, Pa.: Bucknell University Press, 2002.

———. *Novel Relations: The Transformation of Kinship in English Literature and Culture, 1748–1818.* Cambridge: Cambridge University Press, 2004.

Person, Leland S. "Still Me(n): Superman Meets *The Bostonians.*" In Griffin, *Henry James Goes to the Movies,* 99–124.

Petrie, Duncan, ed. *Screening Europe: Image and Identity in Contemporary European Cinema.* London: BFI, 1992.

Pick, Daniel. *Faces of Degeneration: A European Disorder, c. 1848–c. 1918.* Cambridge: Cambridge University Press, 1989.

Pidduck, Julianne. *Contemporary Costume Film: Space, Place and the Past.* London: BFI, 2004.

Pierson, Michele. *Special Effects: Still in Search of Wonder.* New York: Columbia University Press, 2002.

Polanski, Roman. *Roman/By Polanski.* New York: Ballantine, 1984.

Poovey, Mary. *The Proper Lady and the Woman Writer: Ideology as Style in the Works of Mary Wollstonecraft, Mary Shelley, and Jane Austen.* Women in Culture and Society. Chicago: University of Chicago Press, 1984.

———. *Uneven Developments: The Ideological Work of Gender in Mid-Victorian England.* Chicago: University of Chicago Press, 1988.

Potter, Sally. "Immortal Longing." Interview with Walter Donohue. In Vincendeau, *Film/Literature/Heritage,* 57–61.

———. *Orlando.* Based on the book by Virginia Woolf. London: Faber and Faber, 1994.

Prentice, Richard. *Tourism and Heritage Attractions.* London: Routledge, 1993.

Price, Frances. "Beyond Expectation: Clinical Practices and Clinical Concerns." In Edwards et al., *Technologies of Procreation,* 29–52.

Prince, Stephen. "The Essentials of Cinematography." *Movies and Meaning: An Introduction to Film.* Boston: Allyn and Bacon, 1997.

"Profile: New Vampire Movie." Narrated by Beth Accomando. *Morning Edition.* National Public Radio. WVXU, Cincinnati, 26 January 2001. Transcript.

Pym, John. *Merchant Ivory's English Landscape: Rooms, Views, and Anglo-Saxon Attitudes.* New York: H. N. Abrams, 1995.

Radway, Janice A. *A Feeling for Books: The Book-of-the-Month Club, Literary Taste, and Middle-Class Desire*. Chapel Hill: University of North Carolina Press, 1997.

———. *Reading the Romance: Women, Patriarchy, and Popular Literature*. Chapel Hill: University of North Carolina Press, 1991 [1984].

Ramsland, Katherine. "Let the Flesh Instruct the Mind: A *Quadrant* Interview with Anne Rice." *The Anne Rice Reader*, edited by Katherine Ramsland, 55–73. New York: Ballantine, 1997.

Rauch, Alan. *Useful Knowledge: The Victorians, Morality, and the March of Intellect*. Durham, N.C.: Duke University Press, 2001.

Rayns, Tony. "Wilde." Review of *Wilde*, directed by Brian Gilbert. In Vincendeau, *Film/Literature/Heritage*, 186–88.

Riley, Glenda. *Divorce: An American Tradition*. New York: Oxford University Press, 1991.

Rivkin, Julie. *False Positions: The Representational Logics of Henry James's Fiction*. Stanford, Calif.: Stanford University Press, 1996.

Roberts, Bette B. *Anne Rice*. New York: Twayne, 1994.

Roberts, Marilyn. "Adapting Jane Austen's *Northanger Abbey*: Catherine Morland as Gothic Heroine." In Lupack, *Nineteenth-Century Women at the Movies*, 129–39.

Romano, Carlin. "Who Killed Literary Reading?" *Chronicle of Higher Education*, 23 July 2004, B13.

Rose, Jonathan. *The Intellectual Life of the British Working Classes*. New Haven, Conn.: Yale University Press, 2001.

Rosen, Judith. "Love Is All Around You." *Publisher's Weekly*, 8 November 1999, 37–43.

Ross, Andrew. "Uses of Camp." In Cleto, *Camp*, 308–29.

Rothman, Ellen K. *Hands and Hearts: A History of Courtship in America*. New York: Basic Books, 1984.

Rowe, John Carlos. "For Mature Audiences: Sex, Gender and Recent Film Adaptations of Henry James's Fiction." In *Henry James on Stage and Screen*, edited by John R. Bradley, 190–211. Houndmills: Palgrave, 2000.

Rubin, Joan Shelley. *The Making of Middlebrow Culture*. Chapel Hill: University of North Carolina Press, 1992.

Russell, David J. "Monster Roundup: Reintegrating the Horror Genre." In Browne, *Refiguring American Film Genres*, 233–54.

Sadoff, Dianne F. *Sciences of the Flesh: Representing Subject and Body in Psychoanalysis*. Stanford, Calif.: Stanford University Press, 1998.

Said, Edward W. *Culture and Imperialism*. New York: Vintage Books, 1994.

Sales, Roger. *Jane Austen and Representations of Regency England*. London: Routledge, 1994.

Salmon, Richard. *Henry James and the Culture of Publicity.* Cambridge: Cambridge University Press, 1997.

Samuel, Raphael. *Theatres of Memory.* Vol. 1. London: Verso, 1994.

Sanders, Julie. *Adaptation and Appropriation.* London: Routledge, 2006.

Saul, Stephanie. "Birth of Octuplets Puts Focus on Fertility Industry and Risks." *New York Times,* 12 February 2009, late ed., A1, A28.

Schamus, James. "To the Rear of the Back End: The Economics of Independent Cinema." In Neale and Smith, *Contemporary Hollywood Cinema,* 91–105.

Schatz, Thomas. *Boom and Bust: The American Cinema in the 1940s.* History of the American Cinema 6. New York: Charles Scribner's Sons, 1997.

———. *The Genius of the System: Hollywood Filmmaking in the Studio Era.* New York: Pantheon Books, 1988.

———. "The New Hollywood." In Collins et al., *Film Theory Goes to the Movies,* 8–36.

Scott, A. O. "The Invasion of the Midsize Movie." *New York Times,* 21 January 2005, national ed., B1, 22.

Seaman, Barrett. *Binge: What Your College Student Won't Tell You: Campus Life in an Age of Disconnection and Excess.* New York: John Wiley, 2005.

Sedgwick, Eve Kosofsky. *Between Men: English Literature and Male Homosocial Desire.* New York: Columbia University Press, 1985.

———. *The Coherence of Gothic Conventions.* New York: Methuen, 1976.

———. *Epistemology of the Closet.* Berkeley: University of California Press, 1990.

———. *Tendencies.* Series Q. Durham, N.C.: Duke University Press, 1993.

Self, Will. *Dorian: An Imitation.* New York: Grove Press, 2002.

Seltzer, Mark. *Bodies and Machines.* New York: Routledge, 1992.

Sevastakis, Michael. *Songs of Love and Death: The Classical American Horror Film of the 1930s.* Contributions to the Study of Popular Culture 37. Westport, Conn.: Greenwood Press, 1993.

Shanley, Mary Lyndon. *Feminism, Marriage, and the Law in Victorian England, 1850–1895.* Princeton, N.J.: Princeton University Press, 1989.

———. "'One Must Ride Behind': Married Women's Rights and the Divorce Act of 1857." *Victorian Studies* 25 (Spring 1982): 355–76.

Shelley, Mary. *Frankenstein.* Edited by J. Paul Hunter. Norton Critical Edition. W. W. Norton, 1996 [1818].

Shelley, Percy Bysshe. "Introduction" to *Frankenstein,* third edition (1831). In Hunter, *Frankenstein,* 169–73.

———. "Preface" to *Frankenstein.* In Hunter, *Frankenstein,* 5–6.

Shumway, David R. *Modern Love: Romance, Intimacy, and the Marriage Crisis.* New York: New York University Press, 2003.

Simonds, Wendy. *Women and Self-Help Culture: Reading Between the Lines.* New Brunswick, N.J.: Rutgers University Press, 1992.

Sinfield, Alan. *The Wilde Century: Effeminacy, Oscar Wilde and the Queer Movement.* New York: Columbia University Press, 1994.

Skal, David J. *Hollywood Gothic: The Tangled Web of "Dracula" from Novel to Stage to Screen.* New York: W. W. Norton, 1990.

———. *The Monster Show: A Cultural History of Horror.* Rev. ed. New York: Faber and Faber, 1993.

Skal, David J., and Elias Savada. *Dark Carnival: The Secret World of Tod Browning, Hollywood's Master of the Macabre.* New York: Anchor Books, 1995.

Sklar, Robert. *Movie-Made America: A Cultural History of American Movies.* Rev. ed. New York: Vintage, 1994.

Solomon, Aubrey. *Twentieth-Century Fox: A Corporate and Financial History.* Filmmakers, No. 20. Metuchen, N.J.: Scarecrow Press, 1988.

Sonnet, Esther. "From *Emma* to *Clueless*: Taste, Pleasure and the Scene of History." In Cartmell and Whelehan, *Adaptations,* 51–62.

Sontag, Susan. "Notes on Camp." *Against Interpretation and Other Essays.* New York: Dell, 1966.

Spoto, David. *Laurence Olivier: A Biography.* New York: Harper Collins, 1992.

Spring, David. "Interpreters of Jane Austen's Social World: Literary Critics and Historians." In *Jane Austen: New Perspectives,* edited by Janet Todd, 53–72. Women and Literature, New Series. Vol. 3. New York: Holmes and Meier Publishers, 1983.

Squier, Susan Merrill. *Babies in Bottles: Twentieth-Century Visions of Reproductive Technology.* New Brunswick, N.J.: Rutgers University Press, 1994.

———. "Negotiating Boundaries: From Assisted Reproduction to Assisted Replication." In *Playing Dolly: Technocultural Formations, Fantasies, and Fictions of Assisted Reproduction,* edited by E. Ann Kaplan and Susan Squier, 101–15. New Brunswick, N.J.: Rutgers University Press, 1999.

Staiger, Janet. *Perverse Spectators: The Practices of Film Reception.* New York: New York University Press, 2000.

Stam, Robert. *Literature through Film: Realism, Magic, and the Art of Adaptation.* Malden, Mass.: Blackwell Publishing, 2005.

Stanley, Alessandra. "Handsome Stranger? Be Careful. He Bites." *New York Times,* 5 September 2008, late ed., E1, E13.

———. "Oh, Mr. Darcy . . . Yes, I Said Yes!" *New York Times,* 20 November 2005, late ed., sec. 4, 1, 14.

Steele, Valerie. *The Corset: A Cultural History.* New Haven, Conn.: Yale University Press, 2001.

Stepan, Nancy. "Biology and Degeneration: Races and Proper Places." In Chamberlin and Gilman, *Degeneration,* 97–120.

Sterngold, James. "At the Movies: Ideal Time for Wilde?" *New York Times,* 4 June 1999, national ed., E14.

Stewart, Garrett. "Film's Victorian Retrofit." *Victorian Studies* 38, no. 2 (1995): 153–98.

Stocking, George W., Jr. "The Turn-of-the-Century Concept of Race." *Modernism/ Modernity* 1, no. 1 (January 1994): 4–16.

———. *Victorian Anthropology*. New York: Free Press, 1987.

Stoker, Bram. *Dracula*. Edited by Nina Auerbach and David J. Skal. New York: W. W. Norton, 1997.

Stokes, Melvyn. "Female Audiences of the 1920s and Early 1930s." In Stokes and Maltby, *Identifying Hollywood's Audiences*, 42–60.

Stokes, Melvyn, and Richard Maltby, eds. *Identifying Hollywood's Audiences: Cultural Identity and the Movies*. London: BFI, 1999.

Stolberg, Sheryl Gay. "Obama Puts His Own Spin on the Mix of Science with Politics." *New York Times*, 10 March 2009, late ed., A18.

Stone, Lawrence. *Road to Divorce: England, 1530–1987*. New York: Oxford University Press, 1995.

Stone, Lawrence, and Jeanne C. Fawtier Stone. *An Open Élite? England, 1540–1880*. Oxford: Clarendon Press, 1984.

Strathern, Marilyn. "Regulation, Substitution and Possibility." In Edwards et al., *Technologies of Procreation*, 171–202.

———. "A Relational View, 1993." In Edwards et al., *Technologies of Procreation*, 203–16.

Street, Sarah. *British National Cinema*. London: Routledge, 1997.

———. *Transatlantic Crossings: British Feature Films in the United States*. New York: Continuum, 2002.

Strychacz, Thomas. *Modernism, Mass Culture, and Professionalism*. Cambridge: Cambridge University Press, 1993.

Sunder Rajan, Rajeswari. "Fixing English: Nation, Language, Subject." In Sunder Rajan, *The Lie of the Land*, 7–28.

———. *The Lie of the Land: English Literary Studies in India*. Delhi: Oxford University Press, 1992.

Sweet, James A., and Larry L. Bumpass. *American Families and Households*. New York: Russell Sage Foundation, 1987.

Tedmanson, Sophie. "'Pregnant Man' Thomas Beatie Gives Birth for Second Time." *Timesonline*. 10 June 2009. http://www.timesonline.co.uk/tol/news/ world. 15 June 2009.

Thomas, Ronald R. "Specters of the Novel: *Dracula* and the Cinematic Afterlife of the Victorian Novel." In Kucich and Sadoff, *Victorian Afterlife*, 288–310.

Thompson, Emma. *The Sense and Sensibility Screenplay and Diaries: Bringing Jane Austen's Novel to Film*. New York: Newmarket Press, 1995.

Thomson, David. *Rosebud: The Story of Orson Welles*. New York: Alfred A. Knopf, 1996.

Thurston, Carol. *The Romance Revolution: Erotic Novels for Women and the Quest for a New Sexual Identity.* Urbana: University of Illinois Press, 1987.

Tinniswood, Adrian. *The Polite Tourist: Four Centuries of Country House Visiting.* London: National Trust, Harry N. Abrams, 1998.

Troost, Linda, and Sayre Greenfield, eds. *Jane Austen in Hollywood.* Lexington: University Press of Kentucky, 1998.

Tropp, Martin. "Re-creating the Monster: *Frankenstein* and Film." In Lupack, *Nineteenth-Century Women at the Movies,* 23–77.

Tudor, Andrew. *Monsters and Mad Scientists: A Cultural History of the Horror Movie.* Oxford: Basil Blackwell, 1989.

———. "Why Horror? The Peculiar Pleasures of a Popular Genre." In Jancovich, *Horror,* 47–55.

Tuite, Clara. "Domestic Retrenchment and Imperial Expansion: The Property Plots of *Mansfield Park.*" In *The Postcolonial Jane Austen,* edited by You-me Park and Rajeswari Sunder Rajan, 93–115. London: Routledge, 2000.

———. *Romantic Austen: Sexual Politics and the Literary Canon.* Cambridge: Cambridge University Press, 2002.

Turkle, Sherry. *Life on the Screen: Identity in the Age of the Internet.* New York: Simon and Schuster, 1995.

Turney, Jon. *Frankenstein's Footsteps: Science, Genetics and Popular Culture.* New Haven, Conn.: Yale University Press, 1998.

Tyrrell, Heather. "Bollywood versus Hollywood: Battle of the Dream Factories." In *Culture and Global Change,* edited by Tracey Skelton and Tim Allen, 260–73. London: Routledge, 1999.

Urry, John. *Consuming Places.* London: Routledge, 1995.

———. *The Tourist Gaze: Leisure and Travel in Contemporary Societies.* London: Sage, 1990.

Valente, Joseph. *Dracula's Crypt: Bram Stoker, Irishness, and the Question of Blood.* Urbana: University of Illinois Press, 2002.

Van Meter, Jonathan. "Costume Drama." *Vogue,* May 2001, 278–85.

Vanita, Ruth. "*Mansfield Park* in Miranda House." In Sunder Rajan, *The Lie of the Land,* 90–98.

Vicinus, Martha. "'They Wonder to Which Sex I Belong': The Historical Roots of Modern Lesbian Identity." In *Lesbian Subjects: A "Feminist Studies" Reader,* edited by Martha Vicinus, 233–59. Bloomington: Indiana University Press, 1996.

Vincendeau, Ginette, ed. *Film/Literature/Heritage: A Sight and Sound Reader.* London: BFI, 2001.

———. "Unsettling Memories." In Vincendeau, *Film/Literature/Heritage,* 27–32.

Viswanathan, Gauri. "Currying Favor: The Politics of British Educational and Cultural Policy in India, 1813–54." In *Dangerous Liaisons: Gender, Nation, and*

Post-colonial Perspectives, edited by Anne McClintock, Aamir Mufti, and Ella Shohat, 113–29. Minneapolis: University of Minnesota Press, 1997.

Wahrman, Dror. *Imagining the Middle Class: The Political Representation of Class in Britain, c. 1780–1840.* Cambridge: Cambridge University Press, 1995.

Waldrep, Shelton. "The Uses and Misuses of Oscar Wilde." In Kucich and Sadoff, *Victorian Afterlife,* 49–63.

Wallerstein, Judith, and Joan Berlin Kelly. *Surviving the Breakup: How Children and Parents Cope with Divorce.* New York: Basic Books, 1980.

Wasko, Janet. *Hollywood in the Information Age: Beyond the Silver Screen.* Austin: University of Texas Press, 1995.

Watt, Ian. *The Rise of the Novel: Studies in Defoe, Richardson and Fielding.* Berkeley: University of California Press, 1965.

Weeks, Jeffrey. *Sex, Politics, and Society: The Regulation of Sexuality since 1800.* 2nd ed. London: Longman, 1989.

Weitzman, Lenore J. *The Divorce Revolution: The Unexpected Social and Economic Consequences for Women and Children in America.* New York: Free Press, 1985.

Weldon, Fay. "Jane to Rescue." *Guardian,* 12 April 1995, sec. 2, 2–3, 12.

Wexman, Virginia Wright. *Creating the Couple: Love, Marriage, and Hollywood Performance.* Princeton, N.J.: Princeton University Press, 1993.

Whelehan, Imelda. "Adaptations: The Contemporary Dilemmas." In Cartmell and Whelehan, *Adaptations,* 3–19.

White, Edmund. Introduction to *The Picture of Dorian Gray,* by Oscar Wilde, v–xvi. Oxford: Oxford University Press, 1999.

Wicke, Jennifer. "Vampiric Typewriting: *Dracula* and its Media." *ELH* 59 (1992): 467–93.

Wiener, Martin J. *English Culture and the Decline of the Industrial Spirit, 1850–1980.* Cambridge: Cambridge University Press, 1981.

Wilde, Oscar. *The Critic as Artist: The Writings of Oscar Wilde.* Edited by Isobel Murray. Oxford: Oxford University Press, 1989.

———. *The Importance of Being Earnest. The Writings of Oscar Wilde.* Edited by Isobel Murray. Oxford: Oxford University Press, 1989.

———. *The Picture of Dorian Gray.* Edited by Peter Ackroyd. Oxford: Oxford University Press, 1985.

Wilinsky, Barbara. "Discourses on Art Houses in the 1950s." In Hark, *Exhibition,* 67–75.

Williams, Linda. *Hard Core: Power, Pleasure, and the "Frenzy of the Visible."* Berkeley: University of California Press, 1989.

———. *Screening Sex.* Durham, N.C.: Duke University Press, 2008.

———. "Sisters under the Skin: Video and Blockbuster Erotic Thrillers." In *Women and Film: A "Sight and Sound" Reader,* edited by Pam Cook and Philip Dodd, 105–14. Philadelphia: Temple University Press, 1993.

———. "When the Woman Looks." In *Re-Vision: Essays in Feminist Film Criticism,* edited by Mary Ann Doane, Patricia Mellencamp, and Linda Williams, 83–99. AFI Monograph Series. Vol. 3. Frederick, Md.: University Publications of America, 1984.

Williams, Michael. *Crisis and Consensus in British Politics: From Bagehot to Blair.* Houndmills: Macmillan, 2000.

Williams, Raymond. *The Country and the City.* New York: Oxford University Press, 1973.

———. *Marxism and Literature.* Oxford: Oxford University Press, 1977.

Williamson, Milly. *The Lure of the Vampyre: Gender, Fiction and Fandom from Bram Stoker to "Buffy."* London: Wallflower Press, 2005.

Wilmut, Ian, Keith Campbell, and Colin Tudge. *The Second Creation: Dolly and the Age of Biological Control.* New York: Farrar, Straus and Giroux, 2000.

Wilson, Wendy. "Many Changes Afoot among Independents." *Video Business,* 10 March 1995, 1, 8.

Wiltshire, John. "Decolonising *Mansfield Park.*" *Essays in Criticism* 53, no. 4 (October 2003): 303–22.

———. *Recreating Jane Austen.* Cambridge: Cambridge University Press, 2001.

Woolf, Virginia. *The Diary of Virginia Woolf.* Edited by Anne Olivier Bell. 5 vols. New York: Harcourt Brace Jovanovich, 1977–84.

———. *A Room of One's Own.* New York: Harcourt Brace and World, 1957 [1929].

Wright, Patrick. *On Living in an Old Country: The National Past in Contemporary Britain.* London: Verso, 1985.

"Wright's 'Pride and Prejudice' at the Austen Society." Narrated by Kim Masters. *Morning Edition.* National Public Radio. WVXU, Cincinnati, 11 November 2005.

Wyatt, Justin. "The Formation of the 'Major Independent': Miramax, New Line and the New Hollywood." In Neale and Smith, *Contemporary Hollywood Cinema,* 74–90.

Yaeger, Lynn. "Costume Drama." *Travel and Leisure,* May 2001, 142–48.

Young, Elizabeth. "Bods and Monsters: The Return of the Bride of Frankenstein." *The End of Cinema as We Know It: American Film in the Nineties,* edited by Jon Lewis, 225–36. New York: New York University Press, 2001.

Zeffirelli, Franco. *Zeffirelli: The Autobiography of Franco Zeffirelli.* New York: Weidenfeld and Nicolson, 1986.

Zill, Nicholas, and Marianne Winglee. "Literature Reading in the United States: Data from National Surveys and Their Policy Implications." *Book Research Quarterly* 5, no. 1 (Spring 1989): 24–58.

Zoepf, Katherine. "Love on Girls' Side of the Saudi Divide, Separate but Accepting." *New York Times,* 13 May 2008, late ed., A1, A12.

Zukin, Sharon. "Socio-Spatial Prototypes of a New Organization of Consumption: The Role of Real Cultural Capital." *Sociology* 24, no. 1 (1990): 37–56.

Filmography

Abismos de Pasión. Directed by Luis Buñuel. Jorge Mistral and Lilia Prado. Producciones Tepeyac, 1954.

Becoming Jane. Directed by Julian Jarrold. Anne Hathaway, James McAvoy, and Maggie Smith. BBC Films, 2007.

The Bostonians. Screenplay by Ruth Prawer Jhabvala. Directed by James Ivory. Christopher Reeve, Vanessa Redgrave, and Jessica Tandy. Merchant Ivory Productions, 1984.

Bram Stoker's Dracula. Screenplay by James V. Hart. Directed by Francis Ford Coppola. Gary Oldman, Winona Ryder, Anthony Hopkins, and Keanu Reeves. American Zeotrope, Columbia Pictures, 1992.

Bride and Prejudice. Screenplay by Paul Mayeda Berges. Directed by Gurinder Chadha. Aishwarya Rai and Martin Henderson. Pathé, 2004.

Bride of Frankenstein. Directed by James Whale. Boris Karloff, Colin Clive, Ernest Thesiger, and Elsa Lanchester. Universal Pictures, 1935.

Brideshead Revisited. Screenplay by Andrew Davies. Directed by Julian Jarrold. Matthew Goode, Hayley Atwell, Emma Thompson, and Michael Gambon. BBC Films, 2008.

Chinatown. Screenplay by Robert Towne. Directed by Roman Polanski. Jack Nicholson, Faye Dunaway, and John Huston. Paramount Pictures, 1974.

The Claim. Screenplay by Frank Cottrell Boyce. Directed by Michael Winterbottom. Peter Mullan, Milla Jovovich, and Nastassja Kinski. BBC/Pathé, 2000.

Clueless. Screenplay by Amy Heckerling. Directed by Amy Heckerling. Alicia Silverstone, Wallace Shawn, and Paul Rudd. Paramount Pictures, 1995.

Dracula. Screenplay by Garrett Fort. Directed by Tod Browning. Bela Lugosi, Helen Chandler, David Manners, and Edward Van Sloan. Universal Pictures, 1931.

Dracula. Screenplay by W. D. Richter. Directed by John Badham. Frank Langella, Laurence Olivier, Donald Pleasence, and Kate Nelligan. Universal Pictures, 1979.

Emily Brontë's Wuthering Heights. Screenplay by Anne Devlin. Directed by Peter Kosminsky. Juliette Binoche and Ralph Fiennes. Paramount Pictures, 1992.

Emma. Screenplay by Andrew Davies. Directed by Diarmuid Lawrence. Kate Beckinsale, Mark Strong, and Samantha Morton. Meridian Broadcasting, A&E Network, 1996.

Emma. Screenplay by Douglas McGrath. Directed by Douglas McGrath. Gwyneth Paltrow, Toni Collette, and Jeremy Northam. Miramax, 1996.

The Europeans. Directed by James Ivory. Lee Remick and Robin Ellis. Merchant Ivory Productions, 1979.

Eyes Wide Shut. Directed by Stanley Kubrick. Tom Cruise and Nicole Kidman. Warner Bros., 1999.

Frankenstein. Screenplay by Garrett Fort, Francis Edward Faragoh. Directed by James Whale. Colin Clive, Mae Clarke, and Boris Karloff. Universal Pictures, 1931.

Frankenstein Unbound. Directed by Roger Corman. John Hurt, Raul Julia, and Bridget Fonda. Mount Co., Twentieth Century Fox, 1990.

Gods and Monsters. Directed by Bill Condon. Ian McKellen, Brendan Fraser, and Lynn Redgrave. BBC Films, Lions Gate, 1998.

The Golden Bowl. Directed by James Cellan Jones. Daniel Massey, Gayle Hunni-cutt, and Cyril Cusack. BBC, 1972.

The Golden Bowl. Screenplay by Ruth Prawer Jhabvala. Directed by James Ivory. Kate Beckinsale, Nick Nolte, Uma Thurman, and Jeremy Northam. Merchant Ivory Productions, 2000.

Gothic. Directed by Ken Russell. Gabriel Byrne, Julian Sands, and Natasha Richardson. Virgin Vision, 1986.

Great Expectations. Screenplay by Mitch Glazer. Directed by Alfonso Cuarón. Ethan Hawke, Gwyneth Paltrow, and Anne Bancroft. Twentieth Century Fox, 1998.

An Ideal Husband. Directed by Oscar Parker. Cate Blanchett, Minnie Driver, Rupert Everett, Julianne Moore, and Jeremy Northam. Miramax, 1999.

The Importance of Being Earnest. Directed by Oscar Parker. Rupert Everett, Colin Firth, Frances O'Connor, and Judi Dench. Miramax, 2002.

Interview with the Vampire. Screenplay by Anne Rice. Directed by Neil Jordan. Tom Cruise, Brad Pitt, and Kirsten Dunst. Geffen Pictures, 1994.

Jane Eyre. Directed by Robert Stevenson. Orson Welles, Joan Fontaine, and Mar-garet O'Brien. Twentieth Century Fox, 1944.

Jane Eyre. Screenplay by Alexander Baron. Directed by Julian Amyes. Timothy Dalton and Zelah Clarke. BBC, 1983.

Jane Eyre. Screenplay by Hugh Whitemore and Franco Zeffirelli. Directed by Franco Zeffirelli. William Hurt, Charlotte Gainsbourg, and Fiona Shaw. Mira-max, 1996.

Jude. Screenplay by Hossein Amini. Directed by Michael Winterbottom. Christo-pher Eccleston and Kate Winslet. BBC Films, PolyGram, 1996.

Kandukondain Kandukondain. Screenplay by Rajiv Menon. Directed by Rajiv Menon. Aishwarya Rai, Tabu, Ajith, and Mammooty. Sri Surya Films, 2000.

Mansfield Park. Directed by David Giles. Nicholas Farrell and Sylvestra Le Touzel. BBC, 1983.

Mansfield Park. Screenplay by Patricia Rozema. Directed by Patricia Rozema. Frances O'Connor, Jonny Lee Miller, and Harold Pinter. BBC, Miramax, 1999.

Mary Shelley's Frankenstein. Directed by Kenneth Branagh. Kenneth Branagh, Robert De Niro, and Helena Bonham Carter. American Zeotrope, Tristar Pictures, 1994.

Maurice. Screenplay by Kit Hesketh-Harvey. Directed by James Ivory. James Wilby, Hugh Grant, Rupert Graves, and Simon Callow. Merchant Ivory Productions, 1987.

Miss Austen Regrets. Screenplay by Gwyneth Hughes. Directed by Jeremy Lovering. Samuel Roukin, Olivia Williams, and Greta Scacchi. BBC, 2008.

Nosferatu: A Symphony of Horrors. Screenplay by Henrik Galeen. Directed by F. W. Murnau. Max Schreck, Gustav von Wangenheim, Greta Schröder, and Alexander Granach. Prana-Film, 1922.

Orlando. Screenplay by Sally Potter. Directed by Sally Potter. Tilda Swinton, Quentin Crisp, and Jimmy Somerville. Adventure Pictures, Lenfilm, Mikado, Sigma, and British Screen Productions, 1992.

Persuasion. Screenplay by Nick Dear. Directed by Roger Michell. Amanda Root, Ciaran Hinds, and Fiona Shaw. BBC/WGBH; Sony Pictures Classics, 1995.

The Picture of Dorian Gray. Directed by Albert Lewin. George Sanders, Hurd Hatfield, Donna Reed, and Angela Lansbury. MGM, 1945.

The Picture of Dorian Gray. Directed by Glenn Jordan. Shane Briant, Nigel Davenport, and Charles Aidman. Dan Curtis Productions, 1973.

The Picture of Dorian Gray. Adaptation by John Osborne. Directed by John Gorrie. John Gielgud, Jeremy Brett, and Peter Firth. BBC TV, *Play of the Month*, 19 September 1976.

The Portrait of a Lady. Screenplay by Laura Jones. Directed by Jane Campion. Nicole Kidman and John Malkovich. PolyGram, 1996.

Pride and Prejudice. Screenplay by Aldous Huxley. Directed by Robert Z. Leonard. Greer Garson, Laurence Olivier, and Maureen O'Sullivan. MGM, 1940.

Pride and Prejudice. Adaptation by Fay Weldon. Directed by Cyril Coke. Elizabeth Garvie and David Rintoul. BBC, 1980.

Pride and Prejudice. Screenplay by Andrew Davies. Directed by Simon Langton. Colin Firth and Jennifer Ehle. A&E/BBC, 1995.

Pride and Prejudice. Screenplay by Deborah Moggach. Directed by Joe Wright. Keira Knightley, Donald Sutherland, Brenda Blethyn, and Matthew Macfadyen. Focus Features, 2005.

Sense and Sensibility. Screenplay by Emma Thompson. Directed by Ang Lee. Emma Thompson, Kate Winslet, and Hugh Grant. Columbia Pictures, 1995.

Shadow of the Vampire. Directed by E. Elias Merhige. John Malkovich and Willem Dafoe. BBC Films, 2000.

Son of Frankenstein. Screenplay by Wyllis Cooper. Directed by Rowland V. Lee. Basil Rathbone, Boris Karloff, and Bela Lugosi. Universal Pictures, 1939.

Tess. Screenplay by Gérard Brach. Directed by Roman Polanski. Nastassja Kinski, Peter Firth, and Leigh Lawson. Columbia Pictures, 1979.

Van Helsing. Directed by Stephen Sommers. Hugh Jackman and Kate Beckinsale. Universal Pictures, 2004.

Vanity Fair. Directed by Mira Nair. Reese Witherspoon, Gabriel Byrne, and James Purefoy. Focus Features, 2004.

Washington Square. Screenplay by Carol Doyle. Directed by Agnieszka Holland. Jennifer Jason Leigh, Albert Finney, and Maggie Smith. Hollywood Pictures/ Caravan Pictures, 1997.

Wilde. Screenplay by Julian Mitchell. Directed by Brian Gilbert. Stephen Fry, Jude Law, Vanessa Redgrave, and Jennifer Ehle. BBC, 1997.

The Wings of the Dove. Screenplay by Hossein Amini. Directed by Iain Softley. Helena Bonham Carter, Linus Roache, and Alison Elliott. Miramax, 1997.

Wuthering Heights. Screenplay by Charles MacArthur and Ben Hecht. Directed by William Wyler. Merle Oberon and Laurence Olivier. Samuel Goldwyn, 1939.

Wuthering Heights. Directed by Peter Kosminsky. Ralph Fiennes, Juliette Binoche, and Jeremy Northam. Paramount Pictures, 1992.

Index

DIANNE F. SADOFF is professor of English at Rutgers University, New Brunswick, New Jersey. She is the author of *Monsters of Affection: Dickens, Brontë, and Eliot on Fatherhood* and *Sciences of the Flesh: Representing Body and Subject in Psychoanalysis.* She coedited *Victorian Afterlife: Postmodern Culture Rewrites the Nineteenth Century* (Minnesota, 2000).